Losing the Good Portion

Other Books of Interest from St. Augustine's Press

Gerard V. Bradley, *Unquiet Americans*

Joseph Pearce (editor), *Beauteous Truth: Faith, Reason, Literature, and Culture*

Christopher Kaczor, *The Gospel of Happiness:*
How Secular Psychology Points to the Wisdom of Christian Practice

Alain Besançon, *Protestant Nation:*
The Fragile Christian Roots on America's Greatness

John F. Crosby and Stafford Betty,
What Does It Mean to Be a Christian?: A Debate

James V. Schall, *At a Breezy Time of Day:*
Selected Schall Interviews on Just about Everything

James V. Schall, *The Praise of 'Sons of Bitches':*
On the Worship of God by Fallen Men

James V. Schall, *The Regensburg Lecture*

Gary M. Bouchard, *Southwell's Sphere:*
The Influence of England's Secret Poet

Kenneth Baker, *The Mystery of Death and Beyond*

Frederic Raphael and Joseph Epstein, *Where Were We?*

Étienne Gilson, *Theology and the Cartesian Doctrine of Freedom*

Josef Kleutgen, S.J., *Pre-Modern Philosophy Defended*

Charles Cardinal Journet, *The Mass:*
The Presence of the Sacrifice of the Cross

Edward Feser, *The Last Superstition: A Refutation of the New Atheism*

Ernest A. Fortin, A.A., *Christianity and Philosophical Culture in the Fifth*
Century: The Controversy about the Human Soul in the West

Peter Kreeft, *Ecumenical Jihad*

Peter Kreeft, *Socrates' Children: The 100 Greatest Philosophers*

Josef Pieper, *The Christian Idea of Man*

Josef Pieper and Heinz Raskop, *What Catholics Believe*

Karl Rahner, *Encounters with Silence*

Losing the Good Portion

Why Men Are Alienated from Christianity

Leon J. Podles

ST. AUGUSTINE'S PRESS
South Bend, Indiana

Library of Congress Control Number: 2019950154

St. Augustine's Press
www.staugustine.net

To my brothers at the Alpha Omega House,
those who are with us and those who have gone over the Jordan.

Table of Contents

Acknowledgements ix

Preface xi

Introduction 1

Chapter One: Masculinity 7

Chapter Two: The Masculinity of Jesus 22

Chapter Three: The Feminine Christian 43

Chapter Four: The Clergy and Social Control 71

Chapter Five: The Sins of the Clergy 115

Chapter Six: Political Anticlericalism 141

Chapter Seven: Masculine Themes in Christianity 174

Chapter Eight: Targeting Men 213

Chapter Nine: Men and the Future of the Church 241

Selected Bibliography 249

Index 269

Acknowledgements

Many thanks to my wife Maidie and to my friend and hiking partner Skip Eby for listening to me formulate my ideas and for critiquing and proofreading the book. Many thanks to the Fingerhuts, *père et fils*, for their work in the gestation of this book.

Preface

Being a man is difficult in any society; being a Christian man is even more difficult, because the two—being a man and being a Christian—often seem incompatible, or at least in severe tension. My Catholic parents were not observant; my father went to church for baptisms and funerals, but otherwise never attended. I was sent to our parish school and to mass on Sundays, and for some reason it took. The ways of grace are mysterious. I went to a Christian Brothers' high school, where I encountered a physically abusive (and I later suspected sexually abusive) brother and was expelled. I decided to enter a quasi-seminary situation at Providence College, a dormitory for students considering the priesthood, but left abruptly after an unwanted encounter with a homosexual roommate.

Despite all this, I continued to go to mass, to pray, and to immerse myself in the Catholic intellectual tradition. In the early 1970s I was in graduate school at the University of Virginia and visited friends in Washington, D.C.; in both places I encountered the charismatic renewal. UVA students involved in the charismatic renewal or evangelical groups set up the Alpha Omega house in Charlottesville, which I helped renovate and where I lived for a year. It was good to encounter young men who were deeply committed Christians, but still young men.

After I moved to other cities, I noticed an oddity at church. I am of average American male height, but I was frequently the tallest person at church—because everyone else was either female or very old. I was puzzled by this—where were all the other men, especially young men? Puzzling led to researching and researching led to my first book, *The Church Impotent: The Feminization of Christianity*. The title, and publishers choose the title, was misleading and caused some hard feelings. I did not claim that women deliberately drove men out of the church, but that men absented themselves, leaving the church to women and to a male clergy.

But why did lay men desert the pews? In *The Church Impotent* I focused on bridal mysticism, in which all Christians, including males, had to become brides of Christ, not a role that would appeal to most men, although even then I did not think this was a complete explanation. I continued my research and the internet opened up possibilities of research in other languages, with the results you will see in this book.

Is it possible to be masculine and to be a Christian? I think so, although it is hard for anyone to be a Christian, living in the current age of the world, but being transformed by the life of the world to come. I hope this book may help open the doors of the church to men, especially young men, where they may meet the One who wanted to be known as the Son of Man.

I am setting up a website, losingthegoodportion.org, to receive comments, compliments, and brickbats. There I may also post additional material which did not make its way into this book.

Introduction

Men are less religious than women—such is the opinion of saints, scholars, and churchmen. St. Thérèse of Lisieux claimed that women "love God in much larger numbers than men do." Scholars in several disciplines concur. Ferdinand Tönnies in his classic *Gemeinschaft und Gesellschaft* laconically states "women are believing, men, unbelieving." The theologian Karl Rahner observed that women are more pious than men and that they are more frequent churchgoers than men. After a synod of bishops in 1988, Pope John Paul II issued a summary of the synod. After detailing all the ways that women should be further incorporated into the life of the Church, he added: "Many voices were raised in the Synod Hall expressing the fear that excessive insistence given to the status and role of women would lead to an unacceptable omission, that, in point, regarding *men*. In reality, various sectors in the Church must lament the absence or the scarcity of the presence of men, some of whom abdicate their proper Church responsibilities, allowing them to be fulfilled only by women." This simply expands Thérèse's and Tönnies' and Rahner's observations that men are less religious than women. Having made the observation, the pope then proceeded to do nothing about the lack of men. Kenneth Guentert explains the pattern: "The Roman Catholic Church has a rather rigid division of labor. The men have the priesthood. The women have everything else." In many Protestant churches, women are becoming the majority of ministers, so men have nothing.[1]

---

1   Thérèse of Lisieux, *Story of a Soul*, trans. John Clark (Washington, DC: ICS Publications, 1996), 140; Ferdinand Tönnies, *Gemeinschaft und Gesellschaft* (Leipzig: Fues's Verlag, 1887), 167; Karl Rahner, "Der Mann in der Kirche," *Sendung und Gnade: Beiträge zur Pastoral Theologie* (Innsbruck-Wien: Tyrolia-Verlag, 1988), 287; John Paul II, *Christifideles Laici*, Vatican Translation. December 30, 1988. http://www.vatican.va/holy_father/john_paul_ii/apost_exhortations/documents/hf_jp-ii_exh_30121988_christifideles-laici_

Why have men kept their distance from the Western churches? Attempts to explain this situation have usually considered men as the norm, and seek to explain why women differ from this norm, although masculine irreligion is highly unusual in world cultures.[2] In recent years only three books have focused on the question of male absence: my book, *The Church Impotent: The Feminization of Christianity*; Dwight Murrow's *Why Men Hate Going to Church*, which is largely a popularization of my book; and Marta Trzebiatowska's and Steve Bruce's *Why Are Women More Religious than Men?*[3] Trzebiatowska and Bruce, as their title indicates, focus on women from the late nineteenth century to the present. Their assumption, like that of most scholars, is that the greater religiosity of women, and not the lesser religiosity of men, needs explanation.

The greater religiosity of women does not exist in "religion" in general. Many societies have no concept of "religion" in the modern, Western sense; there is simply a way of life, a way which includes raising food, giving birth, waging war, placating the gods, and all other activities of life. The Pueblo Indians, for example, had to use the foreign concept of "religion" to defend their dances by invoking the First Amendment.[4] In historical Judaism and in Orthodoxy, but not in Reformed and Conservative Judaism,[5] lay men have more responsibilities and are more active than women. Islam is a male religion; in some societies almost all men but few women go to mosque.[6] There is little

en.html; Kenneth Guentert, "Kids Need to Learn Their Faith from Men, Too," *U. S. Catholic* 65 (Feb. 1990): 14.

2   For a survey and a bibliography of theories that seek to explain the greater religiousness of women, see Leslie J. Francis and Gemma Penny, "Gender Differences in Religion," in *Religion, Personality, and Social Behavior*, ed. Vassilis Saroglou (New York: Psychology Press, 2014), 313–37.

3   Marta Trzebiatowska and Steve Bruce, *Why Are Women More Religion than Men?* (Oxford: Oxford University Press, 2012).

4   See Tisa Joy Wenger, *We Have a Religion: The 1920s Pueblo Indian Dance Controversy and American Religious Freedom* (Chapel Hill: University of North Carolina Press, 2009).

5   See Sylvia Barack Fishman and Daniel Parmer, *Matrilineal Ascent / Matrilineal Descent: The Gender Imbalance in American Jewish Life* (Waltham, MA: Brandeis University, 2008), 47.

6   Pew Forum, "The World's Muslims: Unity and Diversity," August 9, 2012. http://www.pewforum.org/2012/08/09/the-worlds-muslims-unity-and-diversity-executive-summary/.

evidence in the first millennium of an imbalance of men and women in Christianity. But beginning around the time of Bernard of Clairvaux, there are more and more comments about the greater religiosity of women. Berthold von Regensburg (1220–1272) noticed that women were more at church then men and preached to "you women, who are more merciful than men and go more willingly to church than men and say your prayers more willingly than men and go to sermons more willingly than men."[7] Bishop Brunton (1320–1399) complained that "men, and especially young men, careless about God, withdraw their due service."[8] Later the Dominican Guillaume Pepin (1465–1533) and the Franciscan Michel Menot (d. 1518) agreed with his assessment.[9] Pepin preached that women "are commonly more devout than men," that women are "more avid to hear the word of God than men," and that on feast days women confess and take communion, "while few men do."[10] The clerical encomia of women continued throughout the centuries; in 1880 a Berlin pastor praised women: "They have always become more faithful, more eager and warmer in the love of the Lord."[11] In my previous book I focused on the demographic evidence of the difference in religious participation between men and women[12] and sought

7   Berthold von Regensburg, *Predigten*, Vol. 1, ed. Franz Pfeiffer (Vienna: Wilhelm Braumüller, 1862), 41.

8   Quoted in Gerald Robert Owst, *Preaching in Medieval England: An Introduction to Sermon Manuscripts of the Period 1350–1450* (Cambridge: Cambridge University Press, 1926), 173.

9   Megan C. Armstrong, *The Politics Of Piety: Franciscan Preachers During The Wars Of Religion, 1560–1600* (Rochester, NY: University of Rochester Press, 2004), 106.

10   Quoted in Larissa Taylor, *Soldiers of Christ: Preaching in Late Medieval and Reformation France* (New York: Oxford University Press, 1992), 172. See also Larissa Taylor, "Images of Women in the Sermons of Guillaume Pepin (c. 1465–1533)," *Journal of the Canadian Historical Association* 5, no. 1 (1994): 265–276.

11   Quoted in Hugh McLeod, *Religion and the People of Western Europe 1798–1989* (New York: Oxford University Press, 1997), 35. For McLeod on feminization of religion, see 28–35.

12   Leon J. Podles, "Armies of Women," in *The Church Impotent: The Feminization of Christianity* (Dallas. TX: Spence Publishing, 1999), 1–26. Anecdotal and statistical evidence for the difference could be multiplied twenty-fold; more significantly, only rarely is there little or no difference between the participation of men and women in Western Christian churches.

the cause of male alienation mainly in the tradition that identifies femininity, receptivity, and Christianity.[13] This is certainly one cause, and I trace its further development in modern Christianity in Chapter Three of this current book, but it does not explain the depth and intensity of male hostility to the churches. What is the source of this antipathy? What is the interaction of maleness, or masculinity, and medieval and post-medieval Christianity that creates such a tension?

Maleness has been studied by biologists and masculinity has been studied by psychologists and anthropologists, and I summarize current thought in Chapter One. The essential thrust of masculinity, the male need to establish a masculine identity, is almost universal, and explains many destructive male actions. Societies face the problem of how to direct this male striving for masculinity so that it is constructive.

Three images of Jesus are described in Chapter Two: the Jesus of classical, Mediterranean masculinity, the Jesus of weak or androgynous masculinity, and the Jesus of several varieties of modern masculinities. Jesus lived in a Mediterranean culture that prized masculinity, and the writers of the New Testament are at pains to show how a crucified Jew nonetheless fulfilled the highest ideals of masculinity. The image of Jesus underwent mutations in the second millennium. He sometimes became androgynous or effeminate. In reaction Jesus has more recently been portrayed as a successful businessman, or a fighter for social justice, or a macho fighter, so that he fits in with the image of masculinity in various milieus. In a related development, Christians have long been told they must be feminine to be Christian. In Chapter Three I examine the medieval roots of this belief in Christianized Aristotelianism and I trace it in Pietism, in liberal Protestantism (Schleiermacher), in orthodox Protestantism (Barth), and in Catholicism (von Balthasar).

Men were told by theologians and preachers that they had to become feminine to be Christians, but that is not enough to explain the antipathy that men felt toward the churches. The role of the clergy in social control, the subject of Chapter Four, provoked male rebellion. The clergy, in an attempt to end male violence and sexual irregularities, tried to squelch anything that might excite men, including dancing, drinking, and sports. Men

13   Podles, *Church Impotent*, 113–15.

became suspicious of the clergy who associated mostly with women and had intimate access to women through Catholic confession and Protestant pastoral counseling. Clergymen sometimes abused this access and seduced or raped women. The celibacy of the Catholic clergy created deeper suspicions: men thought that they were not chaste: they were pederasts or homosexuals or seducers. Stories of clerical crimes were seized upon to discredit all clergy. I discuss this in Chapter Four.

The institutional church entered into contests with other forces, and these conflicts gave rise to anticlericalism, which was tinged by the dislike of the clergy as effeminate, effeminizing, and sexually corrupt. Such attitudes were present in the French Revolution, in American anticlericalism, in the Liberal attack on ultramontane Catholicism, in the Nazi attack on Christianity, and preeminently in the Spanish Civil War, which saw the most murderous attack on the clergy in all of history. These painful episodes are discussed in Chapter Five.

Despite these conflicts, men have not totally abandoned the church, and in Chapter Six I look at themes and movements that helped keep men attached to the churches. Christianity and masculinity both sought to initiate a person and so to bring about a rebirth, either as a child of God or as a man. Patristic writers sought to explain the role in the Christian life of *thumos*, the assertiveness and aggressiveness that characterize masculinity. Movements, some of which have continued into the modern era, appealed to masculine ideals: monasticism, chivalry, brotherhoods, the Reformation with its emphasis on spiritual warfare and the role of the father in the family, the Jesuits with their discipline, adventurousness, and delight in contests. In the Protestant world revivalism and fundamentalism had some success in attracting men.

On the continent, where anticlericalism was fiercest, liberal German Catholics in the Krausgesellschaft tried to develop a masculine, Germanic Christianity. The violent conflicts in twentieth-century Europe led to attempts to develop a masculine Christianity; the most successful of these attempts was the Cursillo. In the Anglo-American world Muscular Christianity tried to convince men that religion was not effeminate; it became literalized in the alliance of Christianity and sports, an alliance that would have horrified previous generations of preachers. The Social Gospel wanted a public, masculine Christianity and not a private, sentimental, effeminate one. Business was a male world, and men sought to apply business methods to the churches in the Men and Religion Forward Movement. But even businessmen are fathers, and the emotional themes of fatherhood were taken up by Promise Keepers and the evangelical-charismatic proponents of soft patriarchy.

However, in all of Western Christianity, men remain a minority, and even that minority has a weak attachment to the churches. Men make quasi-religions of politics, of sport, of sex, of masculinity itself, or find a masculine religion in Islam. The churches have long depended on a loyal female constituency. But now women, as they enter into previously male worlds, are also following men out of the church. Unless the churches can reach men, they will continue to decline in numbers and influence in modern and modernizing societies.

Chapter One
Masculinity

"Be a man!"—What could that mean? "Be a woman!" is almost never said. Why do males have to be exhorted to be men? Human beings are, with rare exceptions, unambiguously male or female, so being a male and being a man must be different, although they are closely connected. Women are assumed to be feminine; it is their default state. But men have to work at being manly, or they fail at a task that society or nature or the gods or God has given them. Camille Paglia claims that "a woman simply is, but a man must become. Masculinity is risky and elusive. It is achieved by a revolt against women, and is confirmed only by other men." Wyndham Lewis concurs: "Men were only made into 'men' with great difficulty even in primitive society: the male is not naturally 'a man' any more than the woman. He has to be propped up into that position with some ingenuity, and is always likely to collapse." For the anthropologist David Gilmore, manhood is "the Big Impossible," because it is so difficult to attain and to maintain.[1]

What is this *manhood* that is so difficult to achieve and to keep? Males have a body that is stronger but more susceptible to pathology than a female's, and the course of a boy's development has many more pitfalls than a girl's. If all goes well, the male will transition from the world of the mother to a masculine world of responsible fathers, but part of masculine responsibility is a man's acceptance of his expendability, an acceptance that can easily become self-destructive.

---

1   Camille Paglia, *Sex, Art, and American Culture: Essays* (New York: Random House, 1992), 82; Wyndham Lewis, *The Art of Being Ruled* (Santa Rosa, CA: Black Sparrow Press, 1989), 247; David D. Gilmore, *Manhood in the Making: Cultural Concepts of Masculinity* (New Haven: Yale University Press, 1990), 15.

Maleness

In a mammalian species, the basic template of the body is female. "The female," says J. M. Tanner, "is the 'basic sex' into which embryos develop if not stimulated to do otherwise." Even the primary sex characteristics of males are produced by the action of androgens on a male fetus which initially has female genitals. As Yves Christen explains, "the male can be regarded as a female transformed by testosterone"; the female sex is in a sense the basic sex and therefore "to become a male is a constant struggle."[2] His nipples remind a man that he is fashioned from a female template.

Females have an XX sex chromosome set. One chromosome is the same as the other. Males have an XY sex chromosome set, and the Y chromosome has far fewer genes than the X. The female can supply defects in one X chromosome by the duplicates in the second X chromosome. The male cannot do that. This inability may have deleterious consequences for the male; as Estelle Ramey observes, "about 75% of all genetically mandated abnormalities have a higher incidence in boys than girls." The male-female ratio at conception has been estimated as high as 170 to 100; at birth it drops to 106 to 100. Far more males than females die *in utero*, and the survivors have many more deformities. John Money and Anke Ehrhardt lament that "it is easier for nature to make a female than a male." The Y chromosome is not simply a sex chromosome. It may influence "biological functions throughout life and in every tissue," according to Andrew G. Clark. According to David C. Page, "the cells of males and females are biochemically different," with strong implications for the testing of drugs and possible implications for health and behavior.[3]

2   J. M. Tanner, *Foetus into Man: Physical Growth from Conception to Maturity* (Cambridge, MA: Harvard University Press, 1978), 56; Yves Christen, *Sex Differences: Modern Biology and the Unisex Fallacy*, trans. Nicholas Davidson (New Brunswick, NJ: Transaction Publishers, 1991), 28–29. See also R. J. Stoller, *Presentations of Gender* (New Haven: Yale University Press, 1985), 74.

3   Estelle Ramey, "How Female and Male Biology Differ," in *Women's Health Research: A Medical and Policy Primer*, eds. Florence P. Haseltine and Beverly Greenberg Jacobson (Washington, DC: American Psychiatric Press, 1997), 49; Robert Arking, *The Biology of Aging: Observations and Principles* (New York: Oxford University Press, 2006), 326; John Money and Anke A. Ehrhardt,

The gross structure of the male and female brains also differs, as revealed by MRI imaging: "Maps of neural circuitry showed that on average women's brains were highly connected across the left and right hemispheres, in contrast to men's brains, where the connections were typically stronger between the front and back regions." This corresponds to stereotypical male and female behavior: "men's brains [are] apparently wired more for perception and coordinated actions, and women's for social skills and memory, making them better equipped for multitasking."[4] The converse of multitasking can be called either single-mindedness or obsessiveness, a quality which partially explains why men tend to rise to the top in any area in which they choose to compete, whether computers or cooking.

Brain wiring changes in a major way at puberty, when the male body is flooded with testosterone. Testosterone, which operates on male cells that are biochemically different from female cells, may also explain characteristically male behavior that becomes accentuated after puberty. Human males and males of other species show greater risk-taking and aggression. Men and women are very similar in acting on impulse, but men are far more likely to take risks. Some risk-taking (such as skydiving) requires great deliberation. Researchers therefore have suspected "that this form of

Man and Woman, Boy and Girl: Differentiation and Dimorphism of Gender Identity from Conception to Maturity (Baltimore: Johns Hopkins University Press, 1972), 147; Andrew G. Clark, "Genetics: The Vital Y Chromosome," *Nature* 508 (24 April 2014): 465; David C. Page quoted in Nicholas Wade, "Researchers See New Importance in Y Chromosome," *New York Times*, April 23, 2014. For the consequences of this difference in the chromosomes, see Ramey, "How Female and Male Biology Differ," 49. For the possible role of mitochondria, see S. A. Frank and L. D. Hurst, "Mitochondria and Male Disease," *Nature* 383 (1996): 224; and Duur Aanen, Johannes Spelbrink and Madeleine Beekman, *What cost mitochondria? Maintenance and evolution of mtDNA*. Philosophical Transactions of the Royal Society B. http://rstb.royalsocietypublishing.org/site/2014/mitochondria.xhtml.

4   Ian Sample, "Male and Female Brains Wired Differently, Scans Reveal," *The Guardian*, December 2, 2013. The original study is by Jay N. Gledd, Armin Raznahan, Kathryn L. Mills, and Roshel K. Lenroot, "Magnetic Resonance Imaging of Male/Female Differences in Human Adolescent Brain Anatomy," *Biology of Sex Differences* 3, no. 1 (2012). http://www.biomedcentral.com/content/pdf/2042-6410-3-19.pdf.

impulsive risk-taking—risky impulsivity—is most likely to underlie aggressive and criminal behavior."[5] The combination is dangerous.

Psychologists Maccoby and Jacklin claim that "males are more aggressive," even from infancy.[6] In Andalusia, Julian Pitt-Rivers observed that "the quintessence of manliness is fearlessness, readiness to defend one's own pride and that of one's family. It is ascribed directly to a physical origin and the idiom in which it is expressed is frankly physiological. To be masculine is to have *cojones*."[7] The idiom is widespread. Everyone has noticed that castrated animals are less aggressive. Research has found high testosterone in violent criminals as compared to non-violent criminals.[8] It makes men "rambunctious and impatient," in James Dabbs's characterization. Rambunctiousness is also a characteristic of the hero-criminal. Testosterone leads a man into trouble, but it can also lead him to do feats of extraordinary altruism. Dabbs recounts the story of a petty criminal who broke into a burning house to save children and had to be restrained by firefighters from going back into the house in an attempt to save the last one. He ended up in jail again; he had high testosterone.[9] Audie Murphy risked his life repeatedly to save his fellow soldiers, but in addition to becoming an actor (another high-testosterone occupation), Dobbs points out that he was "in troubles associated with women, gambling, fighting, addiction, and the IRS."[10] As Deborah Blum points out, "aggressive hockey players tend to be high in testosterone; so do virtuoso criminal lawyers."[11] Men in less competitive fields—ministers and farmers—tend to have low testosterone.[12]

5   Catherine Cross, Lee T. Copping, and Ann Campbell, "Sex Differences in Impulsivity: A Meta-Analysis," *Psychological Bulletin* 137, no. 1 (January 2011): 122.

6   Eleanor Emmons Maccoby and Carol Nagy Jacklin, *The Psychology of Sex Differences* (Stanford, CA: Stanford University Press, 1974), 351–52.

7   Julian A. Pitt-Rivers, *The People of the Sierra* (Chicago: University of Chicago Press, 1971), 89.

8   Deborah Blum, *Sex on the Brain: The Biological Differences between Men and Women* (New York: Viking, 1997), 175.

9   James M. Dabbs, *Heroes, Rogues, and Lovers: Testosterone and Behavior*. With Mary Gowin Dabbs (New York: McGraw Hill, 2000), 180.

10 Dabbs, *Heroes*, 190.

11 Blum, *Sex on the Brain*, 176.

12 Dabbs, *Heroes*, 149.

An adolescent cannot mistake cowardice for courage, but he might well mistake foolhardiness for *arête*, manliness. The Greeks thought that irrational aggression was a greater temptation to young men than effeminacy was. As Joseph Roisman observes, Attic "speakers often describe young men as aggressive, haughty, disrespectful of their betters, full of bravado, and preoccupied with drinking, gambling, and sex."[13] Alcibiades, and even Achilles, were not good models for boys, then or now, but too often violence, promiscuity, and crime are the ways males seek to achieve and affirm their manhood. Crime, especially violent crime, is the work of men. Michael Kimmel laments, "from early childhood to old age, violence is the most obdurate, intractable behavioral gender difference."[14] Indeed, Yves Christen goes so far as to claim that the evidence suggests that "criminality is pathological exaggeration of masculinity."[15] Most murderers, and almost all mass murderers, are men.[16] All rapists are men. Almost all robbers, carjackers, stalkers, pedophiles, and hackers are male.[17] Men are both the principal perpetrators *and victims* of violence.[18]

Some neurological conditions are predominantly male. Cambridge psychologist Simon Baron-Cohen sees autism as exaggerated masculinity, in

13 Joseph Roisman, *The Rhetoric of Manhood: Masculinity in the Attic Orators* (Berkeley: University of California Press, 2005), 14.

14 Michael S. Kimmel, *The Gendered Society* (New York: Oxford University Press, 2007), 243.

15 Yves Christen, *Sex Differences*, 89.

16 In the United States at the beginning of the twenty-first century 76% of murderers were men and one-fourth of them under the age of twenty-two (Ronald B. Flowers, *Male Crime and Deviance: Exploring Its Causes, Dynamics, and Nature* [Springfield, IL: Charles C. Thomas, 2003], 102). Worldwide the homicide rate among men is 13.6 and among women 4.0 per 100,000 (Etienne G. Krug, Linda L. Dahlberg, James A. Mercy, Anthony B. Zwi and Rafael Lozano, *World Report on Violence and Health*, Vol. 1 [Geneva: World Health Organization, 2002], 10).

17 For robbers, see Flowers, *Male Crime*, 198; for carjackers, ibid., 202; for stalkers, ibid., 152; for pedophiles, ibid., 226; for hackers, Majid Yar, *Cybercrime and Society* (Thousand Oaks, CA: Sage Publications, 2006), 35.

18 In 2002 in the United States men were 75% of murder victims, and in 89% of the homicide cases, both killer and victim were male (Flowers, *Male Crime and Deviance*, 102).

that autistic persons systematize obsessively and have a relative lack of empathy (but a strong sense of justice).[19] Men also disproportionately suffer from disorders such as schizophrenia, addiction, alcoholism, sexual paraphilias and psychopathy, with its pathological form of empathy.[20] These disorders seem to have a physical substratum; the brains of psychopaths differ from the brains of even other criminals.[21] But any pre-existing physical conditions are exacerbated by the difficulties males encounter in fulfilling their social roles.

The Social Role of the Male

In addition to the physical differences between men and women, and probably more important than them, is the role of the male in human society. Females give birth to males, and this begins a dynamic in personality development. Boys and girls have different developmental patterns because a girl is the same sex as the parent to whom she is closest, her mother, while the boy is a different sex from his mother and may never even know

---

19 Simon Baron-Cohen, *The Essential Difference: Male and Female Brains and the Truth about Autism* (New York: Basic Books, 2004).

20 For schizophrenia see John J. McGrath, "Variations in the Incidence of Schizophrenia: Data versus Dogma," *Schizophrenia Bulletin* 32, No. 1 (2006): 195; for addiction see Mary Shaw, Bethan Thomas, George Davey Smith, and Daniel Dorling, *The Grim Reaper's Road Map: An Atlas of Mortality in Britain* (Bristol: Policy Press, 2008), 19, 40; and Harold E. Doweiko, *Concepts of Chemical Dependency*, 8th Edition (Belmont, CA: Brooks/Cole, 2012), 4; for alcoholism see Katherine van Wormer and Diane Rae Javis, *Addiction Treatment: A Strengths Perspective*, 3rd ed. (Belmont, CA: Brooks/Cole, 2013), 211; for paraphilias see Money and Ehrhard, *Man and Woman*, 148 and Sigrid Güzel, "Ava und Edam: Ist die Partnerschaft zwischen Mann und Frau überhaupt möglich?" *Psyche* 43, No. 3 (1989): 235–36; for psychopathy see Anne Campbell, *Men, Women, and Aggression* (New York: Basic Books, 1994), 79; for empathy see Christian Keyser, *The Empathic Brain*, 215, 207; "Eine fast mystische Verbindung," *Der Spiegel*, July 15, 2013, 124.

21 Sarah Gregory, Dominic Ffytche, Andrew Simmons, Veena Kumari, Matthew Howard, Sheilagh Hodgins, Nigel Blackwood, "The Antisocial Brain: Psychopathy Matters: A Structural MRI Investigation of Antisocial Male Violent Offenders," *Archives of General Psychiatry* 69, no. 9 (2012): 962–72.

his father. A girl, though she must develop her own identity, can model it after her mother's, while the boy must differentiate himself from his mother, or he will never become masculine. As Stephen Ducat describes the process: "Because girls will grow up to become women—thus, they will become like their mother—most of them experience continuity in the inclusiveness of their gender identity" and are also "unburdened by the need to constantly prove their gender."[22] Nancy Chodorow explains that "growing girls come to define and experience themselves as continuous with others; their experience of self contains more flexible or permeable ego boundaries. Boys come to define themselves as more separate and distinct, with a greater sense of rigid ego boundaries and differentiation. The basic feminine sense of self is connected to the world, the basic masculine sense of self is separate."[23] This separation can go too far and become destructive alienation.

To achieve this separation, many societies have developed puberty rituals for boys, rituals that contain the three stages that Arnold van Gennep identified: separation, transition, and incorporation.[24] Among the Australian Kurnai, according to Alfred Howitt, the pattern of separation is vivid: "The intention of all that is done at this ceremony is to make a momentous change in the boy's life; the past is to be cut off from him by a gulf that he can never repass. His connection with his mother as her child is broken off, and he becomes henceforth attached to the men."[25] The initiate is often considered dead[26] and his initiation is a rebirth.[27] Rosalind Miles describes this dynamic: "To be a male is the opposite of being mother. To be a man, the boy must break away from her, and the further

22 Stephen J. Ducat, *The Wimp Factor: Gender Gaps, Holy Wars, and the Politics of Anxious Masculinity* (Boston: Beacon Press, 2004), 31–32.

23 Nancy Chodorow, *The Reproduction of Mothering: Psychoanalysis and the Sociology of Gender* (Berkeley: University of California Press, 1978), 169.

24 See Arnold van Gennep, *The Rites of Passage*, trans. Monika K. Vizedom and Gabrielle L. Caffee (London: Routledge and Kegan Paul, 1960), 75.

25 Alfred W. Howitt, *The Native Tribes of South-East Australia* (London: Macmillan, 1904), 532.

26 Van Gennep, *The Rites of Passage*, 75.

27 See Elsie Clews Parsons, *Pueblo Indian Religion*, Vol. 1 (Lincoln: University of Nebraska Press, 1996), 118.

he travels, the greater will be the success of his journey,"[28] success, that is, in the phase of differentiation from the female. He is born again, but this time of man, not of woman.

According to Miles, this birth, like the first one, is often bloody and violent: "To make the break, however, the boy has to be constantly encouraged, threatened, thrust forward at every turn and side, and never, never permitted to fall back." Boys who undergo this transformation have a lifelong bond with all others who have so suffered. Miles describes the bonding that results from masculine initiation: "No boy, of course, could ever forget an experience like this. . . . The only others able to share his experience will be those who have undergone it with him, pain for pain, blood for blood: that group will then be bonded closer than husband and wife, closer than siblings, closer than mother and child. As the boy is violently disassociated from mother, home, and family, so he is associated, with equal violence, with the group of other boys who will henceforward be from rebirth or death his blood brothers."[29] Men desire an initiation into masculinity, an initiation which requires dying to the old life as a child and being reborn to the new life as a man, even if it entails the possibility of physical death.

The infantile and the feminine, a man feels, are always threatening to drag him back, to keep him from achieving masculinity. Males feel they always have to be on the guard against the temptation to return to the blissful symbiosis and safety of mother and child.[30] Willard Gaylin explains of the boy: "In his search for manhood, any 'feminine' character traits and aspirations will be interpreted as being womanly and therefore threatening. To prove himself a man, a boy must first prove himself *not a woman*. His definition of self is always comparative and contrary." This is especially true of a boy raised without a model of masculinity with which he can identify. Such a boy is insecure in his masculinity and often becomes, as Stephen Ducats puts it, hypermasculine because he needs "to repudiate any aspect of himself that might be construed as feminine." Ducat cites the case of

28 Rosalind Miles, *The Rites of Man: Love, Sex and Death in the Making of the Male* (London: Grafton Books, 1991), 44.

29 Miles, *Rites of Man*, 44, 76.

30 Robert J. Stoller, *Presentations of Gender* (New Haven: Yale University Press, 1992), 17.

the Israeli Kibbutzim. Although theoretically egalitarian, the demands of physical labor meant that men were absent working and women cared for children. A study revealed that only 4% of Israeli soldiers in the 1967 Six-Day War had grown up on a kibbutz, but they accounted for 25% of the fatalities. In a control group of city-raised soldiers, only 45% had feminine scores in a test of unconscious gender identity, while 70% of the men from the Kibbutz "showed responses more typical of women." These men had a stronger identification with their mothers' femininity, but were also more likely to take risks: "By defying concerns for safety, such men are avoiding the feminization they associate with being secure and protected."[31]

The absence of a father often evokes hypermasculine behavior in the boy, because there is no clear path to establishing a masculine identity apart from rejecting the feminine. David Blankenhorn claims that "fatherless boys commit crimes."[32] Obviously other factors influence crime rates, but father-absence in general correlates to higher crime, among both blacks and whites.[33] The presence of a father can offer the boy a different and less destructive path to attaining masculinity.

The Role of the Father

The father separates the son from the mother by being "a wedge between mother and child" and by "inviting and then limiting aggressive displays"[34]; he teaches his son how to use and control aggression. If his father demonstrates empathy and respect for the mother, the boy will learn that both empathy and respect for the feminine are an essential part of being

---

31 Willard Gaylin, *The Male Ego* (New York: Viking, 1992), 26. Ducat, *The Wimp Factor*, 31, 56. See also Kimmel, *Gendered Society*, 53; Scott Coltrane, *Family Man: Fatherhood, Housework, and Gender Equity* (New York: Oxford University Press, 1996), 187–88.

32 David Blankenhorn, *Fatherless America: Confronting Our Most Urgent Social Problem* (New York: Basic Books, 1995), 30.

33 See Paul Raeburn, *Do Fathers Matter: What Science is Telling Us about the Parent We've Overlooked* (New York: Scientific American/Farrar, Straus and Giroux: 2014), 221–24.

34 John Munder Ross, *What Men Want: Mothers, Fathers, and Manhood* (Cambridge, MA: Harvard University Press, 1994), 80.

masculine.[35] As Michael Diamond explains, "boys realize that their dads take care of them as well, they recognize that affection and caretaking are not exclusively feminine qualities. And in recognizing his father as a loving man, the boy himself can embrace love in conflict-free ways as well since he has already embraced the similarities between them [i.e., father and son]."[36] The boy differentiates from his mother but in this scenario does not view qualities such as empathy as being exclusively feminine. Myriam Medzian explains: "When a boy is able from the earliest age to identity with his father, and when that identification includes loving, nurturing, and feeling connected with others, then his developing a masculine identity does not depend on his repressing his identification with his mother and her feminine qualities. He does not need to be contemptuous of a woman to solidify his identity as a man. Having had a nurturant father, he is more likely to be empathetic toward others, including girls."[37] Girls also greatly benefit from an involved father.[38]

When a man becomes a father and is involved with his children, he becomes a better person and helps his children become better persons. His testosterone level drops—and with it many destructive behaviors.[39] One study showed "that prior to fatherhood, the men's identities centered on independence, aggressiveness, and self-concerns, whereas following fatherhood their identities included strong elements of caring and empathy."[40] A man who has

35 See Raeburn, *Do Fathers Matter*, 179–80.

36 Michael J. Diamond, *My Father Before Me: How Fathers and Sons Influence Each Other throughout Their Lives* (New York: W. W. Norton, 2007), 73.

37 Myriam Medzian, *Boys Will be Boys: Breaking the Link between Masculinity and Violence* (New York: Lantern Books, 2002), 90. See also Michael E. Lamb, "How *Do* Fathers Influence Children's Development? Let Me Count the Ways," in *The Role of the Father in Child Development*, ed. Michael E. Lamb, 5th ed. (New York: John Wiley & Sons, 2010), 7.

38 See Raeburn, *Do Fathers Matter*, 160–66.

39 Lee T. Gettler, Thomas W. McDade Alan B. Feranil, and Christopher W. Kuzawa, "Longitudinal evidence that fatherhood decreases testosterone in human males," *Proceedings of the National Academy of Sciences* 108, no. 39 (2011). http://www.pnas.org/content/108/39/16194.full. See also Raeburn, *Do Fathers Matter*, 74–76.

40 David Popenoe, *Life without Father: Compelling New Evidence that Fatherhood and Marriage are Indispensable for the Good of Children and Society* (New York: Free Press, 1996), 79.

a primary identity as a father develops and manifests the qualities that will help his sons also become empathetic, good, family-involved fathers. The absence of fathers in large segments of society therefore contributes to hypermasculine, destructive behavior among boys trying to become men.[41]

The Struggle for Fame

Because his identity is always precarious, a man, more than a woman, needs *kleos,* the fame that gives him escape from non-identity, from oblivion, from being a nobody. Manhood is "the Big Impossible," something that is never finally achieved (except perhaps by an heroic death) and its existence is always precarious. Men want to be recognized, to be honored, and they strive in a thousand ways to have their identity, and their identity specifically as men, acknowledged. The Boy Scout collects merit badges, scientists collect Nobel Prizes, soldiers collect medals, Wall Streeters collect bonuses, thugs collect prison terms, tattoos, scars—anything that establishes identity and encourages others to notice him and affirm him in his masculine identity.

Men are always seeking to prove their manhood by testing themselves against an adversary, whether another man, or society, or nature. As Nancy Dowd explains, "a key part of manhood . . . is constantly to be measured by other men." Charles Darwin concluded that "man is the rival of other men; he delights in competition, and this leads to ambition which passes too easily into selfishness." Testing oneself against other men is crucial to establishing masculinity. Competition of all kinds can help establish masculinity: fighting, sports, music, debates. In the Icelandic sagas we encounter the *ójafnaðarmaðr,* the arrogant man who is always trying to top and dominate someone else. Jacob Burckhardt examined the centrality of *agon* to the Greek world, not just in athletics and arts, but in everything: "the whole of Greek life" was "dominated by the habit of competition." In the world of competitors, there are a few winners and many losers.[42]

---

41   For comparative rates of non-marital births, see Charles A. Murray, *Coming Apart: The State of White America, 1960–2010* (New York: Cox & Murray, 2012), 163, 194, 190–91.

42   Nancy E. Dowd, *The Man Question: Male Subordination and Privilege* (New York: New York University Press, 2010), 21; Charles Darwin, *The Descent of*

Men and women on the average have the same abilities, distributed on a bell curve. But the bell curve for men extends further in both directions. For example, there are more male geniuses, but also more males are severely mentally retarded.[43] Human societies are pyramids. As Synnott points out: "there are relatively few women at the very top, and relatively few at the very bottom: a higher proportion are in the middle."[44] Males, as feminists have noticed, are overrepresented at the top. But they are also overrepresented at the far larger bottom, a fact which is often forgotten.[45] There are far more men homeless[46] and in prison[47] than there are CEOs and senators. If there is a glass ceiling that prevents women from rising to the top, there is no safety net that keeps men from falling into the depths. If anything, men are forced down by systems that penalize their weaknesses.

Will Courtney points out the self-destructiveness of masculinity: "many of the behaviors men use to 'be men' are the same behaviors that increase their risk of disease, injury, and death."[48] Walter Farrell, in *The Myth of Male Power*,[49]

Man and Selection in Relation to Sex, Vol. 2 (London: John Murray, 1871), 326; Jacob Burckhardt, *The Greeks and Greek Civilization*, ed. Oswyn Murray, trans. Sheila Sheen (New York: St. Martin's, 1998), 182.

43 See Roy F. Baumeister, *Is There Anything Good about Men? How Cultures Flourish by Exploiting* Men (New York: Oxford University Press, 2010), 31–34.

44 Anthony Synnott, *Re-Thinking Men: Heroes, Villains and Victims* (Farnham, England: Ashgate, 2009), 206.

45 See Baumeister, *Is There Anything Good about Men?* 17–19.

46 See Joseph Fernandez, "Homelessness: An Irish Perspective," in *Homelessness and Mental Health*, ed. Dinesh Bhugra (Cambridge: Cambridge University Press, 1996), 210; and U.S. Department of Housing and Urban Development, Office of Community Planning and Development, "The 2010 Annual Homeless Assessment Report to Congress," 2011. https://www.hudexchange.info/resources/documents/2010homelessassessmentreport.pdf.

47 In the United States, about 1.1% of all women will eventually go to prison but 9% of all men. However, among Hispanic men, 15.9% will go to prison, and among black men, 28.5% (Ernest Drucker, *A Plague of Prisons: The Epidemiology of Mass Incarceration in America* [New York: New Press, 2011], 94).

48 Will Courtney, *Dying to Be Men: Psychosocial, Environmental, and Biobehavioral Directions in Promoting the Health of Men and Boys* (New York: Routledge Taylor & Francis, 2011), xviii.

49 Warren Farrell, *The Myth of Male Power: Why Men Are the Disposable Sex* (New York: Simon & Schuster, 1993).

and Herb Goldberg, in *The Hazards of Being Male*,[50] have documented that men have more physical and mental diseases, commit more crimes, go to jail more often, and finally die earlier than women: "every critical statistic in the area of longevity, disease, suicide, crime, accidents, childhood emotional disorders, alcoholism, and drug addiction shows a disproportionately higher male rate."[51] Sebastian Junger laments that "statistically, it is six times as dangerous to spend a year as a young man in America than as a cop or fireman, and vastly more dangerous than a one-year deployment at a big military base in Afghanistan. You'd have to go to a remote firebase like KOP or Camp Blessing to find a level of risk that surpasses that of being an adolescent male back home."[52] The worldwide suicide rate among men is almost double that among women.[53] Fewer women and more men are committing suicide.[54] As Synnott says, "men recognize that other men, including themselves, and women, do not value men's lives." Therefore a man does not value his own life; he may volunteer for the Marines or neglect health symptoms that would send a woman immediately to the doctor.

As Synnott observes, "Men are trained to be heroes, and to risk their lives not only for their loved ones, but even for perfect strangers, for their country, for the preservation of law and order . . . and especially for women."[55] As Jonathan Gottschall explains, "if something evil comes through the front door, everyone knows whose job it is to die guarding the family's retreat out the back."[56] Men must cultivate courage to do this, and

50 Herb Goldberg, *The Hazards of Being Male: Surviving the Myth of Masculine Privilege* (New York: Signet, 1987). See also James Harrison, "Warning: The Male Sex Role May Be Dangerous to Your Health," *Journal of Social Issues* 14, no. 1 (1978): 65–86.

51 Goldberg, *Hazards of Being Male*, 5.

52 Sebastian Junger, *War* (New York: Twelve, 2010), 238.

53 Etienne G. Krug et al., eds., *World Report on Violence and Health* (Geneva: World Health Organization), 10.

54 In the United States the rate of suicide among men increased 13% from 1970 to 1996 and *fell* 35% among women (Ronald W. Maris, Alan L. Berman, Morton M. Silverman, *Comprehensive Textbook of Suicidology* [New York: Guilford Press, 2000], 150).

55 Synnott, *Re-Thinking Men*, 113.

56 Jonathan Gottschall, *The Professor in the Cage: Why Men Fight and Why We Like to Watch* (New York: Penguin, 2015), 93.

one aspect of courage is not to make the preservation of one's life the highest priority. Therefore men take risks, and are encouraged to take risks, to test themselves against challenges, whether their opponents are personal or impersonal. Synnott continues: "Self-protection and self-care are not traditional male cultural attributes. They are not mutually exclusive to adventure and altruism, but they are opposed to traditional definitions of masculinity, and normative expectations of male toughness and stoicism."[57] Men must accept their expendability.

Men therefore take on the dangerous work that society needs: most obviously war,[58] but also dangerous civilian occupations. Of the twenty most dangerous civilian occupations, all but one are almost entirely male.[59] In Great Britain 97% of those killed by machinery are males.[60] In the United States, although males constitute only a little more than half of the workforce, they account for nearly all (92%) of fatal injuries on the job. Among law enforcement officers, 95% of those killed in the line of duty are males; 97% of all firefighters killed are males.[61] Men also nurture, but not in the same way women nurture: "Men nurture their society by shedding their blood, their sweat, and their semen, by bringing home food for both child and mother, and by dying if necessary in faraway places to provide a safe haven for their people."[62] Male social dominance must be seen in this context. A man seeks power and wealth and success not for himself, but for

---

57 Synnott, *Re-Thinking Men*, 192.
58 In the American Civil War there were almost no civilian deaths; but 750,000 men died (Guy Gugliotta, "New Estimate Raises Civil War Toll," *New York Times*, April 2, 2012). In the Iraq War, in which women served in the American military, 4261 men and 104 women died. (Anne Leland and Mari-Jana Oberoceanu, *American War and Military Operations Casualties: Lists and Statistics*, Congressional Research Service, 2010). Even in countries in which the civilian population was targeted, men died more often. Of the 26 million Soviet citizens estimated to have died in the Second World War, 20 million were male (Elizabeth Brainerd, *Uncounted Costs of World War II: The Effects of Changing Sex Ratios on the Marriage and Fertility of Russian Women* [Seattle, WA: The National Council for Eurasian and East European Research, 2007], 4).
59 Farrell, *Myth*, 105. See also Harrison, "Warning," 65.
60 Shaw, *Grim Reaper's Road Map*, 62.
61 Courtney, *Dying to Be Men*, 31.
62 Gilmore, *Manhood in the Making*, 230.

others. He is honored for his willingness to serve and to die, for his "selfless generosity, even to the point of sacrifice"[63] and is therefore given charge of the community.[64] As Michael Levin points out, "if sex roles are to be regarded as the outcome of bargaining in which men received dominance in exchange for the risk of violent death, it is hardly clear that they got the better deal."[65] The hero is deified only after his death. But men seek this posthumous honor.

The ideology of masculinity takes different shapes because societies face a variety of challenges. The ancient world of the Mediterranean had its own standards of masculinity. Jesus of Nazareth lived in that society, and those who recorded his life were at pains to show that he met those standards, although in an unexpected way. It is to the masculinity of Jesus and its changing depictions that we will now turn.

63 Ibid., 229.
64 Goldberg, *Hazards of Being Male*, 5.
65 Michael Levin, *Feminism and Freedom* (New Brunswick, NJ: Transaction Books, 1987), 8.

Chapter Two
The Masculinity of Jesus

The broad outlines of masculinity are common to almost all cultures including the Mediterranean one in which Jesus lived, and for which the authors of the gospels and epistles wrote. They wanted to show that Jesus, despite his membership in a conquered people and his ignominious death, was not only masculine according to the general standards of society but indeed exemplified the highest ideals of masculinity, as both pagan and Jewish society understood them. But in modern times the image of Jesus often became feminized; in reaction he has been depicted as exemplifying a type of modern masculinity, whether businessman or athlete.

Greco-Roman Masculinity

Classical writers knew that masculinity was not simply maleness. A male (*mas, homo*) had to become a man (*vir*).[1] Manhood was an unstable combination, difficult to attain and to maintain. A man had to be dominant and active and energetic. But he also had to be self-disciplined and not ruled by his passions. A man had to dominate himself and his passions, to manifest self-control; Stoicism especially emphasized this. Both the divine emperors and the divine man Moses were exemplars of self-control.[2] A man dominated by his passions was effeminate, even if those passions were lust and anger, which might seem to be male passions. For the boy in the classical world, as Colleen Conway summarizes, "to become a man means

---

1   Carlin A. Barton, *Roman Honor: The Fire in the Bones* (Berkeley: University of California Press, 2001), 38.

2   See Thomas Henry Billings, *The Platonism of Philo Judaeus* (Chicago: University of Chicago Press: 1919), 58.

becoming the opposite of wild, evil, and uncontrollable,"[3] and therefore these bad qualities were depicted as feminine, to be rejected by men who strove to be masculine.

A man had to display manly virtues—in fact virtue itself was scarcely distinguishable from manliness. Latin *virtus*, virtue, is derived from *vir*, man; Greek *andreia*, courage, is derived from *aner*, man.[4] For the Latins *virtus* was essentially courage, especially military courage, and was primarily a property of men.[5] A man had to be courageous to bear pain and to suffer death in the service of the community and thereby earn honor. Carlin Barton summarizes the essence of Roman manhood: "Above all, a man willed himself to be expendable."[6] A man received the highest honor when he faced the greatest danger, against impossible odds, to save his people, and in saving them he became their father, for the father was a savior.[7] Barton claims that "the Roman Emperors were aware that the giver of mercy was infinitely more powerful than the guarantor of justice"; Seneca explained that "no one has saved the life of another who was not greater than the one he saved."[8] Not only could the emperor refrain from punishing, he could even decide not to impute the crime. The emperor thereby demonstrated that he was an exemplar of *prautes*, meekness, because his anger was perfectly ruled by reason—at least such was the ideal. The Emperor was the *pater patriae*, and his supremacy was demonstrated by his mercy. Augustus was moved to tears when he received this title from the Senate in 2 B. C.[9]

3   Colleen Conway, *Behold the Man: Jesus and Greco-Roman Masculinity* (New York: Oxford University Press, 2008), 31.

4   See Leon Harold Craig, *The War Lover: A Study of Plato's Republic* (Toronto: University of Toronto Press, 1994); and Angela Hobbs, *Plato and the Hero: Courage, Manliness and the Impersonal Good* (Cambridge: Cambridge University Press, 2000).

5   Catherine Edwards, "The Suffering Body: Philosophy and Pain in Seneca's Letters," in *Constructions of the Classical Body*, ed. James I. Porter (Ann Arbor: University of Michigan Press, 1999), 262.

6   Barton, *Roman Honor*, 47.

7   As Barton explains, "in Roman thought, the father was a savior (*servitor/conservator*) and, conversely, the savior was a father" (*Roman Honor*, 158).

8   Barton, *Roman Honor*, 177.

9   Suetonius, *The Twelve Caesars*, trans. Robert Graves (New York: Penguin Books, 1979), 80.

A man could sorrow. Achilles and Odysseus in the *Iliad* and the *Odyssey* engaged in frequent and copious weeping to the point that commentators were embarrassed.[10] Later Athenians demanded more self-control and thought weeping suitable only to weak women.[11] But not all authors agreed, and Virgil's *Aeneid* is full of the tears of Aeneas and of other warriors. Perhaps the most famous phrase in the *Aeneid* is *sunt lacrimae rerum*. Virgil was imitating Homer, but Roman men seemed to have felt that weeping was not unmasculine, that it showed a strength of *thumos* suitable to a noble masculine character. *Thumos* gave energy to men's grief and pity. According to Barbara Koziak's analysis of Aristotle, through "pity or compassion" one achieves recognition (*anagnorisis*) of the other. This is the basis of political life, of life in common. One "must perceive the nature and extent of human suffering, be disposed through recognition to seeing kinship, and act to reinforce the necessary dependency of citizens on one another."[12] Achilles and Priam at the end of the *Iliad* come together to share mutual sorrow over universal mortality, a mortality of which the warrior, the soldier, the hero are especially conscious.[13]

> Priam sat huddled at the feet of Achilles and wept close for manslaughtering Hektor and Achilles wept now for his own father, now again for Patroclus.[14]

In addition to *virtus* and *andreia*, classical writers had another term that was important to the concept of manliness: *thumos*. Caroline Caswell maintains that θυμός, *thumos*, "inner wind, bearer of consciousness,

---

10 See Barbara Koziak, *Retrieving Political Emotion: Thumos, Aristotle, and Gender* (University Park: Pennsylvania State University Press, 2000), 47.
11 For a discussion of the change, see Hans van Wees, "A Brief History of Tears: Gender Differentiation in Archaic Greece," in *When Men Were Men: Masculinity, Power and Identity in Classical Antiquity*, eds. Lin Foxhall and John Salmon (London: Routledge, 1998), 10–53.
12 Koziak, *Retrieving Political Emotion*, 149.
13 See Lindsey Zachary, "When Men Cry: Male Demonstrations of Grief in 'Beowulf,' 'The Song of Roland,' and 'Sir Orfeo,'" M.A. Thesis, University of Arkansas, 2011. UMI Dissertation Publishing.
14 *Iliad*, 24, lines 509–12, trans. Richard Lattimore (Chicago: University of Chicago Press, 2011), 510–11.

energy, and experience," is derived from *thuo*, θυο, "to rush, run, flow." and is closely associated with the winds. After the early Greek epic *thumos* was restricted from meaning all emotion to meaning primarily "violent emotion."[15] *Pneuma* and *thumos*, both translated as "spirit," have similar derivations. *Pneuma* means breath. The Septuagint uses both *pneuma* and *thumos* or their variations to translate the Hebrew *ruah*, spirit or breath, although *thumos* seems to be used more for the inner forces and emotions of human beings.[16] *Thumos* and *orge* are largely synonymous, and both occur in the New Testament, especially in regard to the anger of God, and are therefore associated with fire.

Thumos was used by the Greeks in several related senses[17]:

1. it is life or animation;[18]
2. it is the seat of the emotions, or emotions in general;[19]
3. it is especially energetic emotion, spiritedness;
4. it is the fiery, energetic impulse to achieve victory and consequent recognition;[20]
5. it is emotion provoked by an obstacle or an evil: anger[21] or grief.

Plato influenced later discussion of *thumos* by his tripartite division of the soul (and of the state, the soul writ large) into reason, desire, and *thumos*,

---

15 Caroline Caswell, *A Study of Thumos in Early Greek Epic* (Leiden: E. J. Brill, 1990), 63.

16 G. Johannes Botterweck, Helmer Ringgren, and Heinz-Josef Fabry, eds., David E. Green and Douglas W. Stott, trans., *Theological Dictionary of the Old Testament*, Vol. 13 (Grand Rapids, MI: B. Eerdmans, 2004), 395.

17 See Jean Frère, *Ardeur et colère: le thumos platonicien* (Paris: Éditions Kimé, 2004).

18 See Barry Sandywell, *The Beginnings of European Theorizing: Reflexivity in the Archaic Age* (London: Routledge, 1996, 102); and Hobbs, *Plato and the Hero*, 8.

19 See Koziak, *Retrieving Political Emotion*, 100; and Sandywell, *The Beginnings of European Theorizing*, 104–05.

20 In Plato's understanding, *thumos* "desires worldly success and reputation" (Hobbs, *Plato and the Hero*, 24).

21 See Kevin White, "The Passions of the Soul," in *The Ethics of Aquinas*, ed. Stephen J. Pope (Washington, DC: Georgetown University Press, 2002), 109.

which in his usage has primarily meanings 3, 4, and 5.[22] Plato thought that *thumos* could serve as an ally of reason against desire, because it opposes injustice and seeks the honorable rather than the pleasurable. But *thumos* needs the guidance of reason in order to play its proper role in the soul and in the state. Plato compared *thumos* to a watchdog, who would run ahead of reason against any stranger. It has to be guided by reason, as the soldiers in the city have to be guided by philosophers, so that they will be hostile to strangers and gentle to citizens.

Thumos as anger was moderated by *prautes*, meekness. Aristotle in *Nichomachean Ethics*, 5 defines *prautes* as the mean between being too angry and not being angry enough. The meek (*praus*) man "feels anger according to the dictates of reason, on proper occasions, and for a proper length of time." It is possible to err either by feeling too little anger or by inappropriate anger. William Barclay discusses the meaning of *praus* and *prautes* in the New Testament. In classical Greek it is used to describe a gentle wind (connecting it to *thumos*) or a spirited horse that has been tamed: "There is gentleness in *praus* but behind the gentleness there is the strength of steel, for the supreme characteristic of the man who is *praus* is that he is a man under perfect control."[23] Marcus Aurelius maintained that "to be lenient (πραον—*praon*) and gentle is more human and thus more manly (αρρενικωτεροη—*arrenikoteron*—virile)" (*Meditations* 11.18),[24] more manly because more self-controlled.

The truly masculine man is therefore also meek. Meekness is the virtue that moderates *thumos*, especially *thumos* as anger, and directs it to the proper manifestation. Aristotle taught that a virtue is the mean between two vices. Courage, for example, is the mean between cowardice and foolhardiness. But the virtue is not in the exact middle; it is closer to one vice than the opposite one, and therefore can be mistaken for that vice (*Nicomachean Ethics*, II.8). Cowardice cannot be mistaken for courage, but

22 Harold Bloom, ed., *The Odyssey* (New York: Infobase Publishing, 2007), 98.
23 William Barclay, *New Testament Words* (Philadelphia: Westminster Press, 1964), 241–42.
24 See Conway, *Behold the Man*, 82, and Mathew Kuefler, *The Manly Eunuch: Masculinity, Gender Ambiguity, and Christian Ideology in Late Antiquity* (Chicago: University of Chicago Press, 2001), 27–28.

foolhardiness can be. Meekness, *prautes*, is the mean between wrath and what I will call spiritlessness. Meekness cannot be mistaken for wrath, but it can be mistaken for spiritlessness, a lack of anger when anger should exist.

True meekness is not only compatible with anger; it makes the person angry when he should be angry and in the manner he should be angry. Therefore Moses, who killed the Egyptian, who called down the plagues upon Egypt, and who commanded that the idolaters be slain without mercy, was the meekest of men (*Numbers* 12.3). Continuing the classical analysis, Aquinas said that without anger the movement of the will against evil is "lacking or weak" (*Summa Theologica* II-II, 158.8). John Chrysostom asserted that "he who is not angry, when he has cause to be, sins."[25] Anger supplies the energy necessary to virtuous combat of evil and to overcoming obstacles to the attainment of the good.[26] Thomas Aquinas held that the "lack of the passion of anger is also a vice" because a person who truly rejects evil will feel anger at it. Anger is a neutral passion, and is "the proper subject matter of the moral virtue of meekness, i.e., that meekness regulates feelings of anger unto the good of reason."[27] In commenting on the *Nicomachean Ethics* Aquinas maintains that "the praiseworthy man is one who is angry about the right things, at the right time, and in due moderation, since he is angry as he should be, when he should be, and as long as he should be."[28] Aquinas, following Aristotle, emphasizes that anger is provoked by an unjust slight, and seeks appropriate vengeance which is an act of justice.[29] It therefore requires the exercise of reason, which, in fallen human nature, anger tends to cloud. Properly exercised anger is praiseworthy, because it gives energy to the contest with evil and enables the person

---

25 Quoted in Peter Kreeft, *Back to Virtue: Traditional Moral Wisdom for Modern Moral Confusion* (San Francisco: Ignatius Press, 1992), 134.

26 See Basil the Great, *On the Human Condition*, trans. Nonna Verna Harrison (Crestwood, NY: St. Vladimir's Seminary Press, 2005), 88–89.

27 Paul Gondreau, *The Passions of Christ's Soul in the Theology of St. Thomas Aquinas* (Scranton: University of Scranton Press, 2009), 429.

28 Quoted in Gondreau, *The Passions of Christ's Soul*, 430. For classical attitudes to anger, see William V. Harris, *Restraining Rage: The Ideology of Anger Control in Classical Antiquity* (Cambridge, MA: Harvard University Press, 2001).

29 Gondreau, *The Passions of Christ's Soul*, 430–32.

to achieve the greatest victory, therefore becoming worthy of the greatest honor.

Thumos motivates the man who seeks honor and recognition.[30] The man dominated by *thumos* is the timocratic man, seeking honor (τιμή, timē) above all.[31] A man should seek the victory that deserves true honor, and he therefore wishes to engage in the most difficult contest that tests all his powers. Socrates implied that philosophy, the love of truth and the struggle to attain it, is the most difficult of all contests. Such a man is superior to the honor-seeking man who relies on the acclaim of those who may judge on false standards and who in any case cannot penetrate beyond the world of appearances and opinions into truth and reality.

Honor is important to men because masculinity is difficult to achieve; men therefore want to be honored in public so that they can be sure that they are masculine, that they have in fact attained the status of manhood. Honor was tested in social interactions and validated by the agonic contest against others.[32] Honor was therefore primarily a quality of men.[33] As Jerome Neyrey points out, a man in antiquity had both a private and a public role, at home and in the public square.[34] The public sphere was inhabited mostly by men, and the men in that sphere represented their kinship group.[35] In that sphere a man could gain honor or experience shame,[36] which in turn would reflect on his kinship group. Honor was also gained in other ways, especially, for Jews, by observing Torah.

---

30 See Hobbs, *Plato and the Hero*, 30, and Francis Fukayama, *The End of History and the Last Man* (New York: Free Press, 1996).

31 See Hobbs, *Plato and the Hero*, 27–30.

32 Jimmy Dale Brewer, *Jesus' Distinctiveness on the Light of Ancient Jewish Masculinity* (Ph.D. Dissertation, Southwest Baptist Theological Seminary, 2010; UMI Dissertation Publishing), 75.

33 Ibid., 76.

34 Jerome H. Neyrey, "Jesus, Gender, and the Gospel of Matthew," in *New Testament Masculinities*, eds. Stephen D. Moore and Janice Capel Anderson (Atlanta: Society of Biblical Literature, 2003), 47.

35 Brewer, *Jesus' Distinctiveness*, 34–35, 47.

36 Brewer, *Jesus' Distinctiveness*, 72.

The Masculinity of Jesus

The writers of the New Testament were faced with a difficulty: how could they show to the classical world that Jesus, a Jewish subject who had undergone the shameful execution of a slave, was in fact the perfect fulfillment of the deepest ideals of masculinity, that he was perfectly self-controlled and displayed proper anger in combating evil; that he dominated the situations he was in; that he displayed courage and was victorious in his contests; that he achieved the most difficult goal and was therefore worthy of the highest honor.[37]

Jesus demonstrated perfect self-control but he did this not by eliminating the passions but by directing them to their proper end. Christians have had a hard time seeing how Jesus could be angry. Deidre Good claims Jesus was never angry.[38] But the Gospels frequently show that Jesus was angry. Paul Gondreau points out that there are five explicit mentions and at least twenty-five indirect references in the Gospels to anger, frustration, or indignation of Jesus—"the Gospels testify more to anger in Jesus' life than to any other emotion."[39] Jesus called his opponents *whited sepulchers*, a *brood of vipers, fit for hell*. He was even angry at Peter: *Get thee behind me Satan!* Even apart from specific mentions of anger, Jesus said that *I have come to cast fire on the earth, and would that it were kindled* and immediately connected this with discord and persecution: *I have come to set a father against his son*. Jesus calls himself *meek and humble of heart*, because his anger was always exercised in accord with reason. According to Gondreau, "more than any other passion, anger readily assists in and accords with Jesus' mission of salvation, which consists in reestablishing the order of divine justice that human sin has perverted."[40] Vengeance, according to Aquinas, is itself a

---

37 See Jerome H. Neyrey, *Honor and Shame in the Gospel of Matthew* (Louisville, KY: Westminster John Knox Press, 1998), 162. Brittany E. Wilson examines the difficulties Luke had in depicting Jesus as conforming to standards of elite classical masculinity in *Unmanly Men: Reconfigurations of Masculinity in Luke–Acts* (New York: Oxford University Press, 2015).

38 See Deidre J. Good, *Jesus the Meek King* (Harrisburg, PA: Trinity Press International, 1999), 86.

39 Paul Gondreau, *The Passions of Christ's Soul*, 37.

40 Ibid., 437.

good: "It is praiseworthy to desire vengeance as a corrective of vice and to preserve the good of justice."[41] In *Revelation* the wrath of the Lamb is revealed, as Jesus, the divine hero, destroys his enemies, and the last enemy to be destroyed is death, which is cast into the fiery furnace. Therefore perfect justice is attained and the kingdom of God established.

Jesus attained honor by being victorious in his contests. Some of his opponents were human. Jesus tested himself in his interactions with other men, starting with his questioning of the doctors in the temple and continuing with his tests of intellect against the Pharisees and Sadducees, discussing politics and theology in a highly public setting to see who would come out on top.[42] As Conway observes, Jesus "betters his opponents in various conflicts and competitions, including those opponents who represent the elite leaders in the community."[43] Jesus' life was a life lived in these public contests; he had no family, no home. Jesus' celibacy and his separation from family life was a masculine separation, the going-forth from the safe world of the family to accept the challenges of the public world. Even for the classical world, both Jewish and pagan, "renunciation of traditional social structures is a form of asceticism, and ascetic practice was itself a means toward ideal masculinity."[44] Celibacy demonstrated self-control of the sexual passions and, by renouncing the consolations of family, an acceptance of hardship.

The Pharisees were not Jesus' most dangerous opponents; he fought Satan and Death in the most public sphere, before the eyes of his Father and of the angels. As David Gilmore wrote of human masculinity, "men nurture their society by shedding their blood, their sweat, and their semen, by bringing home food for both child and mother, and by dying if necessary in faraway places to provide a safe haven for their people."[45] By doing this they earn the right to be honored. For the Romans, "a man willed himself to be expendable . . . and fed the fire of his honor on his own substance."[46]

41 Quoted in Gondreau, *Passions of Christ's Soul*, 434, ST II-II, q. 158 a. 1 ad 3.
42 Brewer, *Jesus' Distinctiveness*, 121.
43 Conway, *Behold the Man*, 95.
44 Ibid., 123.
45 David D. Gilmore, *Manhood in the Making: Cultural Concepts of Masculinity* (New Haven: Yale University Press, 1990), 230.
46 Barton, *Roman Honor*, 40.

Jesus accepted his expendability and emptied himself even to death on a cross, crying out "My God, my God, why have you forsaken me?" As Conway notes, this "agonized cry from the cross is the sound of the cultural expendability of men who are expected to die on demand."[47]

Jesus died to save his people, as many men die in hazardous occupations and warfare. Jesus nourished by giving his own body and blood as true food and true drink. Unlike every other hero, Jesus not only confronted Death but defeated it. Jesus accepted the structure of honor and shame, but he gave it a new meaning.[48] He rejected the narrow ethnocentrism of the kinship group. The primary relationship of the new group was not biological kinship, but relationship to Jesus. His primary relationships are non-family relationships with his disciples, who are his mother and sister and brother. If kinship came into conflict with the commitment to Jesus, kinship had to be sacrificed.[49]

Like Socrates, Jesus despises the common notions of honor and holds out an ideal of true honor which comes from God, who does not judge by appearances and whose standards are infallible. Matthew portrays Jesus as "an ideal, honorable male."[50] His titles of honor—Son of God, Son of David, King of Israel, Messiah, Prophet—are all titles of men operating in the public sphere. As Jimmy Brewer summarizes: "Rather than remaining a social commodity of sorts to be gained at the expense of other men by the approval of a particular set of peers, Jesus presents honor as an award granted primarily by God's recognition of humble service to others."[51] Honor came primarily not from the recognition of other men, but from God the Father.

Jesus suffered crucifixion, the dishonorable death of a slave, but by that means attained *the name that is above all other names*. Paul accepted the classical ideal of masculinity and showed how Jesus fulfilled it and how a

---

47   Conway, *Behold the Man*, 183.
48   See Mary Stewart Leeuwen, *My Brother's Keeper: What Social Sciences Do (and Don't) Tell Us about Masculinity* (Downers Grove, IL: InterVarsity Press, 2002), 5960.
49   Brewer, *Jesus' Distinctiveness*, 135.
50   Jerome H. Neyrey, "Jesus, Gender, and the Gospel of Matthew," in Moore and Anderson, *New Testament Masculinities*, 66.
51   Brewer, *Jesus' Distinctiveness*, 173.

Christian could attain it. A man attained true manhood by a noble death[52] in service to others; Jesus above all did this. His self-emptying of his divinity and his becoming nothing on the cross was the way he saved the world. For Paul, Jesus' seemingly shameful death was in fact understandable, even in classical terms, as an heroic death.[53] By his conquest of death and his resurrection Jesus was established as Lord, *Kyrios*, and his kingdom is universal and eternal.[54] Jesus continues to exercise his self-restraint and clemency, characteristics of the ideal ruler, by restraining his divine anger at the evil of the world, and thereby manifests his manhood.

Jesus fulfills the anthropological model of masculinity, especially as it was understood in the classical world. Coming from an inconspicuous but mysterious and honorable background, Jesus leaves the world of his mother and goes about his Father's business. He overcomes all obstacles to save those entrusted to him, and deserves the highest honor, the title of Lord. He uses his strength to serve others in ways small and great, from washing their feet to raising the dead. Jesus confronts death, passes through it, and defeats it, and is initiated into a new life. His emotions, including his anger and love, are intense, manifesting his *thumos*, but they are always perfectly controlled and reasonable.

The Feminized Jesus

Jesus' masculinity was embodied in the images that Christians made. The East has its image of Jesus. It is of an adult Jewish male, with strong features and hair parted in the middle. It may be based on the image-made-without-human hands (*acheiropoieta*), the mandylion, which may be the Shroud of Turin. Whatever the source, this image of Jesus is ancient, and is found in icons from the fifth-century images of St. Catherine's Monastery on Mount Sinai to the present. The East believes this is a true representation of how Jesus looked, and therefore it cannot be altered. It is a very masculine, Jewish image. The West never developed a theology of images and

---

52 See Peter J. Scaer, "The Glorious Dying of the Son: The Gospel of Luke and Jesus' Noble Death" (*Touchstone*, November 2004).

53 See Conway, *Behold the Man*, 87.

54 See Donald Dale Walker, *Paul's Offer of Leniency (2 Cor 10:1)* (Tübingen: Mohn Siebeck, 2002), 147.

never received (in the theological sense) the Seventh Ecumenical Council of 787 A.D., which restored the icons after the period of iconoclasm. Consequently, the depiction of Jesus has been much freer in the West. Initially it was derived from the Byzantine image; usually Jesus was depicted as a strong, virile man. But more recently Jesus has often been blond, blue-eyed, or feminine. The physical image of Jesus in modern Western devotional art has usually not been masculine; it expresses the soft, "meek" personality that Jesus is often thought to have had. Herman Melville reacted to the popular pictures of Jesus: "whatever they may reveal of the divine love in the Son, the soft, curled. hermaphroditical Italian pictures, in which his idea has been successfully embodied, these pictures, destitute as they are of all brawniness, hint nothing of any power, but the mere negative, feminine one of submission and endurance, which on all hands it is conceded, form the peculiar practical virtues of his teachings."[55] Jesus was shown as feminine because, as we shall see, he was understood as coming to make all mankind feminine, that is, submissive and receptive.

The Sacred Heart

If women were responding to Jesus erotically, as they were encouraged to do in the tradition of bridal mysticism which we will examine in the next chapter, one would think that Jesus would be seen as very masculine. However, this was not the case. The original brutal image of the suffering heart that Margaret Mary Alacoque saw was largely replaced by depictions based on a 1767 painting by Pompeo Batoni for the Church of the Gesù (the Jesuit church) in Rome. It shows Jesus, pointing to his heart, but more importantly gazing outward at the viewer, engaging his (or much more often, her) eyes.[56] The new image emphasizes "the tenderness and accessibility, even the vulnerability"[57] of Jesus rather than his brutal physical sacrifice. The feminine softness and sympathetic gaze of Jesus established a bond between him and those who sought his aid, that is, "primarily women and

---

55 Herman Melville, *Moby Dick, or The Whale* (Bybliotech, 2013), 87.
56 David Morgan, *The Sacred Heart of Jesus: The Visual Evolution of a Devotion* (Amsterdam: Amsterdam University Press, 2008), 23.
57 Ibid., 22.

children."[58] This was a major change, as David Morgan points out, from the original image of the Sacred Heart; it substitutes "closeness and delicacy of feeling for the older passion, devoted personal relationship for penitential anguish."[59] The tone of hymns expressed this:

Sweet Heart of Jesus, we implore
O make us love thee more and more
Sweet Heart of Jesus, make us pure and gentle
And teach us how to do Thy blessed will,
To follow close the print of Thy dear footsteps
And when we fall, sweet heart, O love us still.[60]

Jesus was seen as a gentle, non-threatening, understanding man, everything that ordinary men were not. The devotion to the Sacred Heart was taken up by the Jesuits and used against their enemies, the Jansenists, who were dubious about the devotion to the Sacred Heart on theological grounds.[61] But even the Jesuits were not happy with the effeminate overtones of the devotion. Franz Hattler in 1894 described the image of Jesus in the Sacred Heart cult as "a matchmaker" with a "flirtatiously bowed head, longing eyes, a mouth puckered with kisses," and "foppishly crimped hair."[62] Otto Pfülf found the devotion "too sweet," "like a pious fantasy," that was "more suitable for the souls of women."[63] Richard Burton describes the nineteenth-century French Christ as "curiously androgynous, with his wispy beard, doe-like eyes, and delicate,

---

58 Ibid., 23.
59 Ibid., 24.
60 Katherine Massam, *Sacred Threads: Catholic Spirituality in Australia 1922–1962* (Sydney, Australia: UNSW Press, 1996), 64.
61 Tine van Osselaer, *The Pious Sex: Catholic Constructions of Masculinity and Femininity in Belgium, c. 1800–1940* (Louvain: Leuven University Press, 2013), 101.
62 Quoted in Benjamin Ziemann, *Sozialgeschichte der Religion* (Frankfurt-am-Main: Campus Verlag, 2009), 124.
63 Quoted in Norbert Busch, "Die Feminisierung der ultramontanen Frömmigkeit," in *Wunderbare Erscheinungen: Frauen und katholische Frömmigkeit in 19. und 20. Jahrhundert*, ed. Irmtraud Götz von Olenhusen (Paderborn: Ferdinand Schöningh, 1995), 206.

soft-limbed body."[64] In 1899 in the United States an historian described the image of the Sacred Heart as "a young man in flowing gowns, with soft face, large eyes, small delicate mouth, slightly parted lips, small thin nose, downy beard, long curly hair parted in the middle and falling gracefully to the shoulders, slender hands,"[65] or, as another critic called the image, "a biological Valentine."[66] George Cutten at the beginning of the twentieth century claimed that "Roman Catholic art depicts him [Christ] as most effeminate, and he is always described as the passive sufferer, with hyper-developed emotions."[67]

Such sentiments and images did not appeal to men, as Pius XII recognized, when he criticized those who thought the devotion to the Sacred Heart "a type of piety nourished not by the soul and mind but by the senses and consequently more suited to the use of women, since it seems to them something not quite suitable for educated men,"[68] As a badge, the Sacred Heart had political and therefore masculine implications,[69] but as a devotion it was decidedly non- if not anti-masculine.

64 Richard D. E. Burton, *Holy Tears. Holy Blood: Women, Catholicism, and the Culture of Suffering in France, 1840-1970* (Ithaca, NY: Cornell University Press, 2004), 23.

65 Coleen McDannell, *Material Christianity: Religion and Popular Culture in America* (New Haven: Yale University Press, 1995), 180; Stephen Prothero, *American Jesus: How the Son of God Became an American Icon* (New York: Farrar, Straus & Giroux, 2003), 120.

66 McDannell, *Material Christianity*, 189. See also Prothero, *American Jesus*, 120.

67 George Barton Cutten, *The Psychological Phenomenon of Christianity* (New York: Charles Scribner's Sons, 1908), 296.

68 Pope Pius XII, *Haurietis aquam*, May 15, 1956, Vatican translation. http://www.vatican.va/holy_father/pius_xii/encyclicals/documents/hf_p-xii_enc_15051956_haurietis-aquas_en.html.

69 For the political use of the emblem of the Sacred Heart, see Raymond Jonas, *France and the Cult of the Sacred Heart: An Epic Tale for Modern Times* (Berkeley: University of California Press, 2000); van Osselaer, *The Pious Sex*, 102–03; Lawrence Cole, "The Counter-Reformation's Last Stand: Austria," in Clark and Kaiser, *Culture Wars*, 294–95; Julio de la Cueva, "The Assault on the City of the Levites: Spain," in Clark and Kaiser, *Culture Wars*, 198–99); Patrick Turnbull, *The Spanish Civil War, 1936–1939* (Oxford: Osprey Publishing, 1978), 9; and Michael Seidman, *The Victorious Counter-Revolution: The Nationalist Effort in the Spanish Civil War* (Madison: University of Wisconsin Press, 2011), 171.

The Protestant Jesus

The Congregational minister Jason Pierce asked about Jesus in his 1912
The Masculine Power of Christ, "was he distinctly manly and virile, or was
he effeminate and weak?"[70] In Renaissance art Jesus had been manly and
virile, and Leo Steinberg thinks that his male sexuality was emphasized
to the point that modern viewers are uncomfortable.[71] But the Protestant
Jesus, like the Catholic one, became feminized. The Pre-Raphaelite
Brotherhood wanted to show a masculine Christ, but shied away from
any hint of adult sexuality that a muscular male body might convey. They
therefore showed Jesus as a child (Millais's "Christ in the House of His
Parents") and when they did show an adult Jesus, he was often androgynous. Hunt's well-known "The Light of the World" shows a feminized
Jesus. Hunt used Christina Rossetti as one of the models for the head,[72]
and Jesus wears a soft, rich gown. Bruce Barton complained that "painters
have made Him soft-faced, and effeminate."[73] Francis Peabody, the chaplain for Harvard, complained that artists had made Christ a "pallid sufferer"; a Congregationalist complained of the stained-glass Jesus with
"long hair and women's skirts."[74] Another Congregationalist complained
that artists had shown Jesus as "subdued and meek, calm and effeminate."[75] Robert Warren Conant decried the image of Jesus, "'meek and
lowly' with an expression of sweetness and resignation, eyes often downcast, soft hands gently folded, long curling hair brushed smoothly from
a central parting—all feminine, passive, negative."[76] G. Stanley Hall asked
men what their response was to current pictures of Jesus; men's comments

---

70 Jason Nobel Pierce, *The Masculine Power of Christ: or, Christ Measured as a Man*
    (Boston: Pilgrim Press, 1912), 1.
71 See Leo Steinberg, *The Sexuality of Christ in Renaissance Art and Modern Obli-
    vion* (Chicago: University of Chicago Press, 1996).
72 Mackenzie Bell, *Christina Rossetti: A Biographical and Critical Study* (London:
    Thomas Burleigh, 1898), 19.
73 Bruce Barton, *A Young Man's Jesus* (Boston: Pilgrim Press, 1914), ix.
74 Clifford Putney, *Muscular Christianity: Manhood and Sports in Protestant Ame-
    rica, 1880–1920* (Cambridge, MA: Harvard University Press, 2001), 93.
75 Putney, *Muscular Christianity*, 93–94.
76 Robert Warren Conant, *The Virility of Christ: A New View* (Chicago, 1915), 12.

were that Jesus "looks sick, unwashed, sissy, ugly, feeble, posing, needs a square meal and exercise."[77]

Walter Sallman studied at the Moody Bible Institute in 1914, when the school was involved in the Men and Religion Forward Movement. There the director of night classes, E. O. Sellers, encouraged Sallman to paint a picture of Jesus, "to make Him a real man! Make him rugged, not effeminate. Make him strong and masculine."[78] Sallman painted his Head of Christ in 1940; he intended it to be "a manly one."[79] Not everyone saw it that way. In a 1958 *Christianity Today* article, Robert Paul Roth claimed that this image "was a pretty picture of a woman with a curling beard who has just come from the beauty parlor with a Halo shampoo."[80] David Morgan sees this image of Jesus as depicting the Protestant representation of Jesus as a friend, with the "maternal, feminine characteristics"[81] that Catholics saw in the images of Mary. Women liked this way of depicting Christ, men disliked it.[82] In his inimitable way, Mark Driscoll claims that "the mainstream church . . . has transformed Jesus into 'a Richard Simmons, hippie, queer Christ,' a neutered and limp-wristed popular Sky Fairy of pop culture that . . . would never talk about sin or send anyone to hell."[83] Protestants have tried hard to come up with a masculine image of Jesus; in 1964 Richard Hook painted what has come to be known as the Surfer Jesus[84]—it is popular among evangelicals.

77   Granville Stanley Hall, *Jesus, the Christ, in the Light of Psychology*, Vol. 1 (Garden City, NY: Doubleday, Page, 1917), 28.

78   Erika Doss, "Making a 'Virile, Manly Christ': The Cultural Origins and Meanings of Warner Sallman's Religious imagery," in *Icons of American Protestantism: The Art of Warner Sallman*, ed. David Morgan (New Haven: Yale University Press, 1996), 80.

79   McDannell, *Material Christianity*, 189.

80   Quoted in McDannell, *Material Christianity*, 189.

81   David Morgan, "The Masculinity of Jesus in Popular Religious Art," in *Men's Bodies, Men's Gods: Male Identities in a (Post-) Christian Culture*, ed. Björn Krondorfer (New York: New York University Press, 1996), 257–58.

82   David Morgan, "'Would Jesus Have Sat for a Portrait?' The Likeness of Christ in the Popular Reception of Sallman's Art," in Morgan, *Icons of American Protestantism*, 202.

83   Molly Worthern, "Who Would Jesus Smack Down?" *New York Times*, January 11, 2009.

84   Morgan, *Icons of American Protestantism*, 35–36.

Colleen MacDannell explains the alleged female preference for bad religious art by explaining that in binary systems male equals good, female equals bad.[85] Therefore bad art is called feminine, good art masculine. But the matter is more complicated. Kitschy Catholic art emphasized prettiness and sentimentality. Jesus in the Sacred Heart paintings is a bearded woman. But why would women like bad, sentimental art and a feminized male? What such art appeals to is not a feminine sensibility, but an infantilized sensibility, the "Infantilismus" and "Feminismus" that drove the liturgist Johannes Pinsk to distraction.[86] Women have at times been infantilized by culture and religion. Obedience and receptivity, supposedly the essential characteristics of the feminine, are, on the contrary, characteristics of the immature. A young person can properly be immature; but an adult, man or woman, who is frozen in immature attitudes, is infantilized.

Macho Jesus

Toward the end of the nineteenth century in Germany, the clergy tried to deemphasize the miraculous and to emphasize the pursuit of virtue. Priests appreciated the loyalty of women, but they also wanted to attract men. The Jesuits tried to masculinize the cult of the Sacred Heart. German priests were told not to preach about the visions of Marguerite Marie Alacoque (who was, after all, French) and instead talk of the dogmatic foundations of the devotion. Jesus was to be portrayed as "the ideal of a man," "a man from the sole of his foot to the crown of his head," with "a man's heart, full of solid, manly virtues," and—here is a slightly ominous note— full of love for the Fatherland.[87] The image of Jesus was changed from a

---

85 McDannell, *Material Christianity*, 193–94.

86 Franz Zimmerman quotes this example that Pinsk cites as typical: a Holy Communion picture shows a tabernacle with an open door, "The veil of the tabernacle is half-pushed to the side by a baby Jesus—type: sweet, blonde à la Hollywood!—who mischievously-friendly peeks out, and under it is written, 'Come back soon!'" (*Männliche Frömmigkeit* [Innsbruck: Tyrolia-Verlag, 1936], 41).

87 Norbert Busch, *Katholische Frömmigkeit und Moderne: Die Sozial- und Mentalitätsgeschichte des Herz-Jesu-Kultes in Deutschland zwischen Kulturkampf und Erstem Weltkrieg* (Gütersloh: Kaiser/Gütersloher Verlaghaus, 1997), 217.

safe harbor from the troubles of the world to a spirit that takes the offensive (*Offensivgeist*) against the "enemies of the Kingdom of God." The picture of the Sacred Heart was now shown with crown and scepter.[88] Catholics wanted to break out of their ghetto and participate fully in the national life of Germany. They did not suspect what would happen to Germany from 1914 to 1945.

The business of America is business, and therefore the American Savior was a businessman. Bruce Barton,[89] whose 1925 book *The Man Nobody Knows* became a best-seller, was generally favorable to the Men and Religion Forward Movement, but warned about its tendencies to churchiness. More committed to capitalism than orthodoxy, he seems to have had doubts about miracles, but he knew that Jesus was the model businessman. Barton lauds Jesus for the way he handled the apostles: "He believed that the way to get faith out of men is to show that you have faith in them; and from that great principle of executive management he never wavered."[90] Jesus was popular at the best dinner parties: "There was a time when he was quite the favorite in Jerusalem."[91]

Barton noticed the almost total lack of attention to Joseph, who served as Jesus' earthly father, and traced it to the same tendency that leads Christians to portray Jesus as weak and willowy, instead of the strong carpenter he must have been: "The same theology which has painted the son as soft and gentle to the point of weakness, has exalted the feminine influence in its worship, and denied any large place to the masculine."[92] Barton pointed out that the human idea of Father, which Jesus applied analogously to his heavenly Father, was formed by Jesus' experience of Joseph. Barton constantly attacked holy-card, Sunday-school Christianity for its betrayal of the masculine Jesus: "They have shown us a frail man, undermuscled, with a soft face—a woman's face covered by beard—and a benign but baffled

88 Busch, *Katholische Frömmigkeit*, 218.
89 For a biographical sketch see Charles H. Lippy, *Do Real Men Pray? Images of the Christian Man and Male Spirituality in White Protestant America* (Knoxville: University of Tennessee Press, 2005), 133–42.
90 Bruce Barton, *The Man Nobody Knows: A Discovery of the Real Jesus* (Indianapolis, IN: Bobbs Merrill, 1925), 28.
91 Ibid., 69.
92 Ibid., 40–41.

look, as though the problems of living were so grievous that death would be a welcome release."[93] Barton instead delighted in the Jesus who is a warrior and hero, and noted that the way he motivated men was still a valid principle in modern times. Jesus used the "higher type of leadership which calls forth men's greatest energies by the promise of obstacles rather than pictures of rewards."[94]

Barton also criticized the clericalization of Christian life. Although the Reformers had attacked monasticism and had tried to convince all Christians that they were called to a life of faithful obedience, clericalism crept back into Protestantism. To overcome this, we must "rid ourselves of the idea that there is a difference between *work* and *religious work*."[95] Christians have somehow gotten the idea that only work in or for the Church is pleasing to God, that only the work devoted "to church meetings and social service activities is consecrated."[96] This is a criticism of the attempts to make Christianity attractive to men by providing political and social reform work *within the Church*. Barton did not object to reform motivated by Christian faith and charity, but denied that it had to be under official church auspices to be Christian. Jesus sought "to erase the artificial barrier which men had erected between religion and life, to show that all right living is worship."[97] Barton wanted all Christians to realize that all work is worship; all useful service is prayer: "And whoever works wholeheartedly at any worthy calling is a co-worker with the Almighty in the great enterprise which He has initiated."[98]

In *A Young Man's Jesus*, Barton portrayed Jesus as a strong, energetic, assertive man. Jesus was outraged to find the Temple's "worship desecrated and made the pretext for the oppression of the poor" and this anger "stirred every corpuscle of his young manhood."[99] Barton insisted that Jesus in modern times would "align himself with the foes of Child Labor"[100] and "loose

93   Ibid., 42–43.
94   Ibid., 121.
95   Ibid., 179.
96   Ibid., 179.
97   Barton, *Young Man's Jesus*, 120.
98   Barton, *The Man Nobody Knows*, 180.
99   Barton, *Young Man's Jesus*, 8.
100 Ibid., 115.

the vials of His wrath upon those that share in the blood-profits of the white slave trade,"[101] i.e., sexual trafficking. Such a Jesus is a preacher of the Social Gospel.

Harry Emerson Fosdick sought to portray the masculinity of Jesus in *The Manhood of the Master*. Fosdick noticed the union of opposite qualities in Jesus, in "his heroic and revolutionary fearlessness, his capacity for indignation on the one side, and on the other this deep, friendly tenderness."[102] Jesus' wrath was fearful, especially since it was an expression of his love. Remembering the love of Christ was important, Fosdick admitted, but "a man might better call on the mountains to cover him than to stand naked and defenceless before the indignation which that wrath creates."[103] Fosdick sounded a characteristic note of the twentieth century when he points out that Jesus was tempted, indeed was "the most tempted of all because he had the greatest powers to control."[104]

More recently, Jesus has occasionally been depicted as hyper-masculine. The painter Stephen Sawyer has depicted a macho Jesus: "Sawyer's Jesus is one that many people would never have thought to visualize: Jesus dressed in jeans; Jesus with a heart-shaped tattoo surrounding the word 'Father'; Jesus in a boxing ring, the word mercy printed on his gloves."[105] This is Mark Driscoll's "Ultimate Fighting Jesus."[106] This is the Jesus "who commanded tough fishermen, who cast out the money changers from the temple with a whip, who had the courage and strength to endure the blood sacrifice of his body, who is coming again with an iron rod to punish and rule the earth!"[107] If Bruce Barton's Jesus was a successful middle-aged

---

101 Ibid., 116.
102 Harry Emerson Fosdick, *The Manhood of the Master* (New York: Association Press, 1913), 116.
103 Ibid., 41.
104 Ibid, 88.
105 "Macho Jesus: The New Muscle of the Church," Intentious.com, August 31, 2011. http://intentious.com/2011/08/31/macho-jesus-the-new-muscle-of-the-church/.
106 Brandon O'Brien, "A Jesus for Real Men: What the New Masculinity Movement Gets Right and Wrong" (*Christianity Today*, April 18, 2008). http://www.christianitytoday.com/ct/2008/april/27.48.html.
107 Neil Godfrey, "Gentle Jesus Meek and Mild or Macho-Man Jesus?" *Vridar,*

businessman, Driscoll's Jesus is a late adolescent. This image of Jesus is about as far as possible from the Jesus of current liberal Christianity.[108]

As the image of Jesus varied between the masculine and feminine, so has the image of the Christian. The more recent and the predominant view of the Christian is that he or she should exemplify feminine characteristics, sometimes as a complement to a masculine Jesus, sometimes as an imitation of an androgynous or feminized Jesus. It is to this view we shall now turn.

July 11, 2007. http://vridar.org/2007/07/11/gentle-jesus-meek-and-mild-or-macho-man-jesus/.

108 See O'Brien, "A Jesus for Real Men."

Chapter Three
The Feminine Christian

For almost a millennium Christians have tended to see their primary identity as feminine. It all started with Aristotle for whom all beings consist of
a form and of a matter upon which the form is imposed. He claimed that
the male was completely formed; the female was relatively lacking in form.
The female was more like matter and therefore more able to receive a new
form. If the male seed had been able to impress its form completely on the
female matter, it would always produce a male. If it did not impress the
form completely on the matter, it produced a female. Receptivity, the ability
to receive further forming, was therefore a key characteristic of the female
and consequently of the feminine personality.

The Scholastics, as Prudence Allen has shown in *The Concept of
Woman*, rediscovered and Christianized this Aristotelian analysis of the
female but, unlike Aristotle, saw women's natural receptivity as an advantage. In the order of grace, Christian Aristotelians taught, the woman is
above the man, precisely because of her relatively unformed nature. Prudence Allen explains that "Mary . . . herself became a kind of material for
the formative power of God. Her perfect identity as nonresistant material
for the working of the Holy Spirit led to her complete absorption of the
wisdom of God. Therefore [for St. Albert the Great] it followed that Mary
knew everything that God knew. She was the perfect philosopher, theologian, lawyer, physician, scientist, and so on."[1] What is true of Mary is
true of women in general. Precisely because they are more like the raw
material on which form is imposed, they are more open to being formed
by the Holy Spirit. Men have a form already—a form which gets in the

---

1   Prudence Allen, *The Concept of Woman: The Aristotelian Revolution 750 BC–AD
    1250* (Grand Rapids, MI: William B. Eerdmans, 1997), 383.

way of the shape of Christ that the Holy Spirit wishes to imprint on the human person.

This analysis eventually permeated all medieval discussion of gender. As Ann Astell says, "in the metaphysics of sexuality, every person, male and female, is more feminine than masculine in relation to God—because receptive, dependent, and small."[2] Therefore theologians could use Aristotelian concepts of gender to explain why women, inferior in the realm of nature, are superior in the realm of grace. This analysis has continued to influence theological discourse about women. Both Catholics and Protestant have agreed in seeing the female as the sex more receptive to the action of grace.

Because women are weak, helpless, and trained to obedience, they more easily become Christians, who are likewise weak, helpless, and trained to obedience. Gertrud von le Fort speculates that "perhaps the realization that man's weakness is his real and only strength, his surrender to God's holy will his only true victory he can achieve, perhaps such an awareness is more connate to feminine than to masculine nature."[3] In the Christian paradox, woman's feminine passivity is more valuable than masculine activity: "The receptive, passive attitude of the feminine principle appears as the decisive, the positive element in the Christian order of grace."[4] The subordination of women was long seen as making them more attuned to Christianity. Horace Bushnell, an opponent of women's suffrage, thought that the subordination of women made them more open to religious inspirations: "The woman's nature, being a subject nature, is especially flexible and free to the Christian inspirations, and for this reason, doubtless, it is that more than twice as many women as men are engaged in Christian works and relations."[5]

---

2   Anne W. Astell, *The Song of Songs in the Middle Ages* (Ithaca, NY: Cornell University Press, 1990), 13.

3   Placid Jordan, "Preface," in Gertrud von le Fort, *The Eternal Woman*, trans. Placid Jordan (Milwaukee, WI: Bruce Publishing, 1961), viii.

4   Jordan, "Preface," in von le Fort, *Eternal Woman*, ix.

5   Horace Bushnell, *Women's Suffrage: The Reform against Nature* (New York: Charles Scribner, 1869), 181–82. Bushnell sees Jesus's subordination as manifesting a "womanly nature" (61). See Michiyo Morita, *Horace Bushnell on Women in Nineteenth-Century America* (Lanham, MD: University Press of America, 2004), 64–67.

This approach to the meaning of gender in religion continues to be popular in conservative Christian circles,[6] especially those influenced by C. S. Lewis and Hans Urs von Balthasar. C. S. Lewis maintained that "we are all, corporately and individually, feminine to Him." Ildefons Herwegen argued that the woman because of her natural receptivity can better guard the life of grace and can better reveal "the mystery of receptive grace" than the man can; Romano Guardini agreed that the receptivity, *"das Empfangen,"* of the woman plays a special role. Pius Parsch claimed that "since every Christian is a part, a member of this church, so must his soul bear her characteristics; therefore every Christian soul has something womanly, feminine in it."[7]

Karl Lehman summarized the received analysis among theologians: "The woman is the receiver, she possesses the secret of devotion. Passivity is however not as in ancient philosophy something negative, but in light of Christian grace the most positive. To the woman belong worship, compassion, readiness to sacrifice and ability to serve." Manfred Hauke states that "in relation to God, the soul is receptive, feminine." Franz Xaver Arnold describes "the special inclination which woman has for religion" as "the truly feminine, the will to surrender, the readiness to be receptive." Mary Jo Anderson, in defending the Catholic attitude to women, claims that "women's receptive nature is paramount in understanding women's genius." The essential element in a religious attitude, according to Arnold, is a "passive receptivity," because "in this readiness for self-sacrifice and in this cooperation of the creature, all that is truly religious in humanity is revealed." Of Mary, George T. Montague says that "she is response and instrument." In pronounced feminization of Catholicism in the nineteenth century, in Claude Langlois's analysis, the receptivity of women meant that her duties were "prayer, work, silence, suffering" and above all "docility," which "the clergy demanded of the layman and the superior

---

6 See Paul K. Jewett, *Man as Male and Female* (Grand Rapids, MI: William B. Eerdmans, 1975), 179–88.

7 C. S. Lewis, "Priestesses in the Church," in *God in the Dock: Essays on Theology and Ethics* (Grand Rapids, MI: W. B. Eerdmans, 1994), 239; for Romano Guardini see Teresa Berger, *Liturgie und Frauenseele: Die Liturgische Bewegung aus der Sicht der Frauenforschung* (Stuttgart: W. Kohlhamer, 1993), 55; for Pius Parsch see Berger, *Liturgie und Frauenseele*, 57.

demanded of the religious" but which was the primary duty of the woman as woman.[8]

Hans Urs von Balthasar sees the Aristotelian identification of femininity and receptivity as the key to understanding the structure of Christian belief.[9] Man is the word (*das Wort*); "woman is essentially an answer"[10] (*die Antwort*). As Corinne Crammer summarizes, for von Balthasar, "the feminine is characterized by receptivity (*Empfänglichkeit*), obedience, disponibility, and willing consent to the action of another, or letting be (*Gelassenheit*)."[11] Woman does not initiate; she responds, she answers. Susan Ross correctly says that the phenomenology of von Balthasar and John Paul is "therefore a contemporary development of the traditional approach"

8 Karl Lehmann, "Mann und Frau als Problem der theologischen Anthropologie: Systematische Erwägungen," in *Mann und Frau: Grundproblem theologischer Anthropologie*, ed. Theodor Schneider (Freiburg: Herder, 1989), 70. Manfred Hauke, *Women in the Priesthood? A Systematic Analysis in the Light of the Order of Nature and Redemption*, trans. David Kipp (San Francisco: Ignatius Press, 1986), 304. Hauke concurs with Hans Urs von Balthasar who claims that "every member of the Church, even the priest, must maintain a feminine receptivity to the Lord of the Church" (*New Elucidations*, trans. Mary Theresilde Skerry [San Francisco: Ignatius Press, 1986], 198); F[ranz] X[aver] Arnold, *Woman and Man: Their Nature and Mission*, trans. Rosaleen Brennan (New York: Herder & Herder, 1963), 54–55. Mary Jo Anderson, "Feminine Genius: It's the Church's Stealth Weapon for the Twenty-First Century," *This Rock* (July–August 2005). http://www.catholicculture.org/culture/library/view.cfm?recnum=6709. Arnold, *Woman and Man*, 55-56; George T. Montague, *Our Father, Our Mother: Mary and the Faces of God* (Steubenville, OH: Franciscan University Press, 1990), 85; Claude Langlois, "Féminisation du catholicisme," in *Histoire de la France religieuse*, Vol. 3, *Du roi Très Chrétien à la laïcité républicaine XVIIIe-XIXe siècle*, ed. Phillipe Joutard (Paris: Éditions du Seuil, 2001), 288.

9 As Corinne Crammer notes, "Balthasar reiterates the stereotypes of Western tradition, particularly the ancient Greek tradition of equating the feminine with receptivity" ("One Sex or Two? Balthasar's Theology of the Sexes," in *The Cambridge Companion to Hans Urs von Balthasar*, eds. Edward T. Oakes and David Moss [Cambridge: Cambridge University Press, 2004], 106).

10 Hans Urs von Balthasar, *Theo-drama: Theological Dramatic Theory*, Vol. 3, *The Dramatis Personae: Persons in Christ*, trans. Graham Harrison (San Francisco: Ignatius Press, 1992), 284. See also Crammer, "One Sex or Two?" 97.

11 Crammer, "One Sex or Two?" 98.

which states "that the male represents the 'source' in generation and the female the 'potential.'"[12]

For von Balthasar the nuptial metaphor is central to Christianity. He maintains that "the creature can only be secondary, responsive, 'feminine' vis-à-vis God."[13] Or as Crammer puts it, for von Balthasar, "humanity's appropriate relationship to God is *feminine*, characterized by receptivity for mission and obedience."[14] God is the real actor, the real initiator. Men therefore when they act or initiate are acting in a way contrary to their essential creaturely status; they are only representing, not being, the One who acts and initiates. Priests are masculine insofar as they represent Christ but feminine insofar as they are Christians and brides of Christ.[15] But when women obey and receive, they are acting in accord with their true creaturely status. Mary is the model for discipleship because she is totally receptive. For von Balthasar, "as the archetype of the feminine, Mary displays the paradigmatically feminine qualities as a model for all Christians in relation to God."[16] Not Christ's life, but rather "Mary's life must be regarded as the prototype of what the *ars Dei* can fashion from human material which puts up no resistance to him."[17]

Women outnumber men in Christian congregations. Von Balthasar finds this perfectly appropriate: "We should therefore not be surprised, but rather feel how fitting it is, that normally far more women than men participate in the celebration of the Church's Eucharistic banquet."[18] But the

12   Susan A. Ross, "'Then Honor God in Your Body' (1 Cor. 6:20): Feminist and Sacramental Theology of the Body," in *Horizons on Catholic Feminist Theology*, eds. Joann Wolski Conn and Walter E. Conn (Washington, DC: Georgetown University Press, 1992), 112.

13   Von Balthasar, *Theo-drama: Theological Dramatic Theory*, Vol. 3, 287.

14   Crammer, "One Sex or Two?" 98.

15   See Michele M. Schumacher, "The Unity of the Two: Toward a New Feminist Sacramentality of the Body," in *Women in Christ: Toward a New Feminism*, ed. Michele M. Schumacher (Grand Rapids, MI: William B. Eerdmans, 2004), 223–24.

16   Crammer "One Sex or Two?" 98.

17   Von Balthasar, *The Glory of the Lord*. Vol. 1, *Seeing the Form*, eds. Joseph Fessio and John Riches, trans. Erasmo Leiva-Merikakis (San Francisco: Ignatius Press, 1982), 564.

18   Von Balthasar, "Thoughts on the Priesthood of Women," trans. Adrian Walker, *Communio* 23 (1996): 707.

priesthood is reserved to men, because men represent what they are not, the masculine initiative of God. Men by nature are designed to command, not obey. Influenced by the Aristotelian analysis,[19] John Courtney Murray gave a preordination address to the Jesuits at Woodstock; it was entitled "The Danger of the Vows: An Encounter with Earth, Woman, and Spirit." Murray warned about the danger of "diminished manhood, of incomplete virility" among both religious and men in general. Woman exists to help man be masculine: "Man does not know himself aright until he knows he is the head of woman, set above her, having her under his government. This is his part and person, and if he resigns it, he resigns his manhood . . . it is the woman who puts within the reach of man the act of man—the act of self-rule, through rule of her. It is she who lets him become a man."[20] Women obeys so that man may command—at least if the man is a priest.

There is no place for lay masculinity in this ecclesiastical system.[21] Tina Beattie has pointed out that for von Balthasar, there is "a feminine creation, with the only masculine presence being the priest who represents the divinity of Christ, as therefore of God the Father as the (masculine) origin and source of life."[22] The priest like every Christian man, "must become 'she' in order to remind himself that he is not God."[23] Pope John Paul II in *Mulieris Dignitatem* uses this argument; all human beings—both men and women—are called, through the bridal Church, to be the "Bride" of Christ.

Because von Balthasar identifies receptivity with femininity, he finds femininity in the Trinity. Crammer explores the conundrums this leads to: the Son receives his deity from the Father and is therefore, according to von Balthasar, receptive and therefore super-feminine (and should more

---

19   As Peter McDonough notes in *Men Astutely Trained: A History of the Jesuits in the American Century* (New York: Free Press, 1992), 541, n. 43.

20   Quoted by McDonough, *Men Astutely Trained*, 230.

21   As John O'Donnell says, von Balthasar maintains that "that the Church must avoid everything which is masculine (grasping, active, determining) in its relationship to God and to Christ" ("Hans Urs von Balthasar: The Form of His Theology," in *Hans Urs von Balthasar, His Life and Work*, ed. David L. Schindler (San Francisco: Ignatius Press, 1991), 216–17.

22   Tina Beattie, *New Catholic Feminism: Theology and Theory* (New York: Routledge, 2006), 101.

23   Ibid., 115.

properly be called Daughter?) but is masculine because he represents (a characteristically masculine activity) the Father who acts and is therefore masculine, but in a way the Father is also feminine because he receives his status as a Father because he has generated a son. Von Balthasar's characterization of the Son as receptive and therefore in a way feminine was also maintained by Ludwig Feuerbach. According to Feuerbach, "the Son is begotten, without himself begetting, *Deus genitus*, the passive, suffering, receptive being; he receives his existence from the Father" and "is thus the feminine feeling of dependence in the Godhead."[24]

Feminists have criticized von Balthasar because he has made women supposedly equal but in fact subordinate to men. But at least femininity has a role in von Balthasar's analysis. He has no theology of created masculinity—there is no place for it.[25] Men are supposed to be feminine in relation to God, insofar as they are act (in the Aristotelian sense; that is, not in potency) and are masculine, they are not in their proper role as creatures and disciples. For von Balthasar, Barbara Sain says, "masculinity is either a representation of the divine, which men can never be, or a disposition that hinders their relationship with God."[26] As a result of this, Sain concludes, "Balthasar's theology does not explain how men can relate to God in a positive way, precisely as men."[27] Because all creatures are supposed to be feminine in relation to God, any attempt to relate to God in a non-receptive, that is, characteristically masculine way, leads to a distortion in the creature's relationship with God. Sain concludes: "If creation is meant to be simply feminine before God, then approaching God in a masculine manner

---

24 Ludwig Feuerbach, *The Essence of Christianity*, trans. Marian Evans (London: John Chapman, 1854), 70.

25 Nor does Louis Bouyer, who, following the same line of thought as von Balthasar, writes "the masculine being can therefore be said to be essentially intermediary, and by this fact indefinitely polymorphous. The feminine being, on the contrary, represents, in the realm of the created, the goal, the achievement, the totality" (*Woman in the Church*, trans. Marilyn Teichert [San Francisco: Ignatius Press, 1984], 56).

26 Barbara K. Sain, "Through a Different Lens: Rethinking the Role of Sexual Difference in the Theology of Hans Urs von Balthasar," *Modern Theology* 25, no. 1 (2009): 90.

27 Ibid., 89.

is incoherent or even sinful."[28] Men therefore "are encouraged to look to Mary as a model,"[29] not to Christ.

Perhaps von Balthasar's inability to find a place for created masculinity in the Church explains the curious 2004 document from the Vatican: "Letter to the Bishops of the Catholic Church on the Collaboration of Men and Women in the Church and in the World," signed by Cardinal Ratzinger, then-Prefect of the Congregation for the Doctrine of the Faith. It speaks of the creation of women and of marriage, and of "The Importance of Feminine Values in the Life of Society," but does not, despite the title, speak of masculine values in the life of society or in the life of the Church.[30] John Paul II, in following the identification of receptivity and femininity, sees, according to David Meconi, that holiness is essentially feminine and that "in Christ alone does the feminine structure of holiness become real."[31] To be holy one must, like Christ, be feminine.

Emotion

For Aristotle, Joseph Hartel explains, "male and female are divided according to active and passive powers according to their respective roles in generation."[32] Because the nature of the female is passive, Aristotle says that women are led by their emotions rather than their reason more so than men are. Aquinas follows and elaborates: reason is weaker in women because of the imperfection of their bodily nature, "and therefore, as in many things, they do not govern their passion (affectus) according to reason, but rather are governed by their passions."[33] This

---

28   Ibid., 92–93.

29   Ibid., 83.

30   See Céline Béraud, "Quand les questions de genre travaillent le catholicisme," *Études*, 414 (2011–2012): 213–14.

31   David Meconi, "John Paul II and the Femininity of Holiness," *Faith*, July-August 2005. http://www.faith.org.uk/article/july-august-2005-john-paul-ii-and-the-femininity-of-holiness.

32   Joseph Francis Hartel, *Femina ut Imago Dei in the Integral Feminism of St. Thomas Aquinas* (Rome: Editrice Pontificia Università Gregoriana, 1993), 102.

33   In his *Commentary on the Nichomachean Ethics*, Aquinas says of women: "Et ideo, ut in pluribus, non ducunt affectus suos secundum rationem, sed magis ab affectibus suis ducuntur." Quoted by Hartel, *Femina*, 149.

is so because the female is "a passive power," that is, as Hartel explains, "a principle in any given thing by which it is able to undergo an action."[34] The passivity of the female body allows the active male seed to act on it; this passivity also allows the emotions to act more strongly on the woman than on the man, and therefore she is less governed by reason, and therefore, Aquinas continues, "it is rare that strong and wise women are found." The sensitive power is a passive power, that is, it is reduced to act by something outside itself; as a passive principle, it is stronger in women.[35] Aristotle and the theologians who adopted his analysis provided a "scientific" explanation of why women are more emotional than men, which dovetails with the later view that religion is essentially emotion—an idea that Aquinas would of course have rejected.

The supposed greater emotionality of women has long been a subject of discourse; most people, if asked why women are more religious than men, would probably reply that women are more emotional—therefore implying that religion is mainly a matter of emotion. In the eighteenth century, Bishop Gregoire pointed to the supposed greater emotionality of women: "Men are directed to conviction by reason; women to persuasion by sentiment."[36] If religion is primarily a matter of sentiment, then it will appeal more to women, who are by nature more emotional than men—at least in the view of men, but also of some women, such as Edith Stein, who agreed with the view that emotions were "the center of the woman's soul"[37] (and not, presumably, of the man's) and that this sensitivity "to moral values" means that in the family "the mission of moral and religious education is given chiefly to the wife."[38]

In 1939, a German cleric asked, "Why is religion's access to the soul of a man often so difficult? Why does a woman more easily embrace religion?"[39]

---

34 Hartel, *Femina*, 152.
35 Ibid., 191.
36 Quoted by Ruth Graham in "Women versus Clergy, Women pro Clergy," in *French Women and the Age of the Enlightenment*, ed. Samia I. Spencer (Bloomington: Indiana University Press, 1984), 131.
37 Edith Stein, *Essays on Woman*, trans. Freda Mary Oben (Washington, DC: ICS Publications, 1996), 102.
38 Ibid., 78.
39 Anton Wohlgemuth, *Fragen der Männerseelsorgen*, Band 1 and 2: (Saarbrücken: Saarbrücken Druckerei & Verlag, 1939, 1940), 10.

Another German priest replied that "because her emotional life dominates her, the woman brings greater receptivity and warmth to religion. She comprehends religion more with feeling, while the religious knowledge often remains unclear."[40] Women supposedly feel rather than think, and that, both believers and skeptics agree, is the source of their greater piety.

Sigmund Freud thought that women were more religious than men because they were more feminine, as he understood femininity. In his theory of masculinity and femininity,[41] masculinity is the reality principle, a "correspondence with the real, external world."[42] The masculine, scientific mind is tough: it is able to face such unpleasant realities as the absence of a benevolent Providence that supposedly guides human affairs. Femininity, according to Freud, is the principle of wish-fulfillment, and their femininity causes women to view reality as ultimately promising a fulfillment of our infantile desires for love and safety. Freud wanted all adults, including women, to adopt the reality principle, to become masculine, and to give up the fantasy world of wish fulfillment that Christianity embodies. Freud's "guiding contrast is between wish fulfillment provided by the illusion of a father-God's loving existence and scientifically based resignation to reason and necessity, a resignation which stems from renunciation of childhood wishes."[43] If women would accept the reality principle, they would become tough-minded and give up their immature participation in religion. Modernization was identified with masculinity and rationality, and therefore the religion of women was regarded as retrograde sentimentality. This is often the implied view of many scholars who try to explain the feminization of the churches.

Because the connection of religion, emotion, and femininity was so firmly established in both the scholarly and popular minds, a British clergyman of the mid-nineteenth century was led to lament that "the Christian life has been

---

40 Quoted in Norbert Busch, *Katholische Frömmigkeit und Moderne: Die Sozial-
und Mentalitätsgeschichte des Herz-Jesu-Kultes in Deutschland zwischen Kulturkampf und Erstem Weltkrieg* (Gütersloh: Kaiser/Gütersloher Verlaghaus, 1997)
209.

41 See Judith van Herik, *Freud on Femininity and Faith* (Berkeley: University of
California Press, 1982) and Kirk A. Bingaman, *Freud and Faith: Living in the
Tension* (Albany: State University of New York Press, 2003), esp. 105–29.

42 Van Herik, *Freud on Femininity and Faith*, 55.

43 Ibid., 150.

strangely and mischievously misapprehended as to this, so that men have come to think of it as a state of dreary sentimentalism, fit only for women, or for soft and effeminate men, not calling forth or giving room for the exercise of the sterner and stronger virtues."[44] A substantial tradition in Christianity would say that indeed Christianity is not compatible with masculine qualities, that men must be feminized to become Christians. A feminist novelist has a character say "to bring about true Christian civilization . . . the men must become more like women, and the women more like angels."[45] Many theologians agree.

Sacred Eroticism

Not only were women more emotional than men in the view of theologians, the emotions that women felt in religion were primarily erotic ones. This view of the centrality of *eros* in religion stemmed from the exegesis of the *Song of Songs*, which for centuries was the most commented-on book of the Hebrew Scriptures.

In the Hebrew Scriptures Israel was depicted as the bride of the Lord, and the Christian Scriptures applied this image to Christ and the Church. The image emphasizes the unity of Christ and the Church; they are one body, as husband and wife are one; it emphasizes the care that Christ has for the Church: he nourishes it as his own body. It also emphasizes the exclusivity of the relationship: Christ has only one Church, one Body, and the Church has only one Lord and Spouse.

However, it was natural to see individual Christian virgins as spouses of Christ, and Tertullian speaks of such consecrated women as spouses of Christ, and Athanasius and Ambrose continue this usage.[46] John Bugge sees

---

44 S. S. Pugh, *Christian Manliness: A Book of Examples and Principles for Young Men* (1867), quoted by Sean Gill, "Christian Manliness Unmanned: Masculinity and Religion in Nineteenth- and Twentieth-Century Western Society," in *Men and Masculinities in Christianity and Judaism: A Critical Reader*, ed. Björn Krondorfer (London: SCM Press, 2009), 308.

45 Quoted in Ann Douglas, *The Feminization of American Culture* (New York: Noonday Press, 1998), 108.

46 Mathew Kuefler, *The Manly Eunuch: Masculinity, Gender Ambiguity, and Christian Ideology in Late Antiquity* (Chicago: University of Chicago Press, 2001), 137–39.

a strong influence of Gnosticism in such language, for example in the *Odes of Solomon*, but it entered into common Christian discourse.[47] Bridal imagery was prominent in patristic discussion of the consecrated virgins,[48] who entered a state of life with no earthly husband but with a heavenly bridegroom.[49]

Origen (184–254) was the main transmitter of bridal mysticism to later Christianity.[50] His *Commentary on the Song of Songs* was "the first great work of Christian mysticism."[51] Following rabbinical tradition that saw the bride as Israel, Origen saw the bride as "the Church"[52] or "the whole rational creation"[53] and also (with no explanation for the extension) the individual soul. One suspects unexamined Platonic assumptions[54] because the individualism of this interpretation was contrary to the original image of the community as bride. Origen was very influential, and in the early patristic period the ecclesiological interpretation of the *Song of Songs* slowly gave way to the individual interpretation in which the soul of the Christian is the bride: "the

---

47 John Bugge, *Virginitas: An Essay of the History of a Medieval Idea* (The Hague: Martinus Nijhoff, 1975), 59–60.

48 See Roger Steven Evans, *Sex and Salvation: Virginity as a Soteriological Paradigm in Ancient Christianity* (Lanham, MD: University Press of America, 2003), 111; and E. Ann Matter, "Mystical Marriage," trans. Keith Botsford, in *Women and Faith: Catholic Religious Life in Italy from Late Antiquity to the Present*, ed. Lucetta Scaraffia and Gabriella Zarri (Cambridge, MA: Harvard University Press, 1999), 35.

49 Hildegard Elisabeth Keller, *My Secret Is Mine: Studies on Religion and Eros in the German Middle Ages* (Louvain: Peters, 2000), 33–35.

50 See E. Ann Matter, *The Voice of My Beloved: The Song of Songs in Western Medieval Christianity* (Philadelphia: University of Pennsylvania Press, 1990), 21–22.

51 R. P. Lawson, "Introduction" to *Origen: The Song of Songs, Commentary and Homilies* (Westminster, MD: Newman Press, 1957), 6.

52 Ibid., 38.

53 Ibid., 53.

54 Denys Turner sees "pagan neo-Platonism" (*Eros and Allegory: Medieval Exegesis of the Song of Songs* [Kalamazoo, MI: Cistercian Publications, 1995], 32). Eugene S. Miao also sees Platonism, and points to "the lamentable part played by the mystical interpretation of the Canticle of Canticles in assisting the identification of the Eros motif with the Christian idea of Agape" (*St. John of the Cross: The Imagery of Eros* [Madrid: Playor, 1973], 51).

individual soul of the mystic takes the place of the Church collective."[55] Gregory of Nyssa (335–396) in his commentary on the *Song of Songs* also applied it to the individual soul,[56] as did the later St. Symeon the New Theologian (949–1022). This individualist interpretation died out and in the later patristic period was replaced by Augustine's interpretation of the *Song of Songs* as an allegory of the union of Christ with the new Israel, the Church.[57] However, part of Origen's commentaries on the *Song of Songs* was translated into Latin and had a strong influence on later medieval exegesis.[58]

Bernard of Clairvaux's (1090–1153) writings revived and popularized the bridal metaphor in Western Christianity.[59] Bernard claimed that "if a love relationship is the special and outstanding characteristic of bride and groom it is not unfitting to call the soul that loves God a bride."[60] Having established the principle for the use of such language, Bernard then elaborated. He referred to himself as "a woman"[61] and advised his monks to be "mothers"—to "let your bosoms expand with milk, not swell with passion"[62]—to emphasize their paradoxical status and worldly weakness.[63] Bernard inspired women mystics. Of Juliana of Mount-Cornillon (1192–

---

55 Nelson Pike, *Mystic Union: An Essay in the Phenomenology of Mysticism* (Ithaca, NY: Cornell University Press, 1992), 68.

56 See Jean Daniélou and Herbert Musurillo, *From Glory to Glory: Texts from Gregory of Nyssa's Mystical Writings* (Crestwood, NY: St. Vladimir's Seminary Press, 1979), 152–56.

57 Bugge, *Virginitas*, 64–65.

58 E. Ann Matter, *The Voice of My Beloved: The Song of Songs in Western Medieval Christianity* (Philadelphia: University of Pennsylvania Press, 1990), 12.

59 See James I. Wimsatt, "St. Bernard, the Canticle of Canticles, and Mystical Poetry," in *An Introduction to the Medieval Mystics of Europe*, Paul E. Szarmach (Albany: State University of New York Press, 1984), 77–96.

60 Bernard of Clairvaux, *On the Song of Songs*, Vol. 1, trans. Kilian Walsh (Spencer, MA: Cistercian Publications, 1971), 39.

61 Ibid., 84. See Caroline Walker Bynum, "Jesus as Mother and Abbot as Mother: Some Themes in Twelfth-Century Cistercian Writing," in *Jesus as Mother: Studies in the Spirituality of the High Middle Ages* (Berkeley: University of California Press, 1982), 110–69.

62 Bernard, *On the Song of Songs*, 27.

63 See Caroline Walker Bynum, ". . . And Woman His Humanity," in *Gender and Religion: On the Complexity of Symbols*, eds. Caroline Walker Bynum, Steven Harrell, and Paula Richman (Boston: Beacon Press, 1986), 273.

1258) a thirteenth-century biographer wrote, "Since the writings of blessed Bernard seemed to her so full of mighty flame and sweeter than honey and the honeycomb, she read and embraced them with very much devotion, honouring this saint with the privilege of an immense love. Her whole mind was absorbed with his teaching: she took pains to learn it by heart, and fix in her memory, once and for all, more than twenty of the sermons in the last part of his commentary on the Song, there where he seems to have outstripped all human knowledge."[64] This bridal status of holy women gave them a new status and an added cachet in the male imagination. As Abelard wrote to Heloise, she began to outrank him "on the day she became the bride of his lord while he remained a mere servant."[65]

For the Fathers and Bernard, such bridal imagery was allegorical. But erotic language was highly congenial to women.[66] As Barbara Newman points out, "women with a talent for sublimation need not even give up their eroticism. Beginning in the twelfth century and increasingly thereafter, the brides of Christ were not only allowed but encouraged to engage in a rich, imaginative playing-out of their privileged relationship with God. Christ as a suffering, almost naked young man, was an object of the devotion of holy women."[67] Christ revealed himself to Gertrude of Helfta (1256–1302) as "a youth of about sixteen years of age, handsome and gracious. Young as I then was, the beauty of his form was all that I could have desired, entirely pleasing to the outward eye."[68]

For Hildegard of Bingen (1098–1179), and many others,[69] the bridal union of the soul and Christ is not simply higher than earthly marriage; it

---

64 Quoted by Jean Leclercq, *Monks and Love in Twelfth-Century France: Psycho-Historical Essays* (Oxford: Clarendon Press, 1979), 52.

65 Barbara Newman, *From Virile Woman to WomanChrist: Studies in Medieval Religion and Literature* (Philadelphia: University of Pennsylvania Press, 1995), 6.

66 Keller notices that throughout the Middle Ages "the increasingly exclusive allocation of the female role [of Bride] to female human beings" (*My Secret Is Mine*, 61).

67 Newman, *From Virile Woman*, 6.

68 Gertrude of Helfta, *The Herald of Divine Love*, ed. and trans. Margaret Winkworth (Mahwah, NJ: Paulist Press, 1990), 95.

69 See *The Life of Beatrice of Nazareth*, trans. Roger de Ganck (Kalamazoo, MI: Cistercian Publications, 1991), 100, 195, 225.

replaces it and takes on some of the physical eroticism of the missing sexual union. Margaret Ebner (1291–1361) feels Jesus pierce her "with a swift shot (*sagitta acuta*) from His spear of love."[70] She feels her spouse's "wondrous powerful thrusts against my heart,"[71] and "longed for and greatly desired to receive the kiss just as my lord St. Bernard had received it."[72] In token of her marriage to Christ, Catherine of Siena (1347–1380) wore a wedding ring— the foreskin of Christ (changed by her biographer Raymond of Capua to a golden ring).[73] Teresa of Avila (1515–1582) and John of the Cross (1542–1591) both used erotic love as a metaphor of the relationship of the soul and God.

The devotion to the Sacred Heart of Jesus was suffused with this eroticism. For Gertrude, Christ himself, "my sweetest little Jesus,"[74] is the archer of eros, and his heart is the one we are familiar with from St. Valentine's Day. Jesus tells Gertrude that he aims "arrows of love from the sweetness of my divine heart."[75] In the sixteenth century the devotion became more popular, and in the seventeenth century Margaret Mary (Marguerite Marie) Alacoque (1647–1690) of the Visitandine convent at Paray-le-Monial received revelations of the Sacred Heart, in which Jesus, "the Divine Spouse,"[76] "showed me, if I am not mistaken, that He was the most beautiful, the wealthiest, the most powerful, the most perfect and the most accomplished among all lovers."[77] Her heart was aflame with love for him as his was for her. He unites her to him in his sufferings so that she can join with him in saving sinners. He shows her "a large cross . . . all covered with flowers" and tells her "'behold the bed of My most chaste spouses on which I shall make thee taste all the delights of My pure love.'"[78] She desires to

---

70 Margaret Ebner, *Major Works*, ed. and trans. Leonard Hindsley (New York: Paulist Press, 1993), 156.

71 Ibid., 135.

72 Ibid., 96.

73 Caroline Walker Bynum, *Holy Feast and Holy Fast: The Religious Significance of Food to Medieval Women* (Berkeley: University of California Press, 1987), 246.

74 Gertrude of Helfta, *Herald*, 211.

75 Ibid., 47.

76 *The Autobiography of Saint Margaret Mary Alacoque*, trans. The Sisters of the Visitation (Rockford, IL: Tan Books and Publishers, 1986), 41.

77 Ibid., 40.

78 Ibid., 62.

be united with him through frequent communion, and in praying before the Eucharist, she experiences "how he made me repose for a long time upon His Sacred Breast, where he disclosed to me the marvels of His love and the inexplicable secrets of His Sacred Heart."[79] Their union grows ever closer. One night, "if I mistake not, He kept me for two or three hours with my lips pressed to the Wound of His Sacred Heart."[80]

It is not only twenty-first-century ears that detect a strong erotic note in such language. Henri Grégoire (1750–1831), Constitutional bishop of Blois, detested the *cordicoles* (devotees of the Sacred Heart). He devoted a long chapter in his *Histoires des sects religieuses* to lambasting the proponents of the devotion to the Sacred Heart for their superstitions and follies. Margaret Mary, for example, recounted her amorous conversations, "colloques amoureux" and her espousal to Jesus in "termes si révoltants"[81] that they were suppressed by her editor. Jules Michelet, as always, was suspicious of anything that looked like eroticism in religion.[82]

Bridal mysticism did not disappear in the Reformation.[83] On the contrary, as Sarah Moore discovered, "commentaries and sermons on the Canticles abound in England from the 1580s—the more one looks, the more one finds."[84] Calvinists celebrated the erotic union of the Christian with Christ. In 1673 Edward Pearse follows Bernard's line of thought: "God the Father gives Christ unto the Soul, and the Soul unto Christ; he gives Christ for an Head and Husband to the Soul, and he gives the Soul for a Bride or

---

79   Ibid., 67.

80   Ibid., 82.

81   [Henri] Grégoire, *Histoires des sectes religieuses*, Vol. 2 (Paris: Baudouin Frères, 1828), 253.

82   Raymond Jonas, *France and the Cult of the Sacred Heart: An Epic Tale for Modern Times* (Berkeley: University of California Press, 2000), 21.

83   See Amanda Porterfield, *Female Piety in Puritan New England: The Emergence of Religious Humanism* (New York: Oxford University Press, 1992), 14; and Charles E. Hambrick-Stowe, *The Practice of Piety: Puritan Devotional Disciplines in Seventeenth-Century New England* (Chapel Hill: University of North Carolina Press, 1982), 28–29, 189–90.

84   Susan Hardman Moore, "Sexing the Soul: Gender and the Rhetoric of Puritan Piety," in *Gender and Christian Religion*, ed. Robert Norman Swanson (Woodbridge, Suffolk: Boydell Press, 1998), 177.

Spouse to Christ."[85] Puritan sermons frequently used the metaphor of the Christian as the Bride of Christ and the relationship between Christ and the Christian as that of a man and a woman.[86] Cotton Mather (1663–1728), addressing the Puritans of the late seventeenth century, spoke of God's approach to the soul "under the Notion of a Marriage,"[87] applying to the individual Christian passages from Scripture that refer to the church as bride. Mather, while recognizing that the mystical marriage first referred to the Church, applied it also to each Christian: "Our SAVIOR does Marry Himself unto the Church in general, But He does also Marry Himself to every Individual Believer."[88] The Puritan Thomas Shepard (1605–1649) stated that "all church members are and must be visible saints . . . virgins espoused to Christ."[89]

A Scottish Presbyterian, Samuel Rutherford (1600–1661), rhapsodized that "many a sweet, sweet soft kiss many perfumed, well-smelled kisses, and embracements, have I received of my royal master. He and I have had much love together."[90] John Winthrop (1587–1649) addressed Christ: "O my Lord, howe did my soul melt with joy when thou spakest to the heart of thy poore unworthy handmayd! . . . O my Lord, my love, how wholly delectable are thou! Lett him kisse me with the kisses of his mouthe, for his love is sweeter than wine: how lovely is thy countenance! How pleasant are thy embracings! . . . thou wilt honor me with the societye of thy mariage chamber."[91] Cotton Mather might have reflected that the theme of his book, *The Mystical Marriage: A Brief Essay on the Grace of the Redeemer Espousing the Soul of the Believer*, might explain the lack of men he observed in his congregation.

85   Edward Pearse, *The Best Match; or, The Soul's Espousal to Christ, open'd and improv'd* (London, 1673), 33.
86   See Porterfield, *Female Piety in Puritan New England,* 42–79.
87   Cotton Mather, *Ornaments for the Daughters of Zion* (Boston, 1691), 63.
88   Cotton Mather, *A Glorious Espousal* (Boston, 1719), 11.
89   Quoted by Amanda Porterfield, *Feminine Spirituality in America: From Sarah Edwards to Martha Graham* (Philadelphia: Temple University Press, 1980), 24.
90   Samuel Rutherford, *Joshua Redivivus: or, Three Hundred and Fifty Two Religious Letters* (Glasgow: 1818), 35.
91   Quoted by Moore, "Sexing the Soul: Gender and the Rhetoric of Puritan Piety," 183–84.

Thomas Hooker (1586–1647) helped transmit to New England Protestantism the central ideas of medieval mysticism: the total union of God and the soul, a union best expressed by the erotic imagery of marriage.[92] John Cotton (1585–1652) in his comments on the *Song of Songs* explains that "the publick Worship of God is the bed of loves: where 1. Christ embraceth the souls of his people, and casteth into their hearts the immortal seed of his Word, and Spirit, *Gal.* 4.19. 2. The Church conceiveth and bringeth forth fruits to Christ."[93] Edward Taylor used bridal imagery throughout his meditations: "I then shall be thy Bride Espousd by thee / And thou my Bridegroom Deare Espousde shall bee."[94] The Christian must feel raptures toward his Savior, because "who / Can prove his marriage knot to Christ in's heart / That doth not finde such ardent flames oreflow?"[95] Taylor addresses his Lover, "Thy Pidgen Eyes dart piercing, beames on Love / Thy Cherry Cheeks sende Charms out of Loves Coast, / Thy Lilly Lips drop Myrrh down from above."[96]

Erotic and even sexual metaphors for the relationship of Christ and the soul are used extensively by Puritan writers.[97] Amanda Porterfield notes of Taylor and his religious culture that "God was dominatingly male in the literature and consciousness of Puritans, and in his intimate spirituality, Taylor assumed a complementary feminine stance toward God."[98] As Margaret Masson observes, this stance was in accord with the experience of women but contradicted the experience of men: "whereas for women the resignation to Christ corresponded with their prescribed role of subordination to their husband, for men the requisite behavior in conversion contradicted their conventional

---

92 Porterfield, *Female Piety*, 43–44.
93 John Cotton, *Brief Exposition with Practical Observations upon the Whole Book of Canticles* (London, 1655), 209.
94 Edward Taylor, "Meditation. Cant. 4.8. My Spouse," in *The Poems of Edward Taylor*, ed. Donald E. Stanford (New Haven: Yale University Press, 1960), 39.
95 Taylor, "Meditation. Can. 1.2. Let him kiss me with the Kisses of his mouth," *Poems*, 257.
96 Taylor, "Meditation. Cant.5.13. His Lips are like Lillies, dropping sweet smelling Myrrh," *Poems*, 303.
97 See Richard Godbeer, "'Love Raptures': Marital, Romantic, and Erotic Images of Jesus Christ in Puritan New England, 1670-1730" *New England Quarterly* 68, no. 3 (1995): "Love Raptures," 355–84.
98 Porterfield, *Feminine Spirituality*, 29–30.

roles as dominant, assertive husbands."[99] The metaphor was so common that its lack was noticed. When Samuel Sewall (1652–1730) visited England he liked one preacher's sermon, but the sermon would have been better "if had us'd the Metaphor of Bridegroom and Bride, which heard not of."[100]

Pietism stressed feeling, and women were thought to be more responsive than men to pietistic religion because they had the capacity for feeling. Count Nicolaus Ludwig von Zinzendorf (1700–1760), the founder of the church now known as the Moravians, held that all souls were feminine. In fact, in a December 6, 1748 ceremony (the record of which the Moravians tried to expunge), Christian Renatus von Zinzendorf (the Count's son) declared all single men to be women.[101] Men too were the brides of Christ; the Moravians had found this idea in Bernard of Clairvaux; they therefore "formulated their deep desire for Christ as being in love with Him" using the language of "sexual arousal" and even imagining themselves "in a sexual act with Him."[102] The brothers were Christ's "sweetheart," "darling," or "bride." The brothers consequently did not act very masculine. One observer of the Moravian community of Herrnhut claimed that "the men themselves take on rather effeminate manners."[103] Zinzendorf preached to the Moravians that "in faith we are all sisters."[104] The Moravians were uncertain about how Christian men could be masculine.[105]

99 Margaret W. Masson, "The Typology of the Female as a Model for the Regenerate: Puritan Preaching, 1690–1730," *Signs* 2, no. 2 (1976): 310.

100 Samuel Sewell, *Diary of Samuel Sewell*, Vol. 1 (Boston: Massachusetts Historical Society, 1878), 299. For further examples see Edward S. Morgan, *The Puritan Family: Religion and Domestic Relations in Seventeenth-Century New England* (New York: Harper & Row, 1966), 161–68.

101 Paul Peucker, "Wives of the Lamb: Moravian Brothers and Gender around 1750," in *Masculinity, Senses, Spirit*, ed. Katherine M. Faull (Lewisburg, PA: Bucknell University Press, 2011), 39.

102 Peucker, "Wives of the Lamb," 44. See also Craig D. Atwood, "The Union of Masculine and Feminine in Zinzendorfian Piety," in Faull, *Masculinity, Senses, Spirit*, esp. 25–29.

103 Quoted in Peucker, "Wives of the Lamb," 46.

104 Quoted in Peucker, "Wives of the Lamb," 46.

105 See also Katherine M. Faull's "Temporal Men and the Eternal Bridegroom: Moravian Masculinity in the Eighteenth Century," in Faull, *Masculinity, Senses, Spirit*, 55–79.

Music has always been a way of expressing the erotic sweetness of a relationship with Jesus, from Bach's Cantata *Liebster Jesu* through the 1912 "In the Garden"[106] to the "Jesus is my Boyfriend" tunes of pop evangelicalism. A. Herbert Gray, a Scots chaplain in World War I, objected to "hymns which belong to the same category as the pictures which represent Christ as an almost effeminate figure, and which employ sensuous imagery which is to many quite offensive, 'Jesus Thou art mine and I am Thine—clasped to Thy bosom.'"[107] Herbert E. Douglas notes that religious emotion is "almost exactly like "the 'infatuating' love of the opposite sex and that one can substitute the name of one's lover in many modern choruses about Jesus."[108]

Catholics also continued the tradition of sacred eroticism. In modern times Alphonsus Ligouri (1696–1787) in *The True Spouse of Jesus Christ* claims that "a virgin who consecrated herself to Jesus Christ becomes his spouse" but for other Christians he is only "master, pastor, or father."[109] In the 1865 collection *Les perles de St. François de Sales* the poem "Vive Jesu" appeared. Portions of its eleven pages were quoted by the anticlerical Deputy Paul Bert to demonstrate the perversity of Catholic spirituality: "Long Live Jesus in all my ways / Long live his amorous charms . . . Long live Jesus, when his mouth / Touches me with an amorous kiss . . . Long live Jesus, when his wink / Makes me happily ill . . . Long live Jesus, when his rigors / Reduce my soul to languor."[110] A 1944 Spanish catechism contained prayers such as these for adolescent girls receiving communion: "what do I see. You are already approaching. I feel your heat . . . your breath . . . your life encircles me, that it might absorb me,

---

106 See June Hadden Hobbs, *"I Sing for I Cannot Be Silent": The Feminization of American Hymnody, 1870-1920* (Pittsburgh: University of Pittsburgh Press, 1997), 25.

107 A. Herbert Gray, *As Tommy Sees Us: A Book for Church Folk* (London: Edward Arnold, 1917), 70.

108 Herbert E. Douglas, *Truth Matters: An Analysis of the Purpose Driven Life Movement* (Nampa, ID: Pacific Press Publishing, 2006), 86.

109 Alphonsus de Ligouri, *The True Spouse of Jesus Christ*, ed. and trans. Eugene Grimm (Rockford, IL: Tan Books, n. d.), 18.

110 Quoted by Paul Bert, *La Morale des jésuites* (Paris: G. Charpentier, 1889), 540–41.

penetrate me, make me die" and "Come, Jesus, drench me, penetrate me," and so on.[111]

Germany's most important pastoral theologian of the mid-twentieth century, Franz Xaver Arnold (1898–1969), notes approvingly that "the bridal imagery of medieval mysticism, in contrast with the Scholastic teaching on the 'friendship of God,' portrays the interchange of love between God and man as experienced by the devout individual, representing the soul as a spouse and Christ as her bridegroom."[112] According to Denys Turner, "the Western Christian has traditionally been a female soul in love with her Bridegroom."[113]

Liberal Christianity

As we have seen, the Moravian Pietism of the Herrnhut taught that the bridal metaphor (and in fact sexual intercourse) was the most appropriate metaphor for the relationship of God and the believer.[114] Count von Zinzendorf, the founder of the Herrnhut, held that "all souls are sisters," that God "has created all souls, that the soul is His wife. He created no animos, he formed no masculine soul, among human souls, but only animas, female souls [*Seelinen*] who are His bride, candidates to rest in His arm and in the eternal bedchamber."[115] Bridal mysticism has no place for created masculinity; the believer must be feminine, and men have to develop feminine feelings and qualities to become Christian.

The founder of modern liberal theology, Friedrich Schleiermacher

---

111 Quoted in Manuel Delgado Ruiz, "Anticlericalismo, sexo y familia," in *Familia y relaciones de parentesco: Estudios desde la antropología social*, eds. Dolors Comas and Aurora Echecerría (Valencia: Institut Valencià de la Dona, 1988), 87.

112 Arnold, *Woman and Man*, 20.

113 Turner, *Eros and Allegory*, 25.

114 For the influence of Zinzendorf on Schleiermacher, see Ruth Drucilla Richardson, *The Role of Women in the Life and Thought of the Early Schleiermacher (1768–1806): An Historical Overview* (Lewiston, NY: Edwin Mellen Press, 1991), 38–42.

115 Nikolaus Ludwig von Zinzendorf , *Die an den Synodum der Brüder, in Zeyst von 11. Mai bis den 21. Junii 1757 gehaltene Reden nebst noch einigen andern zu gleicher Zeit in Holland geschehenen Vorträgen*, 208.

(1769–1834), wrote that "I have become a Herrnhuter again, only of a higher order."[116] He thought that Christian piety, "Frömmigkeit,"[117] was essentially emotionality, "Gefühlsbestimmtheit." Schleiermacher accepted the Aristotelian characterization of women as emotional and therefore agreed with the observation of Theodor von Hippel: "Women have God in the heart . . . so it does not matter to them how much or how little speculative reason contributes to this belief."[118] Because women, as the Aristotelian tradition maintained, were more characterized by receptivity and feeling, religion was especially a feminine domain.[119] Theology as a rational activity was a male preserve, but theology was simply a reflection on the emotions. Religion was essentially emotional, and therefore feminine, and therefore most appropriate to the domestic and private sphere,[120] not to the public sphere that was ruled by masculine reason.

Religion was the unmediated feeling of unity with the absolute through discovery of the infinite in the finite, the *Anschauen des Universums.*[121] Women, who have a greater capacity for feeling, therefore have the primary religious experience. Men as thinkers engage in a secondary reflection on this primary experience, and that rational reflection is theology, which as a science is in the masculine public sphere. As for von Zinzendorf, for Schleiermacher all souls are feminine and men must cultivate a feminine capacity for feeling and thereby attain to a secondary naïveté which women have by their feminine nature.[122] Men have to cross the fiery brook of higher

---

116 "Ich kann sagen, daß ich nach Allem wieder ein Herrnhuter geworden bin, nur von einer höherer Ordnung." Quoted by Dorette Seibert, *Glaube, Erfahrung und Gemeinschaft: Der junge Schleiermacher und Herrnhut* (Göttingen: Vanderhoeck & Ruprecht, 2003), 17.

117 "Piety appears as a surrender, a submission to be moved by the Whole that stands over against man" (Schleiermacher, *On Religion, Speeches to Its Cultured Despisers*, trans. John Oman [London: Kegan Paul, Trench, Trübner, 1983], 37).

118 Theodore Gottlieb von Hippel, *Über die bürgerliche Verbesserung der Weiber* (Berlin: 1792), 249.

119 Elisabeth Hartlieb, *Geschlechterdifferenz im Denken Friedrich Schleiermachers* (Berlin: Walter de Gruyter, 2006), 235, 331ff.

120 Ibid., 279.

121 Ibid., 247.

122 Ibid., 335.

criticism to attain what women have, or as Elisabeth Hartlieb puts it, "while the religious development of girls and women is characterized by continuity and a steady development of childhood religious experience and nearness to the divine into a conscious piety, a model of a break and a rebirth is necessary for boys and men."[123] Schleiermacher had observed the feminization and domestication (*Familiarisierung*) of religion in Germany and sought to explain it by the essential nature of man and woman. Women had the private, subjective realm of piety, the home, and charitable works; men had the public, objective realm of theology and office in the church.[124]

In *Christmas Eve Celebration: A Dialogue*,[125] Schleiermacher sets forth his thoughts about religion in the setting of a Platonic dialogue (he was the German translator of Plato), in which each speaker presents views upon which the reader must reflect. Schleiermacher had noticed that the development of the boy into the man is much more discontinuous than the development of the girl into the woman. As Ernestine says, "it seems that men, in contrast to women, tend to lead an odd, wild sort of life between childhood and their better days, a life passionate and perplexed."[126] For women, as Ernestine sees it, "the course of our entire life already lies indicated in our childhood play, except as we grow older the higher meaning of this or that becomes clear."[127] Women have a more unified development.

Leonhardt claims that therefore men are more Christian, because "Christianity is always speaking of a conversion, a change of heart, a new life."[128] Karoline rejoined, "Christ himself . . . was not converted."[129] Christmas, Eduard continues, is the celebration of the immediate union of the human and divine, in which no conversion is needed. Women, both because

---

123 Ibid., 329.
124 Ibid., 281, 283.
125 Friedrich Schleiermacher, *Christmas Eve Celebration: A Dialogue*, ed. and trans. Terrence N. Tice (Eugene, OR: Cascade Books, 2010).
126 Ibid., 41.
127 Ibid., 41.
128 Ibid., 42.
129 Schleiermacher, *Christmas Eve*, 42. Barth thought that this "would have been better left unsaid" (*Church Dogmatics I.2. The Doctrine of the Word of God*, eds. G. W. Bromley and T. F. Torrance, trans. T. G. T. Thomson et al. [New York: T&T Clark International, 2004], 195).

of their greater unity of life and their experience of unity with the child, have a stronger consciousness of the unity of the divine and human, and that is the reason, Eduard continues, "why they are so much more fervently and unreservedly attached to the church."[130] The heart has reasons which the mind knows not, and is a better guide to ultimate reality than reason is.

This explanation of the greater involvement of women in religion became widespread: "It is in the region beyond reason, in the sphere of intuition, of feeling, of aspiration, of that Formless which Goethe declared to be the highest thing in man, that religion finds at once its perennial spring and its impregnable refuge."[131] Following Schleiermacher, Carl Delos Case (1868–1931) claimed: "Man reaches the religious life chiefly by proxy. Religion is natural to woman and often unnatural to man, the more so the more masculine he is,"[132] and in fact "she becomes more of a woman, but he seems to become less of a man, in becoming a Christian."[133] George Coe (1862–1951) saw in this conception of Christianity the explanation for the lack of men: "any large and persistent excess of women in the Churches is chiefly due to a superior adaptation of Church life to the female nature. It is because the Church looks at things with feminine eyes, and calls chiefly into exercise the faculties in which women excel men."[134] These are the passive virtues, which seemed to be more natural to women than to men. Henry Francis Brownson (1835–1913) thought that American Protestants "seriously contend that woman is really of a more angelic character than man; that the Christian virtues and the Christian character are peculiarly feminine; that the human character of our Lord was womanlike; and the better Christian men are, the more like women they become."[135]

130 Schleiermacher, *Christmas Eve Celebration*, 83.
131 Jonathan Brierly, *Ourselves and the Universe* (London: James Clarke, 1903), 114.
132 Carl Delos Case, *The Masculine in Religion* (Philadelphia: American Baptist Publication Society, 1906), 29.
133 Ibid., 30.
134 George A. Coe, *The Spiritual Life: Studies in the Science of Religion* (New York: Eaton and Mains, 1900), 247.
135 Henry F. Brownson, *Orestes A. Brownson's Latter Life: From 1856 to 1876* (Detroit: H. F. Brownson, 1900), 592.

Karl Barth agreed that women were superior precisely because they were receptive and subordinate. In a subtle analysis of the scriptural references to the subordination of woman to man, Barth explains that God's glory is manifested precisely in the utter self-emptying of Jesus on the cross, when he became obedient unto death. The woman, subordinate to the man, is therefore in the same position as Christ, and therefore in the paradoxical reversals of Christianity, she is more glorious and superior.[136] Her receptivity makes her a better hearer of the word. For Barth, the preacher does not preach himself or his own ideas; he must first listen to the word and only then preach it, and only it.

As Paul Fiddes notes, Barth did not realize what this implied: "the perfect hearer of the word is also the most responsible speaker of the word. And in Barth's view, Mary and all womankind are the archetypal listeners. One might say that Barth's logic would lead him to the view that the best preacher is a woman."[137] Woman is subordinate to man as to her head, and all Christians are subordinate to Christ as to their head. Therefore Barth sees that "as living members of the church, man and all other superiors and subordinates in the community have no option but to follow the example of women, occupying in relation to Jesus Christ the precise position which she must occupy and maintain in relation to man."[138] Woman therefore "represents and attests the unity" in which all "are linked as Christians with the one Jesus Christ."[139] Woman and not man is "the type" of all those called into "communion" with Christ.[140] Therefore it is not surprising that Barth, although he wondered about Schleiermacher's lack of masculinity, about his defining religion as "sheer dependence" and his wish "to be a woman," nonetheless finds Schleiermacher "interesting and lovable."[141] Wolfhart

---

136 Karl Barth, *Church Dogmatics III.4: The Doctrine of Creation*, eds. G. W. Bromley and T. F. Torrance, trans. A. T MacKay et al. (1961. London: T and T Clark, 2004), 173.

137 Paul S. Fiddes, "The Status of Woman in the Thought of Karl Barth," in Janet Martin Sosice, ed., *After Eve: Women, Theology and the Christian Tradition* (London: Collins, 1990), 146.

138 Barth, *Church Dogmatics III.4*, 175.

139 Ibid., 174.

140 Ibid., 174.

141 Ibid., 155.

Pannenberg follows this tradition when he writes that "the receptivity accepted in the traditional stylization of the behavior of the sexes as characteristic for the behavior of women 'fits' better as a parable of man's relation to God's saving activity than masculine activity does."[142]

In North America evangelically-minded Protestants who believe that a certain type of conversion experience is necessary to be a real Christian also see masculinity as a serious obstacle. Philip Greven summarizes:

> Evangelicals believed that a truly gracious Christian was a person who was self-denying, will-less, subject and submissive, humble and meek, chaste and pure—all supposedly female attributes. Men, on the other hand, were thought to be naturally superior, willful, active, hardy, industrious, and rational. Yet most evangelicals spent most of their lives denying precisely those attributes of their own temperaments and experiences. In order to be saved, both men and women had to subdue those parts of their being that seemed to be "masculine," and to enhance those aspects of their being that seemed to be "feminine." For many men, one of the central sources of resistance to the experience of being broken and being submitted to the will of God that was necessary for the new birth was their reluctance to relinquish their sense of masculinity. Becoming children of God not only implied the rebreaking of their wills but also a return to the first years of life in which boys and girls were both perceived as feminine.[143]

Among fundamentalists, women, not men, have religious experiences.[144] Men had to give up their hard-earned and highly-valued masculinity to

---

142 Wolfhart Pannenberg, *Jesus—God and Man*, 2nd eds., trans. Lewis L. Wilkens and Duane A. Priebe (Philadelphia: Westminster Press, 1977), 148; see Barth, *Church Dogmatics* I.2, 195.

143 Philip J. Greven, *The Protestant Temperament: Patterns of Child-Rearing, Religious Experience, and the Self in Early America* (Chicago: University of Chicago Press, 1977), 124–25.

144 See Brenda E. Basher, *Godly Women: Fundamentalism and Female Power* (New Brunswick, NJ: Rutgers University Press, 1998), 122.

become Christians. Therefore, according to Greven, "the denial of their masculinity implied in evangelical religious experience and beliefs proved to be a source of persistent inner conflict."[145] Women also had to give up supposedly "masculine" aspects of their personality, but they at least would feel that they were being true to their receptive, docile feminine nature, while men would feel they were acting against the core of their identity as men.

The Christian life—its attitudes, its practices, its emotions—must, in this understanding, become more and more feminine. Tony Walter blames "the macho ethic" that "hinders men from worshipping God."[146] Walter sees this ethic as making men enemies of the Gospel: "Taking up the cross, denying himself, and abasing himself before God is hardly the fulfillment of his masculinity!"[147] Therefore masculinity is evil: "The macho ethic of pride in independence thus appears as a Satanic device for keeping men from faith in Christ, while the feminine ethic appears as a schoolmistress to bring women to faith in Christ."[148] Men must change, not the Church: "It is secular male culture that needs to be challenged and changed, not female church culture."[149]

Only if men become like women can they become Christian. That is the message that was long given to men. Carl Case agreed that was how Christianity was presented: "The modern religious life is far too much a self-abnegation that makes the Christian lose his independence, cultivate only meekness, and subdue his natural assertiveness . . . and obedience to Christ is made synonymous with the loss of manhood."[150] Count Richard Nikolaus Coudenhove-Kalegeri (1894–1972) wrote that "in Europe a holy man is felt to be feminine, while a heathen woman is perceived to be masculine . . . Christian morality is only alien to the European man, not to the European woman. It is much easier for her to be a Christian than for him to be a Christian. The female European can be a Christian without being hypocritical and

---

145 Greven, *Protestant Temperament*, 125.
146 Tony Walter, "Why Are Most Churchgoers Women? A Literature Review," *Vox Evangelica*, 20 (1990): 87.
147 Ibid., 79.
148 Ibid., 87.
149 Ibid., 88.
150 Case, *Masculine in Religion*, 50.

without betraying her instincts."[151] European men thought this because they had been told it for centuries. Walter Ong summarized the received wisdom: "In relation to God . . . we are all, men and women alike, basically feminine. Macho insights reveal nothing of God."[152] Ong uses the pejorative word *macho*; but what he means is that created masculinity is completely irrelevant, indeed an obstacle, in a man's relationship to God. So he sees the "overwhelming femininity of the Roman Catholic Church from the human side"[153] as an inevitable consequence of God's mistake in making males.

In a 2008 internet comment, a young Christian man explained about why young men absented themselves from church: "too many congregations send the message 'holiness = sweetness.' That may be unintentional, but the last thing I want to be as a young Christian is 'sweet.' I'm afraid of ending up as just another Precious Moments figurine!"[154] Men, especially young men, want to be masculine, and the message they get in churches, whether Catholic or Protestant, liberal or conservative, is very often that men must abandon their masculinity and exemplify a caricature of femininity. Sociologists have asked: "Does Masculinity Thwart Being Religious?" Masculinity values risk-taking; religion is for those seeking security.[155] Masculinity is tough-minded, religion is for those seeking comfort; masculinity accepts reality, religion is a fantasy; masculinity is independent, religion demands obedience. Not surprisingly, many men have decided to leave the church to women.

151 Quoted in Bonifaz Wöhrmüller, *Mannhaftes Christentum: Nachdenkliche Kapitel für Männer und Frauen* (Munich: Verlag Josef Kösel & Friedrich Pustet, 1934), 7.

152 Walter Ong, *Fighting for Life: Contest, Sexuality, and Consciousness* (Amherst: University of Massachusetts Press, 1989), 177.

153 Ibid., 178.

154 Robert, Comment on Collin Hansen, "Wanted: Young Men in the Church," *Christianity Today*, May 7, 2008. http://www.christianitytoday.com/ct/2008/marchweb-only/110-52.0.html.

155 Alan S. Miller and John Hoffman, "Risk and Religion: An Explanation of Gender Differences in Religiosity," *Journal for the Scientific Study of Religion* 34, no. 1(1995): 63–65. See John Hoffmann, "Gender, Risk, and Religiousness: Can Power Control Provide the Theory?" *Journal for the Scientific Study of Religion* 48, no. 2 (2009): 232–40; Marta Trzebiatowska and Steve Bruce, *Why are Women More Religious than Men?* (New York: Oxford University Press, 2012), 113–23.

Chapter Four
The Clergy and Social Control

Young males have long caused distress to the more orderly members of society. The Old Shepherd in *The Winter's Tale* complains: " I would there were no age between sixteen and three-and-twenty, or that youth would sleep out the rest; for there is nothing in the between but getting wenches with child, wronging the ancientry, stealing, fighting" (WT.III.3). Bernardino of Siena (1380–1444) had an even more expansive dislike of young males: "If I had sons, this is what I would do with them. As soon as they were three, I would send them all out of Italy, and not allow them to return until they were forty." Leon Battista Alberti (1404–1472) summarized the adult attitude to young men: they are "full of vice, full of license, burdened with needs, give themselves to filthy activities, dangerous, disgraceful for them and for their family."[1]

Persuading or forcing people, especially men, especially young men, to be civilized is a thankless process.[2] The clergy, along with the other forces of order, have long attempted to control the manifestations of youthful male energy. The clergy cooperated with the state to end homicidal

---

1 Bernadino quoted by Elisabeth Crouzet-Pavan, "A Flower of Evil: Young Men in Medieval Italy," in *A History of Young People: Ancient and Medieval Rites of Passage*, Vol. 1, eds. Giovanni Levi and Jean-Claude Schmitt, trans. Camille Naish (Cambridge, MA: Belknap Press of Harvard University Press, 1997), 175; Alberti quoted by Ilaria Taddei, "*Puerizia, adolescenza*, and *giovinezza*: Images and Conceptions of Youth in Florentine Society during the Renaissance," in *The Premodern Teenager: Youth in Society 1150–1650*, ed. Konrad Eisenbichler (Toronto: Centre for Reformation and Renaissance Studies, 2002), p. 23.
2 See Norbert Elias, *The Civilizing Process: The History of Manners*, trans. Edmund Jephcott (New York: Urizen Books, 1978).

violence; they put major efforts into stopping youths from "getting wenches with child." Such efforts were necessary but not popular. But to prevent males from getting excited in any way that might end in violence or sexual irregularities, the clergy also launched frontal attacks on drinking, dancing, sports, fireworks, and indeed almost any form of male pleasure and male sociability that was not under the direct supervision and control of the clergy. To convince men to submit to this level of control, the clergy, especially the Catholic clergy, cultivated an ideology of clericalism that in turn provoked male anticlericalism, which began as hostility and harassment but which, as we shall see in Chapter Six, sometimes turned into murderous persecution.

The history of violence has not been studied much until recently, and the historians who have turned their attention to it have reached startling but well-documented conclusions. Stephen Pinker claims in his exhaustive *The Better Angels of Our Nature*,[3] that violence has declined (although irregularly) throughout the world in the past two millennia. His estimates by necessity are very rough. Robert Muchambled, with better documentation in his *History of Violence*,[4] has shown that in Europe homicide has declined over 90% since the Middle Ages; this decline was the result of efforts by state and church to end young male violence. Histories of violence usually do not comment on one fact because it is so obvious: that violence is almost entirely perpetrated by males.

European Youth and Violence

In the Middle Ages violence among young men in villages was tolerated or even encouraged by villagers: it was "a veritable educational system which linked the proof of manliness to a constant festive confrontation between peers, so as to impress both the girls and the fathers" because boys had to "distance themselves from the feminine world by visible acts of great brutality,"[5]

---

3 Stephen Pinker, *The Better Angels of Our Nature: Why Violence Has Declined* (New York: Viking, 2011).
4 Robert Muchambled, *A History of Violence from the End of the Middle Ages to the Present*, trans. Jean Birrell (Cambridge, England: Polity Press, 2008).
5 Ibid., 46.

acts that sometimes ended in death. Julius Ruff notes that "such violence among social equals and neighbors was, like violence in our own time, largely a male business."[6] Towns tried to control violence because it disrupted commerce. Both state and church later tried to end the occasions for violence by "forbidding dissolute practices, dancing, attending any festivals and taverns during religious services, the abuse of alcoholic drinks, the carrying of weapons, etc."[7]

The Church tried "to impose meditation and prayer"[8] on these violent males. The medieval clergy condemned the secular ideals of honor and vengeance and sought "to promote harmony and humility through life styles that were—ideally—far different from those of most male parishioners."[9] The clergy and monks were forbidden to use weapons (although they sometimes did), and Peter Damien, in addition to attacking clerical sexual crimes, also attacked clerical and secular violence.[10] As Ruth Carras observes, "medieval university students behaved the way young men in groups, from varying social classes, behaved in the Middle Ages and today: they got drunk and rowdy."[11] The universities, the training grounds for clerics, witnessed town-gown disputes that ended in murder. Even village sports between neighboring towns frequently "degenerated into riots."[12] This continued into the nineteenth century, although Victorians tried to romanticize the village festival.[13] In accord with the lesser violence of society, "sports underwent a massive change from violent and sometimes

---

6   Julius R. Ruff, *Violence in Early Modern Europe 1500–1800* (Cambridge: Cambridge University Press, 2001), 125.

7   Muchambled, *History of Violence*, 25.

8   Ibid., 52.

9   Daniel E. Thiery, *Polluting the Sacred: Violence, Faith and the "Civilizing" of Parishioners in Late Medieval England* (Leiden: Brill, 2009), 24.

10   Katherine Allen Smith, *War and the Making of Medieval Monastic Culture* (Woodbridge, England: Boydell Press, 2011), 48.

11   Ruth Mazo Karras, "Sharing Wine, Women, and Song: Masculine Identity Formation in the Medieval European Universities," in *Becoming Male in the Middle Ages*, eds. Jeffrey Jerome Cohen and Bonnie Wheeler (New York: Garland, 2000), 196.

12   Ruff, *Violence*, 168.

13   Jim Obelkevich, *Church and Rural Society: South Lindsey, 1825–1875* (Oxford: Clarendon Press, 1976), 57–61, 160.

homicidal confrontations to regulated spectacles,"[14] although soccer hooligans keep up the connection of violence and sports.

Medieval European youth groups, the "youth abbeys" or "youth kingdoms," were barely tolerated by adult society. The Abbots of Misrule had names such as the Prince of Fools, "the Prince of Improvidence, the Cardinal of Bad Measure, Bishop Flat-Purse, Duke Kickass, and the Grand Patriarch of Syphilitics."[15] The mockery of the youth abbeys sometimes went too far in attacking secular authorities and was suppressed by arrest and even bloodshed. The youth groups monitored the young women who constituted the local marriage market and punished by rough music—the skimmingtons, charivaris, and *Katzenmusik*[16]—those women who reduced the marital chances of the village young men by marrying an outsider or an older man. The youth groups also demonstrated their masculinity through carefully planned gang rapes, usually of a woman who had violated village standards.[17] Gang rape initiated young men into a youth society; in medieval Dijon, perhaps half of male youth had participated in a gang rape.[18] Bishops attacked these practices.[19] But prostitution was accepted as necessary for young males, and indeed for all unmarried men, including clerics.[20]

Demonstrations of courage were also a central purpose of these youth groups, courage "which had to be proven by public displays of fighting prowess and risk taking."[21] These often occurred during feast days. The festivals, at which much of the violence occurred, "were inherently dangerous

14　Pieter Spierenburg, *A History of Murder: Personal Violence in Europe from the Middle Ages to the Present* (Malden, MA: Polity Press, 2008), 171.

15　Natalie Zemon Davis, *Society and Culture in Early Modern France* (Stanford, CA: Stanford University Press, 1961), 98–99.

16　Ruff, *Violence*, 161.

17　Edward Muir, *Ritual in Early Modern Europe* (Cambridge: Cambridge University Press, 2005), 34.

18　Jacques Roussiaud, *Medieval Prostitution*, trans. Lydia G. Cochrane (New York: Barnes & Noble, 1996), 21. See also Muir, *Ritual in Early Modern Europe*, 34.

19　Christopher F. Black, *Italian Confraternities in the Sixteenth* Century (Cambridge: Cambridge University Press, 1989), 48.

20　Roussiaud, *Medieval Prostitution*, 42. Prostitution preserved honorable women from assault.

21　Ibid., 163.

in the eyes of both religious and civil authorities."[22] One Jesuit in the seventeenth century estimated that 1,300 people died each year at festivals in his province.[23] Both Catholics and Protestant clerics objected to the pagan and violent elements of these festivals, especially Carnival, which opposed all that serious clerics stood for: "Order, decency, self-control, and hard work."[24]

Spanish youths celebrated feast days with *pedrades*, in which one group challenged another group to a slingshot battle. For centuries the bishops, especially in Barcelona, tried to stop them.[25] The efforts were unsuccessful. As one Spaniard observed at the beginning of the twentieth century: "When the festive is of greater importance, the afternoon dance is likely to end in a fight. The young men of some parishes club together against those of other parishes, or over love affairs, and after they have danced and drank, they challenge even the very saint of the day, ending in clubbing, fist-fighting, and even in the use of daggers or knives, sometimes resulting in death. The most notable feasts are not deemed a success unless they end in a fight."[26] In 1774 a priest of the Argonne mentioned religious ceremonies after which "one goes to make merry, to dance, to fight, etc."[27] but it was mostly the fun and excitement rather than the danger that provoked clerical ire, although young men regarded fighting as part of the fun.

Homicide and infanticide were lightly punished in the Middle Ages by fines and imprisonment. But Europeans, sickened by the slaughter and chaos of the Thirty Years War, accepted the efforts of the state to end homicide and infanticide[28] by executing both men and women who killed. In the thirteenth century, Europe had 100 murders per 100,000 inhabitants; by

---

22 Ibid., 164.

23 Ibid., 178.

24 Ibid., 179. See the chapter, "Carnival and the Lower Body," in Muir, *Ritual in Early Modern Europe*, 85–116.

25 Henry Kamen, *The Phoenix and the Flame: Catalonia and the Counter-Reformation* (New Haven: Yale University Press, 1993), 210.

26 Manuel Adújar, *Spain of Today from Within* (New York: Fleming H. Revell, 1909), 185–86.

27 Eugen Weber, *Peasants into Frenchmen: The Modernization of Rural France, 1870–1914* (Stanford, CA: Stanford University Press, 1976), 384.

28 For the attempt to end infanticide, see Ruff, *Violence*, 147–55.

the seventeenth century, it had fallen to 10 per 100,000; in 2000 it was .7 in France and England.[29]

Dueling was also a target of reformers.[30] Secular authorities tried to prohibit it. The common people were not allowed to defend their honor (they had none to defend, according to the aristocracy), but the elites thought they had to engage in duels or suffer disgrace. The Council of Trent in 1563 had forbidden dueling, and it was technically illegal in France but tolerated as a way of developing the killer instinct among the state's officers, although occasionally the worst aristocratic murderers were executed.[31] Protestants continued the attack on dueling. The ministers of the Reformed Church in early modern Amsterdam, in an attempt to end dueling, "admonished the secular authorities never to pardon those guilty of manslaughter and forbade their flock to hinder any criminal prosecution."[32] American Protestants later continued the attack; Lyman Beecher led the campaign against dueling after Aaron Burr was killed.[33]

Homicide has often been a response to an attack on honor. A woman's honor is her chastity, and this has been true for millennia; a man's honor has changed over the centuries. In the Middle Ages honor was centered on the body. As Spierenburg explains, "male honor depended on physical courage, bravery, and a propensity for violence."[34] European men have undergone a spiritualization of the sense of honor and consequently are less inclined to react physically if they feel their honor has been attacked. Honor slowly changed from physical deference to connoting "inner virtue," "admirable conduct, personal integrity, or inner sense of right and wrong."[35]

29 Muchambled, *History of Violence*, 17, 276.

30 Muir, *Ritual in Early Modern Europe*, 141–43.

31 Muchambled, *History of Violence*, 166. See Spierenburg, *History of Murder*, 77.

32 Pieter Spierenburg, "Knife Fighting and Popular Codes of Honor in Early Modern Amsterdam" in *Men and Violence: Gender, Honor, and Rituals in Modern Europe and America*, ed. Pieter Spierenburg (Columbus, OH: State University Press, 1998), 123.

33 Randall Balmer and Lauren F. Winner, *Protestantism in America* (New York: Columbia University Press, 2002), 219; Robert Moats Miller, *American Protestantism and Social Issues, 1919–1939* (Westport, CT: Greenwood Press, 1977), 10; Spierenburg, *A History of Murder*, 78.

34 Spierenburg, *History of Murder*, 8.

35 Ibid., 9.

As the concept of honor became more spiritualized, the Christian attitude to male honor softened, and men were sometimes allowed to defend their honor by peaceful means.[36]

Despite all the efforts of Catholics and Protestants, male youth continued to mock the forces of order. Even in the latter part of the eighteenth century, a French cleric complained of youths: "They counterfeit the ceremonies and pay no heed to remonstrances. They run through the village in disguise, dancing, displaying carnival on Ash Wednesday. They enter the sanctuary during services, station themselves between the cross and the priest in processions as though they were clergy, turn their backs to the altar, laugh and talk during services, pound on the benches, fire pistols in church or in front of it on wedding days and holy days, dance in front of the church on the pedestal of the cross, even before catechism and during Advent, and sing obscene songs."[37] Even before the Revolution, the relations of males, especially young males, and the clergy were strained.

Victorian England decided to end the rowdiness and violence of the eighteenth century by changing the law so that it "unceasingly stigmatized and proscribed long accepted modes of *male* behavior."[38] Violence was no longer tolerated. Because men were far more inclined to violent behavior than women, they therefore bore the brunt of the new legal attitudes: "the proportion of men prosecuted at the Old Bailey, which had risen from an eighteenth-century average of about two-thirds to three-quarters in the1820s, rose to almost 90% by the end of the century."[39] Therefore 96% of convicts were male. To counter male violence, evangelicals denounced the cult of honor and physical virility, and emphasized that men should be good workers, husbands, and fathers.[40] The form of homicide practiced by women—child abandonment—was by contrast treated less and less harshly, because women, the angels of the house, to commit such unnatural violence had to have been led astray by men.[41]

---

36 Ibid., 109.
37 Quoted in Muir, *Ritual in Early Modern Europe*, 140.
38 Martin J. Wiener, "The Victorian Criminalization of Men" in Spierenburg, *Men and Violence*, 198.
39 Ibid., 209.
40 Ibid., 201.
41 Ibid., 291.

Campaigns brought the evils of domestic violence to the attention of the public. The behavior of Mr. Punch was no longer acceptable—"in the old Punch and Judy shows . . . Punch was always beating Judy over the head with a club, and would often throw the baby out the window."[42] Ruff describes the typical show that the young (it goes without saying male) adult audience saw: "Punch abusing his neighbor's dog with a stick, and skewering the devil on his own trident. All this was presented with slapstick, scatological humor, and sexual innuendo that caused the audience to laugh at high levels of violence."[43]

Since the Middle Ages, men have committed 90% of murders, but since the Middle Ages the murder rate in Europe has declined 90%, reaching a low point in 1930,[44] because a whole cohort of young men had been killed off in the Great War. Society channeled male aggression into the military, into "just wars" between states and into colonial ventures, in which young men killed the natives rather than their fellow Europeans. With the decline of militarism and colonialism, free-form male violence has been rising again in Europe, usually in the neighborhoods full of alienated young men.

American Youth and Violence

David Courtwright in *Violent Land*[45] describes the connection between youthful masculinity and violence. The American frontier was violent, or rather, only part of it was violent: the part that concentrated armed young men, who had, like all unattached young men, "the sense of expendability that plagues bachelor communities."[46] The murder rate of the frontier was even higher than the homicide rate in medieval Europe. At the height, Leadville, Colorado, had a rate of 105 per 100,000; Bodie, California, had a rate of 116 per 100,000 (around the same period Boston had a rate of 5.8 and Philadelphia 3.2).[47]

---

42 Edward L. Mattil and Betty Marzan, *Meaning in Children's Art: Projects for Teachers* (Englewood Cliffs, NJ: Prentice Hall, 1981), 324.
43 Ruff, *Violence,* 15.
44 Muchambled, *History of Violence,* 210.
45 David T. Courtwright, *Violent Land: Single Men and Social Disorder from the Frontier to the Inner City* (Cambridge, MA: Harvard University Press, 1996).
46 Ibid., 38.
47 Ibid., 81–82.

Mark Twain captured the atmosphere of the frontier in *Roughing It*, and observes the uniqueness of Gold Rush California: "Two hundred thousand *young* men"—"the only population of its kind that the world has ever seen gathered together and it is not likely that the world will ever see its like again."[48] Twain describes the adventure, the risk-taking, the generosity, and the violence of this young male society. The mining camps were up to 92% male;[49] in 1850 among the Euro-American population age twenty to thirty-nine, only 4% were female.[50] It was not the frontier, but a society composed of young men, that produced the violence in which men were both the perpetrators and the victims.

Religious settlements on the frontier were peaceful, because they had a balance of men and women. One of the Mormon towns was named Orderville, which lived up to its name. A community that expects its members to follow standards of behavior is necessary to control young men. Rodney Stark maintains that "religion gains its power to influence behavior to the extent that it is social"[51]; therefore purely personal beliefs of an individual are not very influential in controlling crime; but membership in a moral community is effective. As a result, in highly churched areas, like Provo, Utah, church attendance negatively correlates to delinquency, while in unchurched areas such as Seattle, Washington, there is no correlation because there is no moral community.[52] Richard Stott saw the process occurring in a nineteenth-century village in Indiana, when "churchgoers achieved a critical mass that allowed them to influence the entire village."[53]

Religion could control male violence: "the religious colonies were the most dramatic example of the power of religious conviction to squelch

---

48 Mark Twain [Samuel Longhorn Clemens], *Roughing It* (New York: Harper & Brothers, 1913), 132.

49 Laurie F. Maffly-Kip, *Religion and Society in Frontier California* (New Haven: Yale University Press, 1994), 5.

50 Ibid., 150.

51 Rodney Stark and William Sims Bainbridge, *Religion, Deviance, and Social Control* (New York: Routledge, 1996), 55.

52 Ibid., 74–78.

53 Richard Stott, *Jolly Fellows: Male Milieus in Nineteenth-Century America* (Baltimore: Johns Hopkins Press, 2009), 81.

disorderly behavior. Perhaps that is why, collectively, young single men wanted nothing to do with them."[54] The different rates of religious participation are not just between men and women, but within the sexes as well: "married women were the most faithful churchgoers, young single men the least faithful."[55] Married men tended to follow the lead of their wives in civilizing the West: "Clergyman, female moralists, and their respectable male allies (generally husbands, converts, and Masons) used a variety of means, from petitions to sit-in demonstrations to protest Sabbath-breaking, brothels, dance halls, gambling palaces, and saloons."[56] Their efforts were not appreciated by the young men who were the object of the reform effort. Ministers realized that women were necessary to civilize men, and civilization was a necessary preliminary to converting them.[57] But to ministers' disappointment, revivals failed in the West.[58] The excitement of the frontier and of the Gold Rush was a more than adequate substitute for the excitement of the conversion experience. Prospecting became a rite of passage, an initiation experience.[59]

Although the frontier is gone, the black inner cities and more and more the white underclass (the latter the subject of Charles Murray's *Coming Apart: The State of White America 1960–2010*) contain many young men not under the control of their fathers, young men who therefore have developed a similar culture of expendability and violence, joined to the rejection of religion, which they see as effeminate. The United States has controlled this violence by a massive increase in incarceration; the prison substitutes for the church as an agent of social control. But prisons are not good training grounds for the responsibility and self-control that make a man a good father. So the cycle continues.

The Usual Suspect: Sex

Medieval Europeans, especially in the towns, knew that early marriages could lead to many children and that young men would be hard put to

54 Courtwright, *Violent Land*, 37.
55 Ibid., 35.
56 Ibid., 144.
57 See Chapter Six, "The 'Wondrous Efficacy' of Womanhood," Maffly-Kip, *Religion and Society*, 148–80.
58 Maffly-Kip, *Religion and Society*, 92.
59 Ibid., 134–35.

support such families. Marriages therefore came after a man had trained in a guild and was able to support a family. As a consequence towns had a large population of young, unmarried men, and authorities provided for their needs through the town brothel, thereby "enhancing," as the Council of Augsburg explained, "the good, piety, and honor of the whole commune."[60] Thomas Aquinas, following Augustine, accepted brothels as a way of protecting honorable women from men.[61] The Protestant Reformers rejected this solution, and counseled early marriage, which the secular authorities did not like. The Reformers insisted on closing the town brothel, because in their eyes, according to Lyndal Roper, "men's sexual natures were not uncontrollable" and "male lust could be educated and directed towards marriage."[62]

The era of the Counter-Reformation also saw a new zeal in enforcing chastity for males. Clerical concubinage was almost universal in the Middle Ages but was now vigorously criticized.[63] In the sixteenth century French cities began rejecting prostitution.[64] In Spain both the secular and ecclesiastical courts prosecuted the "raucous boys and young men" and the older men who refused to abide by strict standards of chastity.[65] The Inquisition prosecuted men who claimed that fornication was not a sin.[66] If it was sinful, young men asked, why were there

60 Quoted by Lydal Roper, *The Holy Household: Women and Morals in Reformation Augsburg* (Oxford: Clarendon Press, 1989), 91.
61 *Summa Theologica*, II[a] II[a] 10.11: "in human governments also, those who are in authority rightly tolerate certain evils, lest certain goods be lost, or certain greater evils be incurred: thus Augustine says (*De Ordine* ii.4): *If you do away with harlots, the world will be convulsed with lust*" (trans. the Fathers of the English Dominican Province, revised ed. 1920. New York: Benzinger Brothers, 1948. Reprinted Westminster, MD: Christian Classics n. d.). See Gustavo E. Ponferrada, "Santo Tomás y la prostitución," *Sapientia* (1990): 225–30.
62 Roper, *Holy Household*, 130.
63 Roussiaud, *Medieval Prostitution*, 50.
64 Ibid., 49.
65 Edward Behrend-Martinez, "'Taming Don Juan': Limiting Masculine Sexuality in Counter-Reformation Spain," *Gender and History* 24, No. 2 (2012): 334. doi: 10.1111/j.1468-0424.2012.01685.x.
66 Allyson M. Poska and Elizabeth A. Lehfeldt, "Redefining Expectations: Women and the Church in Early Modern Spain," in *Women and Religion in*

officially sanctioned brothels? These were closed in the 1560s in France[67] and in 1623 by royal decree in Spain.[68] Both Church and state tried to control "the violence and sexuality of legions of men" with a new vigor, even prosecuting aristocrats who seduced lower-class women,[69] and executing men (always men) for bestiality.[70] The common perception of young men of all classes was not positive: "All violated the rules laid down by Christianity and society. All were driven by the same impatience, the same negativity, the same redoubtable desires. All were objects of suspicion and fear."[71]

The Catholic man of the Counter-Reformation was supposed to be continent before marriage and to take St. Joseph as a model in marriage: a responsible, protecting, providing patriarch. Young men would have none of it. They derided those who refused to have sex as "faggots."[72] Picaresque literature contained many examples of youth who rejected social discipline. The popes of Counter-Reformation Rome also tried to rid the city of the prostitution that had so scandalized Martin Luther—but tried without success.[73]

The Reformers tried to stop sexually explicit dancing at weddings, dancing which sometimes led to rape.[74] In France the young men of the village used gang rape to control the girls of the village.[75] Priests took the part

the Old and New Worlds, eds. Susan E. Dinan and Debra Meyers (New York: Routledge, 2001), 38.

67 Tessa Storey, Carnal Commerce in Counter-Reformation Rome (Cambridge: Cambridge University Press, 2008), 243.

68 Behrend-Martinez, "'Taming Don Juan,'" 337.

69 Ibid., 344.

70 Ibid., 343.

71 Crouzet-Pavan, "A Flower of Evil," in Levi and Schmitt, A History of Young People, Vol. 1, 190.

72 Behrend-Martinez, "'Taming Don Juan,'" 346.

73 See Storey, Carnal Commerce, 242.

74 Susan C. Karant-Nunn, The Reformation of Ritual: An Interpretation of Early Modern Germany (New York: Routledge, 1997), 38.

75 Philip T. Hoffman, Church and Community in the Diocese of Lyon: 1500–1789 (New Haven: Yale University Press, 1984), 145. Ruff describes these gang rapes as rites of passage: of the youth groups: "ten or fifteen young men might break into a woman's home to rape her there or to drag her into the street for assault" (Violence, 142).

of the young woman who had been impregnated by a young man and put as much pressure as possible on the young man to marry the woman. The clergy tried to confine sex to marriage. In Andalusia, Stanley Brandes was told that "men avoid the Church because they refuse to believe that their sexual escapades are sinful, or that they should place a strong brake on their sexuality."[76] Laymen also do not believe, as we shall see, that priests are really chaste in their celibacy.

In the seventeenth century in France, reforming clerics sought to control the lives of the laity, and "young men were the chief target of a new sexual ethic."[77] The rigorism of Gallicanism and Jansenism long continued to influence the French clergy, and the Sulpicians who trained diocesan priests worldwide carried these attitudes through much of the Catholic world. This religious attitude was "negative, morose, holding for nothing the present life and turning its back on a world considered as fundamentally evil." This led to an extreme moralism, especially in sexual matters, but also to "an ideal of segregation" which reinforced the "spirit of domination" in the clergy, because the pastor considered his first duty "to shelter his flock" and "to preserve them from every external contamination," whether or not the flock wanted to be sheltered and preserved.[78] Father knew best.

Marriage also became a battleground between men and the clergy. Contraception within marriage was an issue that helped to alienate men from the Catholic Church.[79] By the eighteenth century French families, even observant Catholic ones, were starting to limit the number of their children, and the only way to do this, apart from total abstinence, was *coitus interruptus*, withdrawal before ejaculation. The clergy named this the sin of

---

76 Stanley Brandes, *Metaphors of Masculinity: Sex and Status in Andalusian Folklore* (Philadelphia: University of Pennsylvania Press, 1980), 184.

77 Ralph Gibson, *A Social History of French Catholicism 1789–1914* (London: Routledge, 1989), 11. According to one objective measure, the campaign was successful: the illegitimacy rate in France in the eighteenth century was 1% (Olwen H. Hufton, "The French Church," in *Church and Society in Catholic Europe of the Eighteenth Century*, eds. William J. Callahan and David Higgs, [Cambridge: Cambridge University Press, 1979], 27).

78 Christianne Marcilhacy, *Le diocèse d'Orléans au milieu du XIXe siècle* (Paris: Sirey, 1964), 227–28.

79 Eugen Weber, *Peasants into Frenchmen*, 365.

Onan, "le péché d'Onan," and denounced the married couple who practiced it: "They do not give life, they multiply death, for the husband is a grave-digger and the wife a grave."[80] Since the action was the husband's, the wife was held to be innocent. On the advice of Alphonsus de Ligouri, confessors decided that women were not guilty if their husbands practiced this form of contraception.[81] This decision was based on a fear that rigorism would alienate women and the Church would lose all influence in French society. In 1842 the Trappist (and medical doctor) Pierre-Jean Corneille Debreyne (1786–1867) argued against a rigorist position on the use of contraception because it would alienate women: "The woman can save everything; and perhaps today she is the sole connection that attaches us to religion, to faith, to moral-ity. Break that connection, and perhaps we are done with religion, with faith, with morality. If the woman gets away from us [the *us* seems to be his priest-readers to whom the book is directed] with her everything will disappear and vanish into the abyss of atheism—faith, morality, and our whole civilization."[82] Husbands had to bear the sole responsibility for this form of contraception; they were condemned and were refused absolution when they practiced it.

Men were alienated from the Church by the attempts to end contracep-tion. As Boutry observes: "the denunciation by the church of the crime of Onan wounded the conscience and the decisions of many men" and also "with-out a doubt distanced a great number of them from frequenting the sacra-ments."[83] But the issue of contraception was but one of the sexual issues that men in particular confronted. The attempt to control male sexuality through

80 Quoted in Philippe Boutry and Michel Cinquin, *Deux pèlerinages au XIXe siè-cle: Ars et Paray-le-Monial* (Paris: Éditions Beauchesne, 1980), 593.

81 John T. Noonan, Jr., *Contraception: A History of Its Treatment by the Catholic Theologians and Canonists* (Cambridge, MA: Harvard University Press, 1986), 382.

82 Pierre-Jean Corneille Debreyne, *Essai sur la théologie morale, considérée dans ses rapports avec la physiologie et la médicine* (Paris: Poussielgue-Rusand, 1845), 215–16.

83 Boutry, *Deux pèlerinages*, 593. Jean Quéniart also sees the male role in contra-ception as distancing men from religious practice; see *Les hommes, l'église et Dieu dans la France du XIIIe siècle* (Paris: Hachette, 1878), 230–34. See also Ralph Gibson, "Why Republicans and Catholics Couldn't Stand Each Other in the Nineteenth Century," in *Religion, Politics and Society in France since 1789*, eds. Frank Tallett and Nicholas Atkin (London: Hambledon Press, 1991), 107–20.

the confessional backfired. Anticlerical writers warned French men that they should beware of turning the direction of their wives over to priests, "because through the confessional, where the penitents were mostly women, they exercised power over men's sexuality."[84] Charles Taylor observes that "the combination of sexual repression and clerical control, as it was felt in the practice of confession, drove men away. Clerical control went against their sense of independence, and this became doubly intolerable when the control took the form of opening up the most reserved and intimate facet of their lives."[85] Men had achieved some degree of independence as part of achieving their adult masculinity, and did not want to surrender that independence, especially in sexual matters, to a priest whose masculinity and integrity they suspected.

Attempts (often entirely necessary and justified) to control male sexuality have continued. In the United States the Great Awakenings led to attempts to end prostitution ("White Slavery") both by offering fallen women ways of earning an honest living, by shaming their male customers by publishing their names, and by trying to convince boys of the virtues of chastity. Women led the Purity Crusade and "hoped to change men's carnal nature by early education and conversion."[86] Not only did women try to get the age of consent raised (it was seven in Delaware and ten in many other states),[87] they sometimes seemed to want to abolish sex entirely as a distasteful male activity, like their sisters across the Water, who closed their eyes and thought of England.

The Pledge

Drinking was an obvious source of male disorder and has long been one of the chief targets of clerical reformers, Catholic and Protestant. In France

---

84 W. D. Halls, *Politics, Society and Christianity in Vichy France* (Oxford: Berg, 1995), 10.

85 Charles Taylor, *Dilemmas and Connections: Selected Essays* (Cambridge, MA: The Belknap Press of the Harvard University Press, 2011), 250.

86 Susan Hill Lindley, *"You Have Stepped Out of Your Place": A History of Women and Religion in America* (Louisville, KY: Westminster John Knox, 1996), 97.

87 See Mary E. Odem, *Delinquent Daughters: Protecting and Policing Adolescent Female Sexuality in the United States 1885–1920* (Chapel Hill: University of North Carolina Press, 1995), 14.

the Confrérie of St. Antoine (better known as the Confraternity of the Cow, because its members killed one each year and distributed its meat to the poor) was suppressed in 1845 by the local priest because "he thought the fraternal banquets were too washed down with wine."[88] The members rioted. The Curé of Ars fought the cabarets of his village. They were the center of drinking and often of drunkenness and violence, and the money spent there often reduced families from honest poverty to destitution. The tavern had become a counter-church, a *contre-église*, a center of vice and free-thinking.

In Victorian Britain most working men hated prohibition and rioted against attempts to impose it.[89] The public house was the place where the male working class socialized, and G. K. Chesterton knew it had to be defended against women's objections about its rowdiness and waste. Women insisted that men behave, and Chesterton admitted that "there are very many polite men," but they all were "either fascinating women or obeying them." The female insistence on dignity, according to Chesterton, was "the same that makes women religious."[90] But men by nature, Chesterton implies, are neither very well-behaved nor religious. Attempts by churches to make men behave only drive men further from religion, or as Brian Harrison observed, Christian moral reforming movements "confirmed the irreligious prejudices of secularist working men."[91]

In the United States also, for many "the village church and the village tavern did in fact represent the two great opposing principles, good and evil,"[92] as Daniel Drake said in 1819. In Stott's view, "feminine influence was the key to the success of temperance, because women were the ones who suffered immediately from male drunkenness.[93] At a Baptist church in Alabama, the male membership constituted about 35% of the church, a proportion in line with evangelical churches throughout the South, but

---

88 Weber, *Peasants*, 366.
89 Brian Harrison, "Religion and Recreation in Nineteenth-Century England," *Past and Present* 38 (1967): 112.
90 Gilbert Keith Chesterton, *What's Wrong with the World* (New York: Dodd, Mead, 1912), 175–76.
91 Harrison, "Religion and Recreation in Nineteenth-Century England," 124.
92 Daniel Drake, quoted in Stott, *Jolly Fellows*, 84.
93 Stott, *Jolly Fellows*, 86.

men were the subject of 75% of church disciplinary acts, and the most common reasons for discipline, as church records indicated, were "excess drinking," "too much drinking," "intoxication," and "whiskey making." As Wayne Frank points out, women did not hold church offices, but "they influenced the church's concept of proper ethical conduct and molded Mt. Hebron's use of discipline toward social objectives that helped protect them from violence, drunkenness, and discord."[94]

Prohibition in the United States was the result of the alliance of clergy and women to stop the male drinking that, its enemies claimed, often led to poverty and violence. Although the original temperance societies were male, the movement soon became "largely a female drive against the intemperance and irresponsibility of men."[95] A declining birth rate, the availability of servants, and the lack of direct economic responsibilities gave middle-class women some leisure. Women saw alcohol and poverty as interrelated scourges that wounded the domestic life to which women dedicated themselves.[96] What better use of leisure than to attack such vices?

In 1874 it was observed "for the most part the very people most interested in favor of prohibition are the pious women and the clergy."[97] In America the Women's Christian Temperance Union held pray-ins at saloons during 1873–1874.[98] However, the Episcopalian minister E. A. Wasson claimed that Catholic, Lutheran, and Episcopalian clergy would have nothing to do with Prohibition; it was all the fault of "these Puritan preachers who first stirred up these women and started them on

94 Wayne Flynt, "'A Special Feeling of Closeness': Mt. Hebron Baptist Church, Leeds, Alabama," in *American Congregations*, Vol. 1, *Portraits of Twelve Religious Communities*, eds. James Wind and James W. Lewis (Chicago: University of Chicago Press, 1994), 26, 127, 132.

95 Barbara Leslie Epstein, *The Politics of Domesticity: Women, Evangelism, and Temperance in Nineteenth-Century America* (Middletown, CT: Wesleyan University Press, 1981), 90.

96 See Ruth Bordin, *Women and Temperance: The Quest for Power and Liberty, 1873–1900* (New Brunswick, NJ: Rutgers University Press, 1990), 10–14.

97 Don Fulano, "Christianity and Intemperance," *Common Sense* 1, no. 7 (June 27, 1874): 76.

98 Catherine Gilbert Murdock, *Domesticating Drink: Women, Men, and Alcohol in America, 1870–1940* (Baltimore: Johns Hopkins University Press, 1998), 18. See also Lindley, *"You Have Stepped Out of Your Place,"* 103–06.

their prohibitionist course."[99] The Baptists, Methodists, and Congregation-
alists were supporters of total prohibition; other churches supported temperance, although this sometimes meant total abstinence from alcohol.[100]

Catholic total abstinence was promoted by numerous organizations.
Theobald Mathew ("Father Mathew") joined the Cork Total Abstinence
Society in 1838 and led an extraordinarily successful campaign to encourage
men to take "the pledge." The Jesuit James Cullen founded the Pioneers in
Ireland in 1898 and encouraged (male) Catholics to take the pledge at con-
firmation.[101] The Catholic temperance societies in Toronto were founded
and directed by the clergy, who asked men to pledge complete abstinence
from alcohol, in order to avoid sin and damnation, and also "to provide the
domestic comforts that were made possible by thrift and industriousness"
and to "restore men to the family circle."[102] Apparently, in the clerical mind
women were not prone to alcoholism. Irish Catholic men enjoyed male sociability often, in the view of the clergy, to the detriment of family life: "If
Catholic men were supposed to copy female work habits as well as feminine
maternal instincts, it was because these behaviors were meant to stabilize
the Catholic family by redefining manhood as family oriented."[103]

Sports and Spoilsports

The early Christian church, or at least its teachers, rejected the gladiatorial
and other spectacles as pagan, brutal, and brutalizing.[104] In the Middle Ages

99 E. A. Wasson, "Women and 'Temperance,'" *Pure Products* 7, no. 7 (July 1911):
368.
100 See "Temperance" in *The Catholic Encyclopedia*, Vol. 14 (New York: Robert
Appleton, 1912), 482–93.
101 Elizabeth Malcolm, "Ireland," in *Alcohol and Temperance in Modern History:
An International Encyclopedia*, Vol. 1, eds. Jack S. Blocker, David M. Fahey, and
Ian R. Tyrrell (Santa Barbara, CA: ABC-Clio, 2003), 323.
102 Brian Clarke, *Piety and Nationalism: Lay Voluntary Associations and the Creation
of the Irish-Catholic Community in Toronto, 1850–1895* (Montreal: McGill-
Queens University Press, 1993), 146–47.
103 Paula M. Kane, *Separatism and Subculture: Boston Catholicism, 1900–1920* (Chapel Hill: University of North Carolina Press, 1994), 81.
104 Hoffman, *Church and Community*, 23–46.

and Renaissance, village sports could be brutal: ball games between villages looked more like fights than games and animals were cruelly tortured in bear- and bull-baiting.[105] In France the curés also tried to put a stop to cruel sports at saints' festivals, such as tying a goose up by its neck and then whacking it until it was decapitated.[106] Pope Pius V tried to forbid bull-fighting; he was ignored.[107] Thomas Macaulay's remark about bear-baiting ("The Puritans hated bear-baiting, not because it gave pain to the bear, but because it gave pleasure to the spectators"[108]) is unfair; the clergy were genuinely appalled by cruelty to animals, and knew that by desensitizing men to the sufferings of other creatures it could lead to similar cruel treatment of human beings. Brian Harrison observes of the R.S.P.C.A. in Victorian Britain, that "by encouraging kindness to animals, the Society hoped eventually to civilize manners, and hence to make the masses more receptive to religious instruction."[109]

Although both Catholics and Reformers sometimes found some place for moderate use of sports,[110] on the whole they agreed with Phillip Stubbs, that "a good Christian man will not so idly and vainly spend his golden days."[111] For many centuries most Christians, like Jews, regarded sports as at best a waste of time. Underlying this was a general suspicion of the body.[112]

Because Anglicans and King James I encouraged games on Sunday, the Puritans disliked such sports all the more. Governor William Bradford of Massachusetts was distressed to see that on Christmas Day 1621 boys "were

105 Ibid., 82.
106 Ibid., 134–35.
107 Juan Pedro Viqueira Albán, *Propriety and Permissiveness in Bourbon Mexico*, trans. Sonya Lipsett Rivera and Sergio Rivera Ayala (Lanham, MD: SR Books, 2004), 12.
108 Thomas Babington Macaulay, *The History of England from the Accession of James II*, Vol. 1 (Boston: Phillips, Sampson, 1849), 126.
109 Harrison, "Religion and Recreation in Nineteenth-Century England," 100.
110 See Hoffman, *Church and Community*, 58–82.
111 Shirl James Hoffman, *Christianity and the Culture of Sports* (Waco, TX: Baylor University Press, 2010), 83.
112 Georg Söll, "Sport und Theologie: Chances eines Dialogs," in *Wie human ist der Sport? Theologisch-kirchliche Reflexionen*, ed. Dieter Henke (Munich: Claudius Verlag, 1975), 96–98.

in the street at play, openly; some pitching at the barr, and some at stoole-ball and such like sports."[113] He stopped them. The Puritans, however, encouraged sports that developed martial skills.[114] Thomas Campbell, a founder of the Disciples of Christ, regarded sports as competition for Bible reading and prayer.[115] The French clergy of the nineteenth century disliked sports because they emphasized the body. One curé even denounced the *escarpolette*—the swing—as "one of the vices of his parish."[116]

In the early nineteenth century in England almost all clergy strongly disliked sports. In 1860 the Rev. Samuel Earnshaw saw male alienation from the church as a result of the clergy's attack on "hunting, shooting, fishing, card-playing, billiards, and the theatre."[117] All amusements, but especially male amusements, were suspect, although one Evangelical generously allowed to young men "walks in the country, visits to botanical gardens, and the reading of works of biography and history."[118] Men defiled the Sabbath by making "journeys merely for the sake of pleasure."[119] They indulged in "the shameful practice of rowing machines and boat races on Sunday"[120]; they even had to be corrected for "whistling."[121] But the pubs were open. Robert Southey described the English Sunday: "Yonder goes a crowd to the tabernacle as dismally as they were going to a funeral; the great number are women;—inquire

113 William Bradford, *History of Plymouth Plantation* (Boston: Little, Brown, 1856), 112.

114 Hoffman, *Church and Community*, 87.

115 Clifford Putney, *Muscular Christianity: Manhood and Sports in Protestant America, 1880–1920* (Cambridge, MA: Harvard University Press, 2001), 53.

116 Jean Faury, *Cléricalisme et anticléricalisme dans le Tarn 1848–1900* (Toulouse: Service des Publications de l'Université de Toulouse-le Marial, 1980), 274.

117 Hugh McLeod, "Sport and the Reform of Piety in England: A Case Study," in *Piety and Modernity: The Dynamics of Religious Reform in Northern Europe 1780–1920*, ed. Anders Jarlert (Louvain: Louven University Press, 2012), 58.

118 Ibid., 57.

119 George Burder, in an 1805 sermon, "Lawful Amusements," quoted in Maurice J. Quinlan, *Victorian Prelude: A History of English Manners 1700–1805* (New York: Columbia University Press, 1941), 211.

120 *Statement of the Society for the Suppression of Vice*, 1804, quoted in Quinlan, *Victorian Prelude*, 212.

121 Quinlan, *Victorian Prelude*, 208.

after their husbands at the alehouse, and you will find them besotting themselves there because all amusements are prohibited as well as labor."[122] The church for women, the drinking house for men—a common pattern.

In Great Britain in the last part of the nineteenth and first part of the twentieth centuries, according to Brown, "ball games and especially football, the emerging adoration of males of all ages and social classes between the 1880s and 1920s, were banned from public spaces by by-laws and community expectation. Men were trained to perceive their masculine tendencies, even those promoted by muscular Christianity, as curbed on the Sabbath. Sunday was feminized, and men's games were rendered immoral and illegal."[123] Christians in the United States in the nineteenth century had little use for sports. A minister warned: "Sport, fun, and frolic have no chapter in youth's Book of Life in our day."[124] Another lamented, "our young men are godless. They profane the Sabbath with ball games, bathing and card parties."[125]

Football became popular in the liberal, progressive Northeast United States in the late nineteenth century; the theologically conservative South saw in football a revival of pagan ideals of masculinity, which the churches had long battled in its contemporary incarnation of the murderous Southern code of honor. Southern Christians regarded "male passion as the primary wellspring of sin" and initially denounced football as "animal, barbarous, brutal, savage, and carnal."[126] It created the opposite of the

---

122 Robert Southey, *Letters from England by Don Manual Alvarez Espriella*, Vol. 3, 2nd edition (London: Longman, Hurst, Rees & Orme, 1808), 187.

123 Callum G. Brown, *The Death of Christian Britain: Understanding Secularization 1800–2000* (London: Routledge, 2009), 139.

124 Quoted in Joseph L. Price, "From Sabbath Proscriptions to Super Sunday Celebrations: Sports and Religion in America," in *From Season to Season: Sports as American Religion*, ed. Joseph L. Price (Macon, GA: Mercer University Press, 2002), 18.

125 Quoted in James F. Oates, *The Religious Condition of Young Men* (Chicago: Young Men's Christian Association, n. d.), 10.

126 Andrew Doyle, "Foolish and Useless Sport: The Southern Evangelical Crusade against Intercollegiate Football," *Journal of Sport History* 24, no. 3 (Fall 1997): 327.

college environment that Southern Christians desired: "a pious, highly disciplined collegiate environment that left no room for the passion and frivolity that surrounded intercollegiate football."[127] But the evangelicals have changed their mind, and football, especially in the South, is next to godliness.[128]

But it was not just football that was denounced (with much justice) for its rowdiness and brutality. A Baptist editor in the 1880s condemned baseball as a "murderous game," that is "more brutal than a bull-fight, more reprehensible than a prize-fight, and more deadly than modern warfare."[129] It was as bad as "the "social dance."[130] The dance, more than any other activity favored by young men, aroused clerical ire.

Clerical Choreophobes

Dancing was long an obsession of the clergy of all denominations; it took up far more space in their minds and denunciations than the other characteristically masculine vices of card-playing, horse-racing, theater attendance, bullfighting, etc. Many Fathers disapproved of dancing. The Council of Avignon (1209) prohibited "Dancing in Churches on the Vigils of Festivals."[131] The Council of Paris (1212) forbade dancing "in the Church-yards, or any Consecrated Places."[132] Robert Manning (c. 1290–1340) recounts the story of the Cursed Dancers of Colbeck, who danced in the churchyard on Christmas Eve during Mass and were cursed by the priest to dance for a year without stopping. John Calvin tightened earlier prohibitions against dancing.[133] Luther

---

127 Ibid., 318.

128 For contemporary criticism of sports, see Barry R. Harker, *Strange Fire: Christianity and the Rise of Modern Olympism* (Rapidan, VA: Heartland Publications, 1996), 13.

129 Quoted in Joseph L. Price, "From Sabbath Proscription to Super Sunday Celebrations," in Price, *From Season to Season*, 19.

130 Price, "From Sabbath Proscription to Super Sunday Celebrations," 21.

131 Lewis Ellies Du Pin, *A New Ecclesiastical History*, Vol. 11 (London, 1699), 91.

132 Ibid., 94.

133 Herman J. Selderhuis, *John Calvin: A Pilgrim's Life* (Downers Grove, IL: Intervarsity Press, 2009), 151. Ann Wagner, *Adversaries of the Dance: From the Puritans to the Present* (Urbana: University of Illinois Press, 1997), 27.

saw no reason to prohibit all dancing, especially as it provided an opportunity for courtship,[134] but Evangelical Reformers in Germany denounced the *Bubentänze* (lads' dances) which seem to have been rowdy, leading to "luxury, arrogance, cockiness, contempt for others, indecency, discord, quarreling, murder, adultery, whoring, secret engagements, and other scandals and disgraces"[135]—the original dirty dancing. Perhaps Breughel's village scenes are not exaggerated.

For Catholic villages throughout Europe dancing was not only entertainment but played an important social function. The dances, whether they were ring, line, or couple, "provided an opportunity for young people to meet, to court, and for marriage arrangements to be concluded."[136] Dancing is often stylized courtship. The clergy found such dancing objectionable, especially if dances were held in connection with religious feasts. A priest in Lyon in 1693 lamented that "to see the lewd and violent gyrations of the girls mixed in dance with the young men, does it not seem that one is watching *bacchantes* and savages rather than Christians?"[137] In 1766 François Louis Gauthier assembled condemnations of the dance from Augustine, Basil, Ephraim the Syrian, the Fourth Council of Milan, St. Charles Borromeo, Cardinal Bellarmine, and many others, condemning dancing.[138] Borromeo agreed with those who said that "those who dance often, and accustom themselves to this exercise, commit a mortal sin."[139] Dances and other profane activities (feasts, hunts, tennis) on Sundays and holy days fell under special condemnation.[140] These sacred times should be devoted

---

134 Wagner, *Adversaries of the Dance*, 388.

135 Cyriakus Spangenberg (1528–1604), quoted in Joel Francis Harrington, *Reordering Marriage and Family in Reformation Germany* (Cambridge: Cambridge University Press, 1995), 222.

136 Joyce Riegelhaupt, "Popular Anti-Clericalism and Religiosity in pre-1974 Portugal," in *Religion, Power and Protest in Local Communities: The Northern Shore of the Mediterranean*, ed. Eric R. Wolf (New York: Mouton, 1984), 103.

137 Quoted by Gibson, *Social History*, 20.

138 François Louis Gauthier, *Traité contre les danses et les mauvaises chansons* (Paris: Antoine Boudet, 1766). See Drid Williams, *Anthropology and the Dance: Ten Lectures*, 2nd edition (Champaign: University of Illinois Press, 2004), 92–94.

139 Gauthier, *Traité*, 78.

140 See M. Babin, ed., *Conférences ecclésiastiques du Diocèse d'Angers sur les commandements de Dieu* (Paris: Louis François Delatour, 1771), 451–53.

to church attendance and then "to the reading of a good book, or to some exercise of religion or piety."[141]

The dances that were condemned under the *ancien regime* were the traditional village dances, often line or ring dances. With the advent of the waltz and the polka, which Napoleon's armies brought back from Germany, clerical hatred of dancing rose to a "paroxysm."[142] A Catholic priest of the diocese of Metz published a long treatise against dancing, collecting all the criticisms of dancing onwards from Cicero, who had said that anyone who dances was either drunk or insane. The priest concluded: "It is easy to see that dances are a pomp of the devil, a trap of the impure spirit, an artifice of hell to seduce men, a fire which enflames the hearts of the young, which incites in them every type of disgraceful passion, and which exposes them to the danger of losing their soul."[143] Dancing is next to damnation.

John Vianney, the curé of Ars, was also of this mind, and was determined to extirpate dancing. His vicar, Raymond, explained that in Ars "these young people were crazy about a certain pleasure called dance which they had every Sunday and feast day with a type of drunkenness and fury. The good pastor saw in the dance a block to the growing piety in their hearts. He saw in it the ruin of good morals, a path to debauchery by the adulteration of morals, through the too great liberty that parents too often gave to the young persons who were in the presence of boys."[144] The parents said that they had danced when they were young, that how else were future spouses supposed to meet? John Vianney "deplored such blindness; he wept about it before the Lord; he prayed; he exhorted; he threatened; he menaced with the judgments of God. He refused absolution to those who refused to give up dancing."[145] He told them "if you do not stop going to dances, you are damned" and that "dancing . . . is the chain by which the devil pulls

141 Babin, *Conférences*, 457.
142 Gibson, *Social History*, 91.
143 A Priest of the Diocese of Metz, *Instruction sur la Danse* (Charleville, 1821), 115.
144 Quoted in Boutry and Cinquin, *Deux pèlerinages*, 30–31.
145 Henry Aurenche, *La Passion du Saint Curé d'Ars* (Paris: Novelles Éditions Latine, 1949), 81.

most souls into hell."[146] He had a motto painted on the chapel of St. John the Baptist: "His head was the price of a dance."[147] The young men rebelled.[148] But Vianney prevailed, and his biographer Raymond smugly concludes: "At last the good news went around: there was no longer any dancing at Ars."[149]

Although the girls did not like this change, the men took it hardest.[150] Consequently the confraternities of Ars, which had been primarily male in the eighteenth century, became predominantly female, ranging from 76% to 94% female.[151] The curé of Montreuil-le-Henri in 1830 not only did not admit to Easter communion the young people who went to dances; he also refused communion to parents and masters who did not stop their children and servants from attending dances.[152] Young bachelors above all disliked the ban on dancing.[153] That was of course the group at which the ban was aimed, because "it was by no means uncommon for a dance to culminate in a fight between the champions of two adjoining villages."[154]

The Second Plenary Council of Baltimore, Paragraph 472, condemned "choreas immodestias," and the Third Plenary Council forbad charity dances to benefit any Catholic institution. In 1887 the bishop of Brooklyn forbade "choreis . . . Germanicae" (round dances)"; one vicar-general said that round dances "are forbidden by the natural law," and some priests refused absolution to those who would not give up dancing.[155] The bishop

---

146 Quoted by Christianne Marcilhacy, *Le diocse d'Orléans au milieu du XIXᵉ siècle* (Paris: Sirey, 1964), 255.

147 Alban Butler, *Lives of the Saints: August*, eds. Herbert Thurston and Donald Attwater, (Collegeville, MN: Liturgical Press, 1998), 30.

148 Gibson, *Social History*, 102.

149 Boutry, *Deux pèlerinages*, 32.

150 Gibson, *Social History*, 94.

151 Boutry, *Deux pèlerinages*, 48–49.

152 Marcel Launay, *Le ciel et la terre: L'église au village (XIXᵉ siècle)* (Paris: Cerf, 2009), 72.

153 Jan Art and Thomas Buerman, "Anticléricalisme et genre au XIXᵉ siècle: Le prêtre catholique, principal défi à l'image hégémonique de l'homme," in *Masculinités*, ed. Bruno Benvido (Brussels: Editions de l'Université de Bruxelles, 2009), 329.

154 Muchambled, *History of Violence*, 237.

155 "Round Dances," *The Pastor* 6, no. 11 (1888): 333.

of Le Mans denounced the *saltatio Germanica*, i.e., the waltz, as a mortal sin.[156] Bishop Elder of Cincinnati ordered that "there must be no round dancing at any time."[157] In 1901 the priests of the Albi in France decided that the polka was "truly Satanic" and that the waltz "excited the passions" so "the sacraments were denied to dancers and musicians alike."[158] In 1903 Bishop McCloskey of Louisville canceled a Knights of Columbus picnic because there would be dancing, especially "the shockingly indecent form of the modern dance."[159] Father Brothers of New Jersey declared that "indulgence in the turkey trot, the tango and other objectionable modern dances is as much a violation of the seventh commandment as adultery."[160] Father Hannigan said that if he were a judge, he "would sentence any woman who danced the turkey trot to a year in the penitentiary."[161] Archbishop Spaulding claimed that 19 out of 20 fallen women who came to confession blamed their fall on the dance.[162] Father Luigi Satori of Hagerstown, Maryland, asked Catholic organizations to cease sponsoring dances, because dancing was the "principal" evil— "dancing of any kind, comprehending square dances, which in some respects are worse than round dances."[163] Satori denounced the dance as "a flagrant violation of the Sixth Commandment" in which "syphilitic" men infected innocent girls who ruined their delicate health by the rigors of the dance.[164] Bishop Eugene O'Connell of Marysville, California, and Archbishop Spaulding of Baltimore, following the example of an eighteenth-century bishop of Senez[165]

156　Victor Dechamps, *La vie de plaisirs* (Paris: P.-M Laroche, 1867), 36.

157　W. W. Gardner, *Modern Dancing in the Light of Scripture and Facts* (Louisville, KY: Baptist Book Concern, 1893), 34.

158　Roger Magraw, *France 1815–1924: The Bourgeois Century* (New York: Oxford University Press, 1983), 336.

159　Henry Brown, *The Impending Peril, or, Methodism and Amusements* (Cincinnati, OH: Jennings & Pye, 1904), 42.

160　Quoted by M[ordecai] F. Ham, *Light on the Dance: A Historical and Analytical Treatment of the Subject* (1916), 14.

161　Ham, *Light on the Dance*, 14.

162　Ibid., 14.

163　Luigi Satori, *Modern Dances* (Collegeville, IN: St. Joseph's Printing Office, 1910), 1.

164　Ibid., 24, 58, 52.

165　John McManners, *Church and Society in the Eighteenth-Century France* Vol. 2:

made dancing (like bestiality) a reserved sin that could be forgiven only by a bishop.[166] In 1916, as the First World War raged, Benedict XV reiterated the prohibition against holding benefit dances for Catholic causes.[167]

Clerics expressed three objections to dancing. First, like all amusements, they were a distraction and waste of time. Bishop Felix Vialat of Chalons in 1661 condemned dancing as totally unsuitable for Christians "who are not in this world except to do penitence."[168] In this he echoes Vincent of Beauvais (c. 1190–1264) who condemned dancing because our life is not a time for diversion, especially not for the dance, "but is a time to weep and to cry, because we are here below in a place of exile, in a vale of tears, as if in a prison, and whatever way a man may turn, he sees nothing around him but scenes of affliction."[169] According to the Rev. Jacob Ide (1819), "the question, now to be determined, is, whether rational, and accountable beings, capable of the exalted pleasure of serving and enjoying God, destined to a future and an eternal existence, in which they are to receive according to the deeds done here in the body, have a *right* to spend their precious time, in dancing for mere amusement."[170] The dominant Catholic and Protestant answer was *No*.

Secondly, dancing, as a physical activity, was erotic. As the Baptist Robert Campbell explained: "Sex excitement is the life of the dance."[171] The Jansenist Louis Bailly would not give absolution for sins until the penances were completed: three years for fornication, but also three years for

The Religion of the People and the Politics of Religion (Oxford: Clarendon Press, 1998), 202.

166 Beryl and Associates, ed., *Immorality of Modern Dances* (New York: Everitt & Francis, 1904), 62–63.

167 "The Catholic Ban on Dancing," *The Literary Digest* 52, no. 26 (June 24, 1916): 1849.

168 Gauthier, *Traité*, 70.

169 Ibid., 79.

170 Jacob Ide, *The Nature and Tendency of Balls, seriously and candidly considered, in two sermons, preached in Medway, the first, December 21: the second, December 28, 1818.* (Dedham, MA: M. & W. H. Mann, 1819), 5.

171 Robert C. Campbell, *Modern Evils*, quoted in John Carrara, *Enemies of Youth* (Grand Rapids, MI: Zondervan, 1922), 59.

"dancing in front of the church"[172]—they were equivalent sins. The last and most serious objection was that dancing, like popular procession and pilgrimages, was not under the control of the clergy.[173] Ann Wagner summarizes the sources of the clerical animus against dancing: "an exclusive emphasis on strict rationality, a fear of the passions and the physical body, and an effort to control by avoiding temptation all bespeak a traditional authoritarian theology and morality."[174]

Male Sociability

The youth societies, the youth abbeys, began as a way for society to exercise some control over the activities of young men, but the control was not always successful. The fights that these societies enjoyed were not approved of by their elders, who attempted to outlaw them, accusing the societies of "lasciviousness, license, and debauchery" as well as general violence.[175] Savonarola attacked the vices of young men, the "giovini, ribaldi, scelerati." The young men retaliated; they "would produce rotting asses' skins in church, or bless the faithful with an onion impaled on the point of a sword."[176] They won and Savonarola lost, but their victory was only temporary.

If men wanted to do something on their own, the clergy were against it, whether it was penance or drinking. During the Catholic Reformation, in France as elsewhere, "it was male organizations and customs that were under attack: youth groups, festivities, confraternities."[177] What Gibson says

---

172 Theodore Zeldin, "The Conflict of Moralities: Confession, Sin and Pleasure in the Nineteenth Century," in *Conflicts in French Society: Anticlericalism, Education and Morals in the 19th Century*, ed. Theodore Zeldin (London: George Allen & Unwin, 1970), 27.

173 Caroline B. Bretell, "The Priest and His People: The Contractual Basis for Religious Practice in Rural Portugal," in *Religious Orthodoxy and Popular Faith in European Society*, ed. Ellen Badone (Princeton: Princeton University Press, 1990), 58.

174 Wagner, *Adversaries*, 395.

175 Crouzet-Pavan, "A Flower of Evil," in Levi and Schmitt, *A History of Young People*, Vol. 1, 211

176 Ibid., 218–19.

177 Gibson, *Social History*, 168.

of the Catholic penitential societies was true of all lay male groups; they were "communal, festive, freely mixing the sacred and profane, and hostile to clerical control."[178] In Lyon, as elsewhere, the reformers tried to separate the sacred and profane and also attacked male habits. Men, especially young men, "seemed to be the chief targets of the Church's drive to enforce its new sexual morality."[179] The mixture of sacred and profane in the village festivals, in which village young men played a part, was a constant object of clerical attempts at suppression. Consequently, men were the ones who quarreled with the curés; but women were on good terms with their priests,[180] too good terms, the men suspected.

The men could be serious, profound, and even penitential, as we shall see when examining the Spanish cofradías; but if their activity was not under clerical control, the clergy distrusted it. In the sixteenth and seventeenth centuries in the diocese of Lyon the confraternities of Penitents were harassed by the clergy, who thought they distracted from parish life.[181] After the French Revolution, male confraternities of penitents were revived in France and were immediately attacked by the clergy, who tried to destroy or control them, because of, as one bishop explained, their "ridiculous encroachment on clerical prerogatives."[182]

The male-run village festivals, with their music, dancing, and fireworks, were the object of clerical ire. In many Catholic cultures the men regarded their role in Catholicism as affirming the communal identity of the Catholic people (usually of the village) and bringing down graces upon the community through communal festivals. Through the work and expense of organizing and putting on the festivals, the music, the food, the fireworks, the dancing, men honored God and the saints.[183] The men hired a priest for the necessary sacerdotal roles in the festival, but the clergy did not run the festivals.

178 Ibid., 168.
179 Hoffman, *Church and Community*, 144.
180 Ibid., 144.
181 Ibid., 86.
182 Quoted in Gibson, *Social History*, 57.
183 Enrico Carlson Cumbo, "Salvation in Indifference: Gendered Catholicity among Catholic Immigrants," in *Households of Faith: Family, Gender, and Community in Canada, 1760–1969*, ed. Nancy Christie (Montreal: McGill-Queens University Press, 2002), 224.

Control was the key issue in these conflicts, and they were usually conflicts between the men and the clergy.[184] Fiestas were the occasion for "a contest of wills"[185]: the priest wanted to determine what Catholicism was, and the men had their own ideas. They were willing to let the priest have his version of Catholicism inside the church, with the women and children present (although the men kept a close eye on the women), but outside the church men wanted to maintain their own version of Catholicism. In eighteenth-century Portugal, David Higgs notes, "the church was uneasy with religious festivals and processions that were insufficiently controlled by the clergy."[186] In the Azores the clergy were hostile to the Holy Spirit festival, forbidding its head from speaking from the pulpit, forbidding its members from singing or dancing in church, forbidding clergy from attending the festival, and forbidding women from forming parallel organizations.[187]

In the town of Mesquite in Mexico a social activist priest denounced "folkloric religion," and this affront to their version of Catholicism "provoked the young men of the town into a defiant insistence on raising enough money for an impressive display of fireworks and brass bands."[188] Italians brought their conflicts between priests and the men who put on the *festas* in Canada: "A clerical report of the 1910s, for instance, described a celebration in which clerics and committee members came to blows. In a long tradition of such conflicts, festa committees sometimes hid their saints' statues in saloon lofts and warehouses lest the priests get hold of them."[189]

In São Miguel in Portugal the priest objected to the confraternity spending money on "musicians and fireworks."[190] Many clerics shared this dislike of fireworks,[191] perhaps because they sensed that fireworks were the

184 See Gibson, *Social History*, 78–80.
185 Stanley Brandes, "Conclusion: Reflections on the Study of Religious Orthodoxy and Private Faith in Europe," in Badone, *Religious Orthodoxy*, 189.
186 David Higgs, "The Portuguese Church," in Callahan and Higgs, *Church and Society*, 62.
187 Ibid., 62.
188 David Frye, *Indians into Mexicans: History and Identity in a Mexican Town* (Austin: University of Texas Press, 1996), 113.
189 Cumbo, "Salvation in Indifference," 224.
190 Riegelhaupt, "Popular Anti-Clericalism," 103.
191 See Frye, *Indians into Mexicans*, 114.

visual (and auditory) equivalent and expression of the young male *thumos* that created endless problems. Stanley Brandes, who drily observes that the "Church of Rome does not require the liturgical use of fireworks,"[192] thought that, in the festival he studied, men built and set off the fireworks as an expression of male penetration and explosion. A common Spanish expression for ejaculation is *"tirar un cohete*—to toss a skyrocket."[193] What would a Hispanic feast be without fireworks, especially firecrackers set off during mass to honor God?[194] In Spain the bishops struggled for several centuries to end popular festivities in the church; they often had to compromise, but they insisted: "no 'letting off fireworks inside the cathedral.'"[195] Even the Anglicans warned that "fireworks [at harvest-festivals] are objectionable, as causing a dangerous excitement among young men."[196] Sometimes (as in Palma del Condado in 1973) firework displays ended in fireworks wars between rival confraternities, with damage and serious injuries.[197]

A striking example of the contest between the men who ran festivities and the clerics who wanted to be in charge occurred in the Breton village of La Feuillée in 1907. The village had long had an annual procession on the patronal feast of St. John the Baptist. A small boy dressed in a sheepskin and sandals, imitating John the Baptist, led a sheep decorated with pink cloth roses to the church. Usually a handful of women attended Sunday Mass, but on the feast day several hundred villagers, including a substantial portion of the men, attended. Apparently in the 1906 procession the curé had been the object of some rude remarks, and in 1907 he banned the procession. This was a mistake. "In protest a group of the parish youths

192 Stanley Brandes, *Power and Persuasion: Fiestas and Social Control in Rural Mexico* (Philadelphia: University of Pennsylvania Press, 1988), 110.
193 Ibid., 200.
194 Ibid., 113.
195 Kamen, *Phoenix and the Flame*, 130.
196 Francis Edward Paget, *The Parish and the Priest* (London: Joseph Masters, 1858), 276.
197 Isidoro Moreno Navarro, *Cofradías y hermandades Andaluzas: estructura, simbolismo e identidad* (Seville: Editoriales Andaluzas Unidas, 1985, 90); see also Timothy Mitchell, *Passional Culture: Emotion, Religion, and Society in Southern Spain* (Philadelphia: University of Pennsylvania Press, 1990), 100.

organized a mock procession on 24 June, in which a fox decorated with ribbons was led through the *bourg*, followed by a crowd that forced its way into the church. Here the beribboned fox was 'baptized' in the font. Throughout the parody the mayor ordered the church bells to be rung at full volume."[198] The curé and his assistant fled the village and the bishop put the village under interdict. Eventually a new curé was appointed, and he, exercising discretion, let the procession continue.

In France the clergy, partly under the influence of Romanticism, decided in the latter part of the nineteenth century to make their peace with some practices of popular religion as long as: 1. The clergy were in control; 2. The festive element was eliminated. Men had been frequenters of the old shrines; they stayed away from the new ones. In 1894 the diocese of Cambrai sponsored a pilgrimage to Lourdes, with 5,200 women and 400 men.[199]

Religious festivals and other popular customs were abolished by the Reformers, but disorder continued. Reformers tried to deny young men not only "the sexual license of brothel visits" but also general merriment: "the horseplay of youth, engaging in door-knockings, noisily singing in New Year and prising money from their hearers, dancing, or taking leading roles in carnival frolics." The new authorities of the Reformation also, like the Catholic authorities before them, punished "fighting and rowdy behavior in the streets."[200] The old Adam continued his activities in the new Evangelical Germany.

Clericalism

Both Catholic and Protestant clergy tried to control the laity, a control, in the clergy's view, that was necessary for the good of the laity and for the good of society, and the segment of society that the clergy had the most difficulty controlling and was most determined to control was that of young males. The Christian clergy, like the rabbis and the pagan philosophers,

---

198 Ellen Badone, "Breton Folklore of Anticlericalism," in Badone, *Religious Orthodoxy*, 150.
199 Gibson, *Social History*, 153.
200 Roper, *Holy Household*, 57, 82.

preached the necessity of self-control. If males would not exercise self-control, they needed to be controlled by external authority and had to be convinced to obey that authority. The fundamental virtue of the laity was therefore obedience to the clergy.

The clergy of the Roman Catholic Church made exalted claims for itself.[201] The Donation of Constantine provided a basis for political claims of the superiority of the papacy over all secular powers. Within society, the priest had a unique position. The priest was supposed to be "the intermediary between God, His Church, and the Church's lay subjects."[202] Innocent III claimed that scripture called priests gods: "'Diis non detrahes,' [Ex. 22:28] sacerdotes intelligens, qui propter excellentiam ordinis et offici dignitatem nomine nuncupator"[203] (*You shall not revile gods*, meaning priests, who are called by the name of gods because of the excellency of the order and the dignity of the office). The laity were not convinced. Protestants rebelled against these extreme claims and therefore the Roman Church reaffirmed them in the Counter-Reformation. The clericalist claims influenced the attitudes of priests for centuries, taking odd turns and producing some catastrophic results.

The laity should obey the priest, because even God obeys the priest. God obeys the priest —an extraordinary claim, which was likely to feed narcissism in any man, and to give him an exalted idea of his own authority. In 1907 the Rev. Pierre Chaignon told his fellow priests that they were like Mary, "for the Word of God made flesh puts Himself under our control as He had put himself under hers and obeys us as He deigned to obey her."[204] In 1974 the Rev. John O'Brien claimed "The priest speaks and lo! Christ, the eternal and omnipotent God bows his head in humble obedience to the priest's command."[205]

---

201 Russell Shaw sketches the rise of clericalism in Chapter 2, "A Brief History of Clericalism," in *To Hunt, To Shoot, To Entertain: Clericalism and the Catholic Laity* (San Francisco: Ignatius Press, 1993), 39–81.

202 David Burrows, *The Stereotype of the Priest in the Old French Fabliaux: Anticlerical Satire and Lay Identity* (Oxford: Peter Lang, 2005), 48.

203 Ibid., 49.

204 Pierre Chaignon, *Meditations for the Use of the Secular Clergy*, Vol. 2. Translated L. D. Goesbriand (New York: Benzinger Brothers, 1907), 445.

205 John Anthony O'Brien, *The Faith of Millions: The Credentials of the Catholic Religion* (Huntingdon, IN: Our Sunday Visitor Publishing, 1974), 256.

The clergy would not yield any power to the laity. Pope Pius X gave up all church property in France rather than let it fall under lay Catholic control,[206] and reminded Catholics that the Church is "essentially an *unequal* society, that is, a society comprising two categories of persons, the Pastors and the flock, those who occupy a rank in the different degrees of the hierarchy and the multitude of the faithful. So distinct are these categories that with the pastoral body only rests the necessary right and authority for promoting the end of the society and directing all its members towards that end; the one duty of the multitude is to allow themselves to be led, and, like a docile flock, to follow the Pastors."[207] As Christianne Marcilhacy notes of the priests of Orleans in the mid-nineteenth century, "with the best intentions and with disarming candor priests practiced a spiritual clericalism which extended to all the faithful and which led the priests, not only to identify themselves with religion, but to identify religion with their own person."[208] Therefore dislike of the clergy tended to metamorphose into rejection of Christianity.

Critiques of clericalism came from within the Church. The claims to moral authority contrasted with the obvious corruption of a large segment of the clergy. Catholics such as Boccaccio and Chaucer painted harsh portraits of clerical corruption without questioning the basic structure of the Catholic system. Others questioned the system itself, a questioning that led to the Protestant Reformation and a rejection of the claims of the Catholic clergy. Theoretically, all Christians were priests and all Christians enjoyed liberty of conscience, but Protestant clerics soon decided that the laity needed to be controlled by their betters. As Milton lamented, "New Presbyter is Old Priest writ large."

As a defense against revolutionary and liberal movements of the nineteenth century the hierarchy of the Catholic Church became increasingly centralized. The revolutions and Napoleonic wars had swept away the

---

206 Nicholas Atkin and Frank Tallett, *Priests, Prelates, and People: A History of European Catholicism since 1750* (New York: St. Martin's, 2003), 153.

207 Pius X, *Vehementer nos*, 1906, Vatican translation. http://www.vatican.va /holy_father/pius_x/encyclicals/documents/hf_p-x_enc_11021906_vehementer-nos_en.html.

208 Marcilhacy, *Le diocse d'Orléans*, 256.

survivals of feudal autonomies and privileges, and this allowed the structure of the Church to be simplified. The Pope became the center of Catholic unity and the hierarchy was stiffened to confront the challenges of the age. But this centralization "drained the ranks of the laity of any independence of either thought or act and of any participation save unquestioning obedience."[209] Obedience, as we have seen, was especially appropriate to women, and therefore the image of the femininity of the lay members of the church was increased, even as the hierarchy exercised the masculine role of command.[210] Gibson explains why men rejected and women accepted clerical domination: "A catholicism [sic] so insistent on clerical authority was widely unacceptable to men who prized at least the illusion of being self-determining. Women, by contrast, were much more disposed to accept a hierarchical order and their own subjection within it. This was particularly true of confession...."[211] Confession, or its Protestant equivalent pastoral counseling, was an extremely sore point among men.

In both Catholicism and Protestantism, the assertions of clerical control helped to alienate men from the church. Feminists have complained about the patriarchal authority of the clergy; but men chafed under it even more, because men, more so than women, establish their identity by becoming autonomous and independent. McLeod sees anticlerical movements as a response to churches that were ruled by clerics, especially clerics who tried to direct the public sphere which was reserved to men, and contrasts the churches ruled by ministers with great authority, to the Quakers, who had no clergy, whose men were therefore more involved in administration, and who had a more even balance of the sexes.[212] In the eighteenth century the Quakers lacked a professional clergy, and "men remained actively involved."[213] Susan Juster notes the paradox: when the early Baptists were

---

209 Christine E. Gudorf, "Renewal or Repatriarchalization? Responses of the Roman Catholic Church to the Feminization of Religion," in *Horizons on Catholic Feminist Theology*, eds. Joann Wolski Conn and Walter E. Conn (Washington, DC: Georgetown University Press, 1992), 64.

210 Gudorf, "Renewal or Repatriarchalization?" 64.

211 Gibson, *Social History*, 189.

212 Hugh McLeod, *Religion and Society in England, 1850–1914* (New York: St. Martin's, 1966), 67–68.

213 Marilyn J. Westerkamp, *Women in Early American Religion 1600–1850: The Pu-*

charismatic and unorganized, they had a better balance of men and women than when they became organized and confined governing authority to men.[214] Patricia Bonomi notes the correlation between a professional clergy and the feminization of congregations in Colonial America. The ministers in Congregational churches exerted great authority, and they had predominantly female congregations. Dutch Reformed churches exhibited the same pattern. Where clergy were often absent or lay vestries had great power, as in Anglican Virginia before the Revolution, the congregations seem to have been far less feminized.[215] In London in 1902 the churches with little clerical structure, such as the Quakers, showed the least imbalance of the sexes.[216] The lesser claims of the clergy in Protestantism led some to claim that Protestantism was more masculine than Catholicism. Cutten claims that Catholicism "by the assertion of supreme authority attracted women whose part it is to lean rather than to stand."[217] But Protestantism differed little; the minister could be as autocratic as the pope.

Male Backlash

Male rowdiness led to constant skirmishes between the clergy and young males. Philip Hoffman recounts this 1777 incident in the diocese of Lyon: a youth, Jean Marie Bonnefond, snitched a few cherries from the curé's orchard. This was the last straw for the curé. The young men had been trampling his wheat and stealing his fruit. "Worse, Bonnefond was one of a number of youths who gathered each Sunday in front of the church to play the flute and pound on wine barrels." On the day of the theft, the curé had asked them to stop because he was hearing confessions, but the youths

ritan and Evangelical Traditions (New York: Routledge, 1999), 82; McLeod, Religion and Society, 163.

214 Susan Juster, Disorderly Women: Sexual Politics and Evangelicalism in Revolutionary New England (Ithaca, NY: Cornell University Press, 1994), 123–27.

215 Patricia U. Bonomi, Under the Cope of Heaven: Religion, Society, and Politics in Colonial America (New York: Oxford University Press, 1986), 113-15.

216 Benjamin Ziemann, Sozialgeschichte der Religion (Frankfurt-am-Main: Campus Verlag, 2009), 118.

217 George Barton Cutten, The Psychological Phenomenon of Christianity (New York: Charles Scribner's Sons, 1908), 299.

refused. The curé took a stick, pursued Bonnefond, and gave him a thrashing. The boy filed charges against the curé, who counterfiled charges, because Bonnefond and his friends "danced and sang defamatory songs in front of the curé's house."[218] In villages the youths would leave during mass; the priests would lock the doors; the youths would break them open. The youths of Ars tried to expel their curé, Jean-Marie Vianney (1786–1859), but the forces of order (the adults) defended him.[219] However, his audience remained mostly women. He heard confessions almost all day, devoting 9 to 11 hours to women, 4 to 6 for men.[220]

Protestant pastors also tried to enforce social discipline and thereby provoked male resistance. In 1532 the pastors of Schaffhausen complained that when they tried to end disorders, "the miscreants come beating drums under cover of darkness, and smear the preachers' locks with human excrement."[221] The disorders were "fornication, blasphemy, swear words . . . gambling, drunkenness, and uproar lasting until midnight . . . cries that keep everyone awake."[222] Noise was a male specialty; in 1526 the council of Basel was asked for an edict "so that these insolent rascals cannot enter the church and disturb people with their singing and shouting."[223] Young men went to church to observe and to meet the girls; noise was one way of getting the attention of the opposite sex. An Augsburg edict of 1546 proclaimed: "Lest God should turn his face from us, girls must no longer be courted with musical instruments, or with songs and whistles; moreover, when going to church or elsewhere, any cry, yodel, shout, speech, or song that is indecent or shameful is completely forbidden."[224] Indecent yodeling?

Village louts were not the only men to express their dislike of the church. Even among the aristocracy, contempt shown the Church could

---

218 Hoffman, *Church and Community*, 142–43.
219 See Hugh McLeod, *Secularisation in Western Europe, 1848–1914* (St. Martin's, 2000), 135.
220 Boutry, *Deux pèlerinages*, 64.
221 Quoted in Norbert Schindler, "Guardians of Disorder: Rituals of Youthful Culture at the Dawn of the Modern Age," in Levi and Schmitt, *A History of Young People*, Vol. 1, 240.
222 Quoted in Schindler, "Guardians of Disorder," 241.
223 Quoted in Schindler, "Guardians of Disorder," 260.
224 Quoted in Schindler, "Guardians of Disorder," 276.

have catastrophic consequences. Jean François Le Febre, chevalier de La Barre, was about nineteen years old when he was accused of blasphemy and sacrilege. He had sung blasphemous and bawdy songs, had refused to take off his hat for a Corpus Christi procession, and had (possibly) vandalized a crucifix. For this he was tried in a secular court and condemned. The judgment declared that on July 1, 1766 he "will have the tongue cut out and will then be taken in the said tumbrel to the public marketplace of this city to have his head cut off on a scaffold; his body and his head will then be thrown on a pyre to be destroyed, burnt, reduced to ashes and these thrown to the wind."[225] The Church had asked for a pardon for de La Barre, who was a victim of local intrigues. Voltaire was both horrified by an execution for adolescent folly and fearful for himself, because, when de La Barre's room was searched, in addition to some pornography, a copy of Voltaire's *Dictionnaire Philosophique* was found, and the *philosophes* were being blamed for de La Barre's conduct.[226] The trial and execution did not endear either the *philosophes* or young men to the French union of state and church.

Some men rejected Christianity entirely, with enormous political consequences, as we shall see. But even when men abandoned belief for themselves, they often tolerated religion or even approved of it for women and children, because it would guarantee women's chastity and children's obedience. Therefore many non-practicing French men approved of religion for women and even encouraged them to go to church.[227] The socialist Gustave Téry said his anticlerical father, if pressed, would probably have admitted, "Alas! that it [religion] was excellent for women and children."[228] In Italy "by the side of the male politician, liberal and with that officially

---

225 *Procès du Chevalier de la Barre, décapité à Abbeville, à l'occasion de la mutilation d'un Crucifix* (Hamburg: 1782), 32.
226 Ian Davidson, *Voltaire in Exile: The Last Year, 1753–1778* (New York: Grove Press, 2004), 171.
227 See Marcilhacy, *Le Diocèse d'Orléans*, 215; Gerard Cholvy and Yves-Marie Hilaire, *Histoire religieuse de la France contemporaine*, Vol. 1 (Toulouse: Bibliothèque Historique Privat, 1988), 256; and Hugh McLeod, "Weibliche Frömmigkeit—männlicher Unglaube? Religion und Kirchen im bürgerlichen 19. Jahrhundert," in *Bürgerinnen und Bürger: Geschlechterverhältnisse im 19. Jahrhundert*, ed. Ute Frevert (Göttingen: Vandenhoeck & Ruprecht, 1988), 143.
228 Gustave Téry, *Les cordicoles* (Paris: Édouard Cornély, 1902), vi.

anticlerical, worked in each family of the post-reunification nobility a pious wife, who did not only eagerly go to mass, but led charitable organizations or was involved in a female religious foundation."[229] Hugh McLeod describes the expectations for each sex: "by the latter nineteenth century there were many parts of Western Europe where piety was seen as a normal and desirable part of womanhood, and irreligion as an equally normal part of manhood."[230] Boys at first lived in the religious world of their mothers, but they had to leave it to grow up and become men. Men allowed their sons to be educated in religious schools, because "at least once in his life a man ought to have believed."[231] Manuel Delgado Ruiz says that in Spain strongly anticlerical men who claim to be atheists, but who have pious, observant wives, experience no conflict in the family. The men would not dream of *not* having their children baptized or *not* having them married in a church wedding; but to demonstrate their anticlericalism, during the ceremony the fathers "remain in the portico."[232]

Unbelief was a sign of adult masculinity. In Southern Italy young boys go to church, but in adolescence the boys become less religious and the girls more religious.[233] In one French city, boys were expected to stop going to church after their first communion.[234] In 1927 in the parish of Celles-Évescault near Poitiers, the custom was for a boy to stop going to church when he was old enough to smoke without coughing (*de fumer une cigarette sans tousser*[235])! In Italy boys in Liberal families had a religious education, and then had a rationalist crisis in secondary school, but remained in contact

229 Marco Miriggi, quoted in Manuel Borutta, *Antikatholizismus: Deutschland und Italien im Zeitalter der europäischen Kulturkämpfe* (Göttingen: Vandenhoeck & Ruprecht, 2011), 381.
230 McLeod, *Secularisation*, 135.
231 Borutta, *Antikatholizismus*, 380.
232 Manuel Delgado Ruiz, *Las palabras de otro hombre: anticlericalismo y misoginia* (Barcelona: Muchnik Editores, 1993), 296.
233 Anne Parsons, "Is the Oedipus Complex Universal?" in *Psychological Anthropology: A Reader on Self in Culture*, ed. Robert A. LeVinem (Chichester: John Wiley & Sons, 2010), 13.
234 See Émile Faure and Thomas Puech, *Le Confessionnal* (Paris: Décembre-Allonier, 1869), 64.
235 Robert Favreau, *Le diocèse de Poitiers à le fin du Moyen Âge* (Paris: Beauchesne Éditeur, 1988), 303.

with the religious women in the family.[236] In Spain boys who wanted to be *machote* blasphemed, because, as a counselor to King Alfonso XIII lamented, blaspheming was "a sign of the masculine."[237] This was true outside of Western Europe also. In the mid-nineteenth century "a certain anticlericalism was considered a fundamental component of elite male identity in much of Brazil."[238]

Well before the Quiet Revolution that began in 1960, the French Catholic men of Québec kept their distance from the Church: "men were distant from spiritual life. They considered piety an emotional activity, good for women and children but not for them."[239] In the eighteenth century, before any stirrings of the Enlightenment had reached rural Quebec, the men there liked to display their independence from the Church. At the beginning of the sermon, men would ostentatiously leave the church to go outside to engage in male activities like smoking and drinking, or caring for horses, or fighting over the relative merits of those horses. The church would be left to the priest, the women, and the children. In an anticipation of the French nineteenth-century belief that boys should outgrow religion, Québécois boys made their first public assertion of adult masculinity when they joined the male exodus at the start of the sermon.[240]

---

236 Borutta, *Antikatholizismus*, 381.
237 Delgado Ruiz, *Las palabras de otro hombre*, 33–34. See also Delgado Ruiz, "La antirreligiosidad popular in España," in *La religiosidad popular*, Vol. 1, *Antropología e historia*, ed. Álvarez Santaló, Buxó y Rey, and Rodríguez Becerra (Barcelona: Editorial Anthropos, 1989), 511.
238 Andrew J. Kirkendall, *Class Mates: Male Student Culture and the Making of a Political Class in Nineteenth-Century Brazil* (Lincoln: University of Nebraska Press, 2002), 132–33.
239 Jean-François Roussel, "Roman Catholic Religious Discourse about Manhood in Quebec: From 1900 to the Quiet Revolution," *The Journal of Men's Studies* 11, no. 2 (2003).
240 Ollivier Hubert, "Ritual Performance and Parish Sociability: French-Canadian Catholic Families at Mass from the Seventeenth to the Nineteenth Century," in Christie, *Households of Faith*, 60–61. See also Michael Carroll, *American Catholics in the Protestant Imagination: Rethinking the Academic Study of Religion* (Baltimore: Johns Hopkins University Press, 2007), 108–12. Carroll theorizes that Cajun women were demonstrating their femininity by their displays of piety.

Some men, to the disappointment of their fathers, continued to identify with the religion of their mothers.[241] For those men who stayed within the Church, Christianity developed a way of mitigating the conflict between laymen and clergy: a religious division of labor between believing men and believing women. Inside the church and the home belongs to priests, women, and children. The division is not precisely public-secular and private-religious, although it may develop into that. The church is a public space, and men may carry on their religious activities outside the church. Outside belonged to men, because they wanted to stay away from the clergy and a religious atmosphere that threatened their masculinity. Priests, women, and children had the church; men had their own way of being Catholic. Women went to mass and received the sacraments and thereby "bring home the graces."[242] Men had, as we have seen, the *festa*, the *fiesta*, *la fête*,[243] and, as we shall see, the confraternity.

Men kept their distance (literally) from the church. They recognized the priest's authority inside the church building. In the village of São Miguel in Portugal "when men did enter the church, they barely got beyond the holy water font. More often they stood on the porch or further away just outside the church wall."[244] The Italians in the New World brought from Italy their *mangiapretismo* (literally, *priest-eating*); they thought priests were "lazy, privileged, sexually aberrant in their ambiguous masculinity as celibates, and meddling in their capacity as confessors."[245] An Italian immigrant explained of Italian-American men: "I think no one should mistake their non-church attendance for lack of belief in the Roman Catholic faith .... Basically they dislike the clergy, and if they dislike the Italian clergy they despise the American clergy."[246] This anticlericalism, as Protestants

241 See Paul Seeley, "O Sainte Mère: Liberalism and the Socialization of Catholic Men in Nineteenth-Century France," *The Journal of Modern History* 70, no. 1 (1998): 862–91.
242 Cumbo, "Salvation in Indifference," 210.
243 Ibid., 223.
244 Riegelhaupt, "Popular Anti-Clericalism," 103.
245 Cumbo, "Salvation in Indifference," 209.
246 Edwin Scott Gaustad and Mark A. Noll, *A Documentary History of Religion in America: Since 1877* (Grand Rapids, MI: Wm. B. Eerdmans, 2003), 20.

who tried to convert Italian men discovered, did not mean anti-Catholicism.[247]

Protestant men tended to share in the dislike of the clergy. The *Spectator* in 1888 observed of the Evangelical clergy in England, who were ill-paid: "Power is dear to the souls of all men, and especially to those who may not make money, and are bound by a strict rule of life; and as referees upon all social questions, the clergy were for a time powerful."[248] Because they were males engaging in a contest, the clergy wanted to come out on top, and the contest with men over unacceptable behavior became a contest of wills over all behavior. The clergy reasoned that if they could establish their ascendency over males in all matters, great and small, they would be able to control behavior which definitely needed controlling. But such an attempt to regulate the minutiae of behavior was bound to provoke rebellion. Some men considered the clergy's attempts to end gang rape interference in customary male pleasures; others resented the spiritual relationship their wives had with another man; and still others resented the strict Sabbatarianism that in England forbade even strolling on Sundays and in America forbade sports on Sundays. "The result," as the *Spectator* notes, "was that a positive dislike of it grew up in the young men" and that "the elderly men who were trained by the Evangelical clergy have the least liking for attending church."[249]

Young, small-town Canadian males in the late nineteenth century were often hostile to religion. Robert Gordon Mackintosh mentions a few incidents among boy workers: 'Young Rowdies' disturbed a Primitive [Methodist] service in 1870; and another service in Stallartown in 1885. Two lads were fined two dollars apiece and costs after disturbing a Salvation Army meeting in 1888. Three boys were fined the following year in Springhill for the same reason. "'Unruly' boys attempted to burn the Presbyterian Mission at Nanaimo in 1900."[250] Other towns suffered from the same male attitude. Among unmarried church members, women

---

247 Cumbo, "Salvation in Indifference," 208.
248 "Microscopic Puritanism," *The Spectator* 61 (January 7, 1888): 11.
249 Ibid., 11.
250 Robert Gordon McIntosh, *Boys in the Pits: Child Labor in Coal Mining* (Montreal: McGill-Queens University Press, 2000), 145.

outnumbered men three to one[251] and the young men were sometimes not content to express their disdain by mere aloofness. In Ontario "the police court proceedings of the period regularly included reports of young men and boys who had been arrested and fined for disturbing public worship."[252] The ministers were hostile to male amusements: gambling, drinking, fighting, cockfights, all of which tempted young men even from respectable, church-going families.[253]

Evangelicalism, which in the United States has taken a strong tinge from its major centers in the South, experienced tension between on one side men determined to affirm their masculinity through fighting, drinking, and general hell-raising and on the opposing side the female-majority churches which were determined to civilize males, the fate feared by Huckleberry Finn. Early Methodists in the antebellum South provoked the ire of rowdy males because of their condemnation of "drinking, gambling and swearing,"[254] and, at the start, slavery.[255] The ministers suffered for their rejection of these pillars of Southern male life; sometimes "ministers either lost their lives or felt their lives were threatened."[256]

Southern men did not reject Christianity outright; they sometimes even went to church, but made it clear that they did not like it. Churches were divided by sex, with women and small children on one side and men on the other. The male side of the church was noticeably less attentive. A boy affirmed his entry into manhood by moving from the women's to the men's side of the church. In 1853 a woman complained that "the male members are noted for their regular naps, and after sleeping through the sermon, come kneel and pray as if they had heard it all."[257] In one church in the

---

251 Lynne Sorrel Marks, *Revivals and Roller Rinks: Religion, Leisure, and Identity in Late-Nineteenth-Century Small-Town Ontario* (Toronto: University of Toronto Press, 1996), 31.
252 Ibid., 83.
253 Ibid., 90–91.
254 Charity R. Carney, *Ministers and Masters: Methodism, Manhood, and Honor in the Old South* (Baton Rouge: Louisiana State University Press, 2011), 32.
255 Ibid., 118.
256 Ibid., 119.
257 Ted Ownby, *Subduing Satan: Religion, Recreation, and Manhood in the Rural South, 1865–1920* (Chapel Hill: University of North Carolina Press, 1990), 132.

1870s men and boys sat in the galleries, along with their hounds. In the 1880s a South Carolina minister complained about "certain boys who congregated at the door of the church and by smoking, loud talking and mischievous tricks annoy the congregation."[258] Most men were not so disrespectful; they escorted their women to church, and then stayed outside. Camp meetings were occasions for men to drink, to fight, and occasionally to kill. Southern men are another group of men who feel uncomfortable with the restraints of a church that wants to "civilize," that is, as men saw it, feminize, them. The Southern clergy tried to maintain a degree of church discipline. The men, far more than women, rejected this: "Many wayward males allowed other men to become masters of their conduct. But by accepting expulsion, they asserted their independence."[259]

Independence of mawkish, feminine religion (although not complete rejection of it), was important for Southern men, who adhered to the masculine code of competitiveness and honor.

The attempts of the clergy to make young men responsible, orderly, and obedient were not appreciated. Young men thought that the clergy were trying to make them not just adult (which they might have grudgingly accepted), but feminine. Masculinity was difficult to attain and was precarious once attained, and religion, and specifically Christianity, was felt to be opposed to it and even a threat to it. If the choice were between being Christian and being masculine, many men chose to be masculine. Men were also quick to notice when the clergy failed to live up to the standards they required of laymen. Hypocrisy added to male dislike of the clergy.

---

258 Ibid., 132.
259 Christine Leigh Heyrman, *Southern Cross: The Beginnings of the Bible Belt* (Chapel Hill: University of North Carolina Press, 1997), 216.

Chapter Five
The Sins of the Clergy

Although political differences have been the ostensible cause of anticlericalism, conflicts have often taken on a personal tone that fueled the bitterness and violence of anticlericalism. The clergy have long been suspected by many laymen of not being "authentically" masculine.[1] Both the celibate Catholic clergy and the married Protestant clergy fall under this suspicion. This lack of authentic or "hegemonic" masculinity could take many forms: a clergyman might be physically weak and almost asexual; he could be perverse, a pedophile, a pederast, a homosexual; or he could exploit his office to gain sexual access to women, married and unmarried. These deviations from generally accepted heterosexual masculinity increased the suspicions of laymen who feared both what the clergy might be doing and what the clergy wanted laymen to become: feminine.

J. Reid Meloy theorized that "narcissistic character disorders are prevalent among members of the clergy."[2] Other studies have not shown that there are more narcissists in the clergy than in other professions,[3] but, as

---

1   The poor reputation of the cleric was preceded in Antiquity by the poor reputation of the philosopher. Leon Harold Craig observes that "men who are first of all concerned with being men do not take readily to a way of life they believe will emasculate them" (*The War Lover: A Study of Plato's Republic* [Toronto: University of Toronto Press, 1994], 21).

2   J. Reid Meloy, "Narcissistic Psychopathology and the Clergy," *Pastoral Psychology* 35, no.1 (1986): 50.

3   Jayne Patrick, "Assessment of Narcissistic Psychopathology in the Clergy," *Pastoral Psychology* 38, no. 3 (1990): 173–80; Robert W. Hill and Gregory Yousey, "Adaptive and Maladaptive Narcissism among University Faculty, Clergy, Politicians, and Librarians," in *Altruism, Narcissism, Comity: Research Perspectives from Current Psychology*, ed. Nathaniel J. Pallone (New Brunswick, NJ: Transaction Publishers, 1999), 93–94.

Len Sperry notes, "narcissistic ministers create an incredible amount of havoc in their ministry assignments."[4] In particular, several studies have shown narcissism in clerical sexual abusers, characterized especially by a sense of entitlement.[5] Pamela Cooper-White wrote that she saw "a strong thread of narcissistic problems running through the entire range of clergy offenders."[6]

How valid are these stereotypes? A survey of 1,148 newly ordained Anglican clergy showed they had a characteristically feminine profile in 16 of the 21 personality traits in the Eysenck Personality Profile.[7] A similar survey of Catholic priests in England indicated that priests scored more like women than men in introversion and neuroticism, but more like men than women in psychoticism. That is, priests are more introverted, more neurotic, but also more tough-minded than men in general.[8] Or, one can say that English priests manage to combine the worst features of both sexes—they are introverted, neurotic, and unempathetic. Whether these personality patterns are common in the clergy is not known, but a few such clerics can wreak massive damage, especially as clergy have access to women, the more religious sex.

4   Len Sperry, *Sex, Priestly Ministry, and the Church*, (Collegeville, MN: Liturgical Press, 2003) 89.

5   See Gordon L. Benson, "Sexual Behavior by Male Clergy with Adult Female Counselees: Systemic and Situational Themes," *Sexual Addiction and Compulsivity: The Journal of Treatment and Prevention* 1, no. 2 (1994): 103–118; Leslie Lothstein, "Neuropsychological Findings in Clergy who Sexually Abuse," in *Bless Me Father for I Have Sinned: Perspectives on Sexual Abuse Committed by Roman Catholic Priests*, ed. Thomas Plante (Westport, CN: Praeger, 1999), 59–86; Paul N. Dukro and Marc Falkenhain, "Narcissism Sets Stage for Clergy Sexual Abuse," *Human Development* 21, no. 3 (2000): 24–28.

6   Pamela Cooper-White, *The Cry of Tamar: Violence against Women and the Church's Response* (Minneapolis, MN: Augsburg Fortress, 1995), 137.

7   Leslie J. Francis, Susan H. Jones, Christ J. Jackson, and Mandy Robbins, "The Feminine Personality Profile of Male Anglican Clergy in Britain and Ireland: A Study Employing the Eysenck Personality Profiler," *Review of Religious Research* 43, no. 1 (2001): 14–23.

8   Stephen H. Louden and Leslie J. Francis, "The Personality Profile of Roman Catholic Parochial Secular Priests in England and Wales," *Review of Religious Research* 41, no. 1 (1999): 64.

Unchaste, Perverse, and Effeminate Priests

The celibacy of Catholic priests sets them apart from other men, as it was intended to do. To elevate the priest above the laity, the Church in the Middle Ages tried to enforce (against much resistance) clerical celibacy by declaring clerical marriages to be invalid. The main object was to impress the laity with the spiritual superiority of the clergy, who were able to renounce the powerful human drive of sex. The laity were not always impressed.

Both the *Canterbury Tales* and the *Decameron* contain clerical characters who are corrupt, venal, and perverse. Sacerdotal chastity was impugned by scurrilous medieval fabliaux, which mocked "the moral and financial purity that the Church deemed so important for the clergy."[9] Laymen in the Middle Ages, according to E. N. Swanson, were suspicious of women, "who are portrayed as overly familiar with clerics, to whom they reveal their husbands' secrets, or betray their beds."[10] In sixteenth-century English critiques of the clergy, "the sexual exploitation of women constituted a major part of a standard litany. Belief in widespread homosexual activity, especially in the monasteries where recruitment often focused on adolescents, added a dimension of unnatural vice to these stories."[11] An anonymous priest wrote in *The Reformation of the Emperor Sigismund*, "many priests have lost their livings because of women. Or they are secret sodomites. All the hatred existing between priests and laymen is due to this."[12] Gossip and criticism of priests as "hypocritical, greedy, and oversexed"[13] undermined clerical pretensions and

9 Daron Burrows, *The Stereotype of the Priest in the Old French Fabliaux: Anticlerical Satire and Lay Identity* (Oxford: Peter Lang, 2005), 208.
10 R. N. Swanson, *Religion and Devotion in Europe, c. 1215–1515* (Cambridge: Cambridge University Press, 1995), 305.
11 Richard A. Cosgrove, "The English Reformation: A Programmatic Assessment," in *Anticlericalism in Late Medieval and Early Modern Europe*, ed. Peter A. Dykema and Heiko Augustinus Oberman (Leiden: E. J. Brill, 1993), 571.
12 Translated by Gerald Strauss in *Manifestations of Discontent in Germany on the Eve of the Reformation* (Bloomington: Indiana University Press, 1971), 14–15.
13 Stanley Brandes, "Conclusion: Reflections on the Study of Religious Orthodoxy and Private Faith in Europe," in *Religious Orthodoxy and Popular Faith in European Society*, ed. Ellen Badone (Princeton: Princeton University Press, 1990), 189.

authority; priests were, according to their enemies, guilty of hypocritically "pretending to be above other humans in sexual drives and involvements."[14] Álvaro de Albornoz in 1903 voiced a general male suspicion about celibacy: "Love, forbidden, converts itself into disgusting sodomy."[15]

Confession presented a danger for women. The Fourth Lateran Council, convoked by Innocent III in 1213, in the document *Omnis utriusque sexu* obliged every adult Catholic to go to confession at least once a year. Trent reiterated this obligation. To guide confessors, a series of manuals was written for use by seminarians, and these were a source of much mischief. As the manuals were directed to aspiring confessors they focused on sins, not on virtues. The anticlerical Paul Bert commented on Jean-Pierre Gury's (1801–1866) manual: "If he does not know what is love, not even decency, no more does he know what is delicacy, generosity, friendship, personal dignity, civic duty, love of country: he ignores so thoroughly these noble things, that he does not even know their names."[16] Spanish clergy used the moral theology manual of the Jesuit Tomás Sánchez (1550–1610), who advised the confessor to ask for all details, including the most intimate ones, of sexual sins. This gave rise to the saying of Spanish seminarians, "si quieres saber más que el Diablo, lee a Sánchez en *De matrimonio*"[17]—"If you want to know more than the devil does, read *On Marriage* by Sánchez."

The youthful libertine and later Cardinal Ludovico Sergardi (1660–1726) distinguished his immorality from that of the manuals:

> Moral theology has attained to such a pitch that it is necessary to warn uncorrupted youths from having anything to do with it, lest they entangle themselves in shameful snares and become victims of unchastity. For what abominations (*foeditates*) do not the moral theologians set before the public! Among all the brothels of the Suburra, there is not one that might not be called

---

14   Ibid., 190.

15   Quoted by Paul Aubert, "Luchar contra los poderes fácticos: el anticlericalismo," in *Religión y sociedad en España (siglos XIX y XX)*, ed. Paul Aubert (Madrid: Casa de Velázquez, 2002), 226.

16   Paul Bert, *The Doctrine of the Jesuits* (Boston: B. F. Bradbury, n. d.), xxxv.

17   Luis Martínez Kleiser, *Refranero general ideológico español* (Madrid: Editorial Hernando, 1989), 445.

chaste compared with the contents of these books. I myself, who was a leader of immoral youths and often desecrated my years by unchastity, confess that on reading Sánchez . . . I found myself blushing on more than one occasion, and that his writings have taught me more abominations than I could have learned from the most brazen (*impudentissima*) of prostitutes.[18]

Sánchez's descriptions of sexual perversions surpassed the imagination of even an Italian who was notorious for his youthful sexual adventures. Sergardi, like many prelates, admitted to his sexual activity before ordination, perhaps to establish his masculine *bona fides*, but the sexual activity was normal heterosexual intercourse.

The manuals described an extraordinary range of sexual activities, and anticlericals (who as men did not go to confession) who came upon them thought that priests interrogated women about these activities. Not only did the manuals describe masturbation, fornication, and contraception, they went to great detail about sexual positions and about the use of unusual paraphernalia in sexual activity. Why some of the more bizarre sexual activities were included in the manuals is hard to fathom. Paul Bert accused the authors of the manuals of "erotomania."[19] Willibald Beyschlag in Germany complained that the manual writers "poured out the entirely unspeakable filth of their casuistry of perversion (*Unsucht*) for the purpose of training more confessors."[20] Perhaps the writers wanted to make sure that a priest would not be shocked or taken aback by anything a penitent might tell him. But the anticlericals were correct that the manuals sometimes read like pornography and that the thought of a wife or daughter being asked questions from the manuals is horrifying.

When female piety led to a woman's confessing her sins to a priest, she often aroused the animosity of laymen. The suspicions started as soon as

18 Paul von Hoensbroech, *Fourteen Years a Jesuit: A Record of Personal Experience and a Criticism*, Vol. 2, trans. Alice Zimmern (London: Cassell, 1911), 289; Ludovici Sergardi, *Orationes, Dissertationes, Prolusiones, Epistolae*, Vol. 4 (Lucca: 1783), 205.

19 Bert, *Doctrine of the Jesuits*, 554.

20 Quoted in Róisín Healy, *The Jesuit Specter in Imperial Germany* (Boston: Brill, 2003), 165.

confession became general: "In 1565 the town leaders of Chiari, in the diocese of Brescia, complained angrily to their bishop Domenico Bollani about the friars of S. Bernardino for allowing 'various kinds of impropriety' when hearing women's confessions in convent cells. The accusation did not stem from specific incidents; 'bad rumors' made the men reluctant to let their wives confess to the friars."[21] Male suspicion was not groundless; the bishops of the Council of Trent discussed clergy who tried "to tempt the chastity of virtuous women even during confession and dare abuse this solemn sacrament for seduction."[22]

Nonetheless the Church of the Counter-Reformation placed an even greater emphasis on auricular confession. Stephen Haliczer has examined the practice in Spain; the title of his book, *Sexuality in the Confessional: A Sacrament Profaned*, indicates that all was not well with this sacrament. The clergy were often corrupt—in 1481 in Palencia a third of the cathedral chapter were openly living in sin[23]—and the laity had trouble confessing to men whom they knew were living dissolute lives. However, the laity, especially lay women, went to confession[24] and manuals for confessors seemed to envision female penitents.[25] The Inquisition was responsible for investigating sexual solicitation in the confession—but only solicitation of women.[26] Some priests were corrupt, but even among the well-intentioned, the discussion of intimate matters in the confessional could easily lead to what psychiatrists later experienced: transference.[27] Both priests and psychiatrists sometimes inadvertently become sexually involved with women who pour out their hearts to them. From Augustine onward priests were cautioned about over-familiarity with women, especially the devout, the *dévotes* who tended to monopolize priests' time.[28]

---

21 Wietse de Boer, *The Conquest of the Soul: Confession, Discipline, and Public Order in Counter-Reformation Milan* (Boston: Brill, 2001), 30.
22 De Boer, *The Conquest of the Soul*, 97.
23 Stephen Haliczer, *Sexuality in the Confessional: A Sacrament Profaned* (New York: Oxford, 1996), 11.
24 Ibid., 4.
25 Ibid., 34.
26 Ibid., 64.
27 Ibid., 137.
28 See Tine van Osselaer, *The Pious Sex: Catholic Constructions of Masculinity and*

Even if they stayed away, men could be adversely affected by confession. Anticlerical writers warned French men that they should beware of turning the direction of their wives over to priests, "because through the confessional, where the penitents were mostly women, they exercised power over men's sexuality."[29] The historian Jules Michelet (1798–1874) was the most influential critic of the influence of priests on women. His *Du prêtre, de la femme et de la famille* (1845) went through numerous editions and was translated many times. He warned against the association of women and priests through confession and spiritual direction. Michelet disliked spiritual direction even more than confession because of the length of time director and woman spent together. He also noticed that the language of religion is heavily erotic; one can "mix the two languages, talking of love and devotion at the same time. If you, an invisible witness, heard the conversation of the charming walks, you would not always be able to distinguish who spoke, the lover or the director."[30] The Sacred Heart of Jesus, as we have seen in Chapter Two, was the focus of a fervent devotion: "the heart! The word alone has always been powerful; organ of affections, the heart expresses them in its way, swelling, relieved by sighs. The life of the heart, strong and confused, includes, blends all loves, a word so suitable for the language of double meaning."[31] Eroticism pervaded religious emotion, and unscrupulous priests took advantage of this atmosphere.

Charles Chiniquy (1809–1899) left the Catholic priesthood, became a Presbyterian minister, and warned about confession, during which the priest put to women "questions which the most depraved woman would never consent to hear from her vilest seducer" (he gives a sample of the questions, but only in Latin). This line of questioning allowed the priest to proposition the female penitent. Chiniquy warned that confession also tempted the priest and led him astray; the confessional is "a snare, a pit of perdition, a Sodom for the priest," and yet the husband allows the priest

Femininity in Belgium, c. 1800–1940 (Louvain: Leuven University Press, 2013), 43–47.

29 W. D. Halls, *Politics, Society and Christianity in Vichy France* (Oxford: Berg, 1995), 10.

30 Jules Michelet, *Du Prêtre, de la femme, de la famille* (Paris: Ernest Flammarion, n. d.), 77.

31 Ibid., 164–65.

"to open the heart of his wife, manipulate her soul, and pry into the sacred chambers of her most intimate and secret thoughts." He warns the husband that the priest through the wife's confession "can hear and see your most secret words and actions."[32]

Samuel F. B. Morse, inventor of Morse Code, a proslavery advocate and the author of *Foreign* [i.e,. Catholic] *Conspiracies against the Liberties of the United States*, in 1837 published a book, *Confessions of a French Catholic Priest*,[33] which Morse claims to have edited from what was told him by a French priest who had become a Protestant and had come to the United States, but who wished to remain anonymous because he feared for the well-being of his family in France. The book contains the fears, suspicions, and rumors that the Catholic clergy inspired in France.

The anonymous priest-author as Morse presents him is an appealing figure: sincere and affectionate. He is portrayed as having been led astray by a corrupt world of clericalism. Celibacy, "the unnatural vow,"[34] leads to his biggest problem: hearing the confessions of young women. He falls in love, and is tormented, because in France after 1830 the vow of celibacy was recognized by civil law and he knew he could never marry. His ministry presents ever new temptations to him: "This intercourse of young girls and young unmarried priests is the fullness of immorality; an occasion of glaring disorders or of the most cruel struggles."[35] The priest laments "I ask, is it possible, humanly speaking, for him, a priest, to remain pure, when at twenty-five or thirty years of age he is shut either in the vestry or the confessional with a young woman who reveals to him the secrets of her heart"[36] and whom he often asks for minute details about sexual matters.[37] Many priests seduce their penitents and have mistresses. Priests commit the crimes of "the cities of the plain,"[38] i.e., Sodom, with boys. If a priest is

---

32 Charles Chiniquy, *The Priest, The Woman, and The Confessional*, 36th ed. (Chicago: Adam Craig, 1890), 81,117,119.

33 Samuel F. B. Morse, *Confessions of a French Catholic Priest* (New York: John S. Taylor, 1837).

34 Ibid., iv.

35 Ibid., 60.

36 Ibid., 108.

37 Ibid., 110.

38 Ibid., 136.

discovered in his crimes, "he will be removed, to silence the scandal, and sent to another distant village where he will be unknown; and where, by and by, he will begin again the same mode of life."[39] Morse, whatever the veracity of his source, had picked up the discourse about priests that dominated European anticlerical circles.

The American nativist Nicholas Murray wrote to the Catholic Chief Justice Taney that in Italy "the priests are the corrupters of the people, and mainly through the confessional and the women."[40] Artists also took up the theme. Goya made an engraving with the title, "Auricular confession does nothing but fill the ears of the priest with filth, obscenities, and muck."[41] The Anglo-Catholic revival of confession caused Victorian men to fear for their wives and daughters, if only because priests would meddle in household matters.[42] Confession and sex intertwined in the most famous anti-Catholic fiction of the nineteenth century, Maria Monk's *The Awful Disclosures by Maria Monk of the Hotel Dieu Nunnery of Montreal* (1836). Mark Twain shared the suspicions about confession: "the confessional's chief amusement has been seduction."[43]

If priests were not suspected of seducing women, they were suspected of homosexual activity (which included pederasty). The charges of sexual perversity stemmed largely from a belief that priests were not as masculine as other men, both because of celibacy and because of their interest in religion. Robert E. Goss, a Jesuit whose gay partnership created a controversy, claims that "Catholic priests are public failures of heteronormative male gender in a culture in which religiousness is equated with the feminine and masculinity is equated with male sexuality and

---

39 Ibid., 131.
40 Kirwan [Nicholas Murray], *Romanism at Home: Letters to the Hon. Roger B. Taney* (New York: Harper & Brothers, 1852), 166.
41 See Manuel Delgado Ruiz, "Anticlericalismo, sexo y familia," in *Familia y relaciones de parentesco: Estudios desde la antropología social*, eds. Dolors Comas and Aurora Echecerría (Valencia: Institut Valencià de la Dona, 1988), 85.
42 John Shelton Reed, *Glorious Battle: The Cultural Politics of Victorian Anglo-Catholicism* (Nashville, TN: Vanderbilt University Press, 1996), 195–201.
43 Quoted by Philip Jenkins, *The New Anti-Catholicism: The Last Acceptable Prejudice* (New York: Oxford University Press, 2003), 43. See also 43–45 for similar suspicions.

dominance."[44] Goss sees the tradition of bridal mysticism as a source of this less-than-masculine clerical identity: "many priests are formed in their spiritualities to see themselves as the brides of Christ."[45] Men are suspicious of men who think of themselves as brides.

French anticlericals in the nineteenth century disliked both priests and homosexuals, and associated the two. In this they followed Voltaire, who when he mentioned the clergy would usually insinuate an allusion to pederasty.[46] Anticlerical novelists blamed seminaries for producing homosexuals.[47] Parish priests, with their easy access to women, provoked envy among anticlericals; by contrast, religious, shut up in schools and monasteries, were accused of pederasty and homosexuality. Leo Taxil (the pen name of Gabriel Antoine Jogand-Pages) perpetrated a grand Freemasonic hoax to demonstrate the gullibility of Catholics, including the Pope and Thérèse de Lisieux.[48] In 1880 he founded the Society of Anticlerical Assistance to help families whose children had been sexually abused by priests. The Universal Congress of Free Thought in 1889 declared that "the men who make vows against nature . . . are unworthy to teach youth. The law . . . ought to protect children . . . from the pollution of the pornocrats of the sacristy."[49] These anticlerical French accusations of pedophilia and homosexuality continued in the twentieth century.[50] René

---

44 Robert E. Goss, "Always a Bride, Never a Groom," in *Gay Catholic Priests and Clerical Sexual Misconduct: Breaking the Silence*, eds. Donald L. Boisvert and Robert E. Goss (New York: Haworth, 2005), 132.

45 Ibid., 135.

46 "Les moines chargés d'élever la jeunesse ont été toujours un peu adonnés à la pédérastie. C'est la suite nécessaire du célibat auquel ces pauvres gens sont condamnés" (Voltaire, *Dictionnaire philosophique*, Vol. 1 [Paris, 1819], 258).

47 Philippe Hamon and Alexandrine Viboud, *Dictionnaire thématique du roman de mœurs en France, 1814–1914* (Paris: Presses Sorbonne Nouvelle, 2008), 397.

48 See Robert Ziegler, *Satanism, Magic and Mysticism in Fin-de-siècle France* (New York: Palgrave Macmillan, 2012), 64–73.

49 Quoted in Michel Lagrée, Nicole Lemaitre, Luc Perrin, and Catherine Vincent, *Histoire des curés* (Paris: Fayard, 2002), 285.

50 Jan Art and Thomas Buerman, "Anticléricalisme et genre au XIXᵉ siècle: Le prêtre catholique, principal défi à l'image hégémonique de l'homme," in *Masculinités*, ed. Bruno Benvindo (Brussels: Éditions de l'Université de Bruxelles, 2009), 329.

Rémond explains the line of thought of the anticlericals: "They did not believe that priests could observe the chastity which they had vowed. It is against nature. It constrains them to hypocrisy, to dissimulation. It even leads to crimes against nature. The secret is well guarded. The Church wants to smother the rumors."[51] Priests were men like other men; if only they would marry, their crimes would cease.

The men of the Spanish village that the anthropologist William Christian studied tell "endless stories about the priests' ambiguous sexual position" and make "jokes referring to priests' emasculation."[52] When priests were accused of abusing boys, anticlericals objected not so much to the abuse but to the lack of manliness (*virilidad*) that this type of sexual activity implied. The accusations continue to the present. The journalist Pepe Rodríguez claims that in Spain 95% of priests masturbate, that a majority of Catholic priests have sexual relations,[53] that a third are married or live with a woman,[54] that 7% of priests have sexually abused minors,[55] and that about one in a hundred Spanish men and one in five hundred Spanish women have been sexually abused by a priest or religious.[56] Repeating the themes of the critics of the clergy in the nineteenth century, Enrique Miret Magdalena warns that "no one can place fictive barriers to nature"[57] and María Martínez Vendrell warns that "repression prepares the ground for neurosis."[58] Nature denied leads to perversion and crime, critics of celibacy have maintained for several centuries.[59]

In Spain the main exception to the male detachment from religion has

51 René Rémond, *L'anticléricalisme en France de 1815 à nos jours*, 2nd ed. (Paris: Fayard, 1999), 73.
52 William A. Christian, Jr., *Person and God in a Spanish Valley* (New York: Seminar Press, 1972), 152.
53 Pepe Rodríguez, *La vida sexual del clero* (Madrid: Suma de Letras, 2002), 21.
54 Ibid., 45.
55 Ibid., 155.
56 Ibid., 154.
57 Ibid., iii.
58 Ibid., xiii.
59 For Italian attacks on clerical immorality, see Manuel Borutta, "Anti-Catholicism and the Culture War in Risorgimento Italy," in *The Risorgimento Revisited: Nationalism and Culture in Nineteenth-Century Italy*, eds. Silvana Patriarca and Lucy Riall (New York: Palgrave Macmillan, 2012), 193–200.

been its priests. These men have usually been shielded from the harsh tests that other Spanish men have to undergo to prove their manhood and do not have "the sensitivity wrung out of them and the hardness instilled in them that normally happens in the course of attaining manhood in the village. They are better able to preserve affection for Mary, and in seminary they feel no need to be ashamed of sentimentality."[60] Even laymen who are too visibly pious are called *marica* (sissy), very close to *maricón* (fag).

The Catholic priest in nineteenth-century France was forbidden to wear a beard or mustache, to smoke, to duel, to fight.[61] He was closer to his mother than other men were; he avoided military service, manual labor, and marriage. His whole education led, in the sight of his contemporaries, to a "process of feminization of his habitus."[62] Ecclesiastical authorities were aware of this, but still required priests to wear the soutane (the cassock); men called it the *jupon* (skirt), and the clerics who wore it, *les enjuponées* (the skirted ones).[63] In 1870 the newspaper *Patriote* wrote of seminarians: "let them have the courage to take off their robe, that it can be seen underneath if they are men or if they are hermaphrodites."[64] Anticlericals repeated the saying, "A priest is a man like any other man"—and therefore can't really be chaste. A Spanish widow was blunt: "If they have balls, if they haven't been castrated, then they can't be very different from other men."[65]

But if men thought a priest was chaste, they disliked him all the more. Joyce Riegelhaupt explains this seeming paradox: "a priest who fulfills his vows of chastity and lives a celibate life becomes a more controversial local figure than the married priest—or the priest whose housekeeper is his 'niece' and clearly recognized as his mistress. The issue, especially for male parishioners, was the right of the priest to present himself as 'special,' a

---

60 Christian, *Person and God in a Spanish Valley*, 136.
61 Art and Buerman, "Anticléricalisme," 332.
62 Charles Souad, *La vocation: Conversion et reconversion des prêtres ruraux* (Paris: Les Éditions de Minuit, 1978), 72.
63 Art and Buerman, "Anticléricalisme," 334.
64 Jean Faury, *Cléricalisme et anticléricalisme dans le Tarn 1848–1900* (Toulouse: Service des Publications de l'Université de Toulouse-le Marial, 1980), 272.
65 Ruth Behar, "The Struggle for the Church: Popular Anticlericalism and Religiosity in Post-Franco Spain," in Badone, *Religious Orthodoxy*, 91.

specialness built on a superior moral character (demonstrated through celibacy) which was then used to justify the priest's right to be a 'moral authority.'"[66] Whether hypocritical or sincere, a priest was disliked because of his interference with male pleasures.

Unchaste, Perverse, and Effeminate Ministers

Although Protestantism did not have the issues of auricular confession or clerical celibacy, its ministers sometimes were suspected of effeminacy, perversity, and over-familiarity with women.

The Whig Sydney Smith had observed there were three sexes, "men, women, and clergymen,"[67] and this witticism about a "third sex"[68] became a standing joke. All clerics had to face the "popular stereotype that men of the cloth were neither male nor female."[69] The clergy were seen as exempt from masculine trials and agonies; they were part of the safe world of women. As one layman put it, "life is a football game, with the men fighting it out on the gridiron, while the minister is up in the grandstand, explaining it to the ladies."[70] By the end of the nineteenth century, the weakness and effeminacy of the mainline Protestant clergy had become a commonplace of satire. Thomas Higginson commented on such men:

> One of the most potent causes of the ill-concealed alienation between the clergy and the people, in our community, has been the supposed deficiency, on the part of the former, of a vigorous, manly life. There is a certain moral and physical *anhæmia*, a bloodlessness, which separates most of our saints, more

---

66 Joyce Riegelhaupt, "Popular Anti-Clericalism and Religiosity in pre-1974 Portugal," in *Religion, Power, and Protest in Local Communities: The Northern Shore of the Mediterranean*, ed. Eric R. Wolf (Berlin: Mouton, 1984), 109.

67 Maurice Davies, "Curates," *Belgravia* 29 (1876): 110.

68 Edward C. Lehman, *Gender and Work: The Case of the Clergy* (Albany: State University of New York Press, 1993), 20.

69 Margaret Lamberts Bendroth, *Fundamentalism and Gender: 1875 to the Present*, (New Haven: Yale University Press, 1993), 65.

70 Paul A. Carter, *Another Part of the Twenties* (New York: Columbia University Press, 1977), 53–54.

effectually than a cloister, from the strong life of the age. What satirists upon religion are those parents who say of their pallid, puny, sedentary, lifeless, joyless little offspring, "He is born for a minister" . . . Never did an ill-starred young saint waste his Saturday afternoons in preaching sermons in the garret to his deluded little sisters and their dolls, without living to repent it in maturity.[71]

Lack of masculinity was a sign of a religious personality.

In nineteenth-century New England, ministers of the most important churches were "hesitant promulgators of female virtues in an era of militant masculinity."[72] But the dominant churches of nineteenth-century New England had long been feminized. Not only was the proportion of women in the churches extremely high, both the milieu and the ministers of the church were far more feminine than masculine. Businessmen disdained the clergy as "people halfway between men and women."[73] Ministers found the most congenial environment, not in businesses, political clubs, or saloons, but "in the Sunday school, the parlor, the library, among women and those who flattered and resembled them."[74] Moreover, they were typically recruited from the ranks of weak, sickly boys with indoor tastes who stayed at home with their mothers and came to identify with the feminine world of religion. The popular mind often joined "the idea of ill health with the clerical image."[75] In the vision of Unitarian minister Charles Fenton (1796–1842), playing Sunday school children have replaced stern Pilgrim Fathers and "adult politics have succumbed to infantile piety, *Ecclesia* to a nursery. Masculinity is vanquished in the congregation and, even more significantly, in the pulpit."[76]

71 Thomas Wentworth Higginson, "Saints and Their Bodies," in *The Writings of Thomas Wentworth Higginson*, Vol. 6, *Outdoor Studies* (Boston: Houghton, Mifflin, 1900), 7.
72 Barbara Welter, "The Feminization of American Religion: 1800–1860," in *Clio's Consciousness Raised*, ed. Mary S. Hartman and Lois Banner (New York: Harper & Row, 1974), 22.
73 Ibid., 42.
74 Ibid., 43.
75 Ibid., 89.
76 Ibid., 19.

The supposed effeminacy of ministers also led to a suspicion that those who were unmarried were probably homosexuals or otherwise sexually perverse. In the Church of England the masculinity of Anglo-Catholics was frequently questioned[77] because they were celibate and fussy about ritual.[78] "Effeminate fanatics" and "womanish men" were some of the milder criticisms of these "not conspicuously virile men."[79] *Punch* observed in "Parsons in Petticoats" that "reverend gentlemen 'of extreme High Church proclivities' are very fond of dressing like ladies" and gave them advice on how to protect "the muslin, or alpaca, or tarlatane, or *poult de soie*, or satin, or whatever it is their robes are made of."[80]

If a minister was heterosexual, he was still immersed in a world of women. Orestes Brownson complained about the "female religion" that Protestantism had become.[81] Ann Douglas described the situation: "The nineteenth-century minister moved in a world of women. He preached mainly to women; he administered what sacraments he performed largely for women; he worked not only for them but with them, in mission and charity work of all kinds."[82] When the founder of Wellesley College, Henry Fowler Durant, left the bar to become a minister and "forswore the conflict of the court to work for the Lord, he increasingly entered the realm of women."[83] This realm contained many temptations. A church journal warned of the dangers of giving the clergy, who moved largely in a world of women, unrestricted access to women: "No man in the world has so few conditions imposed upon him at the threshold of society as the clergyman. His passport to social life is

---

77 See Hugh McLeod, "Anticlericalism in Later Victorian England," in *Anticlericalism in Britain c. 1540–1914*, eds. Nigel Aston and Matthew Cragoe (Phoenix Mill, England: Sutton Publishing, 2001), 208–14.

78 Hugh McLeod, *Religion and Society in England, 1850–1914* (New York: St. Martin's, 1966), 154–55.

79 Quoted in Reed, *Glorious Battle*, 211.

80 "Parsons in Petticoats," *Punch*, June 10, 1865, 239.

81 Quoted in Welter, "The Feminization of American Religion," 139.

82 Ann Douglas, *The Feminization of American Culture* (New York: Noonday Press, 1998), 97.

83 Helen Lefkowitz Horowitz, *Alma Mater: Desire and Experience in the Women's Colleges from Their Nineteenth-Century Beginnings to the 1930s* (New York: Alfred A. Knopf, 1985), 43.

almost a *carte blanche*. Women of both states [married and single] and all ages are his companions, socially and professionally. The rules of social intercommunication between the sexes are, in his case, virtually suspended."[84] Because of this intimacy, as *The Pulpit* observed in 1871, "there is no profession, class or avocation, so exposed to or tormented by the devil of sensuality as the ministry. The very sanctity of their office is an occasion of their stumbling. The office is confounded with its occupant, the sanctity of the former is made the possession of the latter. Now, the office is an invulnerable myth; its occupant is a man of like passions with other men."[85] A Methodist Discipline warned ministers: "Converse sparingly, and conduct yourself prudently with women"; and a minister warned other ministers: "You are men, with the passions of men, exposed to the temptations of men, and in the name of God we charge you to remember this matter."[86] Some forgot.

A worldly newspaperman, Nathaniel Willis, noted "the caressing character of the intercourse between the clergy and the women in their parishes whose affections are otherwise unemployed."[87] Another newspaperman, George Thomson, thought that ministers had perfected the art of religious seduction: "So far from a sin, it seems to be an act of duty and of piety to submit to his desires, and when the object is once accomplished, the reward is a devout blessing and thanksgiving, that removes every scruple of conscience and the pleasing duty of comforting a beloved pastor is performed as an act of religious merit."[88] Between 1810 and 1860, at least twenty clergymen were tried for immorality, and half were convicted. The *Police Gazette* had a regular column on clerical scandals.[89]

---

84 William F. Jamieson, *The Clergy as a Source of Danger to the American Republic* (Chicago: W. F. Jamieson, 1873), 292.

85 Ibid., 291.

86 Quoted by Donald G. Mathews, *Religion in the Old South* (Chicago: University of Chicago Press, 1977), 106.

87 Patricia Cline Cohen, "Ministerial Misdeeds: The Onderdonk Trial and Sexual Harassment in the 1840s," in *A Mighty Baptism: Race, Gender, and the Creation of American Protestantism*, eds. Susan Juster and Lisa MacFarlan (Ithaca, NY: Cornell University Press, 1996), 99.

88 Ibid., 102.

89 E. Brooks Holfield, *God's Ambassadors: A History of the Christian Clergy in America* (Grand Rapids, MI: Wm. B. Eerdmans, 2007), 123.

The response of the church authorities was to deny or minimize the accusations. Church authorities simply let the offender transfer to another church or another denomination. The *Chicago Times* criticized "the extreme laxity which has commenced to govern certain denominations in accepting candidates for holy orders, and the mildness with which lesser offenses that infallibly lead to greater ones are excused."[90] The *Chicago Times* also editorialized: "The clergyman, like the physician, has extraordinary facilities for the commission of a certain class of crimes, and those facilities are such as to heap double damnation upon him if he is sufficiently diabolical to make use of them."[91] William F. Jamieson, a nineteenth-century secularist, recounted scandals involving Protestant ministers, and echoed the criticism that had been made about Catholic clerical celibacy: "The pernicious notion that the imaginary influence called 'divine grace' could make the nature of men and women anything else but human nature, has been a prolific cause of crime in 'holy circles' because the barriers of self-restraint have been removed."[92]

As in the later scandals (Billy James Hargis, Jimmy Swaggert, Jim and Tammy Bakker, Ted Haggard), many of the abuses occurred in the "generally sexualized climate" of revivalism.[93] But all denominations had charismatic preachers whose personalities sometimes radiated sexual magnetism to demonstrate that they were indeed men, a fact that their participation in religion might call into question. The evangelical culture of the South demanded a loss of independence and a display of emotion. Southern men rejected "womanish" emotions and feared a religion that "unmanned" its devotees. One Southerner was unhappy when he saw Methodist bishop Thomas Coke, whose "stature, complexion, and voice resembled those of a woman rather than those of a man."[94] Patricia Cohen suspects that in a Christian milieu which was feminized and in

---

90 "Clerical Scandals," *Chicago Times*, reprinted in *The Latter-Day Saints Millennial Star* 34 (1872): 557.

91 Jamieson, *Clergy as a Source of Danger*, 289.

92 Ibid., 190.

93 Susan Juster, *Disorderly Women: Sexual Politics and Evangelicalism in Revolutionary New England* (Ithaca, NY: Cornell University Press, 1994), 37.

94 Quoted in Christine Leigh Heyrman, *Southern Cross: The Beginning of the Bible Belt* (New York: Alfred A. Knopf, 1997), 213.

which the masculinity of religious men was therefore in doubt, ministers might have felt "the need to compensate by overemphasizing traditional masculine prerogatives,"[95] that is, by having sex with their female admirers.

Henry Ward Beecher was the most prominent preacher of his time in America; ferries brought boatloads of tourists to hear him preach in Brooklyn, and he espoused abolition and women's suffrage.[96] In 1872 he was accused of adultery and his trial merited more headlines than the Civil War had. Elizabeth Tollitson confessed to her husband that she had had an affair with Beecher, and in his rage he told the world. His enemies accused Beecher of espousing the "free love" that he had condemned[97] but his congregation rallied around Beecher.[98] At the trial the question was: "Was it possible for a man to seem one way his whole life and yet behave in an entirely different way in private."[99] The jury could not reach a verdict, but most people continued to believe that Beecher had committed adultery with the wife of his best friend. A minister is a man like other men, except he was often worse.

Anticlerical Patriarchs

The Enlightenment sought to base human society on rational universal principles above the sectarian strife and superstition of the Christian churches. The "natural" basis of society was the family, and the "natural" order of the family was the patriarchal family, with the man as the head and the woman as the heart. Jean-Jacques Rousseau in his *Emile* claimed that men and women were radically different and unequal, and that this inequality should be reflected in education and political order.[100] Anticlericals wanted "to modernize marriage as companionate and secular but still

---

95 Cohen, "Ministerial Misdeeds," 83.
96 See Debby Applegate, *The Most Famous Man in America: The Biography of Henry Ward Beecher* (New York: Doubleday, 2006).
97 Ibid., 421.
98 Ibid., 423.
99 Ibid., 450.
100 See Timothy O'Hagan, "Men and Women," in *Rousseau* (New York: Routledge, 1999), 125–39.

patriarchal."[101] The family was sacred for Liberals such as Jules Michelet, who held that "the man, the woman, and the child, the unity of three persons, their mutual mediation,—behold the mystery of mysteries. The divine idea of Christianity, the same as that of Egypt . . . is placing the family on the altar."[102] The family for these conservative Liberals was the basic building block of society. And especially for the male Liberal, the family was a refuge from the conflicts of politics and the competition of business.

Man, as rational, was in charge of the public sphere; woman, as sentimental, was in charge of the private sphere. The differences between man and woman meant that man was best suited for the public sphere, which was one of assertiveness, aggression, war, and violence, and the woman for the domestic sphere, which was one of nurturing and affection. Proudhon, the founder of anarchism, summarized these two worlds as masculine force and feminine beauty. The man and woman became one being; marriage was monogamous and indissoluble. The husband and wife were vowed to one another completely and founded a family. The man was civilized when he became head of a family; he looked to the good of his children and to the future; he became a citizen, and he represented the public face of the family. If the differences between male and female were reduced to the genital difference, there would no longer be a society of families, Proudhon maintained, but a pornocracy, in which men and women were united only by fleeting sexual desire. Without the family, society became an atomized dust of individuals and was ripe for tyranny, against which the family was the strongest protection. For these conservative Liberals, it was therefore of utmost political importance to preserve the difference between the sexes and therefore the unity and stability of the family.

Obviously the churches largely shared this idea, but the Catholic Church in particular was seen as subversive because of its discipline of celibacy for priests and for both male and female religious, and especially for its practice of confession, in which the priest learned the secrets (often sexual) of the family and could develop an intimacy with the wife greater

---

101 Ben Fallaw, "The Seduction of Revolution: Anticlerical Campaigns against Confession in Mexico, 1914–1935," *Journal of Latin American Studies* 45, no. 1 (2013): 91.

102 Michelet, *Du Prêtre, de la femme, de la famille*, 276.

than the husband had. The confessor therefore subverted the unity of the family and was a threat to the existence of society. Anticlericals objected to the clergy from what they considered a higher moral authority, Nature. Therefore anticlericals felt that they, not the clergy, held the high moral ground. The male anticlerical, "whose masculine spirit rejects all vices against nature" is the man who by heterosexual intercourse "without effeminacy (*sin afeminación*) renders homage to Nature."[103]

Jules Michelet warned, as we have seen, of the moral dangers that confession entailed. He also alerted his fellow Liberals as to how the Church's dealings with women threatened the unity of the French family. Who was the real husband?—"If marriage is a union of souls, the true husband was the confessor."[104] Michelet complained that Frenchwomen were under the thumbs of the clergy, who realized that "the direction, the government of women, is the vital point of ecclesiastical power, which they will defend to the death."[105]

Our wives and our daughters are raised and governed by *our enemies*.

Enemies of the modern spirit, of liberty and the future. There is no point in citing one preacher, one sermon. One voice for liberty, fifty voices against . . . Whom are they fooling by such a coarse tactic?

Our enemies, I repeat, in a direct sense. They are by nature envious of marriage and the life of the family. That, I know well, is far less their fault than their misfortune. A dead old system, which functions mechanically, cannot require anything but dead men. Nevertheless life makes its claims in them; they feel cruelly that they are deprived of a family and console themselves by troubling ours.[106]

103 Hernando de Santocraz, in *La Republica*, March 26, 1911, quoted in Juan de la Cueva Merino, *Clericales y anticlericales: El conflicto entre confesionalidad y secularización en Cantabria (1875–1923)* (Santander: Universidad de Cantabria, 1994), 321.
104 Jules Michelet, *Histoire de la révolution française*, Vol. 4 (Paris: Chamerot, 1849), 296.
105 Michelet, *Du Prêtre, de la femme, de la famille*, 11.
106 Ibid., 4.

This clericalism Michelet identified and demonized as "jésuitisme," "l'esprit de mort" ("the spirit of death").[107] Religious life is "a life systematically negative, a life of death," which develops in man "the instincts hostile to life."[108] Priests were the third sex, neither fully man nor woman: "the priest, born a man and strong, but who wants to make himself weak, like a woman, and who thereby participating in both man and woman, is able to interpose himself between them."[109] The priest, only half a man, offers to ally with the woman to change the husband, who saw no need to change.

The spiritual director and the woman were able to converse at great length: "To the director, one tells everything, one speaks of oneself and of relatives, of their affairs, of their interests . . . the confessor is bound by the seal of confession, but the director is not." He can share information, especially with other directors, of what he knows about a household from the wife and the servants. Information is power, and power is what the clergy needs to control society and recalcitrant males. Michelet sarcastically comments on the man who thinks he is lucky to have a religious wife and religious servants who go to confession and to spiritual directors: "Happy is the father of a family, who has such a wife, so virtuous, and such servants, gentle and humble, honest, pious . . . ." He "lives in a house of glass, in which everyone can always look in. Not a word of his is lost. He speaks low, but the acute ear has heard everything. If he writes down his intimate thought, not wishing to speak it aloud, it is read, by whom? One does not know. What he has dreamt on his pillow, he is astonished to hear the next day on the streets."[110]

While Liberal men wanted to be independent of clerics, they wanted women to be dependent on laymen.[111] Laymen and clerics engaged in a tug of war over women over who would be the ultimate influence in women's lives. Both laymen and clerics assumed that women should be ruled by men. The only question was, *Who would be the ruler?* Women were caught

---

107 Ibid., 5.
108 Ibid., 21.
109 Ibid., 14.
110 Ibid., 202.
111 See Luz Sanfelio Gimeno, *Republicanas: Identidades de género en el blasquismo (1895–1910)* (Valencia: Universitat de Valéncia, 2005), 299.

between two powers, but could sometimes achieve some freedom of action by pitting one against the other. Gibson observes: "Men intended that their womenfolk should be under their complete and uncontested control. Women sometimes attempted to evade this domination by looking to the priest as a countervailing locus of power, one they could play off against their husband or father...."[112] The husband might well resent what he saw as interference in his lawful and unique authority over his wife. The priest-turned-anticlerical Chiniquy made explicit men's deepest objections to women's frequenting the confessional: "through the confessional, the priest was much more the husband of the wife than the man to whom she was wedded" and "the husband wants the wife to be *his*—he does not and could not, consent to share his authority over her with anybody: he wants to be the *only* man who will have her confidence and her ear, as well as her respect and her love."[113] Men wanted to be independent, but a man wanted his wife to be dependent on him, and on him alone. And the priest was an interloper. The anticlerical did not want women to go to confession because he did not want a rival. Jean Faury calls this attitude anticlerical machismo.[114]

In 1872 the anticlerical newspaper *La Capitale* warned men about the pious Catholic woman: "The man, who marries such a woman, marries in her place the confessor" with the result that "in place of all the beautiful things that can be learned, your sons learn by heart an endless cascade of broken Latin words that sound worse than Arabic. There is a fight about baptism, there is a fight at each stage of life. You are no longer the father; the father of your sons is the confessor of your wife; you are no longer master of the house; her confessor is." The privacy and intimacy of the family is destroyed: "You have no more secrets; your wife's confessor knows everything . . . he knows what you think, say, write, with whom you talk, what you read . . . what you do in your bedroom."[115] The priest alienated the wife from her husband.

---

112 Ralph Gibson, *A Social History of French Catholicism 1789–1914* (London: Routledge, 1989), 187.

113 Chiniquy, *The Priest, The Woman, and The Confessional*, 122, 127.

114 Faury, *Clericalisme et anticlericalisme*, 272.

115 Quoted in Manuel Borutta, *Antikatholizismus: Deutschland und Italien im Zeitalter der europäischen Kulturkämpfe* (Göttingen: Vandenhoeck & Ruprecht, 2011), 376–77.

In Italy the founder of the Republican Party, Arcangelo Ghisleri (1855–1938) claimed that through the woman the priest influenced the education of future generations and maintained his power. He concluded that the woman must be freed "from the yoke of the priest." This is "the first, the most urgent, the most logical and the holiest of all emancipations" because freeing the woman from the priest "brings her closer to her husband" and "making stronger the holy bonds" of matrimony.[116] Women did not always want to be bound this closely, and would use the cleric as a counterweight to the husband, infuriating the patriarchal republican who wanted the wife to be a mirror image of himself.

German Catholic men were also resentful of the relationship of clergy and women, who shared the same character: "To be a priest and to be a woman means: understanding, bearing fruit in patience, working in generous, selfless love," according to Msgr. Hermann Klens.[117] Priests in confession threatened with the punishments of God husbands who beat their wives or committed adultery. Wives complained to priests that their husbands demanded all too frequent intercourse and the use of contraceptive devices. One priest reported that men felt an envy of God, "who had apparently stolen the place in the heart of his wife, so that he felt himself neglected," and this priest wondered "whether we (the clergy) have not perhaps often brought the husband and wife into a false adversarial position."[118]

In the 1920s Jaime Torrubiano Ripoll, a Catalan Catholic Liberal, lamented the influence of the priest on wives. In the Catholic family, he claimed that "everything is *Father*. The disposal of possessions, the education and formation of the children in their career and in their married and social life, the orientation of the customs of the house, the intimate life of the conscience, the practice and manner of even intimate conjugal relations … everything, absolutely everything, is directed by *Father*" because "the woman, the queen of the family" consults "not with her husband, who in

---

116 Quoted in Borutta, *Antikatholizismus*, 378.
117 Quoted in Doris Kaufmann, *Katholisches Milieu in Münster 1928–1933: Politische Aktionsformen und geschlechtsspezifische Verhaltensräume* (Düsseldorf: Schwann, 1984), 82.
118 Kaufmann, *Katholisches Milieu*, 87.

her mind is inferior to *Father*, but with *Father*." Torrubiano Ripoll warned Spanish husbands to minimize the contact their wives had with priests, because "for your wives you will always be inferior to Father," who not only "represents God," but is surrounded by "tinsel" that excites "feminine sexuality and curiosity."[119]

For anticlericals, the personal is political. All of these critiques would have serious political consequences, especially for the Catholic clergy, who were the objects of heightened suspicions because of the combination of celibacy and confession. The suspicions gave politically anti-clerical regimes a way of attacking the Catholic Church, and many priests had to pay with their lives for the disciplines the Church imposed. The Curé of Ars and the Jansenists were sincere in their rigorism and were respected for their consistency of practice even by those who disagreed with them. But rigorism imposed by those who lead dissolute lives is guaranteed to provoke rebellion. The adulterous Henry Ward Beecher commented on human nature: "I should be sorry to think that everybody was a hypocrite who was different at one time from what he was at another. Men are inconsistent, often, who are not insincere. They are untrue to their own highest ideal, and they act in ways that are contrary to their purposes."[120] A sinner, especially a sexual sinner, may indeed have excellent principles and call people to live up to them; but he should not be surprised that he is accused of hypocrisy.

Catholic Anticlericalism

Anticlericalism was most virulent in Catholic countries. The sexuality of the clergy was attacked in endless caricatures: "Male clergy were shown as effeminate or as hermaphrodites, Jesuits as androgynous, nuns as masculinized."[121] The clergy were, like Jews in Nazi anti-Semitic cartoons, shown as "fanatics, criminals, insane," and finally as "devils, vampires, animals and plants, as reptiles, hydras, snakes, mice, rats...."[122] The clergy were above

---

119 Jaime Torrubiano Ripoll, *Beatería y Religión: Meditaciones de un Canonista* (Madrid: Javier Morata, 1930), 133–34.
120 Applegate, *Most Famous Man*, 471.
121 Borutta, *Antikatholizismus*, 204.
122 Ibid., 209.

all *unnatural* because of their celibacy and their denial of standard models of masculinity. All this dehumanized the clergy, and set the stage not simply for political attacks, but for persecution, assault, and murder. Sexual fear and jealousy gave an edge, sometimes a deadly edge, to anticlerical attacks on the Church.

Whatever sexual activity the clergy may have been engaged in, it was wildly exaggerated by anticlerical men who did not want their wives to have an independent relationship, however spiritual, with another adult male, and who resented the clergy for preaching restrictions on male sexual behavior. Anticlericals, despite their pretensions to be the representatives of Reason, engaged in magical thinking: the clergy were the locus of all evil in the world; if only the clergy were rendered powerless or destroyed, young men would have no more sexual frustrations, prosperity and progress would appear miraculously, and all would be well. The scientist F. J. Raspail thought that the Jesuits were plotting to kill him and were almost certainly the murderers of "Paul-Louis Courier, Eugène Sue, Rosseau, Voltaire, Marat etc. and that they saved Wellington at Waterloo."[123] When critics pointed out there was no evidence for these charges, the anticlericals responded that "the Jesuits had made sure there was none."[124] The absence of evidence was itself evidence.

Jérôme Grévy recognized that the anticlericals made priests and religious a scapegoat. Supposedly rational anticlericals made clericalism "the principal explanation for all evils—past and present—of society. It is not harmless, for example, to claim that the teaching of the Brothers was responsible for the defeat of 1870, that Paul Bert established implicitly a connection between phylloxera and the Jesuits, that the wealth of religious congregations was held responsible for the business crisis of the 1880s."[125] Anticlericalism parallels anti-Semitism. The anticlerical Mexican President Plutarco Elías Calles, whose persecution of the Catholic Church set off the Cristeros rebellion (1926–1929) in which 90 priests and 70,000 people died, ended up as an admirer of Hitler and spent his time "attending the weekly

---

123 Gibson, *Social History*, 111.
124 Ibid., 111.
125 Jérôme Grévy, *Le clericalisme? Voilà l'ennemi! Un siècle de guerre de religion en France* (Paris: Armand Colin, 2005), 58.

séances of the Mexican Circle of Metaphysic Investigations to commune with the dead about his political legacy."[126] As Miguel de Unamuno said of the Spanish, "Our anticlericals are anticlericals of laicism, theologians in reverse,"[127] mirror images of the superstition they claimed to be eradicating.

126 Michael Burleigh, *Sacred Causes: The Clash of Religion and Politics, from the Great War to the War on Terror* (New York: HarperCollins, 2007), 127.
127 Miguel de Unamuno, *De la enseñanza superior en España* (Madrid: Revista Nueva, 1899), 19.

Chapter Six
Political Anticlericalism

Anticlericalism was a major current in nineteenth-century European culture and politics. Where the clergy have had political power, or where they are *imagined* to have had political power, they have been the subject of organized anticlerical campaigns. The clergy exercised their political power not only through public means, such as concordats, education, and property ownership, but also through more personal means such as counseling and confession. And the persons on whom they exercised this personal influence were usually women.

Women as the Agents of the Clergy

Political anticlericalism has long been mostly a male phenomenon in Europe and Latin America: "in countries with religious parties, voters for secular (particularly left, anticlerical, or liberal) parties are disproportionately male, while a large majority of the electorate of the religious parties are usually women."[1] Liberals and Radicals therefore were hesitant to give the vote to women, for they feared that women would be governed by the clergy.[2] In 1907 Georges Clemenceau opposed letting women vote because, he wrote, "the number of [women] who escape the domination of the clergy is ridiculously low. If the right to vote were given to women tomorrow,

---

1   Seymour Martin Lipset, *Revolution and Counterrevolution: Change and Persistence in Social Structures* (New York: Basic Books, 1968), 222.

2   Blanca Rodríguez-Ruiz and Ruth Rubio Marín, "Introduction: Transition to Modernity, the Conquest of Female Suffrage and Women's Citizenship," in *The Struggle for Female Suffrage in Europe: Voting to Become Citizens*, eds. Blanca Rodríguez-Ruiz and Ruth Rubio Marín (Leiden: Brill, 2012), 14–16.

France would immediately jump backwards into the Middle Ages."[3] This was the general sentiment among Liberals. Pope Benedict XV was of the same mind, although he would have put it differently, and in 1919 he came out for women's suffrage.[4] The French Senate in 1922 rejected female suffrage on the grounds that women would vote for clerical parties.[5] Belgian Liberal anticlericals blocked women's suffrage.[6] It was not until 1944 that De Gaulle's provisional government gave women the vote; women voted more for conservatives than men did, but did not always favor the Right.[7]

Spanish anticlericals had a low opinion of women. Edmondo González-Blanco in 1911 claimed that "by far the greatest bulwark of intolerance is the woman," whose "weakness of constitution" and "impoverishment of spirit" is formed in the "swoonings of the confessional."[8] The Spanish anticlerical Republican Manuel Hilario Ayuso wrote in 1931 against women's suffrage: "Today giving the vote to women is absurd, because in the immense majority of towns, the feminine element, for the most part, is in the hands of the priests, who direct feminine opinion, who introduce themselves into the homes and rule in every part."[9] Or as a character in a Miguel

3   James F. McMillan, *France and Women 1789–1914: Gender, Society, and Politics* (London: Routledge, 2000), 228.

4   Susanna Mancini, "From the Struggle for Suffrage to the Construction of a Fragile Gender Citizenship: Italy 1861–2009," in Rodríguez-Ruiz and Marín, *The Struggle for Female Suffrage*, 379.

5   Frank Tallett and Nicholas Aitkin, *Religion, Politics, and Society in France since 1789* (London: Hambledon, 1991), 56.

6   Judith Keene, "Into the Clear Air of the Plaza: Spanish Women Achieve the Vote in 1931," in *Constructing Spanish Womanhood: Female Identity in Modern Spain*, eds. Victoria Lorée Enders and Pamela Beth Radcliff (Albany: State University of New York Press, 1999), 331.

7   Claire Duchen, *Women's Rights and Women's Lives in France, 1944–1968* (London: Routledge, 1994), 40. See Richard Vinen, *Bourgeois Politics in France, 1945–1951* (Cambridge: Cambridge University Press, 1995), 54; and Katherine A. R. Opello, *Gender Quotas, Party Reform, and Political Parties in France* (Lanham, MD: Lexington Books, 2006), 70.

8   Quoted by Paul Aubert, "Luchar contra los poderes fácticos," in Paul Aubert, ed., *Religión y sociedad en España (Siglos XIX y XX)* (Madrid: Casa de Velásquez, 2002), 227.

9   Quoted by Manuel Delgado Ruiz, *Las palabras de otro hombre: anticlericalismo y misoginia* (Barcelona: Muchnik Editores, 1993), 22.

de Unamuno novel claimed, "in the Spain of the henpecked (*calzonazos*) the priests direct the women and the women direct the men."[10] Margarita Nelken gave a more serious explanation, pointing to the passivity that the clergy identified as feminine and therefore demanded of women: "the doctrine of passive resignation and, consequently, of silence in the face of all injustices and all arbitrary acts naturally rules in the Spanish woman who is submitted to the priest."[11] The anticlericals were deeply suspicious of women because women were more religious than men[12] and religion is the opiate of the people, who, so drugged, bear oppression without rebelling.

All over Latin America anticlerical parties opposed giving women the right to vote; conservative parties generally were the ones who gave women the vote, in hopes that it would help the Catholic cause.[13] In Chile, women's suffrage was favored by conservative Catholics, and the anticlerical Liberals and Radicals "vehemently" opposed it.[14] In Mexico "anticlericalism was a strongly male cause" and "the image of the gullible woman, conned (maybe molested) by devious priests, was a commonplace."[15] Mexican revolutionaries in the 1920s and 1930s feared that Mexican women would vote for "reactionary" interests; only four Mexican states granted women the right to vote, and two of them revoked it.[16] One legislator claimed that "if we

---

10 Miguel de Unamuno, *San Manuel Bueno, Mártir*, Kindle Edition, 23.
11 Margarita Nelken, *La condición social de la mujer in España* (Madrid: CVS Ediciones, 1975), 187.
12 See María Pilar Salomón Chéliz, "Devotas mojigatas, fanáticas y libidinosas: Anticlericalismo y antifeminismo en el discurso republicano a fines del siglo XIX," in *Feminismos y antifeminismos: Culturas políticas e identidades de género en la España del siglo XX*, eds. Ana Aguado and Teresa María Ortega López (Universitat de València: PUV, 2011), 71–98.
13 Victoria González and Karen Kempwirth, eds., *Radical Women in Latin America: Left and Right* (University Park: Pennsylvania State University Press, 2001), 13.
14 Lisa Baldez, *Why Women Protest: Women's Movements in Chile* (Cambridge: Cambridge University Press, 2002), 22.
15 Alan Knight, "The Mentality and Modus Operandi of Revolutionary Anticlericalism," in *Faith and Piety in Revolutionary Mexico*, ed. Mathew Butler (New York: Palgrave McMillan, 2007), 34.
16 William H. Beezley and Michael C. Meyer, *The Oxford History of Mexico* (New York: Oxford University Press, 2010), 456.

granted women the right to vote, the Archbishop of Mexico would be the next President of the Republic."[17] Women did not get full voting rights in Mexico until 1953,[18] but in the 1920s, after the Revolution, women put as much social and economic pressure as they could to stop the government from enforcing anticlerical laws. The members of the *Unión de Damas Católicas Mexicanas* and similar women's organizations dressed in black to mourn the persecution of the Church, organized boycotts, raised money and found lodging for priests who had been exiled from their parishes, and visited and fed the priests who were imprisoned.[19]

Anticlerical fears of clerical interference had some basis in reality. In 1885 a priest in the Ardèche told women that "under pain of mortal sin" they must persuade their husbands to vote conservative. In 1897 a husband in Finistère refused to follow his wife's instructions how to vote and who "since that time could have no intercourse with her as a result of clerical proscription."[20] This Lysistrata tactic did not endear the clergy to men. In 1905 a Catholic newspaper, *La Voz de Valencia*, appealed to women: "It is true that the Christian woman does not vote; but she has her husbands, her sons, her brothers, her parents, her [male] friends, her [male] cousins, her dependents, and over all of them she can exercise the smooth but powerful influence of the virtuous woman who makes herself felt with great efficacy. Let those Valencian women who love God and Valencia be encouraged in this electoral apostolate, turning themselves from their proper sphere to dedicated and enthusiastic electoral agents."[21] Even women deputies in the Cortes during the Republic (women could be elected but could not vote) opposed women's

17 Ben Fallow, "The Seduction of Revolution: Anticlerical Campaigns against Confession in Mexico, 1914–1935," *Journal of Latin American Studies* 45, no. 1 (2013): 118.

18 Judith Keene, "Strange Bedfellows: Feminists, Catholics and Anticlericals in the Enfranchisement of Spanish Women," *Australian Feminist Studies* 17, no. 38 (2002): 165.

19 See Patience A. Schell, "Of the Sublime Mission of Mothers of Families: The Union of Mexican Catholic Ladies in Revolutionary Mexico," in *The Women's Revolution in Mexico, 1910–1953*, ed. Stephanie A. Mitchell and Patience A. Schell (Lanham, MD: Rowman & Littlefield, 2007), 99–194.

20 Eugen Weber, *Peasants into Frenchmen: The Modernization of Rural France, 1870–1914* (Stanford, CA: Stanford University Press, 1976), 365.

21 Mónica Moreno Seca, "Mujeres, clericalismo y asociacionismo católico," in

suffrage.[22] The Socialist deputy Margarita Nelken claimed that there was "not a single practicing Catholic woman in the country who had not been interrogated by her confessor about her political ideas and inclinations."[23] Some Socialist deputies ideologically committed to equality and the Catholic deputies who hoped women would vote Catholic combined to give women the vote in 1931.[24] In the 1933 elections women appear to have voted against the Liberals and for rightist, clericalist parties.[25]

In Germany in the 1920s the breakdown in votes for the Catholic Center Party was 60% women, 40% men; the Center Party worried about this "political sickness" and sought to win male votes.[26] Social Democratic women were frustrated that women would vote for the "false" party and criticized women for being "tradition-bound and religious."[27] The more leftist a party was, the less women voted for it. In West Germany, according to a 1953 survey, 60% of all Socialist voters were men, while 58% of the Christian Democrats were women.[28] The initial gender gap in voting was caused by a gender gap in religion; men disproportionately rejected religion and sought to lessen its influence. This pattern continued in the postwar era, 1945–1969, as women voted conservative, but after 1969 the voting patterns of men and women converged.[29]

Clericalismo y asociacionismo católico en España: de la restauración a la transición: un siglo entre el palio y el consiliario, eds. Julio de la Cueva Merino and Ángel Luis López Villaverde (Universidad Castilla-La Mancha, 2005), 115.

22 Keene, "Strange Bedfellows," 165.

23 Quoted in Keene, "Strange Bedfellows," 168.

24 Keene, "Strange Bedfellows," 172.

25 Timothy J. Mitchell, *Betrayal of the Innocents: Desire, Power, and the Catholic Church in Spain* (Philadelphia: University of Pennsylvania Press, 1998), 83.

26 Doris Kaufmann, *Katholisches Milieu in Münster 1928–1933: Politische Aktionsformen und geschlechtsspezifische Verhaltensräume* (Düsseldorf: Schwann, 1984), 77.

27 Birgit Sack, *Zwischen religiöser Bindung und moderner Gesellschaft: Katholische Frauenbewegung und politische Kultur in der Weimarer Republik (1918/1933)* (Münster: Waxman Verlag, 1998), 67.

28 Seymour Martin Lipset, *Political Man: The Social Bases of Politics* (Garden City: Doubleday, 1960), 164.

29 Lydia Gilde, *Frauen und Parteipolitik: Hindernisse und unterstützende Faktoren weiblicher politischer Partizipation* (Munich: GRIN Verlag, 2005), 23.

France

The Enlightenment attacked the superstition and power of the Church. Voltaire signed his letters, "écrasez l'infâme." The Revolution soon took up this cry and turned against the Church and against Christianity. As James McMillan observes, "the sans-culottes were driven by a hatred of priests which is difficult to comprehend but which undoubtedly owed something to sexual jealousy and a perception that priests exercised power over women especially through the confessional, which allowed them to usurp the place which rightfully belonged to husbands."[30] This is a recurrent theme in anticlericalism in Catholic countries. Anticlerical leaders attacked Catholicism and proclaimed that "it is fanaticism and superstition we will be fighting against; lying priests, whose dogma is falsehood ... whose Empire is founded on the credulity of women." Another revolutionary addressed priests: "What you useless buggers, have you not ceased deceiving husbands, seducing their wives and producing bastards?"[31] About 2,000 to 3,000 priests were killed in the Revolution and another 32,000 went into exile.[32]

The French revolutionaries noticed (and disliked) women's greater devotion to Christianity, a devotion that led women to oppose the civil oath of loyalty to the Republic and the later desecration of churches.[33] Marguerite Salvan expressed a general sentiment among women when she proclaimed, "I will defend my religion to the last drop of my blood"[34] (she was in the

30 McMillan, *France and Women*, 26.
31 Richard Cobb, *The People's Armies*, trans. Marianne Elliott (New Haven: Yale University Press, 1987), 450.
32 James McMillan, "'Priest Hits Girl': On the Front Line in the 'War of the Two Frances,'" in *Culture Wars: Secular-Catholic Conflict in Nineteenth-Century Europe*, eds. Christopher Clark and Wolfram Kaiser (New York: Cambridge University Press, 2003), 81.
33 Caroline Ford, *Divided Houses: Religion and Gender in Modern France* (Ithaca: Cornell University Press, 2005), 16–17. See also the chapter, "In Search of Counter-Revolutionary Women," in Olwen H. Hufton, *Women and the Limits of Citizenship in the French Revolution* (Toronto: University of Toronto Press, 1992), 89–130.
34 Geneviève Gabbois, "'Vous êtes presque la seule consolation de l'église': La foi des femmes face à la déchristianisation de 1789–1880," in *La religion de ma*

process of breaking an official's windows). Marie Chabrier warned the revolutionary officials who were trying to administer the civil oath, "Let them come, let them try, those bastards, we'll cut their throats. Religion won't be destroyed."[35] Women's opposition was prominent and vigorous: "they defended calvaries, shrines and churches against the attacks of the dechristianizers; they took the lead in the aftermath of dechristianization in reestablishing and opening churches; and in the enforced absence of the priest, they usurped the role of religious instruction."[36] Were women already more dedicated to religion than men were? Or did they think the police would hesitate to attack women (as later in the *Kulturkampf*)? James McMillan maintains that women's defense of Catholicism made them suspect in the eyes of the revolutionaries, "who acquired the conviction that women were the slaves of superstition and the natural enemies of enlightenment."[37]

The French Revolution and the Napoleonic Wars had weakened or destroyed quasi-independent Catholic power centers, such as the wealthy prince-bishoprics, and therefore gave the Roman Curia the opportunity to promote its vision of Catholicism. These religious changes in the nineteenth century led to an increased feminization of religion, especially in the Catholic Church. This ultramontane Catholicism was popular and devotional; its devotions appealed especially to women. Women in extraordinary numbers entered congregations devoted to active work in the world, especially education and care for the sick. In France the number of women in religion increased from less than 13,000 in 1808 to over 130,000 in 1880.[38] Women developed a special loyalty to the Papacy and were prominent in reviving Peter's Pence.[39]

mère: La rôle des femmes dans la transmission de la foi, ed. Jean Delumeau (Paris: Cerf, 1992), 305.

35 Quoted by Timothy Tackett, "Women and Men in Counterrevolution: The Sommières Riot of 1791," *The Journal of Modern History* 59, no. 4 (1987): 687.

36 Nicholas Atkin and Frank Tallett, *Priests, Prelates, and People: A History of European Catholicism Since 1750* (New York: St. Martin's, 2003), 62.

37 McMillan, *France and Women*, 27.

38 Claude Langlois, "Féminisation du catholicisme," in *Histoire de la France religieuse*, Vol. 3, *Du roi Très Chrétien à la laïcité républicaine XVIIIe–XIXe siècle*, ed. Philippe Joutard (Paris: Éditions du Seuil, 2001), 306.

39 Christopher Clark, "The New Catholicism and the European Culture Wars," in Clark and Kaiser, *Culture Wars*, 22.

The devotion to the Sacred Heart, in addition to its erotic overtones, had a political significance.[40] The badge of the Sacred Heart was worn by the opponents of the Revolution in the Vendée (1793–1796) and later became a symbol of royalism. In 1870 France was traumatized by the defeat of the French army at Sedan. Catholics saw this as divine punishment for France's apostasy and decided to build the Church of the National Vow, Sacré-Coeur on Montmartre. This church became a goal for pilgrimages and a center of opposition to laïcité. The Socialist Gustave Téry attended services where the priest prayed "Lord Jesus, convert the men of France." Téry thought "and the women?"[41] He knew that "it is especially among women that cordicolism [devotion to the Sacred Heart] exercises its ravages."[42] Under the guise of this devotion, anticlericals suspected, the clergy were seeking to reassert its hold on France, and specifically on French men through French women.

The enormous increase in the number of religious women involved in active works such as education meant that more girls than boys were receiving a Catholic education, which also served as a protector of female chastity. In 1807 Napoleon I explained that because of "the weakness of women's brains," school for girls must teach "religion in all its rigor" because it "is the surest guarantee for mothers and husbands."[43] In 1837 about 40% of girls were in Catholic schools, and by 1876 60% of girls were in Catholic

40 For the political use of the devotion to the Sacred Heart in France, see Raymond Jonas, *France and the Cult of the Sacred Heart: An Epic Tale for Modern Times* (Berkeley: University of California Press, 2000). For Spain, see Julio de la Cueva Merino, *Clericales y anticlericales: El conflicto entre confesionalidad y secularización en Cantabria (1875–1923)* (Santander: Universidad de Cantabria, 1994), 328–31; for the Tyrol, see Laurence Cole, "The Counter-Reformation's Last Stand: Austria," in Clark and Kaiser, *Culture Wars*, 294–95; and Lawrence Cole, "Nationale Identität eines 'auserwählten Volkes': zur Bedeutung des Herz Jesu-Kultes unter der deutschsprachigen Bevölkerung Tirols 1858–1896," in *Nation und Religion in der deutsche Geschichte*, ed. Heinz-Gerhard Haupt and Dieter Langewiesche (Frankfurt-am-Main: Campus Verlag, 2001), 480–515.

41 Gustave Téry, *Les cordicoles* (Paris: Édouard Cornély, 1902), 30.

42 Ibid., 54.

43 Quoted in *Women, the Family, and Freedom: The Debate in Documents* Vol. 1, *1750–1880*, eds. Susan Groag Bell and Karen M. Offen (Stanford, CA: Stanford University Press, 1983), 95.

schools. By contrast in 1876 less than 30% of boys were receiving a Catholic education.[44] Anticlericals could not find suitable wives—that is, wives who were not practicing Catholics. Therefore anticlericals were determined to wrest control of education from the Church. In 1880 the Sée law established girls' lycées, not to enable women to enter the professions, but, as Roger Magraw explains, to provide "suitable liberal wives for bourgeois husbands, mothers for future republican children."[45]

Confession was also a way for the clergy to influence politics. A contemporary English observer saw the results of a French election not as an expression of anti-religious sentiments, but as a warning to the curé that "he must not turn the confessional into a vehicle for political propaganda among foolish women."[46] There were few men in the confessional for the curé to influence.

Germany

In the 1840s German men were already aware that women were the mainstay of religion. Therefore the proponents of an independent, national Christianity, such as the *Deutschkatholiken*, tried to detach women from the traditional churches, especially from the Roman Catholic Church.[47] These

---

44 Langlois, "Féminisation du catholicisme," 284. See also Rebecca Rogers, "The Socialization of Girls in France under the Influence of Religion and the Church," in Kraul and Lüth, *Erziehung der Menschen-Geschlechter: Studien zur Religion, Sozialisation und Bildung in Europa seit der Aufklärung*, ed. Margret Kraul and Christoph Lüth (Weinheim: Deutscher Studien Verlag, 1996), 141–43.

45 Roger Magraw, *France 1815–1914: The Bourgeois Century* (New York: Oxford University Press, 1986), 218. *L'Union Républicaine du Tarn* in 1848 lamented that of those who went to confession 90% were women and that the lay school would remedy this situation (Jean Faury, *Cléricalisme et anticléricalisme dans le Tarn*, 1848–1900 [Toulouse: Service des publications de l'Université de Toulouse-Le Mirail, 1980], 271).

46 Eustace Clare Glenville Murray, *Round about France* (London: Macmillan, 1878), 87.

47 See Wayne Detler, "German Catholicism: The Ronge-Czerski Movement, 1844–5," in *Schism, Heresy, and Religious Protest*, ed. Derek Baker (Cambridge: Cambridge University Press, 1972), 341–50.

independent Catholics, whose congregations were about 30–40% women,[48] tried to explain to men the attraction and dangers that women encountered in the ultramontane Catholicism that was gaining ground in Germany. Men were warned that Catholic priests "have focused particularly on women; for in them emotion predominates."[49] The dissenters attacked the celibacy of the clergy and auricular confession. The founder of this German-Catholic Church was Johannes Ronge, who fled to England in the wake of the failures of the 1848 revolutions and died a Unitarian. According to an English contemporary, this new church would do away with "the immorality produced by the forced celibacy of the clergy."[50] "Forced celibacy" would however be replaced by "forced marriage." Priests were expected to marry to demonstrate that they were men. A journal of *Deutschkatholizismus* affirmed: "Whoever ... does not have the courage to reject celibacy also through the deed, him we consider to be a weak man."[51] Herzog notes that the dissenters "established, confirmed, and defined their own masculinity by attacking Catholicism."[52] These German Catholics also attacked "the auricular confession of wives and maidens on the most secret immodest circumstances and subjects, on which a wife would not talk to her husband, or a girl to her own mother, in the shameless, open, and descriptive way which the duty of the confessional imposes on the priest and the female, side by side."[53] The confession was "a place of the most cunning lasciviousness wrapped in the holy cloak of religion" in which women were questioned about "the secrets of the marriage bed."[54] The priest was an interloper in marriage, and intruded himself between the husband and wife,

---

48 Dagmar Herzog, "Religious Dissent and the Roots of German Feminism," in *Gender Relations in German History: Power, Agency, and Experience from the Sixteenth to the Twentieth Century*, eds. Lynn Abrams and Elizabeth Harvey (Durham, NC: Duke University Press, 1996), 8.

49 Quoted in Dagmar Herzog, "Religious Dissent," 91.

50 Samuel Laing, *Notes on the Rise, Progress, and Prospects of the Schism from the Church of Rome Called the German-Catholic Church* (London: Longman, Brown, Green & Longmans, 1846), 44.

51 Quoted in Dagmar Herzog, *Intimacy and Exclusion: Religious Politics in Pre-Revolutionary Baden* (New Brunswick, NJ: Transaction Publishers, 2007), 89.

52 Herzog, *Intimacy and Exclusion*, 89.

53 Laing, *Notes*, 45.

54 Quoted in Herzog, *Intimacy and Exclusion*, 101–02.

"for whom the confessor means more to her than the husband who loves her."[55]

After the defeat of the 1848 revolutions by reactionary forces, the Catholic Church in Germany realized that it was in dire straits. The Church mounted a massive wave of missions, led mostly by the Jesuits and Redemptorists.[56] These missions preached the fundamentals of Christianity with special emphasis on the Four Last Things: Death, Judgment, Heaven, and Hell. The intense emotional atmosphere of these missions was like that of American revivalism. The missions led to an upsurge in religious practice, especially among women. As in France, the number of religious women in Germany increased vastly, and unlike the older contemplative orders, whose members stayed in their convents and prayed, the new orders ran schools, hospitals, and other public institutions.[57]

Liberals maintained that the public sphere was more suitable for men and that the private sphere was more suitable for women. The public masculine sphere was the realm of reason, the state, and politics; the private feminine sphere was the realm of emotion, home, and religion. The entry of women into the public sphere worried Liberals.[58] The influence that the Church had on women was especially dangerous. In the Liberal world view, "due to their incapacity for sustained, disciplined thought, women were seen as more susceptible than men to the irrationalism, excessive emotion, and superstitious nonsense of Roman Catholicism."[59] Like their French equivalents, German Liberals feared that women were consorting with the clergy, the natural enemy of enlightened men. As one anticlerical warned,

---

55 Quoted in Herzog, *Intimacy and Exclusion*, 103.
56 See Michael Gross, *The War against Catholicism: Liberalism and the Anti-Catholic Imagination in Nineteenth-Century Germany* (Ann Arbor: University of Michigan Press, 2005), 35–48; Peter Watson, *The German Genius: Europe's Third Renaissance, the Second Scientific Revolution, and the Twentieth Century* (New York: HarperCollins, 2010), 422–24.
57 Gross, *War against Catholicism*, 211–14.
58 See Michael B. Gross, "*Kulturkampf* and *Geschlechterkampf*: Anti-Catholicism, Catholic Women, and Public Sphere," in *Conflict, Catastrophe and Continuity in German History: Essays on Modern German History*, eds. Frank Biess, Mark Roseman, and Hanna Schissler (New York: Berghahn Books, 1997), 30–31.
59 Gross, *War against Catholicism*, 203.

"One group must on all accounts be guarded from the Jesuits—women! The Jesuit never attacks the dissenter directly. He goes through his wife! Again, German men, guard your women from them. There is no devout Protestant woman, not even a pastor's wife, whom they cannot get around! If we lose the German women, everything is lost; then the children belong to them as well, whom they can model according to their own wishes."[60]

Burghard Assmus asserted that Jesuits had been expelled from parts of Italy in the early modern period because of their reputation as "randy goats." He cited the case of Girard, who had seduced a young girl in the confessional and encouraged all kinds of unchaste activity.[61] In his hysterical anti-Jesuit screed *Jesuitenspiegel*, Assmus concludes with accusations of pederasty. Adam Heuler, S.J. sexually abused seven boys in Constance; he was sent to another school. Viktor Wagner, S.J. abused boys in Munich; he was sent to Lucerne, to replace a teacher who had also abused boys. Wagner openly taught that pederasty was not a sin. His superior hushed everything up.[62]

In 1870 Germany defeated France. At Versailles Wilhelm was declared the emperor of the new German empire. In 1870 the First Vatican Council declared the infallibility of the pope. Although narrowly defined to mean that the pope when he taught as supreme head of the Church could not teach doctrinal error, it was widely interpreted as a political threat to national autonomy. German Catholics were suspected of having divided loyalties, to the point that Liberals even considered revoking the citizenship of Catholics.[63] Liberals feared that ultramontane superstition would triumph, and therefore people must be forced to be free of its influence. At the insistence of the Liberals, the Jesuits were expelled from Germany, the Catholic clergy had to undergo an education in German culture, the German Catholic Church was forbidden to communicate with the Vatican,

---

60   Róisín Healy, "Anti-Jesuitism in Imperial Germany: The Jesuit as Androgyne," in *Protestants, Catholics and Jews in Germany, 1800–1914*, ed. Helmut Walser Smith (New York: Berg, 2001), 168.

61   Róisín Healy, *The Jesuit Specter in Imperial Germany* (Boston: Brill, 2003), 166.

62   Burghard Assmuss, *Jesuitenspiegel: Interessante Beiträge zur Naturgeschichte der Jesuiten* (Berlin: 1904. Berlin: A. Bock Verlag, 1938), 141–42. The Nazis republished older anticlerical screeds.

63   Gross, *War against Catholicism*, 299.

clerical appointments had to be approved by the state, and priests were forbidden by an 1871 law (§130a) to mention politics from the pulpit (this last law was in force until 1953).[64]

The *Kulturkampf* (1871–1875), usually seen as Bismarck's attempt to defeat the rival power of the Catholic Church, had a very strong gender component. Men, far more than women, were detached from religion, especially in its "superstitious," ultramontane form of Roman Catholicism. German Liberals, proponents of rationality, free markets, and independent thought, were strongly anti-feminist[65] and led the attack on the Church. According to Manuel Borutta, "Catholicism was not only associated with internationalism, irrationality and backwardness, but also with femininity, sexual deviance, and sickness."[66] Catholic men in the Center party led the Catholic side in the *Kulturkampf*, but women became more and more active in the defense of the Church. They reckoned that the German empire would be embarrassed to call out Prussian troops against crowds of women wielding umbrellas. Bismarck eventually decided that the battle against the Catholic Church was hurting rather than helping German unity and ended it. But even after the *Kulturkampf*, German Catholic men were content to let women attend the church, while they, like Spanish men, attended the tavern. It was proper for women to be pious, but men were anticlerical; working-class men especially felt they had been betrayed by priests who in response to men's complaints about economic oppression "counseled only prayer, forbearance, and obedience."[67]

Rejection of the 1870 proclamation of papal infallibility led to the establishment of an Old Catholic church in Germany, which was largely a male movement, and the men in it feared the influence of the ultramontane clergy on wives, and through wives on husbands and families.[68] Catholicism

---

64 Margaret Lavinia Anderson, *Practicing Democracy: Elections and Political Culture in Imperial Germany* (Princeton: Princeton University Press, 2000), 101.
65 Gross, *"Kulturkampf* and *Geschlechterkampf,"* 29.
66 Manuel Borutta, "Antikatholizismus, Männlichkeit und Moderne: Die diskursive Feminisierung des Katholizismus in Deutschland und Italien (1850–1900)," Tagung AIM Gender, 5. http://www.ruendal.de/aim/pdfs/Borutta.pdf.
67 Gross, *War against Catholicism*, 221.
68 Angela Berlis, "Celibate or Married Priests: Polemical Gender Discourse in Nineteenth-Century Catholicism," in *Gender and Christianity in Modern Eu-*

was a threat to the manhood of German men. The Liberal Johann Bluntschli in 1872 warned that the "rule of the priests always brings about the castration of the people," that submission to papal authority had historically had an emasculating effect, forcing the "peoples of Europe to sacrifice their manhood."[69] Catholicism was unmanly, according to the Liberals. They accused it of being "international, intolerant, illiberal, medieval, hierarchical," and worst of all, "effeminate."[70] It was suitable only for "weibische Völker," "feminine peoples," not for "the young, vital, masculine (*männlichen*) races." As did Michelet's, Germans' fears centered on the confessional, which reduced the nation to "feminine subservience." There was also a note of jealousy and rivalry; priests got too close to women. Jesuits were not like other men; they were too masculine and commanding in relation to their flock, both males (who should exercise virile independence) and females (who should obey their husbands, not other men) and were also too feminine in relation to their superiors to whom they owed *Kadavergehorsam*, the obedience of a slave.[71]

German anticlericals in the latter part of the nineteenth century continued their attacks, focusing on sexual morality. An 1896 book, *Die Gräuel der Jesuiten*, republished information about pedophilia among the Bavarian Jesuits, information that had become available after the suppression of the Jesuits in 1773. Thirty Jesuits had engaged in "unnatural behavior," the most notorious being Jacob Marell, who committed his crimes in Augsburg at the end of the seventeenth century.[72] Graf Paul von Hoensbroech (1852–1923), who had been a Jesuit, pointed out that within a few decades of the founding of the Jesuits abuses were occurring, and he reported that the Director of the State Archives in Bavaria claimed that there were "hundreds and hundreds" of cases of sexual abuse from the one province of Upper Germany alone.[73]

rope: Beyond the Feminization Thesis, eds. Patrick Pasture and Jan Art (Louvain: Leuven University Press, 2012), 62.

69 Gross, *War against Catholicism*, 207.

70 Beth A. Griech-Polelle, *Bishop von Galen: German Catholicism and National Socialism* (New Haven: Yale University Press, 2002), 27.

71 See Healy, "Anti-Jesuitism in Imperial Germany," 153–81.

72 Healy, *Jesuit Specter*, 169.

73 Paul von Hoehnsbroech, *Fourteen Years a Jesuit*, Vol. 2, trans. Alice Zimmern (New York: Cassell, 1911), 69.

The charges that anticlericals made were the same ones made in France: priests attacked the natural order of the household by subverting the authority of the husband over his wife and children, confessors asked obscene questions and seduced their penitents.[74]

During and after the *Kulturkampf* the Catholic Church was attacked as feminized and perverse. This accusation of effeminacy stung Catholic men, and a reform group in Munich, the *Krausgesellschaft* (named after the liberal-nationalist priest Franz Xaver Kraus), arose which tried to show that masculinity and Catholicism were compatible. Josef Müller, influenced by the modernist theologian Ignaz von Döllinger, sought a non-ultramontane, nationalistic Reform Catholicism. Periodicals such as *Hochland* and *Renaissance* propagated the movement; Herman Schell, author of *Catholicism as the Principle of Progress*, was the intellectual patron. Schell argued for a "nationalistic, masculine-oriented Catholic identity."[75] The modernist priest Joseph Schnitzer, enemy of Rome and the Jesuits, was suspended from the priesthood after the 1907 issuance of the antimodernist encyclical *Pascendi*. His espousal of nationalist Catholicism was popular among university students. The Reform Catholics wanted to remain in the Catholic Church but also embraced the ideal of Positive Christianity, that is, interconfessional cooperation among German Christians, a cooperation based on their racial identity as Germans.

These German Catholics wanted to abolish clerical celibacy, because it kept young men with healthy drives out of the priesthood and let in perverse types, sexually abusive priests such as were exposed in a series of scandals around 1900—scandals which turned out to be baseless. Furthermore, celibacy kept these healthy young German men from reproducing; degenerate types, many of these Catholic reformers went on to say, were reproducing, and should be sterilized. German priests should produce German children because the Aryan race was the purest and most important race and the inferior types were polluting it.[76]

The second head of the Gestapo, Heinrich Himmler, was the son of Gebhard Himmler, tutor to the Wittelsbachs, the Bavarian royal family; Heinrich

74 Healy, *Jesuit Specter*, 162–71.
75 Derek Hastings, *Catholicism and the Roots of Nazism: Religious Identity and National Socialism* (New York: Oxford University Press, 2010), 27.
76 Ibid., 39–42.

remained a devout Catholic until the 1920s. Historians have been puzzled why Nazism arose in Munich; later in the 1930s the conflict between Nazism and the Catholic Church was bitter, but at the beginning Catholic reformers in Munich were espousing nationalist and racial theories and were attacking the sexual deviations of a supposedly celibate clergy. Himmler in 1937 characterized the Catholic priesthood as a "homosexual erotic men's league."[77] The Nazis continued the Liberal criticism of Christianity.[78] The Evangelical Martin Doerne in 1941 wrote that "also in our days the rumor has been spread around, that Jesus Christ has nothing to say and nothing to offer to men and to a manly [i.e., National Socialist] nation."[79] For the Nazis, orthodox Christianity was unfit for men and was, in fact, perverse.

Hitler had been raised a Catholic and attended a Benedictine school. His personal library had about 400 books on the Church, most of which were pornography, "portraying alleged license in the priesthood."[80] According to Hermann von Rauschning, Hitler said he would not make martyrs of the clergy, but that "we shall brand them as ordinary criminals" who have "committed incest."[81] In that way he planned to destroy the Church.

The Nazis were given an unexpected opportunity. Headquartered in Waldbreitbach in the diocese of Trier was a group of lay brothers who called themselves Franciscans, but who had no formal association with the

77 Quoted in Eichard Steigman-Gall, *The Holy Reich: Nazi Conceptions of Christianity, 1919–1945* (Cambridge: Cambridge University Press, 2003), 130.

78 Steigman-Gall claims that "not only did racialist antisemitism find a warmer reception among liberal Protestants than among confessional Lutherans, in many ways racialist antisemitism was born of the theological crisis that liberal Protestantism represented" (*The Holy Reich*, 263). Like Protestant Liberals, Nazis found Catholicism suspiciously unmasculine. Liberals opened the way for the transposition of Christian categories into a nationalist and later racialist context (see Claus Ekkehard Barsch, *Erlösung und Vernichtung: Dr. Phil. Joseph Goebbels* [Munich: Boer, 1987], esp. 306–32).

79 Martin Doerne, *Der Mann vor Gott: Zur Grundlegung kirchlicher Männerarbeit* (Dresden: C. Ludwig Ungelenk, [1941], 20).

80 Timothy J. Ryback, *Hitler's Private Library: The Books That Shaped His Life* (New York: Alfred A. Knopf, 2008), 236.

81 Hermann Rauschning, *Hitler Speaks: A Series of Political Conversations with Adolf Hitler on His Real Aims* (London: Thornton Butterworth, 1939. Reprint, Whitefish, MT: Kessinger, 2006), 60.

Franciscan order, apart from a priest who was their chaplain. These brothers cared for mentally-deficient and mentally-ill people in thirty houses. This was very difficult work, and the brothers were given no training in handling the sexual drives of the patients.[82] In the inflation and unemployment after the First World War many candidates entered this congregation at the age of nineteen or twenty in order to escape total destitution. As the church investigation later discovered, "in blatant contradiction to the rules visits to cells, use of alcohol, disobedience, and even bawdy talk were the order of the day."[83] In a pattern that foreshadowed the catastrophic mismanagement of sexual abuse in the Catholic Church in the latter half of the twentieth century, the church investigation also found that "instead of punishing the guilty person, he was simply transferred to another house ... Yes, it was often held against a brother when he complained about such things."[84] The bishop of Trier investigated and recommended that the congregation be suppressed because of the *scelera*, the crimes that had been committed; Rome agreed and in mid-1937 suppressed the congregation.[85]

But in the meantime the sexual abuse of patients and the homosexual relationships of the brothers had come to the attention of the police. The trials, following Hitler's orders, were held according to legal standards[86] because he wanted them to be convincing; consequently, many of the accused were acquitted. In the first trial, a Franciscan, Pater Leovigill, OFM, who was the confessor at the Waldbreitbach motherhouse and who had used his position to seduce brothers and novices,[87] admitted his guilt and was convicted; he had been previously accused in 1929 but the charges were suppressed under the Weimar Republic.[88]

Scores of brothers were tried and the cases, with all the salacious details, were published in the Nazi newspapers, which enjoyed the unaccustomed

---

82 Hans Günther Hockerts, *Die Sittlichkeitsprozesse gegen katholische Ordensangehörige und Priester 1936/1937* (Mainz: Matthias-Grünewald-Verlag, 1971), 51.

83 Ibid., 51.

84 Ibid., 51.

85 Ibid., 53.

86 Ibid., 217.

87 Ibid., 51.

88 Otto D. Tolischus, "Reich Puts 276 Monks on Trial, Accusing Them of Immorality," *New York Times*, May 27, 1936.

pleasure of expressing moral shock about the sexual activity of Catholic clergy. The *Freiburger Zeitung* denounced the abuse:

> A sequence of horrors .... Monks trespass against cripples .... The lunatic asylum as a place of refuge .... With dragging steps and trembling limbs, physically deformed, these poor victims stood stuttering and weeping before the judge in order to repeat, with horrible gestures, their despairing accusation against the bestial criminal .... All kinds of unnatural lechery .... Debauches of greatest magnitude .... Horrible homosexual crimes .... Thirteen poor crippled children subjected to abominable misdemeanors in the cell of a cloister .... The child raped, and a bunch of roses given to the mother! ... Disgusting shamelessness of a criminal in a priest's cassock ....[89]

The *Nationalzeitung* of Essen claimed that "many cloisters have become hotbeds of homosexuality and that Catholic educational institutions which the pope's encyclical defended have become in reality breeding places of this most horrible vice."[90] The *Völkische Beobachter* said that Germany "cannot tolerate its life and that of its children being poisoned by the activities of a clique which threatens systematically to practice sexual crimes. The Catholic Church has never attempted to put an end to sexual scandals."[91]

The Nazis claimed "that some supposedly erring priests are shown by testimony to have committed new offenses after disciplinary transfers to new parishes."[92] The bishops were accused of concealing these crimes. One Nazi official stated: "This evil cannot be dealt with by concealing it under a cloak of silence or of Christian charity—and in this connection I am unfortunately obliged to point out that ecclesiastical authorities have knowingly laid themselves open to blame by neglecting their office of

89   Edith Roper and Clara Leiser, *Skeleton of Justice* (New York: E. Dutton, 1941), 111.

90   "Berlin Priest Gets Jail Term," *Chester Times* (Chester, PA), April 29, 1937.

91   "Nazi Papers in Drive against Catholic Clergy," *Monessen Daily Independent* (Monessen, PA), April 29, 1937.

92   "Nazi Police Close Catholic Seminary in Morality Drive," AP, *Baltimore Sun*, May 16, 1937.

supervision, and have countenanced a conspiracy of silence. There is no other way of explaining the extent to which this evil has developed."[93] Joseph Goebbels in a speech in the Deutschlandhalle claimed that "in every case the Church has sought to protect the accused, obscure their offenses and either transfer them to some other monastery or smuggle them abroad in order that they might escape the arm of the law."[94] Later behavior of the Catholic hierarchy in the United States lends credence to this accusation.

The moral failings of the abusers and the administrative failings of the bishops allowed the Nazis to take the high moral ground. The *Volkische Beobachter* in 1937 opined: "In the solid mass of so-called 'regrettable individual lapses,' in the over-tolerant attitude of clerical superiors, and in the lying propaganda of this international body under the guidance of Roman or Vatican laws, we perceive symptoms of a disease leading to the complete internal decay of an institution which, up to now, has not achieved its aims among us and never shall."[95] The *Durchbruch* said all Christians shared the guilt of the abusers: "All who today bear the name of Christian share responsibility for all those ecclesiastical sins of past days whose expiation the Lord of righteousness is now completing."[96] According to the State's Attorney, the Church expected natural men to live like angels, but they couldn't, and therefore fell below common decency: "We must not blame the agents of these deeds so much as the system. It is a system which has brought untold misery on mankind .... Perhaps saints can manage to live according to the rules of these Orders; certainly ordinary, natural man will only achieve a sham sanctity."[97] These were staple accusations by critics of Roman Catholicism in general and of celibacy in particular. These themes were at hand and the Nazis picked them up.

---

93 [Walther Mariaux], *The Persecution of the Church in the Third Reich* (1940. [Gretna, LA: Pelican Publishing Company, 2003], 318). The Jesuit Mariaux, himself a German, studied the documents and published this book in English and Spanish in 1940 under the pseudonym *Testis Fidelis*. See Massimo Introvigne, "Goebbels e l'operazione pedofili," *Avvenire*, April 16, 2010.

94 "Goebbels Lashes Catholic Church on Morals Issue," *New York Times*, May 29, 1937.

95 [Mariaux], *Persecution*, 321.

96 Ibid., 321.

97 Ibid., 321.

The Nazis also revived the Liberal attack on confession as dangerous to women. A 1936 cartoon in *Der Sturmer* shows a young German woman in a confessional and a greedy priest staring at her as she says, "But Father, I don't even know the meaning of the sins you are asking me about."[98] Such anticlerical themes could expect to find a resonance in the German public which had heard similar criticisms of the Church for a century or longer.

The Nazi propaganda machine exaggerated the number of abusers. The German bishops pointed out that of the 25,634 priests in Germany, 58 were charged, or one out of 500 priests, or about .2% of priests.[99] As of November 1937, German prosecutors had obtained the convictions of 45 priests, 176 brothers and nuns, and 21 employees, for a total of 242 convictions—somewhat less than the 7,000 figure that the Nazi press had told the public.[100] At this point the trials were stopped because they were backfiring and were in fact solidifying Catholic lay support for their bishops and priests.[101]

As far as I have been able to discover, these were the last public accusations of sexual abuse by clerics in German-speaking countries until 1995, when Cardinal Hans Groër of Vienna was accused. Beginning in 2010 a massive number of accusations of immorality were made against German priests and monks; either the behavior of the clergy had deteriorated since the 1930s, or the Nazis had not succeeded in uncovering widespread corruption, as hard as they had tried.

Many Protestants, concerned about the lack of masculinity in the Church, went along with the Nazi critique of supposedly effeminate Christianity and formed the *Glaubensbewegung Deutsche Christen*.[102] The movement, which was deliberately given a confusing name, had a half-million members and occupied influential positions in the Evangelical Church. In the Church elections of 1933, two-thirds of the votes went to the German Christians. They began to reconstruct the Church on national, racial lines,

---

98 Ibid., 443.
99 Ibid., 306.
100 Ibid., 305.
101 Hockerts, *Die Sittlichkeitsprozesse*, 214.
102 For the history of this movement, see Kurt Meier, *Die Deutschen Christen* (Göttingen: Vandenhoeck & Ruprecht, 1964) and Michael Burleigh, *Sacred Causes: The Clash of Religion and Politics from the Great War to the War on Terror* (New York: HarperCollins, 2007), 201–12.

removing as far as possible the racially impure (i.e., Jews) to build a new church based on blood, not belief. Influenced by liberal theology, they saw revelation as not confined to the Bible but continuing in history, specifically in the history of Germany.[103] They sought, like the missionaries in foreign lands, to acculturate Christianity to the new National Socialist Germany. The rituals of the Church celebrated the German racial community.

The new German Church would be a manly Church. A German Christian flyer proclaimed: "We want a kind of Christianity with which one can do something in life, a Christianity of which our youth will say: that it is alive, there is heroism there. That it is not 'only' for old women, but for the life-affirming men of the Third Reich."[104] The Church was to be no longer feminine and weak but *männlich* and *mannhaft*, manly, virile, strong, vigorous, brave, resolute. To be manly was to be a soldier, "to fight ruthlessly, to exhibit hardness and heroism, to follow orders with discipline and enthusiasm."[105] A pastor proclaimed that he wanted "a church of men, not a church of women of both sexes."[106] The German Christians proclaimed themselves as "the storm troopers of the church."[107] A German Christian leader explained that Christianity was not "something for the weak," but was "aggressive" and "appropriate for men."[108] Even a German Christian woman said that women did not want "a soft Christianity of feelings."[109]

Opponents of the German Christians acknowledged that men were absent from the Church; the Confessing Church, *die Bekennende Kirche*, was almost entirely a feminine movement, which was led by a few active men. The lack of men forced the ordination of women: "Because of the high

---

103 For the role of liberal theology in opening the way to radical redefinitions of Christianity, see Kala Poewe, *New Religions and the Nazis* (New York: Routledge, 2006), 21–22, 178 (note 16). Both Roman Catholic authoritarianism and the Protestant orthodoxy of Barth were seen as obstacles to the new German faith.

104 Quoted in Doris L. Bergen, *Twisted Cross: The German Christian Movement in the Third Reich* (Chapel Hill: University of North Carolina Press, 1996), 61.

105 Bergen, *Twisted Cross*, 63.

106 Ibid., 63.

107 Ibid., 65.

108 Ibid., 66.

109 Bergen, *Twisted Cross*, 68.

preponderance of women, the Confessing Church decided to ordain women theologians [technically a consecration rather than an ordination][110] and to give them the spiritual direction of parishes."[111] Women were at the forefront of Christian resistance to Nazism, because a "malaise" afflicted men and dampened their commitment to Christianity.[112]

But men were also absent from German Christian services, which had two-to-one or three-to-one ratios of women to men, and even from neo-pagan services, which seem to have been dominated by women. The German Christians tried to masculinize worship by hymns with martial rhythms and words about dying for the Fatherland. The Nazis increasingly kept their distance from all forms of Christianity, even from the fawning attentions of the German Christians. After 1945 the German Christians blended back into the Evangelical Church, which continues to have a deficit of men. As one German Christian later lamented, "this group [men] is innerly cold toward the church and for the most part toward Christianity as well."[113]

Spain

Spanish anticlericalism has a long history. *Lazarillo de Tormes*, the anonymous sixteenth-century picaresque Spanish novel, has caustic remarks about priests, and Cervantes in *Don Quixote* casts a suspicious eye at the hermit and his "housekeeper." Aubert maintains that since the Middle Ages "masculine aggression [has been] directed at priests, who are accused of being lazy because they are not manual workers, of being perverse because in confession they receive very intimate confidences and because they are permanent witnesses of human weaknesses; of being intruders because they mix themselves into the intimacy of the couple and exercise moral pressure on their sexual behavior. This explains the distrust of the woman, who is

---

110 See Victoria Barnett, *For the Soul of the People: Protestant Protest against Hitler* (New York: Oxford University Press, 1992), 168.

111 Hans-Ulrich Wehler, *Deutsche Gesellschaftsgeschichte 1914–1949* (Munich: Verlag C. H. Beck, 2003), 805.

112 Michael Phayer, *Protestant and Catholic Women in Nazi Germany* (Detroit, MI: Wayne State University Press, 1990), 238.

113 Bergen, *Twisted Cross*, 218.

considered weak and impressionable and suspected of being, in the household, a factor in clericalism and intolerance."[114]

To these attitudes was added a modern dislike of the Church both because it was superstitious and because it upheld the oppressive ancient regime. The Church was therefore doubly an obstacle to rationality and progress. Both bourgeois men and working-class men disliked the clergy.[115] As in France, in Spain when boys grew up and disidentified from the feminine world of their mothers, they also rejected the religion that the mother professed. In the lives of nineteenth- and twentieth-century anticlericals, a common pattern emerged: "The male child typically started his life under the influence of his mother, aunts, and female caretakers in general, absorbing their 'fussy, sentimental, almost superstitious beliefs.' Many boys were allowed and even encouraged to dress up as priests and pretend to say mass. But with the onset of puberty and peer-bonding with male cousins or friends, the erstwhile little angel learned to mock feminine piety, and indeed to reject anything that might seem 'sissy.'"[116] The world of men, especially working-class men, was a world without religion. For a man to be outstandingly religious was considered shameful. A man is humiliated, *pasar vergüenza*, if he is in debt, or "if he is seen in church holding a rosary, or sitting in the front benches in church."[117] Devout Spanish men wear the hood in penitential procession lest they be seen as demonstrating their piety too publicly.[118]

The Spanish wife is not the head of the family, but in Spain she "assumes control of all affairs pertaining to the spiritual well-being of the household: the masses for the dead, the children's prayers, the husband's annual communion, and the negotiations with the important divine

---

114 Aubert, "Luchar contra los poderes fácticos," 227.

115 See David D. Gilmore, *The People of the Plain: Class and Community in Lower Andalusia* (New York: Columbia University Press, 1980), 150.

116 Timothy Mitchell, *Betrayal*, 43. See also Julio Caro Baroja, *Introdución a una historia contemporánea del anticlericalismo español* (Madrid: Colección Fundamentos, 1960), 120–21.

117 Carmen Lisón-Tolosana, *Belmonte de los Caballeros: A Sociological Study of a Spanish Town* (Oxford: Clarendon Press, 1966), 338.

118 Timothy Mitchell, *Passional Culture: Emotion, Religion, and Society on Southern Spain* (Philadelphia: University of Pennsylvania Press, 1990), 103–04.

figures."[119] She is the matriarch, at least in all spiritual matters: "The woman is expected to be more religious than the man and to fulfill her religious duties more punctiliously. The wife/mother has to elicit blessings for her children and husband by her prayers. She puts pictures and images of her favorite saints in places of honor, and at times she may force the husband not to overlook his religious obligations. If a child is ill she, never the father, will light small lamps or candles before the image of the Virgin or will recite the Rosary or commission a holy hour."[120] Male attitudes to the religiosity of their women varied. Some saw such piety as a guarantee of feminine chastity. In 1890 Emilia Pardo Bazán pointed out that Spanish men, even if they were "deists, atheists, skeptics and rationalists" wanted "their daughters, sisters, spouses, and mothers" to be nothing else than "pure Catholics."[121] But they did not want their womenfolk to be *beatas*—fanatics—who were caricatured in anticlerical periodicals and novels. A woman was devout not because she freely chose to be so—a woman's "intellectual and spiritual autonomy" was not recognized by anticlericals—but because of "the dominion which a priest exercised over her."[122] Many men deeply resented this supposed dominion.

The first outbreak of murderous anticlericalism occurred in the 1830s. The Jesuits were regarded as supernaturally powerful and cunning, and therefore everything that went wrong was their fault, since they controlled everything. When cholera broke out in Madrid, the proletariat blamed the Jesuits for poisoning the water supply.[123] The mob gathered in the Puerta del Sol and shouted, "veneno, veneno, mueran los jesuitas, mueran los frailes"—*poison, poison, kill the Jesuits, kill the religious*—and murdered eighty priests and brothers.[124] The Grand Master of Spanish Freemasonry called

---

119 William A. Christian, Jr., *Person and God in a Spanish Valley* (Princeton: Princeton University Press, 1989), 135.
120 Lisón-Tolosana, *Belmonte de los Caballeros*, 309.
121 Emilia Pardo Bazán, "La mujer española," *La España Moderna* 17 (May 1890): 110.
122 María Pilar Salomón Chéliz, "Devotas mojigatas, fanáticas y libidinosas: Anticlericalismo y antifeminismo en el discurso republicano a fines del siglo XIX," in Aguado and López, *Feminismos y antifeminismos*, 96.
123 Mitchell, *Betrayal*, 35.
124 Teófanes Egidio, Javier Burrieza, and Manuel Revuelta, *Los Jesuitas en España u en el mundo hispánico*, Vol. 1 (Madrid: Marcial Pons, 2004), 300.

the slaughter of the clergy a "castigo merecido"[125]—a punishment they deserved.

Spanish folklore had numerous proverbs and stories that mocked sexual predation by priests[126] and prepared the Spanish for more modern anticlerical propaganda. French anticlerical literature, especially Michelet's *Le prêtre, la femme, et la famille*, directly influenced Spanish anticlericals. An anticlerical woman in 1910 denounced "the Church, which with its unmarried priests brings unrest to families and societies, the Church, which places celibates in the confessional [and] introduces spurious ideas into the family."[127] Confession to priests by women was especially dangerous. The Spanish popular press in the first part of the twentieth century disseminated tales of clerical sexual malfeasance. The priest was both a threat to the family and an agent of reaction. Anticlericals feared "that Catholic women colluded with priests in order to turn Spanish children against Liberalism, and specifically, Republicanism."[128] Gil Blas de Santillán (the pseudonym of the Freemason and ex-priest Segismundo Pey de Ordeix) in 1910 warned that women penitents "are the soul of clericalism, the life of the priest, the strength of the Church, the secret behind all its influence, its prosperity, and the power of the Jesuits."[129] Convents accepted young women over the objections of their parents—and their suitors. The 1901 play, *Electra*, by Benito Pérez Galdós, is about the struggle of a young man, Maximo, to fight off a sinister priest who tries to put Maximo's beloved into a convent. The play helped to precipitate violence and martial law.[130] Maximo proclaims about the Church: "Let us meet the enemy with a bold face. Let us destroy him, if we can or let ourselves be destroyed by him ... but all at once, in a single onslaught, at one stroke ... Either him or us .... Set

---

125 Egidio, Burrieza, and Revuelta, *Los Jesuitas*, 302.
126 Mitchell, *Betrayal*, 10–11.
127 Miryam, "Anticlerical Women: What We Want," in *Modern Spain: A Documentary History*, ed. Jon Cowans (Philadelphia: University of Pennsylvania Press, 2003), 109.
128 Enrique A. Sanabria, *Republicanism and Anticlerical Nationalism in Spain* (New York: Palgrave Macmillan, 2009), 124.
129 Quoted in Sanabria, *Republicanism*, 131.
130 Mitchell, *Betrayal*, 58.

fire to the house, set fire to Madrid."[131] Fire was the favorite tool of anticlerical violence.

José Nakens and other anticlericals detected a strong erotic element in many Catholic devotions. Nakens felt that men could not compete with the emotions aroused by devotion to the Sacred Heart of Jesus; women "shuddered in orgasmic delight simply by contemplating and empathizing with the pain and suffering of the image of Christ ... and by anticipating a union with him in heaven."[132] Anticlericals thought this unfair competition: bliss should be experienced in the marriage bed, not in an imaginary heaven. As in Michelet's complaints, there is an unmistakable note of jealousy in the Spanish anticlericals' attitude toward the Church.

José Álvarez Junco explains the "envidia," envy, that the anticlericals felt toward "el gran macho dominador de la colectividad feminina," the "great male dominator of the feminine community," that is, the priest: "Let us reconstruct the picture: It is a matter of a patriarchal and discriminatory society, in which the clergy has at its disposal various means of access to the women, means unavailable to the normal man; the priest talks to the women alone and about intimate matters, he seduces them with his speech from the pulpit, he influences their conduct in themes so delicate for other men such as the conjugal life."[133] Whatever their personal success with women, Liberals had less access to the female public and failed to attract women to their ideas, and they blamed the clergy for this failure.

The Spanish had a suspicion that clerical celibates were not in fact sexually continent. Such suspicions were fed by purported exposés such as the 1896 book by a defrocked priest:

> *THE SECRETS OF CONFESSION. Revelations, mysteries, crimes and monstrosities; sacrileges, aberrations and absurdities; misery, social, and religious problems, and human extravagances; immoralities of conservative and ultramontane morality, and other excesses or sins*

---

131 Benito Peréz Galdós, *Electra* Act V, Scene v. Project Gutenberg, ebook 28002.
132 Sanabria, *Republicanism*, 140.
133 José Álvarez Junco, *Alejandro Lerroux: El emperador del paralelo* (Madrid: Editorial Síntesis, 2005), 344.

heard from penitents during long experience in the confessional by Constancio Miralta, presbyter.[134]

The author, whose real name was José Ferrándiz Ruiz, churned out a series of pornographic books on Catholic life. *El Motín*, an anticlerical journal, blamed extortion and sexual abuse by priests for turning the natives of the Philippines against the Spanish.[135]

Even more disliked than the corruption of women was the corruption of male youth by priests. In the nineteenth century the clergy were accused of poisoning wells; in the twentieth century they were accused of being "poisoners of youth, promoters of an insane hypocrisy in sexual matters and in frequent cases practitioners of vice in consequence of a forced celibacy contrary to nature."[136] Celibacy caused and cloaked "an environment saturated by satyriasis, homosexuality, nymphomania, sadomasochism, pederasty, whoremongering."[137] The clerical sexual attack on heterosexual masculinity was felt to be but one front of a broader attack on the masculinity of the laity.

Anticlerical rhetoric became more heated. The criticism in the anticlerical press was not directed against the power and wealth of the Church (it had largely lost both by the end of the nineteenth century) but against the sexual behavior of the clergy. Celibacy was unnatural, the anticlericals maintained—it was a form of repression, a "negation of life" that led to perversion. The clergy was called a monster, an "unclean baboon," "repugnant toads," "an octopus" with "tentacles"[138]—all images that were used in anticlerical cartoons.[139] The clergy were dehumanized and became scapegoats

---

134 Quoted in Mitchell, *Betrayal*, 39.

135 Sanabria, *Republicanism*, 136.

136 Francisco Vázquez García and Andrés Moreno Mengíbar, *Sexo y razón: Una genealogía de la moral sexual en España (siglos XVI–XX)* (Madrid: Akal, 1997), 257–58.

137 Manuel Delgado Ruiz, *La ira sagrada: Anticlericalismo, iconoclastia y antirritualismo en la España contemporánea* (Barcelona: Editorial Humanidades, 1992), 62.

138 Junco, *Alejandro Lerroux*, 345.

139 See Michel Dixmier, Jacqueline Lalouette, and Didier Pasamonik, *La République et L'Église: Image d'une Querelle* (Paris: Éditions de la Martinière, 2005).

for all Spain's failures; the clergy became "a symbol of everything hateful that existed in the world"[140] and, as a poet in 1904 proclaimed, exterminating them would be "a panacea for our ills."[141]

Clericalism tried to annihilate "virile souls," and therefore burning religious houses would be proper activity for "times of virility."[142] The monster must be destroyed with fire. Much of this was simply rhetoric designed to stir up anticlerical voters, but it did much more than that. Alejandro Lerroux in 1906 called upon the *jóvenes barbaros*, the young savages of Spain to "sack the decadent and miserable civilization of this luckless land, destroy its temples, finish off its gods, lift up the veil of the novices and elevate them to the category of mothers in order to make the race more virile. Don't stop at tombs or altars. There is nothing sacred in this world. The people are the slaves of the Church. The Church must be destroyed. Fight, kill, die!"[143] Such rhetoric ignited a conflagration of masculine *thumos* among the *jóvenes barbaros*. During the Tragic Week in Barcelona in 1909, rioters burnt eighty religious buildings. Mobs disinterred nuns from their graves in the cloister, and a workman "did an obscene dance as he carried a corpse."[144] This was but a hint of the barbarity to come.

The anticlericals continued and intensified their campaign against the Church. The anticlerical newspapers of Madrid had a daily circulation of one million and regularly featured vicious anticlerical cartoons. The newspaper *La Traca* in 1933 sponsored a competition to decide what to do with the clergy. The answers were ominous: "The majority of the responses—

In the cartoon by Alfred Le Petit in *Le Grelot*, May 6, 1883, 96, "The morals of the Jesuits," a policeman is conducting a young priest to prison for offenses against decency as an older priest points to heaven and comforts him, "Courage, my son. Up there, there are young boys, but no policemen."

140 Julio de la Cueva Merino, *Clericales y anticlericales: El conflicto entre confesionalidad y secularización en Cantabria (1875–1923)* (Santander: Universidad de Cantabria, 1994), 331.

141 Ibid., 332.

142 Junco, *Alejandro Lerroux*, 348.

143 Quoted in Manuel Revuelta González, *El anticlericalismo español en sus documentos* (Barcelona: Editorial Ariel, 1999), 123.

144 Joan Connelly Ullman, *The Tragic Week: A Study of Anticlericalism in Spain 1875–1912* (Cambridge, MA: Harvard University Press, 1968), 247.

of which 'geld them' was almost unanimous—were in this style: 'What you do with grapes: you hang the good ones, and you crush the bad ones underfoot until there's not a drop of blood left' and 'Put them on the power cables, douse them with gasoline, set them on fire and afterward make sausages out of them to feed the animals with.' Or 'Castrate them. Grind them. Boil them. Shred them. Throw them into a manure pit.'"[145] This was not simply venting, as the actions of these anticlericals soon demonstrated.

Anticlericals had an obsession with the sexuality of priests. In 1931 Ángel Samblancat, a deputy, a journalist, and the owner of a Barcelona condom store, said in the Cortes: "And finally we are supporters of humanizing the priest, marrying him off, so that he can know what is good (*laughs*), marrying off the priest, Señor Deputies, so that he can know what is purgatory (*laughs*); and we are supporters of humanizing the priest by making him a father in fact and not in name only, making him the father of living creatures, of living beings, and not of children unknown and unacknowledged (*laughs and shouts*)."[146] The clerical deputies walked out, and even the Republican politician Manuel Azaña said that Samblancat had said "mil atrocidades," a thousand atrocities.[147]

In 1936 an orgy of murder directed at the Catholic Church stained the Republican side at the beginning of the Civil War and propelled the Church into an alliance with Franco.[148] A third of the churches of Madrid were burned in three days. The violence was almost all male-on-male. Republicans killed 283 nuns but 6,549 priests and male religious.[149] This represented one of every seven priests in Spain and one in four in the areas controlled by the Republicans.[150] There was an unmistakable note of sadism

145 Delgado Ruiz, *La ira sagrada*, 54–55.
146 Quoted in González, *El anticlericalismo español en sus documentos*, 136.
147 Manuel Azaña, *Diarios completos: monarquía, república, guerra civil* (Barcelona: Editorial Crítica, 2000), 309.
148 See Stanley G. Payne, *The Spanish Civil War* (Cambridge: Cambridge University Press, 2012), 111–18.
149 Mary Vincent, "'The Keys of the Kingdom': Religious Violence in the Spanish Civil War, July–August 1936," in *The Splintering of Spain: Cultural History and the Spanish Civil War, 1936–1939*, ed. Chris Ealham and Michael Richards (Cambridge: Cambridge University Press, 2005), 86.
150 Stanley G. Payne, *Spanish Catholicism: An Historical Overview* (Madison: University of Wisconsin Press, 1984), 169.

in the Republican atrocities. Priests were not simply killed—they were "hanged, drowned, suffocated, burned to death, or buried alive"; they were tortured to death, with "a morbid fixation on genitalia."[151]

> The corpses of priests found without eyes, tongues, or testicles. In several cases, the body had been castrated, either pre- or post-mortem, and the genitals stuffed into the victim's mouth .... The 'morbid fixation with genitals' was ... the product of machismo, which was in turn reflected in the anticlerical obsession with the sexuality of the cloister.[152]

> In 1936, the use of sexual temptation in the torture and humiliation of priests was widespread. Half-naked women were brought to tantalize and mock a 27-year-old curate from Banyeres; a prostitute named "Nona" was brought into the gaol to tempt and to mortify the deacon of Junquera; another priest in his twenties, in Barcelona, punched the face of a woman promising him marriage and freedom. Marriage in these cases was clearly a euphemism for sex .... In this horrible search for tumescence and ejaculation which would have "proved" his masculinity, the brother's own words are telling: "I am as much a man as you. But I am a religious."[153]

The mummified corpses of nuns and priests were displayed in obscene poses on the altars of ransacked churches. Militia did obscene things with

151 Julio de la Cueva, "Religious Persecution, Anticlerical Tradition and Revolution: On Atrocities against the Clergy during the Spanish Civil War," *Journal of Contemporary History* 33, no. 3 (1998): 356. Maria Thomas recounts some of this "gruesome sexual torture" (*The Faith and the Fury: Popular Anticlerical Violence and Iconoclasm in Spain, 1931–1936* [Portland, OR: Sussex Academic Press, 2013], 102).
152 Vincent, "'The Keys of the Kingdom,'" 78. See incidents in Antonio Moreno, *Historia de la persecución religiosa en España* (Madrid: Biblioteca de Autores Cristianos, 1961), 611–13; see also Gwynne Lewis, "Political Brigandage and Popular Disaffection in the South-east of France, 1795–1804," in *Beyond the Terror: Essays in French Regional and Social History, 1789–1815*, eds. Gwynne Lewis and Colin Lucas (Cambridge: Cambridge University Press, 1983), 218.
153 Vincent, "'The Keys of the Kingdom,'" 88.

statues of the Virgin. The anticlerical propaganda that had circulated in Spain found its ultimate expression in this revolutionary violence. A "vulgar, masculine, working-class power ... targeted its seeming antithesis, the priest."[154] Marxism and materialism were expressed not just in a disdain for religion, but in an active and destructive hatred of anything and anyone that purported to represent a non-material reality, whether it was a church building or a celibate priest.

Everything connected with Catholicism had to be destroyed, preferably with fire.[155] Anticlericals, almost all young men, burned churches and searched homes for religious images and piled everything in heaps which they set ablaze. The anarchists boasted that "we have lit our torches and applied the purifying fire to all the churches."[156] In Andalusia the "young men" organized church burnings to "ignite" the masses.[157] In Aravena the men stripped the church, gathered all the crucifixes, paintings, statues, chalices, and images into a huge pile and "set [it] ablaze" and dynamited the church, totally gutting it.[158] They detained their Catholic enemies and "wanted to burn them alive with no trial."[159]

These were not simply political murders. Something far deeper and more elemental was at work.[160] Poor men in Spain felt that their masculinity was doubly dishonored. They could not be providers for their families: they were landless and dependent on Catholic landowners. The landowners thought they were good Christians because they gave charity to the poor; but what the poor, especially the men among them, wanted was respect.

154 Ealham and Richards, *Splintering of Spain*, 89.
155 Maria Thomas notes the "cathartic purpose" of destruction by fire: "Its capacity to destroy utterly the religious icons offered symbolic proof that the pernicious influence of the Church was being expunged from the landscape forever" (*The Faith and the Fury*, 134).
156 *Solidaridad Obrera*, August 20, 1936, quoted by Julio de la Cueva, "Religious Persecution," 367.
157 Richard Maddox, *El Castillo: The Politics of Tradition in an Andalusian Town* (Urbana: University of Illinois Press, 1993), 157.
158 Ibid., 155.
159 Ibid., 154.
160 See David D. Gilmore, "The Anticlericalism of the Andalusian Rural Proletarians," in Álvarez Santaló, Buxó y Rey, and Rodríguez Becerra, *La religiosidad popular*, Vol. 1, 478–98.

The men saw that the Church, the priests, could attract women and would interfere in male sexual pleasures, even in marriage. The revolutionaries were not ideologists, but wanted recognition, independence, and respect, so that they could be respected by others as men and respect themselves as men.[161] They rejected priests and looked down upon the weakness of women who submitted to priests, reaffirming "the secular, agonistic ethos of honor at the core of traditional representations of masculine identity."[162] Catholicism attacked men's honor *precisely as men* and therefore had to be destroyed.

Timothy Mitchell[163] and Pierre Conard[164] think that sexual repression by the Spanish church created rage which eventually burst forth in the horrors of the Civil War. Young men have to disidentify from their mothers to establish their masculinity. In European society (which lacks authoritative initiation rituals), masculinity is always precarious and must be carefully maintained. Young men express their masculinity in very disruptive ways, and women, the Church, and society at large are always trying to tame them. In Manuel Delgado Ruiz's analysis, these three forces which seek to tame masculinity are interchangeable in the masculine imagination, and the clergy bore the brunt of Spanish men's fear of being emasculated by women.[165] The Spanish man perceived the Church not simply as feminine, but as "feminizante," feminizing,[166] and therefore not simply an environment inappropriate to a man, but "openly dangerous for the integrity and prestige of his masculinity."[167] Masculinity and its sexual expression had become so important, even so sacred, to the anticlerical men of Spain that they sought to defile and destroy all that seemed to oppose it in any way, especially a depraved, hypocritical Church that destroyed families and practiced unnatural vices.

---

161 See Maddox, *El Castillo*, 155–64. See Brian D. Bunk, *Ghosts of Passion: Martyrdom, Gender, and the Origins of the Spanish Civil War* (Durham, NC: Duke University Press, 2007), 126.

162 Maddox, *El Castillo*, 161.

163 Mitchell, *Betrayal*, 106–10.

164 Pierre Conard, "Sexualité et anticléricalisme (Madrid 1910)," *Hispania* 31 (1971): 103–31.

165 Delgado, *Las palabras*, 302.

166 Ibid., 34.

167 Ibid., 23.

In 1940 the victorious Franco said that "Spain will be devoted to the Church by means of the woman,"[168] but he would have to rely only on the women. Even after his victory and the triumph of National Catholicism, when demonstrating that one was a Catholic might help keep a man out of jail (or from some worse fate), men stayed away from church. In the early 1940s "in some cities, only 3% of the adult male population regularly attended religious services."[169] Even as secularization has taken hold in Spain and church attendance has declined in all groups, the difference between men and women remains constant.[170]

In 1990 the Jesuit Ignacio Ellacuría and his companions were murdered by the Salvadoran military. A government official, Jesús María Rodés, the director of the school of the autonomous police of Catalonia and a member of a communist party, claimed that the Ellicuría was "not an innocent victim" because he belonged to "a religious organization of paramilitary character," that is, the Jesuits.[171] A Socialist politician wants members of Opus Dei banned from holding public office.[172] Pope Benedict XVI took note of these attitudes, and during his visit to Santiago de Compostela in November 2010 told the press that "there has been born in Spain a forceful and aggressive secularism such as existed in the 1930s."[173]

In recent decades aggressive secularism has mostly confined itself to legal and propaganda attacks on churches, especially conservative churches. The sexual irregularities and crimes of the clergy continue to provide ammunition for anticlericals. But not all men have abandoned the churches as inimical to their masculinity, and in the next two chapters I will consider the themes and movements that have kept some men attached to the churches.

---

168 Ibid., 47.
169 Wayne H. Bowen, *Spain during World War II* (Columbia: University of Missouri Press, 2006), 223.
170 Pablo Brañas-Garza, "Church Attendance in Spain (1930–1992): Gender Differences and Secularization," *Economics Bulletin* 26, no.1 (2004).
171 "Presión Justificada," *El País*, November 19, 1989.
172 José Ignacio Moreno Iturralde, "Gómez y la intolerancia," *ABC*, August 7, 2012.
173 Adrián Sack, "El Papa criticó el 'secularismo agresivo' que existe en España," *La Nación*, November 7, 2010.

Chapter Seven
Masculine Themes in Christianity

Basic themes in Christian life closely parallel themes in masculinity: initiation, conflict, rebirth, honor. For this reason, Christian life can be portrayed as a masculine way of life, as a fulfillment of masculinity, as "true" masculinity. Paul's remark about there being neither Jew nor Greek, male nor female in the new creation has been misunderstood: Christians were the true Israel, and all Christians, including women, were masculine. However, this masculinity was not a natural masculinity, but rather a participation in the masculinity of the Son. Movements in Christianity which incorporated masculine themes helped keep some men attached to the churches, despite the clergy's attempts to make men give up male pleasures and make men feminine.

Initiation

Boys have to die to their old nature, often through a violent initiation, and be reborn as men. Regeneration, the second birth, was also central to Christianity: in baptism a person dies with Christ and is born again as a new creature. In defending masculine initiation rites, David Thomas notes that "Christianity is based upon a story of sufferings, followed by resurrection, redemption, and ascent into a better life that is an uncanny parallel of the narrative enacted in almost all ritual initiations."[1] Like the crucifixion this rebirth is a struggle, an *agon*. The Western Church gave the name *sacramentum* to its liturgical actions.[2] The *sacramentum* was the oath sworn by

1   David Thomas, *Not Guilty: The Case in Defense of Men* (New York: William Murrow, 1993), 57.
2   *Sacramentum* may also refer to the oath of the gladiator. See Victor C. Pfitzner,

the soldier inducted into the army. He put aside all civilian concerns and henceforth devoted his life entirely to military affairs. Soldiers called civilians *pagani*, hicks, and Christians took over the term to describe those who had not enlisted in the army of Christ.[3] As Mathew Kuefler notes, this confirmed that Christians were masculine, "whose daily struggles against sin and temptation—against the unmanliness of vice within themselves—were identified as warfare against evil."[4]

The Christian is called to imitate Jesus, an imitation that implies the possibility of martyrdom. Tertullian compared martyrdom to a second baptism, a baptism of blood.[5] The martyr was a soldier, a "miles Christi."[6] Tertullian was the first to use this image extensively: "it is our battle to be summoned to your tribunals that there, under fear of execution, we may struggle for the truth. But the day is won when the object of the struggle is gained. This victory of ours gives us the glory of pleasing God."[7] In the paradoxical reversals of Christianity, "true manliness is found in apparent unmanliness"; the martyr, like Christ, gains the victory "in the very act of being defeated."[8]

The martyr was also an athlete. The Greek world was obsessed with sports and competition. Plato and later philosophers had little use for this attitude and tried to demonstrate that the philosopher was the "true athlete

"Was Paul a Sports Enthusiast? Realism and Rhetoric in Pauline Athletic Metaphors," in *Sports and Christianity: Historical and Contemporary Perspective*, eds. Nick J. Watson and Andrew Parker (New York: Routledge, 2013), 97.

3   Mathew Kuefler, "Soldiers of Christ: Christian Masculinity and Militarism in Late Antiquity," in *Men and Masculinities in Christianity and Judaism: A Critical Reader*, ed. Björn Krondorfer (London: SCM Press, 2009), 246–47.

4   Ibid., 239.

5   *Scorpiace* VI (*Ante-Nicene Fathers*, Vol. 3, *Latin Christianity* [Peabody, Massachusetts: Hendrickson Publishers, 1996], 639). Perhaps Tertullian alludes to Mithraism; see Mathew Kuefler, *The Manly Eunuch: Masculinity, Gender Ambiguity, and Christian Ideology in Late Antiquity* (Chicago: University of Chicago Press, 2001), 114.

6   Ibid., 112.

7   "Apologeticus," in *The Writings of Tertullian*, Vol. I, *Ante-Nicene Christian Library*, eds. Alexander Roberts and James Donaldson (Edinburgh: T & T Clark, 1969), 138. See also Kuefler, *Manly Eunuch*, 109–12.

8   Kuefler, *Manly Eunuch*, 115.

of god."[9] In the struggle for control of the passions the philosopher "becomes the victor in the true Agon of life with its task of gaining αρετε" (arete— fortitude or manliness).[10] The Jews did not have athletic competitions, but Philo followed the philosophers in describing holiness "as the contest for virtue in the struggle against the passions and vices"[11] and *Maccabees* characterizes the martyred Jews as athletes who were victorious in the contest.[12] Paul used athletic imagery extensively, and the narratives of the martyrs described them as the new athletes of God.

Like a Greek athlete, the Christian trained himself (*ascesis*) to win a contest. Like a Roman athlete, the Christian manifested courage. The Roman gladiatorial games set a model for citizens to emulate. Pliny the Younger explained that the games were "to inspire them [the Romans] to face honorable wounds and look scorn on death, by exhibiting love of glory and desire for victory even in the persons of criminals and slaves."[13] Romans deeply admired courage, and thought that if mere gladiators could show such courage, how much more should a Roman citizen show. A Roman was supposed to be a man and display manly qualities, especially the four cardinal virtues: prudence, justice, temperance or self-control, and fortitude or manliness (ἀηδρεία).[14]

L. Stephanie Cobb explains, "being a Christian required a person to act like one; being a Christian meant being a man."[15] The martyr is the new athlete, the new soldier. His (and her) passion is not passive, but active, a battle. The martyr displayed all the masculine virtues, especially self-control

---

9 See Victor C. Pfitzner, "We are the Champions! Origin and Development of the Image of God's Athletes," in *Sport and Spirituality*, eds. Gordon Preece and Robert Hess (Adelaide: ATF Press, 2006), 49–64; and Patrick Kelly, *Catholic Perspectives on Sports: From Medieval to Modern Times* (Manwah, NJ: Paulist Press, 2012), 99–106.

10 Victor C. Pfitzner, *Paul and the Agon Motif: Traditional Athletic Imagery in the Pauline Literature* (Leiden: E. J. Brill, 1967), 28.

11 Ibid., 39.

12 Ibid., 61–62.

13 Pliny the Younger, *Letters and Panegyricus*, trans. Betty Radice. Loeb Classical Library (Cambridge, MA: Harvard University Press, 1990), 393.

14 L. Stephanie Cobb, *Dying to Be Men: Gender and Language in Early Christian Texts* (New York: Columbia University Press, 2008), 61–62.

15 Cobb, *Dying to Be Men*, 124.

and fortitude. The Church felt, therefore, that martyrdom was, properly speaking, a masculine activity, even for women. While awaiting execution in the year 202, Perpetua had a dream in which an angel came to her and anointed her so that she became, mystically, a man, exclaiming, "facta sum masculus."[16] All Christians, including women, are called to be athletes of Christ, soldiers against Satan, and to act in a masculine fashion in the spiritual realm.[17] A Latin hymn praises a martyr: "poenas cucurrit fortiter / et sustulit viriliter"; or in the nineteenth-century translation, "For thee through many a woe he ran, / In many a fight he played the man."[18]

Monks and Ascetics

After the age of the martyrs, preachers stressed that anyone who battled sin was also a soldier of Christ.[19] Chastity and sexual renunciation, according to Jerome, make one a true soldier of Christ.[20] Origen developed the allegory of the warrior as a soldier of Christ.[21] His battle against his strong sexual desires doubly demonstrated a Christian's manliness.[22] The spiritual life was understood as a battle; even prayer and the liturgy were seen as a type of warfare.[23] The monks became

16 Edward C. Malone, *The Monk and the Martyr: The Monk as the Successor of the Martyr* (Washington, DC: Catholic University of America Press, 1950), 67.

17 See Kerstin Aspergren, *The Male Woman: A Feminine Ideal in the Early Church* (Stockholm, Almquist and Wiksell, 1990).

18 Quoted by Rachel Moriarty, "'Playing the Man'—the Courage of Christian Martyrs, Translated and Transposed," in *Gender and the Christian Religion: Papers Read at the 1996 Summer Meeting and the 1997 Winter Meeting of the Ecclesiastical History Society*, ed. R. N. Swanson (Woodbridge, England: Boydell Press, 1998), 10.

19 Kuefler, *Manly Eunuch*, 117–24.

20 Ibid., 174–75.

21 Katherine Allen Smith, *War and the Making of Medieval Monastic Culture* (Woodbridge, England: Boydell Press, 2011), 19.

22 Kuefler, *Manly Eunuch*, 281. See also Jacqueline Murray, "Masculinizing Religious Life; Sexual Prowess, the Battle for Chastity, and Masculine Identity," in *Holiness and Masculinity in the Middle Ages*, eds. H. Cullum and Katherine J. Lewis (Toronto: University of Toronto Press, 2004), 24–42.

23 Smith, *War*, 28–37.

the new athletes of Christ,[24] the soldiers of Christ,[25] the successors to the martyrs.[26] *The Teaching to Monks (Doctrina ad monachos)*, ascribed to Athanasius, even claims that the monk is more of a soldier than the martyr: "The martyrs were often consummated in a battle lasting for only a moment; but the monastic institute obtains a martyrdom by means of a daily struggle."[27] The Irish monks saw both the ascetic life and the life of the pilgrim as a form of martyrdom.[28] Anthony battled demons in the desert in a "contest,"[29] in "many wrestlings" against "destructive demons."[30] Benedict finds warfare a natural metaphor for monasticism and recurs to it frequently in his Rule. The battle is fought against the devil. As David Brakke explains "whether he was fighting demons or his own passions or both, the monk imagined himself as an *agōnistēs*, a 'fighter,' 'contender,' or 'combatant'—a masculine figure. He was a gladiator in the arena facing down demonic beasts or a soldier in the army of Christ arrayed against the demonic army of Satan."[31]

Later monks continued to think of themselves as soldiers. The *Anonymous Life of St. Cuthbert* refers to God's soldier, *militis*.[32] Bede speaks of Cuthbert as an athlete and of his life as a warfare.[33] Cuthbert seeks out

24　See Michael Novak, *The Joy of Sports: End Zones, Bases, Baskets, Balls, and the Consecration of the American Spirit*, rev. ed. (Lanham, MD: Madison Books, 1994), 29.

25　Smith, *War*, 89–96.

26　See Jean Leclercq, François Vandenbroucke and Louis Bouyer, *The Spirituality of the Middle Ages*, trans. by the Benedictines of Holmes Eden Abbey (London: Burns & Oates, 1968), 183.

27　Malone, *Monk and the Martyr*, 57.

28　See Bertram Colgrave, *Two Lives of Saint Cuthbert: A Life by an Anonymous Monk of Lindisfarne and Bede's Prose Life*, ed. and trans. by Bertram Colgrave (Cambridge: Cambridge University Press, 1985), 315.

29　Athanasius, *The Life of Antony and the Letter to Marcellus*, trans. Robert C. Gregg (New York: Paulist Press, 1980), 35.

30　Ibid., 69.

31　David Brakke, *Demons and the Making of the Monk: Spiritual Combat in Early Christianity* (Cambridge, MA: Harvard University Press, 2006), 182.

32　*Two Lives of Saint Cuthbert*, 98.

33　"Athleta, militiae celestis" (*Two Lives*, 180).

waste places as a scene of battle.[34] His withdrawal from ordinary life is not to seek peace but to engage in battle, the contest that is the way of life of a hermit.[35] Monks were, accruing to Edward Malone, "the champions of the Church who carry on the battle with evil spirits, and with the spirit of evil in the world. They are forever engaged in a wrestling match with their own passions; they are running a race for which they expect an incorruptible crown; the world is the arena in which they engage in a spirited contest with all that is opposed to the will of God."[36] The monastic life was an agonic life, one of conflict. The monk did not flee from human society to find safety in solitude, but like the hero went out into the wilderness to confront the forces of evil and fought them to rid himself and the world of all traces of evil. Emperor Henry in the eleventh century referred to monks as those *sub regula sancti Benedicti deo militantes*, fighting for God under the rule of St. Benedict.[37] According to David Brakke, "the monk chose to enlist at the front lines of the cosmic battle between good and evil."[38] The spiritual battle in which monks participated was not against flesh and blood but against demons. It was, Evagrius explained, "the battle that takes place in the intellect."[39]

The monk underwent an initiation to prepare him for the battle. The reception of the candidate was regarded as a mystery, a *mysterion*, closely parallel to the initiation of baptism.[40] The baptismal creed had a threefold affirmation of the Trinity and a corresponding threefold rejection of the world, the flesh, and the devil. Parallel to the baptismal liturgy, the monastic

---

34   "But when he had fought there in solitude for some time with the invisible enemy, by prayer and fasting, he sought a place of combat farther and more removed from mankind, aiming at greater things" (*Two Lives*, 214, 215).

35   "Heremeticae conversationis agonem" (*Two Lives*, 266).

36   Malone, *Monk and the Martyr*, 90.

37   Quoted in Scott Wells, "The Warrior Habitus: Militant Masculinity and Monasticism in the Henrician Reform Movement," in *Negotiating Clerical Identities: Priests, Monks and Masculinity in the Middle Ages*, ed. Jennifer D. Thibodeaux (New York: Palgrave Macmillan, 2010), 62.

38   Brakke, *Demons*, 241–42.

39   Ibid., 183.

40   See Leclercq, Vandenbroucke and Bouyer, *The Spirituality of the Middle Ages*, 18; see also Malone, *Monk and the Martyr*, 121.

profession according to the customs of St. Pachomius required a threefold "renunciation of the world, his parents, and himself."[41] This may be the root of the medieval definition of monasticism as the life of poverty, chastity, and obedience. The candidate received a new identity as part of his initiation and was given a new name and new clothes, the habit of the professed religious. Monastic profession is a rebirth[42] and like baptism and martyrdom causes the remission of sins.

This conflict requires *andreia*, manliness, even in women. Because this manliness was not physical, even women could attain it. Jerome wrote to Lucinius after he and his wife had taken a vow of celibacy: "You had a companion in the flesh, now in the spirit: from a wife to a sister, from a woman to a man (*de femina, virum*), from a subordinate to an equal."[43] Like the female martyrs who were virilized by their struggle, women who engaged in the intellectual combat became men. Amma Sarah said to two anchorites "by nature (*phusis*) I am a woman, but not by thought," and to other men she said "it is I who am a man, you who are women."[44] Bishop Gregory of Tours explained that God "gives us models not only men, but even the lesser sex, who fight not feebly, but manfully (*viriliter*); He brings unto His celestial kingdom, not only men who fight as they should, but also women, who with success exert themselves in the struggle."[45] Participation in struggle, *agon*, established a masculine identity.[46]

---

41 Malone, *Monk and the Martyr*, 126.
42 Paul Evdokimov points out: "The Old Slavic word for monk, inok, derives from inoi, meaning 'other,' which corresponds well to the symbolism of baptismal rebirth" (*Woman and the Salvation of the World: A Christian Anthropology on the Charisms of Women*, trans. Anthony Gythiel [Crestwood, NY: St. Vladimir's Seminary Press, 1994], 106).
43 *Patrologia Latina* 22. 670. See Mary Harlow, "In the Name of the Father: Procreation, Paternity and Patriarchy," in *Thinking Men: Masculinity and its Self-Representation in the Classical Tradition*, eds. Lin Foxhall and John Salmon (New York: Routledge, 1998), 17.
44 Brakke, *Demons*, 185.
45 Quoted by Katherine Allen Smith, "Spiritual Warriors in Citadels of Faith: Martial Rhetoric and Monastic Masculinity in the Long Twelfth Century," in Thibodeaux, *Negotiating*, 93.
46 See Gillian Clark. "The Old Adam: The Fathers and the Unmaking of Masculinity," in Foxhall and Salmon, *Thinking Men*, 177–78.

Fasting was a struggle in which men were called to compete and show themselves men, and fasting was usually seen in light of the struggle for chastity.[47] Monks had to fight manfully against the disordered inclinations of the body, usually called concupiscence, and affirmed their masculinity by struggling against these inclinations and establishing self-control. To be sexually licentious was to be effeminate. For the monk, as Ruth Karras explains, "both those [sexual] desires and the successful struggle to overcome them were signs of masculinity."[48] A medieval romance praised the knight Hugh of Lincoln who became a monk, because he "laid aside the burden of earthly soldiering for heavenly ... He donned armour against the flesh, soldiered against himself, and himself overcame himself."[49] Gerald of Wales tells numerous stories in his *Gemma Ecclesiastica* of men who fought sexual temptations: St. Benedict by rolling in nettles, St. Amonius by piercing his body with a red-hot iron, Godric, whose desires were so strong "that many times the seminal fluid was even discharging itself through natural channels," by immersing himself in freezing water.[50] The point of these stories is that sexual desire in these religious men was so strong that it had to be tamed by extraordinarily severe means—the severity of the means proving the extreme virility of the men.[51]

As monks were drawn from the upper classes and the upper classes were increasingly dominated by the ethos of chivalry, the already-existing metaphor of spiritual battle was reinforced by the portrayal of monasticism as a heavenly chivalry. Monks, like Bernard, came from knightly families

47　See Ruth Mazo Karras, "Thomas Aquinas' Chastity Belt: Clerical Masculinity in Medieval Europe," in *Gender and Christianity in Medieval Europe: New Perspectives*, eds. Lisa M. Bitel and Felice Lifshitz (Philadelphia: University of Pennsylvania Press, 2008), 56–57.

48　Ruth Maxo Karras, *Sexuality in Medieval Europe: Doing unto Others* (New York: Routledge, 2005), 43. See Jacqueline Murray, "Masculinizing Religious Life: Sexual Prowess, the Battle for Chastity and Monastic Identity," in Cullom and Lewis, *Holiness and Masculinity*, 26.

49　Quoted in Murray, "Masculinizing," 30; see also 37.

50　Gerald of Wales, *The Jewel of the Church [Gemma Ecclesiastica]*, trans. John J. Hagen (Leiden: E. J. Brill, 1979), 163–64.

51　See Jacqueline Murray, "One Flesh, Two Sexes, Three Genders" in Bitel and Lifshitz, *Gender and Christianity*, 34–51 and Karras, "Thomas Aquinas's Chastity Belt," 52–67.

or had even been knights themselves,[52] and understood chivalry and monasticism in terms of each other, uniting the two in such heights of medieval literature as *The Quest of the Holy Grail*.

Chivalry

John of Salisbury in his *Policraticus* wishfully described the purpose of knighthood: "To protect the church, to attack infidelity, to reverence the priesthood, to protect the poor, to keep the peace, to shed one's blood, and, if necessary, to lay down one's life for one's brethren."[53] This was Chaucer's "verray parfit gentil knight" who fought in just wars against the enemies of Christendom, who manifested valor, "Trouthe and honour, freedom and curteisye," yet "of his port as meek as is a mayde." This was the rarely-attained ideal, but even the ideal was in tension with Christianity. Robert Higgs claims with some justification that "knighthood ... was imposed on Christian doctrine, not organic to it, the founders of chivalry misapplying a few athletic and martial metaphors in the Epistles and transforming the shepherd-warrior David into a companion knight of medieval Crusaders and even Caesar himself."[54] Knights were pious, at least in their own eyes, but they lived by the sword. As one medieval author put it, "if God wishes, we can acquire our salvation by the exercise of arms just as well as we could by going ourselves over to contemplation and eating nothing but roots."[55] Chivalry was "the male aristocratic form of lay piety" which simply "downplayed or simply ignored most strictures" that were "not compatible with their sense of honour and entitlement."[56] This "lay independence" sometimes matured into anticlericalism.[57]

---

52 Richard W. Kaeuper, *Chivalry and Violence in Medieval Europe* (New York: Oxford University Press, 1999), 68; see also Smith, *War*, 52–57.

53 Quoted in Richard W. Southern, *The Making of the Middle Ages* (New Haven: Yale University Press, 1953), 114.

54 Robert J. Higgs, *God in the Stadium: Sports and Religion in America* (Lexington: University Press of Kentucky, 1995), 316.

55 Quoted by Ruth Mazo Karras, *From Boys to Men: Formations of Masculinity in Late Medieval Europe* (Philadelphia: University of Pennsylvania Press, 2003), 42.

56 Kaeuper, *Chivalry*, 47.

57 Ibid., 52.

As for the warriors of antiquity, honor, *timē*, was for the knight his chief goal, honor won by outstanding deeds of arms, as it had been won by his models in the ancient world. The knight thought that for him as a Christian warrior the pain and sufferings of war were the *ascesis*, the penance that conformed him to the Passion of Christ.[58] The knight, in his own view, imitated Christ the warrior who conquered Satan and Christ the Suffering Servant who bled for his people.[59] The monk claimed to be a fighter in the *militia Christi*, but the knight saw his own way as superior. If the monk underwent an initiation and a rebirth, so did the knight, especially if he took up the cross and became a Crusader. The ceremony of making a knight generally included a ritual bath as part of the transformation of a squire into a knight; a bishop assured crusaders that their hardships in battle had caused them to be "reborn of a new baptism of repentance."[60]

The knight saw his fighting in a just conflict as an imitation of Christ; the clergy sometimes disagreed.[61] The gospel seemed to enjoin non-violence: "He who lives by the sword will perish by the sword." Augustine had provided the framework for judging that a war might be just. But for several centuries, penitentials prescribed penalties for anyone who had killed, whether the homicide was justified or not.[62] The clergy were dependent on the knights for maintaining order in society and began to claim that the knight's violence was licit, as long as he was directed by the clergy.[63] In Spain the attempt to regain territory that had been conquered by the Moslems was seen as a holy war; it began the long pushback against the

---

58 See Derek A. Rivard, *Blessing the World: Ritual and Lay Piety in Medieval Religion* (Washington, DC: Catholic University of America Press, 2009), 158.

59 Richard W. Kaeuper, *Holy Warriors: The Religious Ideology of Chivalry* (Philadelphia: University of Pennsylvania Press, 2009), 34.

60 Quoted by Kaeuper, *Holy Warriors*, 241, n. 22.

61 For the peace movement see Kaeuper, *Chivary*, 73–81, and Kaeuper, *Holy Warriors*, 13–17.

62 Nikolas Jaspert, *The Crusades*, trans. by Phyllis G. Jestice (New York: Routledge, 2006), 14. See Ernst-Dieter Hehl, "War, Peace, and the Christian Order," in *The New Cambridge Medieval History*, Vol. 4, *c.1024–c.1128, Part 1*, eds. David Luscombe and Jonathan Riley-Smith (Cambridge: Cambridge University Press, 2004), 186–89; Erdmann, *Origin of the Idea of a Crusade*, 16.

63 Kaeuper, *Chivalry*, 66.

Moslem conquest of Christian lands. From this sprang the idea of the Crusade.[64] The clergy decided that the best use of the irrepressible violence of knights was to direct it against an external enemy, the Saracens, who had conquered vast stretches of the Christian Empire, including the Holy Land.[65] Pope Urban II proclaimed the first Crusade in 1095; the crusade would be an armed pilgrimage,[66] and like the pilgrimage, would gain indulgences *under certain conditions*.

The knights did not always pay attention to this qualifier, and they heard what was most compatible with their own mentality: that crusading brought about the forgiveness of sins and that the knight who died in the crusade would immediately enter heaven. Jacques de Vitry preached: "Those crusaders who prepare themselves for the service of God, truly confessed and contrite, are considered true martyrs while they are in the service of Christ, freed from venial and also mortal sins, from all the penitence enjoined upon them, absolved from the punishment for their sins in this world and the punishment of purgatory in the next, safe from the tortures of hell, in the glory and honor of being crowned in eternal beatitude."[67] The clergy began proclaiming that the crusader was a martyr,[68] and like the martyr, would enter Paradise immediately, and could also benefit his family and deceased relatives.[69] What knights *thought* the clergy were saying is summarized by the speech of the pope in the romance, the *Song of Aspremont*:

He who goes now against this foe to fight
And for God's sake should lose his mortal life,

---

64 See Erdmann, *Origin of the Idea of a Crusade*. See also Allen J. Frantzen's comments in *Bloody Good: Chivalry, Sacrifice, and the Great War* (Chicago: University of Chicago Press, 2004), 41–42.

65 Rodney Stark, *God's Battalions: The Case for the Crusades* (New York: HarperOne, 2009), 3–4.

66 Andrew Holt, "Between Warrior and Priest: The Creation of a New Masculine Identity during the Crusades," in Thibodeaux, *Negotiating Clerical Identities*, 188.

67 Jacques de Vitry, "Sermo II," in Christopher T. Maier, *Crusade Propaganda and Ideology: Model Sermons for the Preaching of the Cross* (Cambridge: Cambridge University Press, 2000), 113.

68 Kaeuper, *Chivalry*, 68.

69 Kaeuper, *Holy Warriors*, 78.

God waits already for him in Paradise
With crowns and laurels for the soldier of Christ;
He shall sit us at his own right-hand side;
Without confession, all the sins of your lives
On God's behalf I now collect and shrive;
Your penance is to fight with all your might![70]

The key matters of repentance and contrition were not always remembered, perhaps because knights, although willing to die in defense of Christendom, were not willing to confess their sins to a priest and to accept direction from him. Crusades began to resemble jihad, although the two types of holy war may have independent origins in their respective religions.[71]

Christian knighthood was united with monasticism in the military orders. After the First Crusade the idea grew up for an order of laymen who would combine fighting with monastic observance. The clergy were forbidden to fight and to shed blood; but the laymen who took vows of poverty, chastity, and obedience were not ordained and were not clerics and therefore were not subject to this prohibition. The Templars were the first such order.

Bernard of Clairvaux, popularizer of bridal mysticism in his *Sermons on the Song of Songs*, justified religious violence in *On the New Christian Militia*,[72] which he wrote for the Knights of the Order of the Temple. He felt some discomfort in both books, for he realized that he was innovating and that his innovations needed a defense. Bernard insists that "to inflict death or to die for Christ is no sin," and he defends the Christian knight against charges of manslaughter: "If he kills an evildoer, he is not a mankiller, but, if I may so put it, a killer of evil." Bernard claims he does not mean "that the pagans are to be slaughtered when there is any other way to prevent them from harassing and persecuting the faithful, but only that it now seems better to

70 Quoted by Kaeuper, *Holy Warriors*, 101.
71 See Jaspert, *The Crusades*, 77; see Emmanuel Sivan, *L'Islam et la Croisade: Idéologie et propagande dans les réactions musulmanes aux Croisades* (Paris: Librairie d'Amerique et d'Orient, 1968).
72 Bernard of Clairvaux, *Treatises III: On Grace and Free Choice; In Praise of the New Knighthood*, trans. Daniel O'Donovan and Conrad Greenia (Kalamazoo: Cistercian Publications, 1977).

destroy them." Bernard cites John the Baptist's advice to soldiers to be content with their pay as implying the legitimacy of killing and goes so far as to characterize the knight who dies in warfare as "a martyr."[73]

Not everyone approved this new type of religious life. Walter Map wrote that the Templars "take up the sword for the protection of Christendom, which was forbidden to Peter for the defence of Christ. There Peter was taught that peace should be sought by patience. I do not know who taught these to overcome force with force. They take up the sword and perish by the sword. They nevertheless assert: 'all laws and all law codes allow the repelling of force by force.' He, however, rejected that ruling, who, when Peter was striking a blow, refused to call on the legions of angels."[74] There were other voices of criticism,[75] but on the whole, the new idea of warfare inspired by religion and directed by clerics became a dominant ideology. After the failure of the Crusades the knights came under the control of centralizing monarchies and warfare became secular. The twentieth century was to witness the unexpected revival of the imagery and concept of the crusade, to some extent in the First World War, and more explicitly in the Spanish Civil War.

Jesuits

Ignatius was a soldier who sought honor in battle.[76] He was wounded and during his convalescence in Pamplona was deprived of his usual reading, the chivalric romances which Cervantes mocked in *Don Quixote*. His conversion was brought about by reading a version of the *Legenda aurea* that emphasized the chivalric nature of Christianity. At first he tried to be a better Christian by following both the crusading and chivalric ideals. He met a Moor on the road (and *moro* also meant sodomite[77]) who, by denying

73   Bernard of Clairvaux, *In Praise of the New Knighthood*, 134, 135.
74   Quoted in Alan Forey, *Military Orders from the Twelfth to the Early Fourteenth Century* (Toronto: University of Toronto Press, 1992), 204.
75   See also Erdman, *The Origin*, 229–68.
76   See *Autobiography*, in *Ignatius of Loyola: Spiritual Exercises and Selected Works*, ed. George E. Ganss (New York: Paulist Press, 1991), 68.
77   Juan Goytisolo, *Tradición y disidencia* (2002. México City: Fondo de Cultura Económica, 2003), 43.

that Mary remained a virgin *in partu,* was not sufficiently respectful of Mary for Ignatius's taste: "At this, various emotions came over him and caused discontent in his soul, as it seemed he had not done his duty. They also aroused his indignation against the Moor, for it seemed that he had done wrong in allowing the Moor to say such things about Our Lady, and that he ought to sally forth in defense of her honor. He felt inclined to go in search of the Moor and stab him with his dagger for what he had said."[78] Ignatius came to a crossroad. He decided to let his donkey choose the way. If the donkey chose the road that the Moor had taken, Ignatius would catch up with him and kill him. If the donkey chose the other way, Ignatius would let the matter go. The donkey, fortunately for the Moor, chose the other way. Ignatius then proceeded to Montserrat, near Barcelona. There "Ignatius once and for all exchanges the dagger for a pilgrim's staff at the altar of Our Lady."[79]

Ignatius was now "the new soldier of Christ,"[80] but more than that, a pilgrim. Ulrike Strasser explains the significance of this change: "The contrasting phallic images of dagger and staff are emblematic of a shift in masculine identities. The dagger stands for a life of warfare, aggression, and the defense of women's honor. The pilgrim's staff stands for a life of service to God, wandering the earth, forgoing violence. By trading one for the other, Ignatius is changed from a soldier to a soldier of Christ. He will continue to be brave but will now be brave on behalf of God. He will no longer think of 'a certain lady' but pledge all his loyalty to the Queen of Heaven."[81]

Ignatius, in his *Spiritual Exercises*, did not use the tradition of bridal mysticism. He uses "bride" to refer only to the Church, not to the Christian.[82]

78   Ignatius, *Autobiography*, 74.
79   Ulrike Strasser, "'The First Form and Grace': Ignatius of Loyola and the Reformation of Masculinity," in *Masculinity in the Reformation Era*, eds. Scott H. Hendrix and Susan C. Karant-Nunn (Kirksville, MO: Truman State University Press, 2008), 60.
80   Ignatius, *Autobiography*, 77.
81   Ulrike Strasser, "'The First Form and Grace': Ignatius of Loyola and the Reformation of Masculinity," in Hendrix and Karant-Nunn, *Masculinity in the Reformation Era*, 60.
82   Ignatius uses the image in such passages as "in Christ the Lord, the bridegroom, and in His spouse the Church" (*Exercises*, 160).

Even in a passage in which he compares Satan to a "false lover"[83] who seduces the soul, he does not develop the logical parallel of God as a true lover who woos the soul. Instead, Ignatius returns to the older patristic models of spiritual warfare. He compares the Christian to a knight who is addressed by an earthly king: "It is my will to conquer all the lands of the infidel. Therefore, whoever wishes to join with me in this enterprise must be content with the same food, drink, clothing, etc. as mine. So, too, he must work with me by day, and watch with me by night, etc., that as he had a share in the toil with me, afterwards, he may share in the victory with me."[84] This military experience, of being comrades and followers of an earthly prince, is the analogy that Ignatius chooses to help the Christian understand his role in the drama of salvation. Christ speaks to each Christian: "It is my will to conquer the whole world and all my enemies, and thus to enter into the glory of my Father. Therefore, whoever wishes to join me in this enterprise must be willing to labor with me, that by following me in suffering, he may follow me in glory."[85] The Christian is forced to choose between the two standards, "the one of Christ, our supreme leader and lord, the other of Lucifer, the deadly enemy of our human nature."[86] The Jesuits always felt that life was a struggle, whether a warfare with evil or a contest between self and God. Alonso de Orozco, echoing patristic and monastic language, warned "that he who would see the face of the most powerful Wrestler, our boundless God, must first have wrestled with himself."[87]

Elizabeth Rhodes claims that "aggression" is the hallmark of the Society, agreeing with Balbino Marcos who says that the Jesuit spirituality is marked by "struggle, combat, and activity" (*lucha, combate, actividad*).[88]

---

83 Ignatius, *Exercises*, 145. Ignatius also compares Satan to "a woman" because he "is a weakling before a show of strength, and a tyrant if he has his will" (*Exercises*, 145).

84 Ibid., 43.

85 Ibid., 44.

86 Ibid., 60.

87 Quoted by Robert Harvey, *Ignatius Loyola: A General in the Church Militant* (Milwaukee: Bruce, 1936), 149.

88 Elizabeth Rhodes, "Join the Jesuits, See the World: Early Modern Women in Spain and the Society of Jesus," in *The Jesuits II: Cultures, Sciences, and the Arts*, eds. John W. O'Malley, Gauvin Alexander Bailey, Steven J. Harris, and T. Frank Kennedy (Toronto: University of Toronto Press, 2006), 35.

But it was also an adventure: An early Jesuit, Jerónimo Nadal, explained that "the principal and characteristic dwelling of Jesuits is ... in journeying."[89] Ignatius in his autobiography referred to himself as a pilgrim and the novices made pilgrimages as preparation for their missionary journeys.[90]

The Jesuits, unlike the Cistercians, Dominicans, and Franciscans, never had a female branch. As Robert Harvey notes, "With the exception of one brief episode ... there was no consideration given to the founding of a female order in connection with the company of Jesus."[91] Although much of Ignatius's initial support came from women—his "efforts met with a greater response among the women than in any other quarter"[92]—he wanted his followers to steer clear of them: "All familiarity with women was to be avoided, and not less with those who are spiritual, or wish to appear so."[93] Jesuits, however, did in fact serve as confessors and spiritual directors to women, a role that would contribute to male hostility against them.

The Jesuits until the end of the twentieth century also stressed the agonic element in education; Barry Harker notes: "The Jesuits encouraged the agonic motive so immoderately in their schools that pupils lived in a veritable war footing with each other. Eventually, the refined competitive system of the Jesuits, with its endless competitions, public recitations, and prize giving was imported virtually in its entirety into the Catholic universities."[94] The discipline at Jesuit schools and colleges was almost military in its strictness—bed checks and compulsory chapel. Education was a battle: "A military rhetoric of battle and struggle, and a continuing immersion

89 Quoted by Peter McDonogh, *Men Astutely Trained: A History of the Jesuits in the American Century* (New York: Free Press, 1992), 22.

90 John W. O'Malley, *The First Jesuits* (Cambridge, MA: Harvard University Press 1993), 271.

91 Robert Harvey, *Ignatius Loyola: A General in the Church Militant* (Milwaukee, WI: Bruce, 1936), 182.

92 Heinrich Boehmer, *The Jesuits: An Historical Study*, trans. Paul Zeller Strodach (Philadelphia: Castle Press, 1928), 40.

93 Quoted by Harvey, *Ignatius Loyola*, 192.

94 Barry R. Harker, *Strange Fire: Christianity and the Rise of Modern Olympism* (Rapidan, VA: Hartland Publications, 1996), 103.

in competition as a mode of learning."[95] The manual *Teaching in Jesuit High Schools* claimed that the "spirit of rivalry" is in "the fibre of the American boy. All his life he will be facing competition, which seems to go fiercer as the years go by. To form the habit of flinching and shying away from competition will do the youth more harm than learning the attitude of welcoming it and facing it."[96]

The Jesuits cultivated a masculine atmosphere in the Society. "A continuing need to prove one's manhood through contest ... seems to have typified Jesuit manhood."[97] In 1954 a Jesuit gave a sermon (on Mary!) which managed to include these phrases: "militant loyalty," "struggle," "fighting man," "commander of Christ," "fighting force," "fought to turn the tide," "turned back a tide," "became a fighting issue," "militantly," "glorious army of militants."[98]

As the Jesuit Walter Ong noticed, males are characterized by agonistic behavior; a man is always testing himself against something or someone.[99] Academic life in the West was for millennia adversative.[100] Latin was the language of learning, and Latin was a language used almost exclusively by men, and learning Latin was a male initiation ritual entailing physical punishment. Oral disputation, defending a thesis, was the primary means of instruction. But in two years, 1967–1968, the School of Divinity of St. Louis University ceased using Latin as a language of instruction, dropped the thesis method as a method of instruction, dropped circles and disputations together with oral course examinations as integral parts of it program, and admitted women.[101] Ong sees all these developments as a final rejection of the male, adversative method of learning in its last bastion, the Roman

95 Steven Rosswurm, *The FBI and the Catholic Church, 1935–1962* (Amherst: University of Massachusetts Press, 2009), 47.

96 Quoted in McDonogh, *Men Astutely Trained*, 422.

97 Rosswurm, *FBI and the Catholic Church*, 45.

98 Ibid., 48.

99 Walter J. Ong, *Fighting for Life: Contest, Sexuality, and Consciousness* (Amherst: University of Massachusetts Press, 1989), 75.

100 See Blythe McVicker Clinchy, "Issues of Gender in Teaching and Learning," in *Teaching and Learning in the College Classroom*, eds. Kenneth A. Feldman and Michael B. Paulsen (Boston: Pearson Custom Publishing, 1998), 167–69.

101 Ong, *Fighting for Life*, 139.

Catholic seminary. In the larger church the Second Vatican Council replaced polemic and adversative stances toward other churches, other religions, and the world in general with conciliatory gestures—and Latin was replaced by the *mother* tongue.[102]

Peter McDonough and Eugene Bianchi comment on "the movement from a masculine to a more feminine manner discernible among both Jesuits and former Jesuits" and how "the ethos of religious practitioners like the Jesuits has shifted from masculine assertiveness to a feminine emphasis on conciliation and healing."[103] In 1986 the Jesuit Curia admitted that the Ratio Studiorum recommended competition, but said that now, "although a Jesuit school values the stimulus of competitive games, it urges students to distinguish themselves by their ability to work together, to be sensitive to one another, to be committed to the service of others shown in the way they help one another" and rejects "an atmosphere of academic competition."[104] The *Jesuit Education Reader* boasts how programs "have helped create on our campuses an atmosphere of friendship, care, and appreciation rather than the usual one of competition and criticism."[105] In 2002 the Jesuit William Neenan observed that "all Jesuit universities have more female than male undergraduate students. In several the percentage approaches two-thirds of the total enrollment."[106]

Confraternities

From the beginning of the Christian era men have formed brotherhoods. Most of these groups were assimilated to the lower clergy and were therefore celibate. But brotherhoods of laymen also existed. Some had economic functions, such as the guilds which also had attendant religious activities

---

102 Ibid., 170–71.

103 Peter McDonough and Eugene C. Bianchi, *Passionate Uncertainty: Inside the American Jesuits* (Berkeley: University of California Press, 2002), 296.

104 Quoted in Vincent J. Duminuco, ed., *The Jesuit Ratio Studiorum: 400ᵗʰ Anniversary Perspectives* (New York: Fordham University Press, 2000), 200.

105 George W. Traub, *A Jesuit Education Reader* (Chicago: Loyola Press, 2008), 378.

106 William B. Neenan, "Sports and Jesuit Universities: A Winning Combination," *Conversations on Jesuit Higher Education* 21 (2002): 8.

for their members. Others, the confraternities, had a specifically religious character.[107] They undertook works of charity and both celebrated feasts and did penance in a characteristically masculine way, that is, some would say, to excess. The Flagellants, making public an old private practice, whipped themselves through the streets "in order to avert God's anger by assimilating themselves with Christ through sharing in his sufferings."[108] These public penitents were all male.[109] The penitential fraternities were the successors to the Crusades, which had begun as a penitential exercise. Penance, and not killing, was their central spiritual value.[110] Those who did not go on crusade could join a confraternity, whose male members often did not get along well with the clergy.[111] Penitents engaged in a close imitation of Jesus, even to the shedding of blood, and took upon themselves the sufferings of the world. In Europe these male religious organizations have died out: "The confraternities of penitents were absorbed by the third orders, which recruited their own members primarily among women."[112] Women did not do public penance.

The spiritual currents inspired by Francis of Assisi influenced attitudes to penance. As a youth he was a leader in revels and sought fame in battle. After his conversion his generosity took a different direction. Francis was not influenced by bridal mysticism—he never quoted the *Song of Songs*.[113] Christ was not his lover; Francis instead was the lover of Lady Poverty. Christ was the Bridegroom of Lady Poverty, and Francis was her knight. Francis sought to imitate the *kenosis* of Christ, the self-emptying that culminated in crucifixion and death. Francis' imitation of Christ was made visible in his stigmata. This Franciscan spirituality that sought to share in

---

107 See Frederick DeLand Leete, *Christian Brotherhoods* (New York: Eaton & Mains, 1918).
108 André Vauchez, *The Laity in the Middle Ages: Religious Beliefs and Devotional Practices,* ed. Daniel E. Bornstein, trans. Margery J. Schneider (Notre Dame: University of Notre Dame Press, 1993), 123.
109 Ibid., 123.
110 Ibid., 49.
111 Ibid., 115.
112 Ibid., 127.
113 Jacques Delarun, *Francis of Assisi and the Feminine* (Saint Bonaventure, NY: Franciscan Institute Publications, 2006), 160.

the sufferings of Christ was one of the fonts for the affective, penitential movements which attracted men.

The ethos of the penitential brotherhoods was that there was "an open route of communication between God and man, a route that could be traversed through repentant pilgrimage and corporate suffering." The penances were intended "to expiate collective guilt and to obtain divine pardon and clemency for the community."[114] Confraternities of penitents who engaged in public flagellation became extremely popular in Spain and authorities sought to limit their number. Men had to be restrained: "Authorities also felt compelled to restrain zealous young men from too frequent self-flagellation, finally forbidding public scourging on saints' days" and confining it to Holy Week, the Santa Semana, and a few other rare occasions.[115]

Confraternities of all types were and are present throughout the Catholic world.[116] They are voluntary lay associations, mostly of men, although sometimes women could join, although their role is not always clear. The confraternities offered mutual aid: a decent burial and prayers and penance for the living and the dead. The solidarity of all Christians, on earth, in purgatory, and in heaven was reinforced and celebrated. The confraternities expressed the fullness of the Communion of the Saints.[117] As a fifteenth-century Italian confraternity member, Francesco de Largi, explained to his fellow-members: "My very dear brothers, I wish to pray for you and your salvation without ceasing, so that in praying for one another we would merit to acquire divine grace in this world and glory in the next world, and so will be observed forever, as it has been promised, the mutual love for one another."[118] The confraternities also sponsored fiestas and built

---

114 Maureen Flynn, "Baroque Piety and Spanish Confraternities," in *Confraternities and Catholic Reform in Italy, France, and Spain*, eds. John Patrick Donnelly and Michael W. Maher (Kirksville, MO: Truman State University Press, 1999), 238.

115 Flynn, "Baroque Piety," 238.

116 See Albert Meyers and Diane Elizabeth Hopkins, *Manipulating the Saints: Religious Brotherhoods and Social Integration in Postconquest Latin America* (Hamburg: Wayasbah, 1988).

117 Catherine Vincent, *Les confréries médiévales dans le royaume de France XIIIᵉ – XVᵉ siècle* (Paris: Albin Michel, 1994), 187.

118 Quoted in Vincent, *Les confréries*, 70.

and carried floats in processions; their social life included feasts, dancing, and drinking. The annual dinner was of great importance; it was "quasi-liturgical,"[119] like an *agape*. A sixteenth-century Frenchman said that the communal banquets of the confraternities promoted "peace, concord, and amity" and in Zamora a confraternity claimed that "love always increases at social gatherings and banquets."[120]

A conflict between clerics and laymen has long marked the history of confraternities in the Catholic world.[121] In the later medieval period, even confraternities that had been founded for clerics became mostly lay, and most members were male[122] and exhibited an anticlerical attitude.[123] Confraternities seem to have been popular among men precisely because they were not under clerical control. Men joined them voluntarily, elected their own officers, and largely ran their own affairs.[124] The clergy did not like such independence; they "were suspicious of chapels operating independently from the parish church, separating so many men from the other parishioners, leaving the women and the children to the curé—foreshadowing of nineteenth- century pattern of religious practice."[125]

The French clergy critiqued the social activities of the confraternities as frivolity and debauchery, "les festins et le ripaille,"[126] according to the

119 Vincent, *Les confréries*, 171.
120 Allyson M. Poska, "From Parties to Pieties: Redefining Confraternal Activity in Seventeenth-Century Ourense (Spain)," in Donnelly and Maher, *Confraternities and Catholic Reform*, 233.
121 See José Sánchez Herrero, *La Semana Santa de Sevilla* (Madrid: Sílex, 2003), 21.
122 Christopher Black, "Introduction: The Confraternity Context," in *Early Modern Confraternities in Europe and the Americas*, eds. Christopher Black and Pamela Gravestock (Aldershot, England: Ashgate, 2006), 1.
123 Paul Trio, "Lay Persons in Power: The Crumbling of the Clerical Monopoly on Urban Devotion in Flanders, as a Result of the Rise of Lay Confraternities in the Late Middle Ages," in Black and Gravestock, *Early Modern Confraternities*, 53–56.
124 See Sánchez Herrero, *La Semana Santa*, 21.
125 John McManners, *Church and Society in Eighteenth-Century France*, Vol. 2, *The Religion of the People and the Politics of Religion* (New York: Oxford University Press, 1998), 178.
126 Quoted by Vincent, *Les confréries*, 171.

Archbishop of Reims. Clergy denounced these useless expenses, "soutirages d'argent,"[127] which could have been put to better use, that is, in supporting the activities of the clergy or perhaps in building bridges.[128] In fifteenth-century Italy, the clergy did not like "their independence from clerical leadership,"—obviously the most important objection—"their use of laymen to preach and interpret the Gospel, or for allegedly drunken and immoral behavior at their feasts and festivals"—the most frequent complaint.[129] Severe penitential observances, confraternity members maintained, were needed because even the men in confraternities were caught up in male competition, conflict, and sensuality.[130]

The Reformers had no more use for the confraternities than the Catholic clergy did: Luther denounced confraternity activities as "banquets and drinking bouts."[131] Confraternities disappeared in Protestant areas and were the target of clerical reforms in Catholic areas: "Catholic Reformers sought to ensure that confraternities became agents of the new spirituality as well as the new church government and control."[132] In 1604 Pope Clement VII issued the bull *Quaecunque*, which severely limited the lay independence of confraternities by extending clerical control over them.[133] In Italy the Counter-Reformation was ambivalent about confraternities; the chief fear of church authorities was that "parishioners would be distracted from their parish church, and the authority of parish priest and bishop be lessened."[134]

The pre-eighteenth-century confraternities were manifestations of an "exclusively male piety" that bishops feared would perpetuate "a type of superparochial congregationalism"; later in the eighteenth century the

---

127 Vincent, *Les confréries*, 171.
128 Ibid., 172.
129 Christopher F. Black, "Confraternities and the Parish in the Context of Italian Catholic Reform," in Donnelly and Maher, *Confraternities*, 7.
130 See Timothy Mitchell, *Passional Culture: Emotion, Religion, and Society in Southern Spain* (Philadelphia: University of Pennsylvania Press, 1990), 46, 92.
131 Quoted by Vincent, *Les confréries*, 189.
132 Black, "Confraternities and the Parish," 35.
133 Poska, "From Parties to Pieties," 224; Flynn, "Baroque Piety," 241.
134 Christopher F. Black, *Italian Confraternities in the Sixteenth Century* (Cambridge: Cambridge University Press, 2003), 62.

penitential confraternities "were no longer exclusively male or extra-parochial,"[135] but they appear to have been predominantly so. For example, in Provence the confraternities of penitents had their own chapels and chaplains, who said mass for them on Sunday. Maurice Agulhon describes the situation: "The 'normal' situation was that the parish priest preached to women and children, while the men kept away, satisfied in their conscience with the mass that their chaplain had said for them, perhaps a little fast … and in any case without a sermon."[136] In France in the eighteenth century men started deserting the confraternities for the Masonic lodges, and the confraternities became organizations of women.[137] With the male confraternities gone, this was the situation in the nineteenth century: "the women at the mass, but the men in some group or society, where one found oneself among men."[138] The French Revolution had fulfilled the hierarchy's wish to abolish the male confraternities, but when the confraternities disappeared or became clericalized, the men left also, losing their main tie to the church.

In the first part of the nineteenth century, male penitential confraternities revived to some extent, especially in Southern Europe, but the clergy "distrusted their independence and disapproved of their activities," which "included 'dancing and drinking.'"[139] But on the whole men avoided religious confraternities because the confraternities were "clerically dominated."[140] In mid-nineteenth-century Orléans, the clergy were hostile to many if not all male fraternities, in which they saw "no religious value" and claimed the confraternal feasts were "feasts of debauchery more than

---

135 Andrew E. Barnes, "The Transformation of Penitent Confraternities over the Ancien Régime," in Donnelly and Maher, *Confraternities*, 136.

136 Maurice Agulhon, *Pénitents et Francs-Maçons de l'ancienne Provence* (Paris: Fayard, 1968), 126. See Timothy Tackett, *Priest and Parish in Eighteenth-Century France* (Princeton: Princeton University Press, 1977), 199, 200.

137 Claude Langlois, "Féminisation du catholicisme," in *Histoire de la France religieuse*, Vol. 3, *Du roi Très Chrétien à la laïcité républicaine XVIIIᵉ–XIXᵉ siècle*, ed. Phillipe Joutard (Paris: Éditions du Seuil, 2001), 291. See also Agulhon, *Pénitents et Francs-Maçons*, 206–11.

138 Agulhon, *Pénitents et Francs-Maçons*, 126.

139 Nicholas Atkin and Frank Tallett, *Priest, Prelates, and People: A History of European Catholicism since 1750* (New York: Oxford University Press, 2003), 113.

140 Ibid., 114.

devotion: and that the members very often did not make their Easter duty."[141] In 1853 the bishop of Arras, Pierre-Louis Parisis, forbade the diversions and feasts of the confraternities and suppressed thirty-eight of them. Men resented this action, and, as Yves-Marie Hilaire points out, the bishop thereby "precipitated the decline of a traditional form of male sociability in Artois; whatever were his intentions, he probably contributed to distancing men from the church" and the pious associations encouraged by the church were "populated essentially by women."[142]

In El Salvador for centuries the *cofradías* were the center of parish life and were "male-dominated" and centered on devotion to the Passion. The clergy disliked them, not because of unorthodoxy, but because of "the autonomy of the brotherhoods and local communities and their frequently anticlerical attitudes." When the economy of El Salvador became dominated by coffee plantations, local farms and communities were expropriated and the bishops were therefore able to end local autonomy and end the power of the *cofradías*. The clergy got control of religious practice, which therefore declined, "especially among adult men."[143]

In Canada the clergy's insistence on exercising "constraint" on "lay initiative" severely limited the temperance societies of the nineteenth century.[144] The devotional confraternities of the nineteenth century, almost entirely female, were tightly controlled by the clergy in Canada, but attempts to found societies for men on the same basis failed. The clergy had to draw back and to allow men's organizations "to select their own leaders."[145] The young men's literary societies decided to include tugs of war,

---

141 Christianne Marcilhacy, *Le diocèse d'Orléans au milieu du XIXᵉ siècle* (Paris: Sirey, 1964), 318.

142 Yves-Marie Hilaire, *Une chrétienté au XIXᵉ Siecle? La vie religieuse des populations de diocèse d'Arras (1840–1914)*, Vol. 1 (Lille : Publications de l'Université de Lille, 1977), 411.

143 Anna L. Peterson, *Martyrdom and the Politics of Religion: Progressive Catholicism in El Salvador's Civil War* (Albany: State University of New York Press, 1997), 46–47.

144 Brian Clarke, *Piety and Nationalism: Lay Voluntary Associations and the Creation of the Irish-Catholic Community in Toronto, 1850–1895* (Montreal: McGill-Queens University Press, 1993), 151.

145 Ibid., 92.

banjo clubs, free tobacco, billiards, concerts (interspersed with boxing) etc., and were therefore moderately successful. Not everyone approved. The *Catholic Weekly Review* complained "it is difficult to understand why some clubs are called 'Catholic.'"[146] However, when the Toronto clergy tried to get men to join the St. Vincent de Paul Society, most men found the demands on both time and behavior too severe. Men were told they had to lead austere lives in service to the poor, but men "saw no conflict between being a faithful Catholic and indulging in a few drinks in the company of friends at their favorite tavern."[147]

In Spain the *cofradías* and *hermandades* which carried out the external cult often combined fervor with militant and political anticlericalism.[148] In Spain the fate of the *hermandades* has been strongly affected by anticlericalism and political developments. Their public function was to bear the floats during Holy Week and other festivals. During the 1936–1938 Civil War they were suppressed; after Franco's victory they were revived as part of National Catholicism. At the end of the dictatorship and in the turmoil following the Second Vatican Council they declined; but then they enjoyed a massive revival, especially in Andalusía. Isodoro Moreno, an anthropologist at the University of Seville, studied them in the 1970s and returned to the subject in the 1990s to consider this unexpected revival. His analysis is important to understanding why anticlerical men participate in and defend activities of popular Catholicism, or perhaps lay Catholicism would be a less invidious term.

The Second Vatican Council adopted a central European attitude to Catholic life and was hostile to popular religiosity. José Sanchéz Herrero claims that "for Spain the Council represented the incorporation of religiosity in a direction opposed to the traditional Hispanic religiosity."[149] Everything was to be pared down, simplified, all the accretions and popular developments—novenas, processions—abolished. In Spain, after the Second Vatican Council, priests generally ended the outdoor processions over

146 Ibid., 94.
147 Ibid., 107–09.
148 Delgado Ruiz, *Las Palabras de otro hombre: anticlericalismo y misoginia* (Barcelona: Muchnik Editores, 1993), 23.
149 Sánchez Herrero, *La Semana Santa*, 308.

which they had control in an attempt to make religion more rational, "less mysterious and magical."[150] The bishops came back from Rome eager to purify the Spanish Church, and the clergy began the purification by abolishing Corpus Christi processions and even burning popular images just as the anticlericals had done in the Civil War. The bishops tried to convert the *cofradías* into social welfare organizations and wanted the members to give up their demonstrative public piety and accept the new stripped-down liturgy.[151]

After the socialist party, the PSOE, attained power in 1982, it remained anticlerical but decided, by encouraging the *hermandades* and other popular Catholic activities, to demonstrate it was *not* anti-religion.[152] The Spanish Left decided to follow the analysis of Antonio Gramsci and to regard popular religion as a necessary part of culture. The Socialists began lavishly promoting the processions and other activities of the confraternities, so that the populace would see in the Left not an iconoclastic enemy, but "the great defender of popular religion."[153] This popular religion is celebrated in the streets and fields, "outside of the churches and the immediate authority of the clerics."[154] Therefore the Socialists can support it without supporting the clergy; indeed, by supporting the confraternities they undermine the authority of the clergy.

The Spanish bishops took note and decided to adopt a more conciliatory attitude toward popular religiosity. They encouraged the brothers to engage in charitable activities (which had always been part of the purposes of the *cofradías*)

150 Stanley Brandes, *Metaphors of Masculinity: Sex and Status in Andalusian Folklore* (Philadelphia: University of Pennsylvania Press, 1980), 196.
151 Sánchez Herrero, *La Semana Santa*, 316.
152 Dionisio Borobio, *Hermandades y cofradías: entre pasado y futuro* (Barcelona: Centre de Pastoral Litúrgica, 2003), 25.
153 Sánchez Herrero, *La Semana Santa*, 317. See also Javier Escalera Reyes, "Hermandades, religión oficial y poder en Andalucía," in *La religiosidad popular*, Vol. 3, *Hermandades, romerías y santuarios*, eds. León Carlos Álvarez Santaló, Maria Jesús Buxó y Rey, and Salvador Rodríguez Becerra (Barcelona: Editorial Anthropos, 1989), 458–69; and Antonio Ariño Villarroya, "Las relaciones entre las asociaciones festeras y la institución eclesiástica: Una aproximación a la lógica de la religión popular" (ibid., 473, 482).
154 Isidoro Moreno, *Las hermandades Andaluzas: Una aproximación desde la antropología* (2nd ed. Seville: Universidad de Sevilla, 1999), 192.

and to attend liturgical celebrations in the church, something even pious Spanish men have long been reluctant to do. Although almost all members join a *cofradía* for motives closely connected with Catholic faith, and also believe that they should participate in religious acts, they have a more distant attitude to Sunday mass. When asked "Do you think it is necessary to be practicing [i.e., to attend Sunday mass] to be a member [cofrade]?" 42% of members answer *No*.[155]

Dionisio Borobio, a liturgical scholar, has tried to assure the *cofradías* that "rather than intending to suppress them, the ecclesiastical authority intends to control them, given their social and cultural importance."[156] The bishops wished to shape and use the *cofradías* for their own purposes. The bishops also began the process of extending their control over the confraternities by feminizing them. Confraternities had had women members and auxiliaries, but men had run them independently of the clergy. The bishop of Seville in 2011 ordered the *cofradías* to accept women on equal terms[157]; what this has resulted in in the past is that a largely male association would become a largely female association. The head of the cultural association in Puig de Missa, Antonio Marí Ferrer, observes of the local *cofradías*, "there are ... many women. The men are less constant. They go to football or somewhere else and are more absent. The women are always there. My mother is in El Cristo de la Oración and I believe that 90% of the members of this brotherhood are women."[158]

Confraternities were a way in which men expressed both their independence and solidarity, independence from authorities which sought to run men's lives and solidarity with fellow men, often precisely as men. In southern Italy the male religious societies, the *fratelli*, had a strong sense of "lay autonomy and group solidarity."[159] In Spain membership in a *hermandad*

---

155 Borobio, *Hermandades y cofradías*, 99.

156 Ibid., 54.

157 "Mujeres cofrades de toda España aplauden el decreto de Asenjo" (*ABC*, February 4, 2011).

158 "Los hombres son poco constantes, las mujeres están ahí siempre," *Diario de Ibiza*, May 4, 2011.

159 Enrico Carlson Cumbo, "Salvation in Indifference: Gendered Catholicity among Italian Immigrants," in *Households of Faith: Family, Gender, and Community in Canada, 1760–1969*, ed. Nancy Christie (Montreal: McGill-Queens University Press, 2002), 210.

establishes a sense of communal identity. The activities of the *cofradías* create a feeling of a collective Us, "symbolized by a hermandad, by images and popular rituals, which, although they in turn develop from religious elements, are not totally controlled by the clerics and religious hierarchies, nor do they respond to a religious utilitarianism or to any other type of utilitarianism."[160] Although there is no central register, there seem to be about 5,000 *cofradías* in Spain with about one million members.

The community fostered by the *hermandad* is a masculine community based upon shared suffering. In Monteros, as elsewhere in Andalusia, men do not go to church, because the priest is in control inside the building; but in the outdoor procession of the *Señor de Consuelo*, a painting of the Crucifixion, men are in control and participate enthusiastically, setting off fireworks along the way. Only boys are allowed the difficult task of carrying the large painting in its heavy frame through the streets. The painting is an emotional one: "One has only to look at the painting of the crucified Christ, his head hung pitifully sideways, his eyes downcast, to recognize that he is a man who has sacrificed greatly." The boys, suffering under the weight, thereby "at once display power and suffering, [and] identify closely with the Son of God." Men, in seeing the image of the Crucified see also the destiny of all men to be a sacrifice. They honor, in some sense, a "self-portrait, a supernatural image of themselves."[161] In Christ, as in men who fulfill their masculinity, there is a union of power and weakness, because men are strong only so that they may give of themselves to others, even to the point of death.

The confraternities were exported to the Spanish and Portuguese New World and flourished there. In some places they became the main way the Church was organized. The fiestas, which sometimes included elements of African or Indian religion, were immensely popular, and were also the object of clerical criticism because of expense, drunkenness, debauchery, and violence. In the United States the Penitentes of New Mexico have long attracted attention and clerical opposition, even before the United States annexed the area.[162]

---

160 Moreno, *Las hermandades Andaluzas*, 185.
161 Brandes, *Metaphors of Masculinity*, 201, 202.
162 For the practices of the Penitentes, see Leon Podles, *The Church Impotent: The*

In America in the late nineteenth century various brotherhoods were founded with the intention of reaching young men, or as the prayer of the Episcopal Brotherhood of St. Andrew put it, "grant that young men everywhere may be brought into the Kingdom of Thy Son."[163] The most famous was the Gideons, organized by commercial travelers who wanted Christian fellowship and later took up the work of placing Bibles in hotel rooms.[164] Catholics also founded the Knights of Columbus, the Catholic Order of Foresters, and temperance organizations, and the male organizations, in contrast to other Catholic organizations, "enjoyed enormous liberties."[165] In England the Catenian association was established in 1908 as a venue for male, middle-class, Catholic men. It has spread to the Commonwealth and now has 11,000 members. Alana Harris notes that it is "unique among Catholic societies in not allowing ordained priests or male religious to become members," and "has consistently resisted clerical control."[166]

The Reformation

Most scholars recognize the rejection of the religious feminine by the Reformation: "The Reformation substantially purged Christianity of its feminine elements, leaving men and women alike faced with a starkly masculine religion"[167] (although such a change coexisted with the continued emphasis on bridal mysticism, as we have seen). Paul Tillich claims that "the spirit

---

Feminization of Christianity (Dallas, TX: Spence Publishing, 1999), 145–47; and Harry Sylvester's novel *Dayspring* (1945. San Francisco: Ignatius Press, 2009).

163 Frank Graves Creesey, *The Church and Young Men* (Chicago: Fleming H. Revell, 1904), 118.

164 Clifford Putney, *Muscular Christianity: Manhood and Sports in Protestant America, 1880–1920* (Cambridge, MA: Harvard University Press, 2001), 67.

165 Ibid., 88.

166 Alana Harris, "'The People of God Dressed for Dinner and Dancing?' English Catholic Masculinity, Religious Sociability, and the Catenian Association," in *Men, Masculinities, and Religious Change in Twentieth-Century Britain*, eds. Lucy Delap and Sue Morgan (New York: Palgrave Macmillan, 2013), 55.

167 Peter N. Stearns, *Be a Man! Males in Modern Society*, 2nd ed. (New York: Holmes & Meier, 1990), 39.

of Judaism with its exclusively male symbolism prevailed in the Reformation."[168] The return to biblical and patristic models of spirituality led once again to a portrayal of the life of the Christian as a battle, a spirituality that was essentially masculine. Luther, rejecting most of the comforting medieval devotions to saintly intercessors, mediators, and protectors, returned to a stark view, like that of Ignatius of Loyola, of humanity caught between God and the Devil. The war was inescapable: "Christ and Satan wage a cosmic war for mastery over Church and world. No one can evade involvement in this struggle. Even for the believer there is no refuge—neither monastery nor the seclusion of the wilderness offer him a chance for escape. The Devil is the omnipresent threat, and exactly for this reason the faithful need the proper weapons for survival."[169]

The Lutheran branch of the Reformation, because of its emphasis on *agon*, on struggle, led to a Christianity that was far more masculine than medieval Catholicism had been: "The overwhelming image of both God and the believer in Luther's writings is a masculine one. ... True faith is energetic, active, steadfast, mighty, industrious, powerful—all archetypally masculine qualities in the sixteenth (or the twentieth) centuries. God is Father, Son, Sovereign, King, Lord, Victor, Begetter, 'the slayer of sin and the devourer of death' —all aggressive, martial, and totally male images. With the home now the center of women's religious vocation, even the imagery of the Church becomes masculine, or at least paternal and fraternal."[170] The church became a brotherhood, a church of the brethren.

168 Paul Tillich, *Systematic Theology*, Vol. 3 (Chicago: University of Chicago Press, 1963), 313.

169 Heiko A. Oberman, *Luther: Man between God and the Devil*, trans. Eileen Walliser-Schwarzbart (New Haven: Yale University Press, 1989), 104. Calvin too "interpreted the Christian life as a ceaseless struggle with the powers of evil within both the self and the world" and he therefore prayed to God, "'since thou proposest to us no other end than that of constant warfare during our whole life ... may we be ever armed and equipped for battle'" (William J. Bouwsma, "The Spirituality of John Calvin," in *Christian Spirituality: High Middle Ages and Reformation*, ed. Jill Rait with Bernard McGinn and John Meyendorff [New York: Crossroad, 1987], 331).

170 Merry Wiesner, "Luther and Women: The Death of Two Marys," in *Disciplines of Faith: Studies in Religion, Politics, and Patriarchy*, eds. Jim Obelkevich, Lyndal Roper, and Raphael Samuell (London: Routledge & Kegan Paul, 1987), 103.

The Reformation emphasis on conflict was supplemented by a more peaceful emphasis on patriarchy. Calvin explained that the husband and wife were equal, but that the wife was functionally subordinate to the husband, whose authority was like that of Christ, an authority of service and sacrifice.[171] Calvin, while stressing paternal authority, condemned domestic violence, and under his influence Geneva made wife-beating a crime.[172] Lutheranism placed a new emphasis on the role of the father — "Protestant theologians increased his status and responsibility."[173] But this new emphasis on the role of the father meant that the man had new duties and responsibilities that were not always easy to fulfill. Protestant preachers knew that "their patriarchs were vulnerable ... needing structure for the sexual fulfillment, and requiring care from their spouses. When they misbehaved in relationships, men received less sympathy and consideration than did women, because men were held to high standards of public responsibility and quickly blamed when they violated those standards."[174] Not all men were able to or wanted to fulfill their newly-enhanced role of patriarch.

French Reformed communities sought to integrate men into the life of the church in several ways. They stressed the role of the father in conducting family prayers ("C'est le père qui le préside"[175]) and in teaching religion to his children.[176] Raymond Mentzer summarized the new role of fathers: "Ideally, they brought their offspring to the temple for induction into the community of believers, officiated at family prayers every evening, guided sons and daughters in their marriages, and ensured the correct

171 André Bieler, *L'homme et la femme dans la morale calviniste* (Geneva: Labor et Fides, 1963), 36, 48–49.
172 Julius R. Ruff, *Violence in Early Modern Europe 1500–1800* (Cambridge: Cambridge University Press, 2001), 132–33.
173 Robert James Bast, *Honor Your Fathers: Catechisms and the Emergence of a Patriarchal Ideology in Germany, 1400–1600* (Leiden: Brill, 1997), 92.
174 Scott H. Hendrix, "Masculinity and Patriarchy in Reformation Germany," in Hendrix and Karant-Nunn , *Masculinity*, 87–88.
175 Paul de Félice, *Les protestants d'autrefois, vie interior d'églises, mœurs et usage* (Paris: Librarie Fischbacher, 1897), 86.
176 Raymond A. Mentzer, "Masculinity and the Reformed Tradition in France," in Hendrix and Karant-Nunn, *Masculinity*, 125.

belief and proper behavior of every one living under the ancestral roof."[177] In the public life of the community the laymen were given prominent roles. In the Middle Ages, midwives had often baptized children (which they were permitted to do in an emergency) because of the fear of infant mortality. Calvin ended the practice of allowing women to baptize and insisted that the child be baptized at Sunday worship and that the father be present.[178] Men also served as the consistory of the local church and had the responsibility for the preparations of the quarterly celebration of the Eucharist. The elders would examine church members to assure they know the catechism and then gave them a token. At the service an elder would collect the token, an elder would supervise the communicants as they approached the table, and an elder would often administer the cup.[179] These were all roles given only to adult laymen.

Counter-Reformation Catholics recognized the weak presence of the father in the Christian image of the family and promoted Joseph as the model for Christian manhood. In the medieval Church marriage was in a chaotic state, and in response to that difficulty, Hispanic Catholics may have imitated the Protestant promotion of "the patriarchal, nuclear family."[180] The image of the Holy Family that consisted of Ann, Mary, and Jesus was supplemented or replaced by the Holy Family as Joseph, Mary, and Jesus.[181] Joseph had long been shown as a bumbling old man who did not

177　Mentzer, "Masculinity and the Reformed Tradition in France," in Hendrix and Karant-Nunn, *Masculinity*, 137.

178　Calvin wrote in a letter "Unless they are impeded by business, fathers are ordered to attend," quoted in Susan C. Karant-Nunn, "'Suffer the little children to come unto me, and forbid them not': The Social Location of Baptism," in *Continuity and Change: The Harvest of Late Medieval and Reformation History*, eds. Robert J. Bast and Andrew C. Gow (Leiden: Brill, 2000), 369. See Mentzer, "Masculinity and the Reformed Tradition in France," in Hendrix and Karant-Nunn, *Masculinity*, 123; "Il fallait que le père vint lui-même au temple" (De Félice, *Les Protestants*, 187).

179　Mentzer, "Masculinity and the Reformed Tradition in France," in Hendrix and Karant-Nunn, *Masculinity*, 128–29.

180　Charlene Villaseñor Black, *Creating the Cult of St. Joseph: Art and Gender in the Spanish Empire* (Princeton: Princeton University Press, 2006), 79.

181　Sara F. Matthews Grieco, "Models of Female Sanctity in Renaissance and Counter-Reformation Italy," in *Women and Faith: Catholic Religious Life in Italy*

comprehend what was happening to Mary; he was now shown as a strong young man who protected the child Jesus, and indeed in Spanish art he replaced Mary as the primary one who held the Christ Child.[182] But the priest, not the father, in fact remained the main spiritual influence in the family, as anticlericals bitterly complained.

Revivalism

Luther stressed the inward drama of the Christian who had to accept the free gift of justification. Conversion is prominent in what one might call the conservative wing of American Protestantism: revivalism, fundamentalism, and evangelicalism. In Winthrop Hudson's classic definition, evangelism is "a theological emphasis upon the necessity for a conversion experience as the beginning point of a Christian life, while revivalism is a technique developed to induce that experience."[183] As Schleiermacher's character Leonhardt in *Christmas Eve Celebration* noted, this process of conversion is parallel to the crisis that adolescent males often go through and indeed is parallel to the pattern of male development.[184]

Revivalism had roots in Methodism, and it seems that early Methodism appealed about equally to men and women. In East Cheshire, Methodist societies had "about 55 percent female membership," which "closely matches the sex ratio as a whole in textile manufacturing centres."[185] Revivalism did not flourish in England, but it became the predominant form of Protestantism after it had been transplanted to the colonies. The series of revivals that began in the eighteenth century modified the demographic composition

from Late Antiquity to the Present, ed. Lucetta Scaraffia and Gabriella Zarri (Cambridge, MA: Harvard University Press, 1999), 161–62.

182 Black, *Creating the Cult of St. Joseph*, 59.

183 Winthrop S. Hudson, *American Protestantism* (Chicago: University of Chicago Press, 1972), 78.

184 Friedrich Schleiermacher, *Christmas Eve Celebration: A Dialogue*, ed. and trans. Terrence N. Tice (Eugene, OR: Cascade Books, 2010), 41.

185 Gail Malmgreen, "Domestic Discords: Women and the Family in East Cheshire Methodism, 1750–1830," in *Disciplines of Faith: Studies in Religion, Politics, and Patriarchy*, eds. Jim Obelkevich, Lyndal Roper, and Raphael Samuel (London: Routledge & Kegan Paul, 1987), 60.

of the church in America, which in the seventeenth century, as we have seen, was largely female. It also affected religious feelings and their expression. Bridal mysticism, although it was common to Puritan and pietist, was supplemented by a different form of the religion of the heart, one that resonated more closely with masculine concerns. Herbert Moller maintains that "revivalism ... was an emotionalized religion based on inner experience, but of a peculiar American type. Unlike the mystical movements of Europe, it did not center around asceticism and divine love, but rather around sin, repentance, and redemption; instead of stressing the humanity of Christ and the intimate love relationship between God and man, it aroused fear and trembling through hell-fire oratory."[186] It was therefore more masculine.

In the First Great Awakening of the eighteenth century, the one identified with the Calvinism of Jonathan Edwards, women still made up the majority of new church members: "In over half of the churches the proportion of women at admission increased from previous levels or remained in line with the church's historical appeal."[187] But sometimes the percentage of men joining the church increased over the low percentage of the pre-revival period: "On occasion, however, the Great Awakening did redress the severe imbalance of females over males in new membership, and in several towns even tipped it decidedly in the latter's direction."[188] In the Low Country South Carolina revival of 1803–1804, ministers feared that the proportion of women, already a large majority in evangelical churches, would increase, but learned that "white men would always convert in greater numbers in revival settings than in the regular course of church life."[189]

---

186 Herbert Moller, "Sex Composition and Correlated Cultural Patterns of Colonial America," *William and Mary Quarterly*, 3rd series, 2 (1945): 152.

187 Gerald F. Moran, "Christian Revivalism in Early America" in *Modern Christian Revivals*, eds. Edith L. Blumhofer and Randall Balmer (Urbana: University of Illinois Press, 1993), 52–53.

188 Moran, "Christian Revivalism," 53. See also Terry D. Bilhartz, *Urban Religion and the Second Great Awakening: Church and Society in Early National Baltimore* (Rutherford, NJ: Fairleigh Dickinson University Press, 1986), 97.

189 Stephanie McCurry, *Masters of Small Worlds: Yeoman Households, Gender Relations, and the Political Culture of the Antebellum South Carolina Low Country* (New York: Oxford University Press, 1995), 150.

Revivalist preaching had a special appeal for men. Chad Gregory notes that "conservative revivalists and fundamentalists sought to channel pristine, male energy."[190]

Charles Grandison Finney, the preacher who began the Second Great Awakening, the wave of revivals that set the evangelical tone of American Protestantism, was a Freemason, and his conversion experience in 1821 closely resembled the fraternal initiation he had gone through when he became a Mason. Mark C. Carnes compares fraternalism and revivalism: "Both revivalism and fraternalism depend upon an agency outside the individual to generate a personal transformation; both depicted man as inherently deficient; and both invoked grim visions of death and hell to precipitate an emotional response that could lead men to an unknowable and distant God."[191] The anguish and the hellfire-and-brimstone sermons of the revivals were a change from the calm rationality, Unitarianism, and Universalism of the older churches. The Christ of the Revivalists "was a sinless Messiah slain to satisfy the wrath of a righteous God."[192] Conversion is an experience comprehensible to men who follow the ideology of masculinity, who know that the meaning of life can only be found in a test that leads to a kind of death and to a rebirth as a new type of being.

During the Second Great Awakening the percentage of men who joined the church also increased,[193] but it was not as high as in the First. Women were the majority of the participants in the revival, but the percentage of men in revivals was higher than the percentage of men in the churches.[194] This revival, unlike that of the eighteenth century, appealed to

190 Chad Alan Gregory, "Revivalism, Fundamentalism, and Masculinity in the United States, 1880–1930." Ph.D. University of Kentucky, 1999, i.

191 Marc C. Carnes, *Secret Ritual and Manhood in Early America* (New Haven: Yale University Press, 1989), 72.

192 Terry D. Bilhartz, "Sex and the Second Great Awakening: The Feminization of American Religion Reconsidered," in *Belief and Behavior: Essays in the New Religious History*, eds. Philip R. Vandermeer and Robert Swierenca (New Brunswick, NJ: Rutgers University Press, 1991), 125.

193 See Bilhartz, *Urban Religion*, 21–22.

194 See David William Kling, *A Field of Divine Wonders: The New Divinity and Village Revivals in Northwestern Connecticut, 1792–1822* (University Park: Pennsylvania State University Press, 1993), 10; Susan Hale Lindley, *"You Have Stepped out of Your Place": A History of Women and Religion in America* (Louis-

the more mature: "Married adult males were more likely to convert than young unattached males; females were more likely to convert than males; and of any single group (considering gender and marital status), married females were the most likely to convert."[195] That more married men than unmarried converted suggests that wives had more to do with male conversions in this Awakening than in the previous one.[196]

In the brief but intense revival of 1858, brought on by the tensions that led to the Civil War, there was an unusually high percentage of men. The *Christian Advocate* noted that often "the majority of the converts [were] males."[197] Although the revival preached the old gospel, it used new methods: "It relied heavily upon businessmen, business methods, and the business outlook."[198] This was a harbinger of Moody's approach and that of almost all later evangelists. During Wilbur Chapman's crusade in Boston in 1909, he emphasized that Christianity was sound business and attracted mostly male audiences.[199] In the revivals of the twentieth century, men also seem to have been attracted to conversion at a rate that has exceeded that of non-revival periods, although women have remained the majority of the converts. This relative success among males was not limited to Protestants, for whom revivals were almost an institution. The Roman Catholic Church had a tradition of mission preaching which was imported to America, and it also seemed to have more success reaching men than regular services.[200]

Nevertheless, the revivals did not reach the completely unchurched; they were most popular among church-goers. Revivalists were frustrated that churchgoers occupied the chairs and sometimes asked them to stay

ville, KY: Westminster John Knox, 1996), 59–69; and Bilhartz, "Sex and the Second Great Awakening," 122.

195 Kling, *Field of Divine Wonders*, 170.

196 See ibid., 217.

197 *The Christian Advocate*, March 4, 1858, quoted by Richard Carwardine, *Transatlantic Revivalism* (Westport, CN: Greenwood Press, 1978), 169.

198 Marion L. Bell, *Crusade in the City: Revivalism in Nineteenth-Century Philadelphia* (Cranbury, NJ: Associated University Presses, 1977), 169.

199 Margaret Lamberts Bendroth, "Men, Masculinity and Urban Revivalism: J. Wilbur Chapman's Boston Crusade, 1909," *The Journal of Presbyterian History* 75, no. 4 (1997), 236.

200 Jay Dolan, *Catholic Revivalism: the American Expedience 1830–1900* (Notre Dame, IN: University of Notre Dame Press, 1978), 121.

away to make room for the unchurched. Those who were not already members of churches often came from families that had church members, or were children and adolescents from Sunday schools. The down-and-outers, the utterly profane, the deists and skeptics, did not go to revivals, and this group was almost entirely male. Revivalism did not seem to have any long-term impact even on more receptive males. If it added members to the churches in the short run, it led to a falling off as enthusiasms cooled. Among Catholics, priests who preached the parish missions knew that there was a large group of "mission Catholics" who came to church only for missions and then stayed away until the next mission. Conversion is a peak experience, and even men who want initiation find it impossible to live permanently on the mountaintop. Terry Bilhartz seems to be correct in his assessment that evangelical revivalism "retarded but failed to arrest the male fallout in nineteenth-century congregations."[201]

Fundamentalism

Fundamentalism is innately combative. Edith Blumhofer describes it as "a masculine, macho movement that railed against softhearted, effeminate Christianity" (and fundamentalists saw Billy Graham as a proponent of this effeminate Christianity).[202] It used the rhetoric of war: "attacking, battling troops, Christian soldiers, and boot camps."[203] As Jerry Falwell admitted, "one thing fundamentalists do better than anything else is fight. It's all we know how to do, and if there isn't an issue, we'll start one."[204] Carol Flake observed that "it was the genius of evangelical preachers to make the born-again experience seem a masculine rite of passage. Christianity was like a team, an army into which one was initiated, with Jesus as the commander."[205] Men, fundamentalists realized, love a good fight.

201 Bilhartz, "Sex and the Second Great Awakening," 126.
202 David Edwin Harrell, Jr., "American Revivalism from Graham to Robertson," in Edith Waldvogel Blumhofer and Randall Balmer, *Modern Christian Revivals* (Urbana: University of Illinois Press, 1993), 197.
203 Ibid., 197.
204 Ibid., 197.
205 Carol Flake, *Redemptorama: Culture, Politics, and the New Evangelicalism* (Garden City, NY: Anchor Press, 1984), 92–93.

Fundamentalism, according to Margaret Lamberts Bendroth, attempted to be self-consciously masculine and reacted against the effeminate liberal churches.[206] Both fundamentalists and liberals had predominantly female constituencies.[207] But liberals were effeminate, according to the fundamentalists, because they refused to acknowledge the conflict, the battle between good and evil, in the world, and tried to make Christianity a mild religion of progress and enlightenment. Bendroth describes fundamentalism as "a means of separation, a way to declare superiority over the domesticated faith that shunned open conflict with the world, the flesh, and the devil."[208]

Because the surrounding culture regarded religion as feminine, the self-proclaimed masculinity of fundamentalism is a result, in Mark Muesse's view, of male fundamentalists' anxiety about their masculinity.[209] Like other Christians, they must assume a receptive, i.e., feminine, attitude in relationship with God. They also must renounce some of the vices by which men try to demonstrate they are men. Fundamentalist men are expected to be chaste before marriage and faithful within marriage, and fundamentalist sermons try to exercise social control over men; "the vices put on parade were those that tended to lure husbands rather than wives away from respectability: drinking, gambling, whoring, cursing, immoral conduct."[210] Mark Muesse sees the military, aggressive rhetoric of fundamentalism as an attempt to counterbalance this stress on the abandonment of common male behavior. Fundamentalism "offered men a hypermasculine world view, with a rationalistic theology, a universe of clearly demarcated boundaries and order, a sense of control and a militant outlook."[211]

As North American religion has migrated south to Latin American

---

206 Margaret Lamberts Bendroth, *Fundamentalism and Gender: 1875 to the Present* (New Haven: Yale University Press, 1993), 64.
207 See ibid., 90.
208 Ibid., 19.
209 Mark W. Muesse, "Religious Machismo: Masculinity and Fundamentalism," in *Redeeming Men: Religion and Masculinities*, eds. Stephen B. Boyd, W. Merle Longwood, and Mark W. Muesse (Louisville, KY: Westminster John Knox, 1996), 89–102.
210 Flake, *Redemptorama*, 92.
211 Muesse, "Religious Machismo," 100.

cultures, it has become more and more Pentecostal. Protestants are simply called *evangelicos*, and they emphasize to a greater or lesser extent separation from the world. Catholic groups by contrast emphasize solidarity and blame crime on exploitative social structures. Protestants emphasize conversion, the renunciation of the world, the flesh, and the devil, and personal reform; they offer men a clean break from the world of the gang, from destructive machismo, which includes sports, drinking, drugs, womanizing, and violence. They offer men "the sense of rebirth—becoming a new creature—that is central to Pentecostalism's promise of salvation from social ills through conversion."[212] This emphasis on individual responsibility seems to be more effective in changing lives than the Catholic attempts to reform broad structures.[213] Dissolute males were to be reborn as Christian patriarchs. Patriarchy is one of the movements explicitly aimed at men, movements we will consider in the next chapter.

212 Jon Wolseth, *Jesus and the Gang: Youth Violence and Christianity in Urban Honduras* (Tucson: University of Arizona Press, 2011), 120.

213 See Edward Orozco Flores, *God's Gangs: Barrio Ministry, Masculinity, and Gang Recovery* (New York: New York University Press, 2014), 91–103.

Chapter Eight
Targeting Men

As Christians became aware of the alienation of men from Christianity, they developed strategies that targeted males. Older movements had faded: monasticism and the Jesuits had become marginal among Catholics; Reformation calls to a battle against Satan had given way to accommodation to the surrounding culture. Newer movements have emphasized the contest that men engage in to prove their masculinity and gain honor; the most recent ones concentrate on the healing of relationships, especially relationships within a family. Usually movements combine the two emphases, combat and empathy, which are uneasy partners.

Christian Heroism

The European wars of the twentieth century forced Christians to experience violence on an unprecedented scale. After 1889 French seminarians were obliged to serve one year in the army, and in the First World War priests were drafted into the medical service and also served as chaplains; after 1917 they served in the front lines. Military service, at least as far as public image, "a virilisé le pretre," gave the priest a virile image.[1] Jean Badelle (1917–1941), secretary-general of the *Jeunesse Étudiante Chrétienne*, challenged the youth of France: "The religion of the catacombs implies adventure, even imprudence ... the martyrs ran to torture with a youthful spirit. It is necessary to put oneself back into the presence of this audacity and this enthusiasm of irresistible youth to recover the true Christian

---

1   Paul Airiau, "Le prêtre catholique masculin, neutre, autre? Des débuts du XIXᵉ siècle au milieu du XXᵉ siècle," in *Hommes et masculinités de 1789 à nos jours*, ed. Regis Revenin (Paris: Éditions Autrement, 2007), 199.

movement."² This was to be a "virile and strong" Christianity, but with a heroism of love, not of force.³ It would replace the Christianity of the "dolorism of the Sacred Heart, the excess of Marian devotion" with the "adult person of Jesus Christ."⁴

After the defeat in World War I, German Catholics sought a new ideal of masculinity to attract youth to the Church. Irmtraud Götz von Olenhusen maintains that "without doubt the First World War was the catalyst that made the feminine model of religious identity for the young appear as completely unsuitable for the times, not to say dubious."⁵ The veneration of Mary was in part downplayed, and in part re-presented as the veneration of a strong woman, "who treads on the head of the serpent" and was "fearful as an army ready for battle."⁶ Christ the Hero became the model for the young Catholic.⁷ The former patron of youth, St. Aloysius Gonzaga, had been celebrated because he combined an intense religiosity with a physically weak constitution. There was an unsuccessful attempt to portray him as a stern ascetic with a "hidden, unbendable will,"⁸ but he was replaced by St. Michael the Archangel, who was shown defeating the dragon and was therefore a better model for "a young, strong hero."⁹

The liturgy was considered more masculine than popular devotions.¹⁰

2 Jean Badelle, quoted by Alain-René Michel, *Jeunesse étudiante chrétienne face au nazisme et à Vichy 1938/1944* (Paris: Presse Universitaire Septrion, 1988), 197.

3 Bernard Comte, *L'honneur et la conscience: Catholiques français en résistance 1940/1944* (Paris: Les Éditions de l'Atelier, 1998), 262.

4 Étienne Fouilloux, "Femmes et catholicisme dans la France contemporaine: Aperçus historiographique," *Clio*, 1-1995. http://clio.revues.org/498.

5 Irmtraud Götz von Olenhusen, "Geschlecterrollen, Jugend und Religion: Deutschland 1900–1933," in *Erziehung der Menschen-Geschlechter: Studien zur Religion, Sozialisation und Bildung in Europa seit der Aufklärung*, eds. Margret Kraul and Christoph Lüth (Weinheim: Deutscher Studien Verlag, 1996), 244.

6 J. Sträter, quoted in Götz von Olenhusen, Geschlecterrollen," 251.

7 Götz von Olenhusen, "Geschlecterrollen," 242.

8 J. Mammacher, quoted in von Olenhusen, "Geschlecterrollen," 249.

9 Irmtraud Götz von Olenhusen, *Jugendreich Gottesreich Deutschesreich: Junge Generation, Religion und Politik 1928–1933* (Cologne: Verlag Wissenschaft & Politik, 1987), 83–84.

10 How the liturgy was more "masculine" than sentimental, "effeminate" popular

In the liturgical movement, the Risen Body of Christ was the focal point, and therefore the dignity of the body was emphasized, as was the importance of health. Urbanus Bomm, the abbot of Maria Laach, said that because the liturgy used bodily things—word and song and gesture—it "sanctified the body"; the state of the body and health were made valuable and desirable through this, because "through them the celebration of the holy Mysteries is guaranteed."[11] Before the Nazi takeover the Catholic sports organization for young men had 700,000 members.[12] Its prewar head, Ludwig Wolker, claimed that "the will of the Creator, to see strong men and joyous natures walking under the sun, finds expression on the earth through the true sportsman."[13] Because man is a union of body and soul, he must therefore "also in his body, also in sport serve the glory of God."[14]

Christians had to be strong to face the threat of Nazism. The *Sturmschar* was founded as an elite for the Catholic youth organizations.[15] It used military imagery—songs, uniforms, banner, and marches—but did not have a military purpose. As the threat of civil war grew in Germany after 1932, Catholic Action took an explicitly military direction. The Catholic Liga in Münster proclaimed, "for the storm columns of the Most High Lord of Hosts there is no repose and no rest."[16] Adolescent Christians incorporated the *Führerprinzip* into their organizations. They saw Christ as the true Führer.

One form looms from yesterday to today,
One form does not falter!

devotions was not always clear. Was it more objective, having greater *Sachlichkeit*, or did it inspire awe? See Andrea Meissner, "Against 'Sentimental' Piety: The Search for a New Culture of Emotions in Interwar German Catholicism," *German History* 32, no. 3 (2014): 393–412.

11 Götz von Olenhusen, *Jugendreich*, 80.

12 Ludwig Wolker, "Mein Weg zum Sport," in *Geist und Ethos in Sport: Reden und Aufsätze von Prälat Ludwig Wolker im deutschen Sport*, ed. Martin Söll (Düsseldorf: Verlag Haus Altenberg, 1958), 7.

13 Wolker, "Das Gemeimnis des Sports," in Söll, *Geist und Ethos*, 21.

14 Wolker, "Vom Ethos des Sportes, " in Söll, *Geist und Ethos*, 62.

15 See Götz von Olenhusen, *Jugendreich*, 89–96 and Franz Henrich, *Die Bünde katholischer Jugendbewegung* (Munich: Kösel Verlag, 1968), 249.

16 Doris Kaufman, *Katholisches Milieu in Münster 1928–1933* (Düsseldorf: Schwann, 1984), 11.

Christ!
He stands confident of victory!
He holds out his hand to us and goes forward!
He is everything:
Beginning and goal and leader to the goal,
Strength and way! King of the coming age![17]

Such young Christians were willing to battle in the streets against the Nazis; but Catholic adults saw this as mere bravado and generally submitted to the new regime.

Cursillo

In the intensifying anticlerical and antireligious atmosphere of Spain in the 1930s, the men of Catholic Action started planning a massive pilgrimage to Santiago de Compostela to take place in 1937. According to Kristy Nabhan-Warren, this pilgrimage "distinguished itself in its embodied hypermasculinity and a championing of Christ and his male apostles."[18] To prepare the young pilgrims, little courses (*cursillos*) were developed. The pilgrimage was delayed by the Spanish Civil War and World War II and did not occur until August 1948.[19] But the *cursillos* continued; they had become a preparation for the pilgrimage of life. Catholic leaders on the island of Mallorca continued developing and giving these courses for young men, the group "most alienated from the Church."[20] The Cursillo movement confronted this situation in Spain: "Religious apathy was prevalent among men in Spain. Church going had long been considered a pious need of women

---

17 Hermann Ühlein, *Kirchenlied und Textgeschichte: literarische Traditionsbildung am Beispiel des deutschen Himmelfahrtsliedes von der Aufklärung bis zur Gegenwart* (Würzburg: Verlag Königshausen & Neumann, 1995), 180.

18 Christy Nabhan-Warren, *The Cursillo Movement in America: Catholics, Protestants, and Fourth Day Spirituality* (Chapel Hill: University of North Carolina Press, 2013), 32.

19 Marcene Marcoux, *Cursillo: Anatomy of a Movement* (New York: Lambeth Press, 1982), 8.

20 Ivan Rohloff, *The Origins and Development of Cursillo* (Dallas, TX: National Ultreya Publications, 1976), 85.

and children. It was often considered childish or effeminate for men to be devout in their faith."[21]

The Cursillo sought to help men find joy in the faith, to show initiative, and to be largely free from clerical control.[22] Eduardo Bonnin, the founder of Cursillo, according to Nabhan-Warren, wanted "to create manly, strong, but also emotionally connected soft patriarchal Christian soldiers for Christ—men who would be better husbands, fathers, and Christians."[23] As we shall see, Promise Keepers and the evangelical-charismatic churches also have this aim.

The religion of the cursillista would be based on an experience of love: "In the cursillos the truth enters into the head and explodes into the heart."[24] The Cursillo often produces a profound experience of *metanoia*, of rebirth, of transformation. Using language reminiscent of revivalist Protestantism, one cursillista explained: "I was born again ... I was filled with love, and I knew that God loved me ... My old self died, and my new self is able to see the lovable in each person and to see the unlovable as lovable."[25] The Cursillo, in the view of the anthropologist Marcene Marcoux, follows a classic initiation ritual, a "rite of passage"[26] which leads to a personal transformation. The program is secret and deliberately upsets preconceptions and keeps participants off balance. It lasts four days, and the cursillista is told that every day after that is the Fourth Day, because it is a new life. He is initiated into a new community, and attends the Ultreyas (from the Spanish word *Ultreya*, the motto of the Camino de Santiago: "Ever Onward)."

The participant is asked to review his past life; this often leads to a public confession of sin. This allows "the men to overcome the *machismo*, or male ego, that often prevented them from confessing to a priest. Indeed, baring their souls to other men made the telling of sins in the confessional much easier. By the same token, committing oneself to a new life before

---

21 Ibid., 19.
22 Nabhan-Warren, *Cursillo Movement*, 44–45.
23 Ibid., 154.
24 Rohloff, *Origins and Development*, 37.
25 Marcoux, *Cursillo*, 91.
26 Ibid., 111.

their fellow men became a matter of honor."[27] One study reported: "It has made active participation in Church life respectable for Mexican American men, and laid the basis for a social apostolate contrasting with the individualistic piety in much of Latin religious worship."[28] A Franciscan priest thought the Cursillo attracted men because it challenged them and called "for a lifestyle that demands what only a virile man can give .... To be a Christian is not possible for a moral or spiritual weakling."[29] The Chicano activist Armando Rendón recounts his experience:

> Within the social dimension of the Cursillo, for the first time in many years I became reimmersed in a tough, macho ambiente. Only Spanish was spoken. The effect was shattering ....
>
> Because we were located in cramped quarters, with limited facilities, and the cooks, lecturers, priests, and participants were men only, the old sense of machismo and camarada was revived and given new perspective.
>
> Reborn but imperfectly, I still had a lot to learn about myself and my people.[30]

The Cursillo is both masculine and communal and ends not just in a changed individual but in a man seeking to change society. César Chávez was a cursillista, as were many of the leaders of the California Migrant Mission Program.

27 Gilberto M. Hinojosa, "Mexican-American Faith Communities in Texas and the Southwest," in *Mexican Americans and the Catholic Church, 1900–1965*, eds. Jay Dolan and Gilberto Miguel Hinojosa (Notre Dame, IN: University of Notre Dame Press, 1997), 117.
28 Leo Grebler, Joan W. Moore, Ralph C. Guzmán, and Jeffrey Lionel Berlant, *The Mexican-American People: The Nation's Second Largest Minority* (New York: Free Press, 1970), 468.
29 Quoted in Dolan and Hinojosa, *Mexican Americans*, 224.
30 Quoted in Anthony M. Stevens-Arroyo, "From Barrios to Barricades: Religion and Religiosity in Latino Life," in *The Columbia History of Latinos in the United States since 1960*, ed. David Gregory Gutiérrez (New York: Columbia University Press, 2004), 315.

Very early the Cursillo was changed "from a youth's movement to a men's movement."[31] It aimed to reach stable community leaders, mostly married, from twenty-five to fifty-five. Originally the Cursillo targeted primarily men, because of the "presumption that women were already religious and had little need for the Cursillo."[32] When women saw the changes in their husbands, they too wanted to have a cursillo, and eventually cursillos were given for women: "The Cursillo movement began as a male-only movement, but when Mexican-American men began to manifest changes in their lives, their wives wanted to have the same experience."[33] The Cursillo has spread beyond Hispanic Catholicism into Protestant denominations.

Muscular Christianity

S. S. Pugh in 1867 lamented that "the Christian Life has often been strangely and mischievously misapprehended as to this, so that men have come to think of it as a state of dreary sentimentalism, fit only for women, or for soft and effeminate men, and not calling forth or giving room for the exercise of the sterner and stronger virtues."[34] Charles Spurgeon saw that this mistaken idea had become widespread: "There has got abroad a notion, somehow, that if you become a Christian, you must sink your manliness and turn milksop .... Young men, to you I would honestly say that I should be ashamed to speak to you of a religion that would make you soft, cowardly, effeminate, spiritless."[35] These Christians desired a Christianity that exemplified manliness, as they understood it.

31 Rohloff, *Origins and Development*, 98.
32 Ana María Díaz-Stevens, "Latinas and the Church," in *Hispanic Catholic Culture in the U.S.: Issues and Concerns*, eds. Jay Dolan and Allan Figueron Deck (Notre Dame, IN: University of Notre Dame Press, 1994), 261.
33 Kristy Nabhan-Warren, *The Virgin of El Barrio: Marian Apparitions, Catholic Evangelizing, and Mexican American Activism* (New York: New York University Press, 2005), 140.
34 S. S. Pugh, *Christian Manliness: A Book of Examples and Principles for Young Men* (London: Religious Tract Society, n. d.), 94–95.
35 Charles H. Spurgeon, *A Good Start: A Book for Young Men and Women* (Morgan, PA: Soli Deo Gloria Publications, 1995), 24.

The phrase "Muscular Christianity" originated in a review of Charles Kingsley's *Two Years Ago* (1857), which gave this name to Kingsley's union of "physical strength, religious certainty, and the ability to shape and control the world around one."[36] The suspicion that religion had become feminized and, in High Church circles, effeminate led Victorians to seek a masculine Christianity.[37] This variety of Christianity shunned asceticism, especially celibacy and virginity, in which it detected perversion. Charles Kingsley despised Cardinal Newman and wrote *Water Babies* as a popular defense of Christian marriage and progeny and, beyond that, of the unity of church and world, sacred and secular.[38] Kingsley and his like-minded friends wanted men to be Christian without being too religious, because religion, in its ascetical Roman, monastic, Tractarian forms, was identified with femininity. Kingsley preached "godliness and manliness," but not "saintliness," which is "not God's ideal of a man, [but] an effeminate shaveling's ideal."[39] Kingsley disliked the popular images of St. Francis de Sales and St. Vincent de Paul, because "God made man in His image, not in an imaginary Virgin Mary's image."[40] Kingsley's charges, as we have seen, were provoked by the long-standing identification of femininity, receptivity, and Christianity.

Kingsley was an early proponent of the motto "Be All You Can Be," because manly potential should be fulfilled, not denied.[41] Kingsley advised a friend to preach to men "that Christ is in them, a true and healthy

36 Donald E. Hall, "Introduction" to *Muscular Christianity: Embodying the Victorian Age*, ed. Donald E. Hall (Cambridge: Cambridge University Press, 1994), 7.

37 See Norman Vance, *The Sinews of the Spirit: The Ideal of Christian Manliness in Victorian Literature and Religious Thought* (Cambridge: Cambridge University Press, 1985).

38 Vance, *Sinews of the Spirit*, 16. For a discussion of the exchanges between Newman and Kingsley, see Bruce Haley, *The Healthy Body and Victorian Culture* (Cambridge, MA: Harvard University Press, 1978), 95–119.

39 Charles Kingsley, *Charles Kingsley: His Letters and His Age*, Vol. 1 (London: Henry S. King, 1877), 204.

40 Ibid., 204.

41 David Rosen writes: "For Kingsley, the ideal of self-actualization, the fulfillment of manly potential, becomes a moral imperative" ("The Volcano and the Cathedral: Muscular Christianity and the Origins of Primal Manliness" in Hall, *Muscular Christianity*, 35).

manhood, trying to form Himself in them, and make men of them."[42] Mysticism was abhorrent to Kingsley because it was effeminate. He disliked talk about Christ as the bridegroom of the soul, because in both Catholicism and Puritanism, "the soul is talked of as a bride—as feminine by nature, whatever be the sex of its possessor. This is indeed only another form of the desire to be an angel," who is usually imagined as "a woman, unsexed."[43]

The Romantics had begun to reevaluate the importance of energy and emotion as opposed to self-control. Kingsley expounded the necessity of the expression of *thumos*, the male energy that found expression in violence and in sex. The male self was not to be denied, but affirmed, because it was a creation of God. Virtue was not limited to feminine behavior. David Rosen explains that for Kingsley, "current ideas of human perfection had derived from female nature, so that to be virtuous, a man had to imitate a woman and so repress parts of his natural force that sought expression."[44] Masculine energy, Kingsley maintained, was a creation of God and should not be repressed: "when a man acts from impulse ... his flesh is at harmony with, and obeys, his spirit."[45] Kingsley said that by exercise he cultivated his "thumos, (translate as you will—wrath, spirit, pluck, or otherwise), which Plato says is at the root of all virtues. I have indulged for a while that savage element which ought to be in the heart of every man; for it alone gives him the energy by which he civilizes himself."[46]

Muscular Christianity wanted Christian men to develop healthy, sturdy bodies and therefore develop the characteristics of strength, courage, and endurance that would enable them to preach the Gospel and bring about the Kingdom. Stories of missionaries emphasized their heroism and endurance in an attempt to appeal to "young men, the section of the population thought to be most distant from the churches."[47] Beyond these

---

42 Kingsley, *Charles Kingsley: His Letters*, Vol. 1, 399.

43 Ibid., 259. See Laura Fasick, "Charles Kingsley's Scientific Treatment of Gender," in Hall, *Muscular Christianity*, 93.

44 Rosen, "The Volcano and the Cathedral," 33.

45 Quoted by Rosen, "The Volcano and the Cathedral," 34.

46 Charles Kingsley, *Sir Walter Raleigh and His Time with Other Papers* (Boston: Ticknor & Fields, 1859), 424.

47 Hugh McLeod, *Religion and Society in England, 1850–1914* (New York: St. Martin's, 1966), 150.

emotional objections to feminized religion lay a broad church emphasis on ethics, a "liberal religious awareness which crystallized ... into a vigorously combative Christianity involving urgent ethical and spiritual imperatives."[48] Not the priest or the monk, but the Christian gentleman, was the ideal.[49] This gentlemen has great and even savage energy, but he puts it at the service of a higher cause: building a Christian civilization.

Not all were in agreement with this program. Cardinal Newman mistrusted such an attempt. He wrote: "There have been those Protestants whose idea of an enlightened Christianity has been a strenuous antagonism to what they consider the unmanliness and unreasonableness of Catholic morality, an antipathy to the precepts of patience, meekness, forgiveness of injuries, and chastity. All this they have considered a woman's religion." Newman claimed that this attitude leads logically to Islam.[50] Newman's quarrel with Kingsley was part of his quarrel with activist, reforming Christianity, which led to his refusal to support Cardinal Manning's campaign for temperance legislation. Religion was supernatural, or it was nothing, and manliness was a merely natural phenomenon. If manliness could make a good man, what need was there for the priesthood—or for Christianity, for that matter.

Sports

Muscular Christianity was literalized in Christian sports.[51] As we have seen, the Christian churches were long suspicious of amusements, especially male amusements such as sports. Attitudes changed first in England. A mania for sports began in the public schools in the mid-nineteenth

---

48 Vance, *Sinews of the Spirit*, 3.

49 Ibid., 17–26.

50 John Henry Newman, *An Essay in Aid of a Grammar of Assent* (London: Longmans, Green, 1917), 248–49.

51 For useful bibliographies of Christianity and sports, see Nick J. Watson and Andrew Parker, "Sports and Christianity: Mapping the Field," in *Sports and Christianity: Historical and Contemporary Perspectives*, ed. Nick J. Watson and Andrew Parker (New York: Routledge, 2013), 9–81; and Jim Parry, Simon Robinson, Nick J. Watson, and Mark Nesti, *Sports and Spirituality: An Introduction* (New York: Routledge, 2007), 221–45.

century and spread to the working classes. The body and the soul were both God's work, and both should be cultivated. In 1858 a headmaster, G. E. L. Cotton, said: "God was the creator of our bodies as well as of our minds. His workmanship included physical as well as mental powers and faculties. In developing both we served Him who made us, no less surely than when we knelt in prayer."[52] The clergy did not participate in the drunkenness, swearing, and sexual immorality of men, but they were as masculine as any athlete. Anglican clergymen who had developed a taste for sports while at school brought their enthusiasm to their parishes. Boxing was especially popular.[53] In *Edwin Drood* Dickens satirized such Anglicans as the Rev. Septimus Crispackle, who practiced his feints, "while his radiant features teemed with innocence, and soft-hearted benevolence beamed from his boxing gloves."[54]

The YMCA was founded in London in 1844 and initially forbade all amusements; it came to the United States in 1851 and soon used amusements and sports to attract young men.[55] In fact basketball was invented in the YMCA. In the United States in latter part of the nineteenth century, churches began changing their attitudes to the body and consequently to exercise and sports, Clifford Putney claims, because of the influence of German Higher Criticism.[56] Liberal theologians led the way to a reversal of the Protestant attitude to sports. In the North churches and colleges were influenced by Social Darwinism, which saw in violent sports the way to train men for the conflict of life. Evangelicals continued to regard sports with suspicion. A Congregationalist paper opined: "The law of God requires that we love our neighbor and seek his good. If then, under the pretense of recreation, we contrive to injure our neighbor in any way; or expose him to personal inconvenience or suffering, we are no longer excusable, but criminal."[57]

---

52 Quoted in McLeod, *Religion and Society*, 152.
53 McLeod, *Religion and Society*, 151.
54 Charles Dickens, *The Mystery of Edwin Drood* (New York: Oxford University Press, 1999), 7.
55 Clifford Putney, *Muscular Christianity: Manhood and Sports in Protestant America, 1880–1920* (Cambridge, MA: Harvard University Press, 2001), 64–72.
56 Putney, *Muscular Christianity*, 54.
57 Review of *A Plea for Amusements*, by Frederick W. Sawyer, *The New Englander* 9 (1851): 355.

Football especially for Southern Evangelicals was "a symbol of materialism, fanaticism, modernity, and liberalism."[58]

Evangelicals came to accept sports as necessary to appeal to the most difficult constituencies to evangelize, "the sterner sex"[59] and young men, although they continued to have grave doubts about the most violent sports, such as boxing.[60] Evangelicals tried to steer a middle course, "different from gloomy monkishness on one hand, and from so-called muscular Christianity on the other," as the *Missionary Herald* put it in 1873.[61] The body was temple of the soul and needed to be cultivated and perfected. Health was nigh to godliness. The YMCA lost its evangelical coloring as it emphasized character-building and service over doctrine and conversion, because, as Theodore Roosevelt said, the YMCA "has tried not to dwarf any of the impulses of the young, vigorous man."[62] Fundamentalists tended to regard all sports as a part the world from which Christians should withdraw.[63]

The ministry too needed to be masculinized. Too often, the Unitarian minister Thomas Wentworth Higginson (1823–1911) claimed, the laity are alienated from the clergy because the clergy lack a "vigorous, manly life."[64] The Protestant minister was primarily a preacher of the Bible, and to be a preacher he had to be above all a scholar, a time-consuming vocation. Early nineteenth-century Protestant attitudes to sports were not that different from Orthodox Jewish attitudes: they were a waste of time. The Congregationalist minister Washington Gladden (1836–1918) remembered that

58 Shirl Hoffman, *Good Game: Christianity and the Culture of Sports* (Waco, TX: Baylor University Press, 2010), 94.

59 Samuel Earnshaw, "The Traditions of the Elders," 1860, quoted in Dominic Erdozain, *The Problem of Pleasure: Sport, Recreation and the Crisis of Victorian Religion* (Woodbridge, England: Boydell Press, 2010), 149.

60 Tony Ladd and James A. Mathisen, *Muscular Christianity: Evangelical Protestants and the Development of American Sport* (Grand Rapids, MI: Baker Books, 1999), 85.

61 Quoted in Erdozain, *The Problem of Pleasure*, 149.

62 Quoted in David Setran, *The College "Y": Student Religion in the Era of Secularization* (New York: Palgrave Macmillan, 2007), 129.

63 Ladd and Mathisen, *Muscular Christianity*, 85.

64 Thomas Wentworth Higginson, "Saints and Their Bodies," in *The Writings of Thomas Wentworth Higginson*, Vol. 6, *Outdoor Studies* (Boston: Houghton, Mifflin, 1900), 6.

when he was twelve years old, "he mentally debated the question of conversion, under the impression that the change involved the sacrifice of baseball,"[65] and the Unitarian minister Edward Everett Hale (1822–1909) said that for the Puritans "to play at cricket was a sin."[66] The clergy came to the realization that their sedentary, scholarly way of life was an obstacle to reaching men. Allen Stockdale, the "Pitching Parson," in 1913 advised ministers to "lose the sickly white color of the speculative realm of study, and to take on the more attractive brown of the actual life of men" because "men are liable to lose respect for your traditional position when they lose respect for your muscles."[67]

If the preacher could be an athlete, why couldn't the athlete be a preacher? Billy Sunday played center field for the Chicago White Stockings, and in 1891 went to work for the YMCA and was eventually ordained by the Chicago Presbytery in 1903, although he had no real theological education.[68] He preached the old-time religion, he railed against "the awful malignity of strong drink,"[69] but his main attraction was his style. He was colloquial and used sports metaphors and broke furniture and choked the devil.

Churches began building athletic and recreational facilities, and by this means sometimes were successful in attracting the young, especially "young men," to church activities.[70] Founded in 1954, the Fellowship of Christian Athletes uses coaches and athletes to evangelize other athletes. Its website explains its mission: "To present to athletes and coaches and all whom they influence the challenge and adventure of receiving Jesus Christ as Savior and Lord, serving Him in their relationships and in the fellowship of the church." It was aimed at boys and young men. In 1973, Dave Hannah

---

65 Washington Gladden, *Moral Aspects of Social Questions* (Boston: Houghton, Mifflin, 1886), 253.

66 Edward Everett Hale, "Public Amusement for Rich and Poor," in *Addresses and Essays on Subjects of History Education and Government* (Boston: Little, Brown, 1900), 347.

67 Quoted in Putney, *Muscular Christianity*, 56.

68 Putney, *Muscular Christianity*, 59.

69 William T. Ellis, *"Billy Sunday": The Man and the Message* (Philadelphia: John C. Winston, 1917), 80.

70 Putney, *Muscular Christianity*, 63.

assured Athletes in Action members, "Christianity is for men. It's not a crutch, but a vital, living relationship with God. Through this experience, day by day, he allows us to maximize our mental preparation to meet life as men and as athletes." But like many religious organizations, sports ministries ended up attracting women more than men: "Over the following decades ... female Christian athletes would become the dominant population in sports ministry organizations."[71]

The Social Gospel

Christians in the Anglo-American world did not face military challenges, but they saw a need for heroism in confronting the evils of society. The Christian Socialist F. D. Maurice rejected the interpretation that saw the Sermon on the Mount as recommending "passive or feminine qualities" and which therefore discouraged "all the qualities which have been most conspicuous in heroes who have struggled for freedom." Political Christianity, which in Europe was at the service of the various churches, took a different form in the United States. Men were called to work and fight not for particular churches but for Christian principles. Walter Rauschenbusch, at the beginning of the twentieth century, claimed the failure to preach the Social Gospel was the reason "that our churches are overwhelmingly feminine." Rauschenbusch followed the traditional analysis that women are domestic and religious; men are public and therefore irreligious: "Men's life faces the outward world, and his instincts and interests lie that way. Hence, men crowd where public questions get downright discussion. Our individualistic religion has helped to feminize our churches." Men would find their rightful Christian place in the public, political world. Those who emphasized Christian social action also stressed that Christian men must be masculine and active.[72]

---

71 Annie Blakeney-Glazer, *Faith on the Field: A Cultural Analysis of Sports Ministry in America*, Ph.D. Dissertation 2008, University of North Carolina at Chapel Hill, 79. http://dc.lib.unc.edu/cdm/ref/collection/etd/id/2362.

72 Frederick Denison Maurice, *Social Morality* (London: Macmillan, 1869), 460; Walter Rauschenbusch, *Christianity and the Social Crisis* (Louisville, KY: Westminster/John Knox, 1991), 367.

The Social Gospel was the religious wing of the Progressive Movement; it sought to prepare the way for the coming of the Kingdom of God on earth by means of social reforms.[73] When faced with social problems, the question it asked itself was *What would Jesus do?* Josiah Strong explained that the kingdom of God is Christ's "social ideal, to be realized here in the earth when his prophetic prayer shall have found its fulfilling answer ... and God's will is done in earth even as it is done in heaven."[74] This was a Christianity of action, not of doctrine or of sentiment. The Southern Baptist Convention in 1915 proclaimed: "Some think of the Kingdom of God as narrow, effeminate and sentimental. The exact opposite is true. It is broad, masculine, and practical .... So long as there is social inequality, industrial justice or political crime, the kingdom of God is not yet fully come.... The kingdom of God is not a Sunday affair. It must pervade the factory that runs six days a week as well as the Sunday morning service."[75] Religion was a public matter for men who would fight for justice.

Action would attract men, who wanted challenge, not comfort, in their religion.[76] Josiah Strong declared that "there is not enough of effort, of struggle, in the typical church life of today to win young men to the church.... Eliminate heroism from religion and it becomes weak, effeminate. Is there no significance in the fact that two-thirds of the church-membership today are women, that for every young man in the church there are two young women?"[77] The fight against social evils would attract men to "a masculine concept of the church and church leadership."[78] Frederick

73 For a recent account of the main leaders see Gary Dorrien, *Social Ethics in the Making: Interpreting an American Tradition* (Chichester: Wiley-Blackwell, 2011), 60–143.

74 Josiah Strong, *The Times and Young Men* (New York: Baker & Taylor, 1901), 233.

75 Philip Hamburger, *Separation of Church and State* (Cambridge, MA: Harvard University Press, 2002), 380.

76 See Stephen Prothero, *American Jesus: How the Son of God Became a National Icon* (New York: Farrar, Strauss and Giroux, 2003), 95–97. For both Billy Sunday and Rauschenbusch, Jesus "was a courageous man of action" (ibid., 97).

77 Strong, *The Times and Young Men*, 179–80.

78 Janet Forsythe Fishburn, *The Fatherhood of God and the Victorian Family: The Social Gospel in America* (Philadelphia: Fortress Press, 1981), 169.

DeLane Leete maintained that "men have discovered and the fact is attractive to them that Christianity means a fight, that its object is war à la outrance."[79] The Social Gospel was a religion of action so it needed strong, healthy men, but the body was a means, not an end, because the fight was against social evils, not military action against fellow men.

The Social Gospel called men to fight the ills of society—the robber barons, gross inequality, dangerous working conditions, child labor—so that "great burdens of wrong will be lifted, and deadly vices will be swept away."[80] But those deadly vices included male activities such as drinking.[81] Washington Gladden proclaimed that "the liquor problem was inextricably bound up with the general problem of establishing the Kingdom of God on earth."[82] Prohibition was a goal of the Progressive Movement.[83]

Liberation theology can also be seen as a variant of the Social Gospel. Some Catholic clergy of Latin America grew weary of their role as chaplains to a women's society. They found themselves conducting devotions while upper-class Catholics ground down the poor. Even worse, the ideal of a passive, obedient, suffering Christ was used as an opiate for the masses. The cruel rich, liberation theologians thought, should feel the wrath of God. Machismo could be harnessed against the evil in society: "If social protest is man's work, they [liberation theologians] believe that the fiery Christ will replace the 'effeminized' version. Did not Christ chase the money changers from the temple?"[84]

---

79 Frederick DeLane Leete, *Christian Brotherhoods* (Cincinnati, OH: Jennings and Graham, 1912), 388.

80 Leete, *Christian Brotherhoods*, 392.

81 See Paul Allen Carter, *The Decline and Revival of the Social Gospel: Social and Political Liberalism in American Protestant Churches 1920–1940* (Ithaca, NY: Cornell University Press: 1956), 33–34.

82 Quoted in Anne-Marie E. Szymanski, *Pathways to Prohibition: Radicals, Moderates, and Social Movement Outcomes* (Durham, NC: Duke University Press, 2003), 189.

83 Mara Laura Keire, *For Business and Pleasure: The Regulation of Vice in the United States 1890–1933* (Baltimore: Johns Hopkins Press, 2010), 136–40.

84 Marvin Goldwert, "Machismo and Christ: The New Formula," *Contemporary Review* 145 (1984): 185.

Men and Religion Forward Movement

The Social Gospel helped produce an unusual revival, the Men and Religion Forward Movement of 1911–1912.[85] Rauschenbusch, the most prominent proponent of the Social Gospel, stated that "the Men and Religion Forward Movement has marked a definite advance of the social gospel in the Christian Church in America."[86] Gail Bederman, in her study of the movement, notes that "the messages were often traditional, but the method of presentation was highly unorthodox. As often as possible, organizers bought ads on the sport pages, where Men and Religion messages competed for consumers' attention with ads for automobiles, burlesque houses, and whiskey.... The entire revival, from beginning to end, was occasionally depicted as one big advertising campaign."[87] Like modern revivalism, the Men and Religion Forward Movement used business techniques. Unlike revivalism, it tried to bring men into a mainline Protestantism that did not emphasize emotional peaks, but a slow, steady acceptance of responsibility in the church and society.[88] The Movement also avoided doctrinal controversies and concentrated on practical cooperation across denominational lines. All churches experienced an increase in male membership, the Episcopal church most of all.[89]

Its proponents covered a spectrum of orthodoxy. Some were classic evangelicals, but the search for suitable church work for men led them to ally with the proponents of the Social Gospel. Urban and political reform under church auspices was the heart of the Social Gospel, which also provided work suitable for men: the protection of the weak and interaction

85 See L. Dean Allen, *Rise Up, O Men of God: The "Men and Religion Forward Movement" and the "Promise Keepers"* (Macon, GA: Mercer University Press, 2002).

86 Walter C. Rauschenbusch, "The Conservation of the Social Service Message," in *Messages of the Men and Religion Movement*, Vol. 2, *Social Service,* (New York: Association Press, 1912), 121.

87 Gail Bederman, "'The Women Have Had Charge of the Church Work Long Enough': The Men and Religion Forward Movement of 1911–1912 and the Masculinization of Middle-Class Protestantism," *American Quarterly* 41 (1989): 444.

88 Allen, *Rise Up, O Men of God,* 120.

89 See Bederman, "Men and Religion," 454.

with the world of business and politics. The family had to be protected from the corrosive influences of modern life.[90] The father, although his religion was supposed to be sane, calm, rational, and steady, was not supposed to be just a distant authority figure and a provider, but a companion to his sons: "It is just as important that the father should play with and be the father to his boy as for him to see that he has good food, warm clothing, and a comfortable bed to sleep in."[91] Appeals to men's desires to be good fathers became increasingly prominent in attempts to reach men.

Promise Keepers

Promise Keepers, although it uses many revivalist techniques,[92] bears a strong resemblance to its predecessor, the Men and Religion Forward Movement, as Charles Lippy has pointed out.[93] Most importantly, both seek to encourage men to be involved with their families. Lippy thinks "that Promise Keepers is simply trying to carve out a place for men in the domestic sphere that allows them to retain a male identity, just as Men and Religion Forward and advocates of male domesticity did."[94]

In 1990 Bill McCartney,[95] head football coach at the University of Colorado, had a conversation with an official of the Fellowship of Christian Athletes that gave him the idea for Promise Keepers, and he chose the name

90   Allen, *Rise Up, O Men of God*, 113–23.
91   Cence A. Barbour, *Making Religion Efficient* (New York: Association Press, 1912), 30.
92   See Michael A. Longinow, "The Price of Admission? Promise Keepers' Roots in Revivalism and the Emergence of Middle Class Language and Appeal in Men's Movements," in *The Promise Keepers: Essays on Masculinity and Christianity*, ed. Dane S. Claussen (Jefferson, NC: McFarland, 2000), 44–46.
93   Charles H. Lippy, "Miles to Go: Promise Keepers in Historical and Cultural Context," in *Men and Masculinities in Christianity and Judaism: A Critical Reader*, ed. Björn Krondorfer (London: SCM Press, 2009), 321–32. See also Charles H. Lippy on Promise Keepers in *Do Real Men Pray? Images of the Christian Man and Male Spirituality in White Protestant America* (Knoxville: University of Tennessee Press, 2005), 187–97.
94   Lippy, "Miles to Go," 329.
95   For the career and family difficulties of William McCartney, see Lippy, *Do Real Men Pray?* 197–205.

in 1991. Promise Keepers leaders noticed that men in modern America differed from women in that men had trouble developing close relations; men tended to be isolated and loners.[96] Promise Keepers sought to make men emotionally expressive to overcome this alienation.[97] McCartney said that "we want to help men heal the lost and broken relationships in their lives. We want to see fathers and sons reunited in love and repentance .... we want to see men fall down before God and repent of their past sins .... I truly believe that there is not a single wound that cannot be healed, not a single heart that cannot be softened, through the love of Jesus Christ."[98] Allen sees this therapeutic approach (as opposed to the business methods of the Men and Religion Forward Movement) as a consequence of the American commitment to therapy as the solution to life's problems.[99] Men were told that they should defend their families by personal involvement; previously men had been told to become active in social reform. Promise Keepers also uses metaphors from sports and warfare to motivate men to act. Men are competitive and Satan is the enemy.

The feminization of the Church and the feminization of men are targets of Promise Keepers' criticism.[100] A key part of the feminization of men, according to Promise Keepers, is the lack of conviction. The masculine male is independent of the opinion of others; he is a principled man. But the problem with our society is, according to a statement by two Promise Keepers, that "many men who grow up in a feminized environment skip over independence and opt for over-dependence" and they therefore are "codependent" on "others for validation of his or her beliefs or values."[101]

Promise Keepers are also well aware of the tendency of men to be overly independent, to be alienated and unempathetic. They look to Christ as a model in overcoming the tendencies of masculinity to go wrong: "Christ nurtures; men can nurture. Christ experienced fear; men can be

96 Allen, *Rise Up, O Men of God*, 209.
97 Ibid., 213.
98 Quoted in Allen, *Rise Up, O Men of God*, 171–72.
99 Allen, *Rise Up, O Men of God*, 228–29.
100 See Ken Abraham, *Who Are the Promise Keepers? Understanding the Christian Men's Movement* (New York: Doubleday, 1997), 106–10.
101 Bryan W. Brickner, *The Promise Keepers: Politics and Promise* (Lanham, MD: Lexington Books, 1999), 80.

afraid. Christ cried; men can cry. Christ doubted; men can have doubts. Christ was intimate with other men; men can be intimate with other men."[102] Promise Keepers follows the evangelical tradition in seeing Jesus as the model of the perfect man. Since Jesus perfectly exemplifies masculinity, what Jesus did is therefore a model for men. His self-sacrifice is the central motif, but also important is his display of emotions. What Jesus did was perfect, so men can do the same things and remain masculine, or rather become truly masculine. Michael Messner acknowledges that Promise Keepers offers men a secure identity as Christian fathers, and that "a man who is secure in his position as a man has no need for alcohol, has no need to destroy his own body or other men's bodies through violence, has no need to resort to sexual promiscuity to prove himself."[103] Women are often happy to cede symbolic headship of the family for this vast improvement in male behavior.

Promise Keepers has a revivalist cast,[104] with mass meetings that ask for a commitment to the faith. It focuses especially on married men, and among them on those who have some sense of responsibility and are willing to listen to spiritual advice on how to fulfill the responsibilities of marriage. Promise Keepers does not reach the unchurched male; "Ninety-percent of the stadium goers" were "evangelical, Pentecostal, or charismatic," a third were Baptists, and "four-fifths claimed they attended services weekly."[105] These men have already made a reconnection to the feminine in marriage, and it is this connection to the feminine that the leadership of Promise Keepers is using to bring men back into a closer relationship with the Church. The long-range success of Promise Keepers is, however, doubtful. Revivalist attempts to reach men may have some initial success, but they founder in their attempts to

---

102 Ibid., 86.
103 Michael A. Messner, *Politics of Masculinities: Men in Movements* (Lanham, MD: AltaMira Press, 2000), 34.
104 See Michael J. Chrastra, "The Religious Roots of the Promise Keepers" in Claussen, *The Promise Keepers*, 20; Longinow, "The Price of Admission?" 40–55; Kenneth Clatterbaugh, *Contemporary Perspectives on Masculinity: Men, Women, and Politics in Modern Society* (Boulder, CO: Westview Press, 1997), 177–93.
105 Edward L. Gambill, *Uneasy Males: The American Men's Movement 1970–2000* (New York: iUniverse, 2005), 192.

develop stable commitments.[106] Men may be attracted by the crisis atmosphere, but they discover it is impossible to live day to day in a crisis.[107] In addition, Promise Keepers faces the problem that the church life to which it is attempting to attract men continues to be feminized and therefore tolerable only by men who have a strong connection to religious women.

Soft Patriarchy

Conservative Protestantism, according to Brad Wilcox, "domesticates men"[108] by connecting men to a community which stresses family responsibilities.[109] About 50% of conservative Protestant men attend church frequently (several times a month), compared to 39% of mainline Protestant men and 7% of men not affiliated with a church.[110] Conservative churches emphasize men as patriarchs; they also help men get more emotionally involved with their wives and children. Consequently, according to Wilcox, "churchgoing conservative Protestant family men have the lowest rates of domestic violence of any major religious group in the United States."[111] Such men, while disciplining their children, are spending more time with them and are more expressive emotionally both with their children and their wives than mainline Protestants and unaffiliated men are.[112] Men take

106 For its rise and decline, see Gambill, *Uneasy Males*, 185–204.

107 See Abraham, *Who Are the Promise Keepers*, 153–54.

108 W. Bradford Wilcox, *Soft Patriarchs, New Men: How Christianity Shapes Fathers and Husbands* (Chicago: University of Chicago Press, 2004), 13. See also Brasher, *Godly Women: Fundamentalism and Female Power*, 168, and Frances Fitzgerald, *Cities on a Hill: A Journey through Contemporary American Cultures* (New York: Simon & Schuster, 1986), 141.

109 For the demographic profiles of churches see Wilcox, *Soft Patriarchs*, 71, and Callum Brown, *Religion and the Demographic Revolution: Women and Secularisation in Canada, Ireland, UK and USA since the 1960s* (Woodbridge, England: Boydell Press, 2012), 84.

110 Wilcox, *Soft Patriarchs*, 16.

111 Ibid., 207.

112 Ibid., 10, 13. See also Colleen McDannell, "Beyond Dr. Dobson: Women, Girls, and Focus on the Family," in *Women and Twentieth-Century Protestantism*, eds. Margaret Lamberts Bendroth and Virginia Lieson Brereton (Urbana: University of Illinois Press, 2002), 122.

more responsibility, including emotional responsibility, for their families because of the largely symbolic headship they receive.[113] Scott Coltrane sees evidence that "in societies where men develop and maintain close relationships with young children, hypermasculine displays and competitive posturing are rare."[114] Women and children benefit from men's participation in these churches; the problem remains of how to get men to participate, especially men who follow the rules of machismo in Hispanic cultures.

Evangelicalism has had more success than Catholicism in detaching Hispanic men from machismo, and one strategy it has used is to call men to take responsibility for their families, to be the heads of their families, to be patriarchs.

> The discipline and order of the family in Pentecostalism emerges from the emphasis on patriarchal authority in both the home and the church. The notion of the father as the caring but strict head of the household parallels the pastor's role as head of the church. The reinforcement of the nuclear family, in fact, is central to the vision (and the success) of Pentecostal churches throughout the Americas. In the face of disintegrating families, irresponsible husbands, and undisciplined children, Pentecostal churches often present a healing solution: a place for each member of the family in an orderly, hierarchical, and stable structure, supported and mirrored by the church itself, and sharply opposed to the corrupt outside world.[115]

The strategy of evangelicalism in Latin cultures has been to build up the family and to separate it from the corrupt and violent structures of society, hoping that as more and more families follow Christian patterns the larger society will be influenced for the better.

113 Wilcox, *Soft Patriarchs,* 173.
114 Scott Coltrane, *Family Man: Fatherhood, Housework, and Gender Equality* (New York: Oxford University Press, 1996), 188.
115 Anna Peterson, Manuel Vásquez, and Philip Williams, "Christianity and Social Change in the Shadow of Globalization," in *Christianity, Social Change, and Globalization in the Americas,* eds. Anna L. Peterson, Manuel A. Vásquez, and Philip J. Williams (New Brunswick, NJ: Rutgers University Press, 2001), 11.

Although Catholics also want men to be responsible fathers, they have had less success in achieving this than conservative Protestants have. This may be because both the Catholic Church and mainline Protestants, according to some observers, "emphasize the family the least of all the traditions we studied."[116] Instead these churches focus on social justice, seeking to correct the underlying structural problems that lead to poverty, drunkenness, and family abandonment.[117] However, such an approach is long-term and may not succeed, while individual reformation of the man, the goal of conservative Protestantism, produces immediate, visible benefits for the family and for the woman, as the man stops drinking, gambling, fighting, and womanizing and instead devotes his time and money to his wife and children. For conservative Latino Evangelicals there is no doubt that male and female roles are divinely ordained, and that fatherhood "is a divinely commissioned responsibility and authority."[118] Such a message has not been proclaimed by Catholics and liberal Protestants, who tend to follow Western feminist prescriptions for social reform.

In Colombia, and in many developing countries, family life has been severely disrupted by the difficult transition from a peasant to a money economy. Conversion to an evangelical or charismatic church leads men to reaffirm traditional sex roles, but in a manner that benefits their families. Elizabeth Brusco points out that Western feminists and Third World feminists often disagree about sex roles, because in the Third World "traditional systems may be more effective in providing for the fulfillment of women's basic needs and goals and allocating status to their activities, even when they remain separate from the activities of men."[119] The St. Joachim's Catholic Men's Organization in Zambia promotes a traditional model of man as the responsible head of a family. This is foreign to Western gender equality. But, as Adriaan S. van Klinken observes, Zambian "women seem to be more interested in concrete and significant changes in the behaviour of men than in the question whether

---

116 Peterson, Vásquez, and Williams, "Christianity and Social Change," 11.
117 Ibid., 29.
118 Jose Leonardo Santos, *Evangelicalism and Masculinity: Faith and Gender in El Salvador* (Lanham, MD: Lexington Books, 2012), 54.
119 Elizabeth Ellen Brusco, *The Reformation of Machismo: Evangelical Conversion and Gender in Colombia* (Austin: University Press of Texas, 1995), 141.

men adhere to an abstract ideal of gender equality."[120] Concretely, men who convert to a Christianity that demands responsible male headship stop abandoning their families and squandering their money.

Jose Santos studied the interaction of evangelicalism and masculine ideals in violent post-war El Salvador. Evangelicals in El Salvador (who have fundamentalist, Pentecostal, and Holiness traits) have attracted equal numbers of men and women,[121] unlike most other religious groups in the Americas. Evangelicals tell a compelling narrative in which men reject a masculine code of violence, honor, drinking, and promiscuity in order to become patriarchs, servant leaders who dedicate themselves in self-giving, affectionate love to their wives and children and to society at large. They separate themselves from the masculine "world," rejecting even the universal passion for soccer, and begin a new, Christian life. Pentecostalism too "stands for the domestic table over against the street and the bar and the machismo culture of violence and indulgence."[122]

In the United States black churches especially feel the lack of men; Jeremiah Wright, the controversial pastor of President Obama's church in Chicago, recognizes that black men "are a pitiful minority in most Black congregations."[123] Afro-American pastors have to deal with the social disintegration that irresponsible and criminal male behavior causes; they try to convince men to be responsible patriarchs. James Meeks built up his church by teaching "every real man should take leadership in the church and in his home, because God designed him to be in charge."[124]

120 Adriaan S. van Klinken, "Imitation as Transformation of the Male Self: How an Apocryphal Saint Reshapes Zambian Catholic Men," *Cahiers d'Études africaines* 53, no. 209–10 (2013): 137. https://adriaanvanklinken.files.wordpress.com/2012/05/2013-imitation-as-transformation-of-the-male-self.pdf.

121 Santos, *Evangelicalism and Masculinity*, 83, 104.

122 David Martin, "Evangelical Expansion in Global Society," in *Christianity Reborn: the Global Expansion of Evangelicalism in the Twentieth Century*, ed. Donald M. Lewis (Grand Rapids, MI: Wm. B. Eerdmans, 2004), 293.

123 Jeremiah A. Wright, Jr., "Foreword," in Jawanza Kunjufu, *Adam! Where Are You? Why Most Black Men Don't Go to Church* (Sauk Village, IL: African American Images, 1994), vi.

124 James Meeks, "Building a Church with Men," in *Man Power: The New Revival in America: The Call to African American Men for Spiritual Renewal*, ed. Edwin Lewis Cole (Nashville, TN: Thomas Nelson, 1997), 172.

Churches for Men

Caitlin Leffingwell visited churches in Hartford, Connecticut, in 2011–12. The congregations of the mainline churches were predominantly female. But one, in the Southern Baptist tradition, had 30 men and 22 women, mostly educated young adults. The pastor explained the male presence in his church, or rather the male absence in most churches: "Instead of being invited into 'the risky adventure that the church should be' through reliance completely on the Holy Spirit as a kingdom is formed, the call to be a Christian has become a call to comfort, a 'come to my bosom' in which many worship songs sound more like 'prom songs for Jesus.'"[125] The pastor believed that men and women had different roles, and that when women started taking over men's roles in the church, men were altogether too willing to turn responsibility over to them. Therefore it helped that the pastor was male, and indeed a young male.

Seeker-friendly churches make men their primary target. Men are ultra-sensitive to authority and infringements on their hard-won independence.[126] Bill Hybels, the founder of Willow Creek Church, names them "seekers"—those who were on a spiritual journey, looking for adventure. Willow Creek uses rock music, entertainment, and a deliberately unchurchy atmosphere with no religious symbols. The typical seeker is "Unchurched Harry," or as the Catholic priest Michael White names him, "Timonium Tim."[127] White and his assistant Tom Corcoran at the Church of the Nativity in Timonium, Maryland, aim at the de-churched Catholic man, because "we're convinced that if we can get Tim on the discipleship path, his wife will happily join him and his kids will have a far better shot at staying active through their teen and adult years."[128]

---

125 Caitlin Leffingwell, "Eternal Insurance—No Boys Allowed! Understanding Gender Disparities in Church Attendance through a Study of Churches in Hartford, Connecticut" (University of Connecticut, Honors Scholar Thesis, Paper 250, 2012), 30. http://digitalcommons.uconn.edu/srhonors_theses/250.

126 James B. Twitchell, *Branded Nation: The Marketing of Megachurch, College, Inc., and Museum World* (New York: Simon & Schuster, 2004), 101.

127 Michael White and Tom Corcoran, *Rebuilt: Awakening the Faithful, Reaching the Lost, and Making Church Matter* (Notre Dame, IN: Ave Maria Press, 2013), 72.

128 Ibid., 74.

Mark Driscoll, the former pastor of Mars Hill Church, worried about the immature American "guy" culture: "Those guys tend not to go to church. If those guys do show up at church, it's usually just to find a couple of gals to break the commandments with. And the Church doesn't really know what to do with them, so the least likely person in America to go to church is a guy in his 20s who is single. Without knowing what to do with those guys, they commit crimes, they get women pregnant, they're a drain on social services, they don't raise their kids, they don't contribute to church, they're not getting ready to lead the next generation. I'd say it's nothing short of a crisis, it's a real problem."[129] Driscoll speaks to young men bluntly their own language about sex and has therefore shocked many evangelicals.[130] His use of coarse and comic language about Scripture to overcome the reluctance of young men to listen to the Gospel also has drawn much criticism.[131]

Driscoll also likes the use of Mixed Martial Arts (also known as Cage Fighting) to attract young men to church and to show that Christianity isn't for wimps. Brandon Beals, a pastor of a church in Washington State, says that he agrees that "compassion and love" are important, but "what led me to find Christ was that Jesus was a real fighter."[132] This approach has been roundly criticized, but its goal is not to make men hypermasculine, but to reach men who are macho and put them on the path to becoming Christians and responsible and affectionate fathers and husbands. Driscoll courts controversy with his approach, but his pastoral advice to men is to cultivate intimacy. He insists that a man, like Jesus, must be both "tough and tender," or one might say, meek and macho:

129 Roxanne Wiemann, "Mark Driscoll Says Just Grow Up," http://www.relevant-magazine.com/god/church/features/22807-mark-driscoll-wants-you-to-grow-up.

130 See Gerry Brashears, quoted in Collin Hansen, *Young, Restless, Reformed: A Journalist's Journey with the New Calvinists* (Wheaton, IL: Crossway Books, 2008), 145.

131 See John MacArthur, "Grunge Christianity? Counterculture's Death-Spiral and the Vulgarization of the Gospel," *Pulpit Magazine*, December 11, 2006. http://media.sermonaudio.com/mediapdf/42408014482.pdf.

132 R. M. Schneiderman, "Flock Is Now a Fight Team in Some Ministries," *New York Times*, February 2, 2010.

As men, we are to be tough in defending the week, oppressed, abused, and poor, fighting for justice and mercy .... We are to be tough in carving out safety and protection for women and children in a world that abuses then.

As men, we are to be tender in comforting the hurting, encouraging the downcast, and teaching the simple. We are to be tender with our wives, loving them as Christ does the church. We are to be tender with our children, kissing them on the head, often telling them that we love them, and providing continuous assurance that we truly consider them gifts from God. We are to be tender with those who are already broken by their sin and needing godly counsel and help.[133]

A man must exemplify both *thumos* and *prautes*, like a merciful king, who is tender and compassionate not because he is weak, but because he is strong. Like many preachers, Driscoll did not follow his own advice, and self-destructed because of his bullying and duplicity.[134]

Men's intensity, their *thumos*, is essential to their masculinity. Both Catholic and Protestant clergy have usually done their best to damp it down, rather than to use it to give energy to Christianity. Churches offer comfort and safety, a refuge from the world. The Scots chaplain A. Herbert Gray wanted men to hear this message: "that the biggest and bravest of men is calling them to a great adventure that will involve many risks, that will tax all their resources—that God Himself needs them and will use all that is most daring in them for His ends."[135] That is also John Eldredge's point in his occasionally erratic *Wild at Heart*.[136] God has placed the fire of

---

133 Mark and Grace Driscoll, *Real Marriage: The Truth about Sex, Friendship and Life Together* (Nashville, TN: Thomas Nelson, 2012), 44.

134 Michael Paulson, "A Brash Style that Filled Pews, Until Followers Had Their Fill," *New York Times*, August 22, 2014. http://www.nytimes.com /2014/08/23/us/mark-driscoll-is-being-urged-to-leave-mars-hill-church.html?_r=0.

135 A. Herbert Gray, *As Tommy Sees Us: A Book for Church Folk* (London: Edward Arnold, 1917), 47.

136 John Eldridge, *Wild at Heart: Discovering the Secret of a Man's Soul* (Nashville, TN: Thomas Nelson, 2001).

thumos in man; like all fire it is dangerous, but it gives light and heat to a cold world.

Karl Rahner asked "What should a masculine Christianity look like?"[137] James E. Dittes examines the masculine drive to transcendence. Because of the physical and psychological development of the male, every "man experiences life as given to him as incomplete."[138] This emptiness produces a desire for self-transcendence through death and rebirth. Men are always looking for this experience, upsetting the settled routines of life, going on pilgrimages and adventures, changing careers, committing themselves obsessively to work or play or sex in a hope of finding the beyond out there. Men seek to be reborn and receive new powers. Men seek power because they love: "We men are gripped with a passion to control because we are gripped with a passion to save."[139] Because he is a man, he knows that life is full of sorrow and wants to protect those he loves from that sorrow. Every man is a soldier and a priest. He wants to bring salvation, "to save life from its sorrow by summoning the transcendent."[140] But men look almost anywhere but to Christianity for the transcendence for which they long.

137 Karl Rahner, "Der Mann in der Kirche, " in *Sendung und Gnade: Beiträge zur pastoral Theologie*. 5th edition (Innsbruck-Vienna: Tyrolia-Verlag, 1988), 292.

138 James E. Dittes, *Driven by Hope: Men and Meaning* (Louisville, KY: Westminster John Knox, 1996), 9.

139 Ibid., 67.

140 Ibid., 69.

Chapter Nine
Men and the Future of the Church

Male alienation from Christianity has been an important source, perhaps the main source, of the declining influence of the churches. Men have resented the attempts of the clergy to make them abandon their hard-earned masculinity and become like women. Churches therefore have had as their main constituency women and children, but now women are following men out of the church, taking their children with them. At the end of the nineteenth century in Germany, Franz Xaver Wetzel observed that "the example of the father works almost infallibly on the children. So pastors and mothers can raise the boys and girls in faith and the fear of God, can keep them in piety and virtue—but too soon comes the grown-up son, the mature daughter and says 'I am following the example of my father, so it will be a lot more fun. One doesn't have to pray so much, one can allow oneself a lot. In my father's path I will be free of all moral constraints. Away with the superstitions of the mother! Long live the father's freer, happier spirit!'"[1] The father's world is more attractive than the mother's world, to the girls as well as to the boys. In Norman Rockwell's depiction of this situation in his *Saturday Evening Post* cover from May 16, 1959, the mother and children are dressed and off to church, while the father stays home in his pajamas and reads the Sunday paper. The boy looks at him. But soon the girl will look at him too.

Bill Hybels of Willow Creek Church wanted to reach the unchurched. In his survey of the neighborhood he discovered that "the impediment to family faith was, in a word, men."[2] If men go to church, "women follow,

---

1 Franz Xaver Wetzel, *Leitsterne für die männliche Jugend und strebsame Männer* (Ravensburg: Dorn'sche Verlagsbuchhandlung, 1896), 297–98.
2 James B. Twitchell, *Branded Nation: The Marketing of Megachurch, College, Inc., and Museum World* (New York: Simon & Schuster, 2004), 101.

children in tow."[3] Belgian Catholics had noticed this, and *The Messenger of the Sacred Heart* pointed out that "when the man is a Christian, then the whole family is; the opposite is not true; when you have the women and the children, often the man still resists."[4] The Rev. Watts Ditchfield warned clergymen in early twentieth-century England that if they did not reach men but concentrated on women and children: "the lack of men in his church will have convinced the children (while they are children) that it is unmanly to go to Church. On the other hand, if he gets the men, *they* will see that the children attend Sunday school, who in their turn will be more likely to become church goers as they become older."[5]

The father is the key to transmitting religion to the next generation. A 1994–1995 Swiss survey[6] (and Switzerland is a multi-religious, multi-national society) produced intriguing results. If the father is a regular practitioner, he has an overwhelming influence on the practice of his children; in fact, surprisingly, more children are practicing if the father is a regular practitioner and the mother is irregular or non-practicing than if both parents are regular churchgoers. If the father is an irregular practitioner and the mother is regular, only 3.4% of the children are regular practitioners; if the father is non-practicing and the mother is regular, only 1.5% of the children are regular practitioners. Unless the father is practicing, the children are lost to the church. The authors of *Young Catholic America* summarize their findings: "Committed Catholic fathers are not a sufficient condition for producing children who will be committed Catholics down the road.

3   Twitchell, *Branded Nation*, 101.

4   Quoted by Tine van Osselaer, "From That Moment On, I Was a Man: Images of the Catholic Male in the Sacred Heart Devotion," in *Gender and Christianity in Modern Europe: Beyond the Feminization Thesis*, eds. Patrick Pasture and Jan Art (Louvain: Leuven University Press, 2012), 124.

5   J. E. Watts Ditchfield, "Men's Services in the Church of England," in *The Religious Life of London*, ed. Richard Mudie-Smith (London: Hodder & Staughton, 1904), 303.

6   Werner Haug and Philippe Wanner, "The Demographic Characteristics of Linguistic and Religious Groups in Switzerland," in *The Demographic Characteristics of National Minorities in Certain European States*, Population Studies, No. 31, Vol. 2, eds. Werner Haug, Paul Compton, Youssef Courbage (Strasbourg: Council of Europe Publishing, 2000), 154.

However ... having a committed Catholic father seems to be a necessary condition." That is, "the faith of Catholic fathers is powerfully determinative of the future faith of their children."[7]

If the churches cannot attract and keep men, they eventually will not have women or children either, and they will wither. "Even when controlling for the proportion of older participants, a higher proportion of women in the congregation is associated with decline rather than growth. As was the case for younger adults, the congregation that is able to attract larger proportions of men, who also tend to be less religiously active, is the exceptional congregation—and is more likely to grow,"[8] as C. Kirk Hadaway concludes from an analysis of church surveys. The greater the percentage of males in the congregation, the healthier a congregation is. Callum Brown points out that the British churches with the highest percentage of women are declining faster than more conservative churches which have a higher proportion of men[9] (although they too are declining). Many women apparently have come to like a "feminized" environment even less than men do.

James Wellman's study of a group of churches in the Pacific Northwest of the United States, a highly unchurched region, found that the mainline churches were 53% female and 47% male, but that the evangelical churches were 40% female and 60% male.[10] The evangelical churches were almost by definition mission-oriented, and they were successful in growing (by 90% in five years)[11] and in reaching men. Although, like other mainline churches,

---

7   Christian Smith, et al., *Young Catholic America: Emerging Adults in, Out of, and Gone from the Church* (New York: Oxford University Press, 2014), 124, 125.

8   C. Kirk Hadaway, "FACTs on Growth: A new look at the dynamics of growth and decline in American congregations based on the Faith Communities Today 2005 national survey of congregations." http://faithcommunitiestoday. org/sites/all/themes/factzen4/files/CongGrowth.pdf.

9   Callum G. Brown, *Religion and the Demographic Revolution: Women and Secularisation in Canada, Ireland, UK and USA since the 1960s* (Woodbridge, England: Boydell Press, 2012), 262–63.

10 James K. Wellman, Jr., *Evangelical vs. Liberal: The Clash of Christian Cultures in the Pacific Northwest* (New York: Oxford University Press, 2008), 51.

11 Wellman, *Evangelical vs. Liberal*, 48. The liberal pastors feared growth and did not want larger congregations; their churches, not surprisingly, were generally not growing (134).

the Presbyterian Church USA (PCUSA) is in decline, not all congregations are declining. In 2005–6, congregations that were over 50% male actually *grew*, while congregations that were 40–50% male were down 1.5% and congregations that were less than 40% male were down 2.09%.[12]

The Departure of Women

The gap between men and women in church participation is narrowing in some highly secularized milieus, but not because men are becoming more active. Women are beginning to reject the traditional model of femininity as a form of infantilization. As women enter public life, they tend to adopt masculine attitudes, including the masculine suspicion of religion. Thomas Reese, the Jesuit editor of *America*, fears the loss of women: "The growing alienation of educated Catholic women from the Church is especially critical for the future since women traditionally filled the churches in Europe and Latin America and were more deferential than men to clerical influence."[13] But women no longer want to be passive recipients of clerical direction.

Christof Wolf has analyzed the difference between German men and women in terms of religious observance, age, cohort, and population of place of residence. In older cohorts, the differences between men and women are substantial as the members of that cohort age. But in the youngest cohort, the difference between male and female observance disappears in the cities. As a result "the pews, which the women leave behind empty in the Church, are not filled by men. The defeminization of the church is not a 're-masculinization.' It is much more a general detachment from the Church."[14] In Italy also the historical gap between the sexes is closing. Sandro Magister notes the decline in church attendance among

12 David. T. Olsen, *The American Church in Crisis: Groundbreaking Research Based on a National Database of Over 200,000 Churches* (Grand Rapids, MI: Zondervan 2008), 103.

13 Thomas J. Reese, *Inside the Vatican: The Politics and Organization of the Catholic Church* (Cambridge, MA: Harvard University Press, 1998), 276.

14 Christof Wolf, "Zur Entwicklung der Kirchlichkeit von Männern und Frauen 1953 bis 1992," in *Religion und Geschlecterverhältis*, eds. Ingrid Lukatis, Regina Sommer, and Christof Wolf (Opladen: Lesker & Budrich, 2010), 81.

young Italians: "The collapse is so clear that it also wipes out the differences in religious practice between men and women—the latter of whom tend much more to be practicing—typical of previous generations. Among the youngest, very few of the women go to church, on a par with the men."[15] As attendance at mass approaches zero, the male and female rates are converging.[16]

Church involvement in the United States has begun to follow the same pattern. From 1991 to 2012, church involvement by men has declined 6 percentage points among men, but among women 11 percentage points; volunteer work at church has declined 6 percentage points, but among women 9 percentage points. Bible reading among women has declined 10 percentage points, so that now more men than women (41% to 40%) read the Bible every week.[17] As George Barna notes, "the religious gender gap has substantially closed."[18] But it has closed not because men have become more like women, but because women have become more like men.

Some cohorts of women may have surpassed men in alienation from religion. In examining the data of religious commitment since 1987, William C. D'Antonio, Michele Dillon, and Mary L. Gautier find that "it has become quite evident that women's long-standing loyalty to the Church and commitment to Catholicism can no longer be taken for granted. On key indicators of commitment—weekly Mass attendance, attitudes about the importance of the Church in their lives, and whether they might ever leave the Church—Catholic women show a steep trajectory of decline over the past 25 years. This decline is such that women's levels of commitment to the Church are now on a par with men's, whereas in 1987, women's

15 Sandro Magister, "Who Goes to Mass and Who Doesn't: The Uncertain Tomorrow of Catholic Italy," chiesa.expressonline.it, August 6, 2010.

16 Jean Twenge sees the same phenomenon in the United States. See Danielle Paquette, "Why more young women than ever before are skipping church," *Washington Post*, May 27, 2015, http://www.washingtonpost.com/blogs/wonkblog/wp/2015/05/27/why-more-young-women-than-ever-are-skipping-church/.

17 "Twenty Years of Surveys Show Key Differences in the Faith of America's Men and Women," barna.org. August 1, 2011.

18 "Comments on the August 1 Barna Update," georgebarna.com.

commitment far exceeded men's."[19] Patricia Wittberg found that millennial Catholic women (i.e., those born between 1981 and 1995), "are slightly more likely than Catholic men their age to say that they never attend Mass."[20]

The ordination of women has not stopped the departure of women and may inadvertently contribute to it. As Charles Lippy observes, "as Protestant religious institutions were opening the ranks of the clergy and other leadership positions to women," they are thereby "unwittingly cementing even more the cultural equation of that which is generally accepted as religious as being feminine rather than masculine."[21] As early as the mid-1970s, Episcopalians recognized that "the ordained ministry may become a profession chiefly for women, like nursing."[22] In 2012 the majority of Canadian United Church ministers were women, and 80% of ordinands are now women. In 2007 and again in 2010 a majority of those ordained for the Church of England were women, and the London School of Economics sociologist David Martin claims that "it is obvious that over time the priesthood will become increasingly a female occupation."[23] Since the Episcopal Church has opened

19 William V. D'Antonio, Michele Dillon, and Mary L. Gautier, *American Catholics in Transition* (Lanham, MD: Rowman & Littlefield, 2013), 13–14. For example, in 1987, 52% of Catholic women attended weekly Mass, while 35% of Catholic men attended. The corresponding figures for 2011 are 31% of women and 30% of men.

20 Patricia Wittberg, "A Lost Generation?" *America*, February 20, 2012. http://americamagazine.org/issue/5129/article/lost-generation.

21 Charles H. Lippy, *Do Real Men Pray? Images of the Christian Man and Male Spirituality in White Protestant America* (Knoxville, TN: University of Tennessee Press, 2005), 221.

22 Constance H. Buchanan, "The Anthropology of Vitality and Decline," in *Episcopal Women: Gender, Spirituality and Commitment in an American Mainline Denomination*, ed. Catherine M. Prelinger (New York: Oxford University Press, 1992), 313.

23 For Canada in 2012 see David Ewart, "United Church Glass Ceiling?" Resources for Worship, Leadership, and Congregational Health, September 11, 2012, http://www.davidewart.ca/2012/09/united-church-glass-ceiling.html. In 2007 the Rev. Michael Webster said that in his United Church congregation, "women outnumber men three to one—and by United Church standards, that's a lot of men" ("Where the Guys Aren't," *UC Observer*, June 2007) http://www.ucobserver.org/living/2007/06/where_the_guys_arent/. For England in 2007 see Ruth Gledhill, "More women than men are being ordained to Anglican priesthood," *London Times*, November 14, 2007. http://www.the-

the ministry to women, the candidates tend "to be increasingly female, predominantly middle-aged," and more frequently than in the past, "openly homosexual." Missing are "young, usually married men."[24] A male clergy will not necessarily attract laymen—it has not done so in the past; but a female clergy may further cement the identification of Christianity and femininity. In England in 2010 women were 55% of the congregation, in 2012, 63%.[25] If the ministry eventually reflects the congregation, especially the active members of the congregation, the vast majority of those ordained will be women.

What churches have not done is ask themselves whether women are simply imitating men in departing from the church, and whether women have generally the same motives as men for departing. Mainline denominations seem content to be shrinking women's clubs. Adair T. Lummis of Hartford Theological Seminary concluded a presentation on the absence of men in the Episcopal Church with this observation: "Denominations and congregations have survived long without a balance of men to women in the pews. If real men support the church financially and approve of their family members attending, why be concerned that men are not present? Solution: let the jocks be and let the more spiritually advanced women and men both people and manage the congregations!"[26] She articulates what seems to be a widespread attitude.[27] But if men reject Christianity as

times.co.uk/tto/faith/article2098750.ece ; for England in 2010 see Myles Collier, "Ordained Women Priests Outpace Men in Church of England," *Christian Post*, June 2, 2010. http://www.christianpost.com/news/ordained-women-priests-outpace-men-in-church-of-england-77553/; Martin is quoted in Collier, "Ordained Women."

24 Buchanan, "The Anthropology of Vitality and Decline," 31.

25 Collier, "Ordained Women."

26 Adair T. Lummis, "Men's Commitment to Religion: Perceptions of its Nature, Nurture, and Consequences," paper delivered at the Annual Meeting of the Society for the Scientific Study of Religion, October 2002. http://hirr.hartsem.edu/bookshelf/lummis_article2.html.

27 Diane Knippers claims that "radical feminism is the dominant ideology that controls mainline seminaries; indeed our theological schools are in the grips of a kind of feminist fundamentalism that brooks no dissent or opposition" ("Fatherhood in the Mainline Protestant Tradition," in *The Faith Factor in Fatherhood: Renewing the Sacred Vocation of Fathering*, ed. Don E. Eberly [Lanham, MD: Lexington Books, 1999], 117).

detrimental to their masculine identity, women too will reject it as detrimental to their equality with men. Women demand to enter into male-dominated areas; men do not demand to enter female-dominated fields, and this failure causes women to suspect that such areas are inferior, whether the area is housework, elementary school teaching, or the Christian churches.

Perhaps some lessons can be drawn from my survey of male alienation from the church, and these lessons now apply to women as well. Men value their independence and resent clerical domination. The movements that reach men are mostly lay-led and lay-governed. The clergy should treat men and women as responsible adults, capable of running their own affairs. Movements that have reconnected men to the churches have often faded away because men find the atmosphere of everyday church life too feminine, and drift away. Avoidance of erotic hymns and concentration on masculine concerns in preaching (work, sexuality, family) would help.

The hardest group to reach is completely unchurched young men, and this group is growing as fewer men have childhood experiences of church and marry later, if at all. This group is dominated by *thumos*, by the energy that fuels anger, passion, and the desire for masculine honor. How to tap this energy for Christianity, how to show men that the highest honor is to be honored by God is the key to reaching young men.

Movements that have reached men have focused upon the person of Jesus Christ, not as the Bridegroom, but Leader and Friend. Friendship is more intimate than sexual love, it is one soul in two bodies, the friend is another self, friends have all things in common. Men suffer from the existential loneliness that is the lot of every human being, and more so because of their drive to independence. Men seek to overcome this loneliness in the comradeship of fraternal movements, of fascism, of communism, of terrorist groups, of gangs, of war. Such ways are deceiving and destructive. Men will not accept Christianity because it is socially useful, although in general Christians make good, law-abiding, family-centered citizens. Men accept Christianity because it resonates with their deepest longings, both their desire to be truly masculine, in the highest and deepest sense, and their longing for communion, not to be alone in an empty universe, but to have a companion and friend in the adventure of life and in the adventure that begins after this life.

Selected Bibliography

I have included what I regard as the most important books and articles on the general topics treated in this book, especially treatments in books other than in English.

Abraham, Ken. *Who Are the Promise Keepers? Understanding the Christian Men's Movement*. New York: Doubleday, 1997.

Airiau, Paul. "Le prêtre catholique masculin, neutre, autre? Des débuts du XIXᵉ siècle au milieu du XXᵉ siècle." In Revenin, *Hommes et masculinités*, 191–207.

Allen, L. Dean. *Rise Up, O Men of God: The "Men and Religion Forward Movement" and the "Promise Keepers."* Macon, GA: Mercer University Press, 2002.

Allen, Prudence. *The Concept of Woman: The Aristotelian Revolution 750 BC–AD 1250*. Grand Rapids, MI: William B. Eerdmans, 1997.

Art, Jan and Thomas Buerman. "Anticléricalisme et genre au XIXᵉ siècle: Le prêtre catholique, principal défi à l'image hégémonique de l'homme." In Benvido, *Masculinités*, 323–37.

Aston, Nigel and Matthew Cragoe. *Anticlericalism in Britain c. 1540–1914*. Phoenix Mill, England: Sutton Publishing, 2001.

Atkin, Nicholas and Frank Tallet. *Priests, Prelates, and People: A History of European Catholicism since 1750*. New York: St. Martin's, 2003.

Badinter, Elisabeth. *XY: On Masculine Identity*. Translated by Lydia Davis. New York: Columbia University Press, 1995.

Badone, Ellen, ed. *Religious Orthodoxy and Popular Faith in European Society*. Princeton: Princeton University Press, 1990.

Baron-Cohen, Simon. *The Essential Difference: Male and Female Brains and the Truth about Autism*. New York: Basic Books, 2004.

Barton, Bruce. *A Young Man's Jesus*. Boston: Pilgrim Press, 1914.

Barton, Bruce. *The Man Nobody Knows: A Discovery of the Real Jesus*. Indianapolis, IN: Bobbs Merrill, 1925.

Barton, Carlin A. *Roman Honor: The Fire in the Bones*. Berkeley: University of California Press, 2001.

Baumeister, Roy F. *Is There Anything Good about Men? How Cultures Flourish by Exploiting Men*. New York: Oxford University Press, 2010.

Beattie, Tina. *New Catholic Feminism: Theology and Theory*. New York: Routledge, 2006.

Bederman, Gail. *Manliness and Civilization: A Cultural History of Gender and Race in the United States, 1880–1917*. Chicago: University of Chicago Press, 1995.

Bendroth, Margaret Lamberts. *Fundamentalism and Gender: 1875 to the Present*. New Haven: Yale University Press, 1993.

Bendroth, Margaret Lamberts and Virginia Lieson Brereton, eds. *Women and Twentieth-Century Protestantism*. Urbana: University of Illinois Press, 2002.

Bieler, André. *L'homme et la femme dans la morale calviniste*. Geneva: Labor & Fides, 1963.

Bitel, Lisa M. and Felice Lifshitz, eds. *Gender and Christianity in Medieval Europe: New Perspectives*. Philadelphia: University of Pennsylvania Press, 2008.

Black, Christopher and Pamela Gravestock, eds. *Early Modern Confraternities in Europe and the Americas*. Aldershot, England: Ashgate, 2006.

Borobio, Dionisio. *Hermandades y cofradías: entre pasado y futuro*. Barcelona: Centre de Pastoral Litúrgica, 2003.

Borutta, Manuel. *Antikatholizismus: Deutschland und Italien im Zeitalter der europäischen Kulturkämpfe*. Göttingen: Vandenhoeck & Ruprecht, 2011.

Borutta, Manuel. "Antikatholizismus, Männlichkeit und Moderne: Die diskursive Feminisierung des Katholizismus in Deutschland und Italien (1850–1900)." Tagung AIM Gender. http://www.ruendal.de/aim/pdfs/Borutta.pdf.

Bouyer, Louis. *Woman in the Church*. Translated by Marilyn Teichert. San Francisco: Ignatius Press, 1984.

Boyd, Stephen B., W. Merle Longwood, and Mark W. Muesse, eds. *Redeeming Men: Religion and Masculinities*. Louisville, KY: Westminster John Knox, 1996.

Brakke, David. *Demons and the Making of the Monk: Spiritual Combat in Early Christianity*. Cambridge, MA: Harvard University Press, 2006.

Brandes, Stanley. *Metaphors of Masculinity: Sex and Status in Andalusian Folklore*. Philadelphia: University of Pennsylvania Press, 1980.

Brasher, Brenda E. *Godly Women: Fundamentalism and Female Power*. New Brunswick, NJ: Rutgers University Press, 1998.

Brewer, Jimmy Dale. "Jesus' Distinctiveness in Light of Ancient Jewish Masculinity." Ph. D. Dissertation, Southwest Baptist Theological Seminary, 2010. Anne Arbor, MI: ProQuest, UMI Dissertation Publishing, 2011.

Brickner, Bryan W. *The Promise Keepers: Politics and Promises*. Lanham, MD: Lexington Books, 1999.

Brizendine, Louann. *The Male Brain*. New York: Broadway Books, 2010.

Brown, Callum. *Religion and the Demographic Revolution: Women and Secularisation in Canada, Ireland, UK and USA since the 1960s*. Woodbridge, England: Boydell Press, 2012.

Brown, Callum G. *The Death of Christian Britain: Understanding Secularization 1800–2000*. London: Routledge, 2009.

Brusco, Elizabeth E. *The Reformation of Machismo: Evangelical Conversion and Gender in Columbia*. Austin: University of Texas Press, 1995.

Bunge, Gabriel. *Dragon's Wine and Angel's Bread: The Teaching of Evagrius Ponticus on Anger and Meekness*. Crestwood, NY: St. Vladimir's Seminary Press, 2009.

Bunk, Brian D. *Ghosts of Passion: Martyrdom, Gender, and the Origins of the Spanish Civil War*. Durham, NC: Duke University Press, 2007.

Burrows, David. *The Stereotype of the Priest in the Old French Fabliaux: Anticlerical Satire and Lay Identity*. Oxford: Peter Lang, 2005.

Burton, Richard D. E. *Holy Tears. Holy Blood: Women, Catholicism, and the Culture of Suffering in France, 1840–1970*. Ithaca, NY: Cornell University Press, 2004.

Bynum, Caroline Walker. *Jesus as Mother: Studies in the Spirituality of the High Middle Ages*. Berkeley: University of California Press, 1982.

Bynum, Caroline Walker, Steven Harrell, and Paula Richman. *Gender and Religion: On the Complexity of Symbols*. Boston: Beacon Press, 1986.

Callahan, William J. and David Higgs, eds. *Church and Society in Catholic Europe of the Eighteenth Century*. Cambridge: Cambridge University Press, 1979.

Campbell, Anne. *Men, Women, and Aggression*. New York: Basic Books, 1994.

Carnes, Mark C. *Secret Ritual and Manhood in Early America*. New Haven: Yale University Press, 1989.

Carney, Charity R. *Ministers and Masters: Methodism, Manhood, and Honor in the Old South*. Baton Rouge: Louisiana State University Press, 2011.

Case, Carl Delos. *The Masculine in Religion*. Philadelphia: American Baptist Publication Society, 1906.

Chiniquy, Charles. *The Priest, the Woman, and the Confessional*. 36th ed. Chicago: Adam Craig, 1890.

Chodorow, Nancy. *The Reproduction of Mothering: Psychoanalysis and the Sociology of Gender*. Berkeley: University of California Press, 1978.

Christen, Yves. *Sex Differences: Modern Biology and the Unisex Fallacy*. Translated by Nicholas Davidson. New Brunswick, NJ: Transaction, 1991.

Christian, Jr., William A. *Person and God in a Spanish Valley*. New York: Seminar Press, 1972.

Christie, Nancy, ed. *Households of Faith: Family, Gender, and Community in Canada, 1760–1969*. Montreal: McGill-Queens University Press, 2002.

Clark, Christopher and Wolfram Kaiser, eds. *Culture Wars: Secular-Catholic Conflict in Nineteenth-Century Europe*. New York: Cambridge University Press, 2003.

Clatterbaugh, Kenneth. *Contemporary Perspectives on Masculinity: Men, Women, and Politics in Modern Society*. Boulder, CO: Westview Press, 1997.

Claussen, Dane S. *The Promise Keepers: Essays on Masculinity and Christianity*. Jefferson, NC: McFarland: 2000.

Clawson, Mary Ann. *Constructing Brotherhood: Class, Gender, and Fraternalism*. Princeton: Princeton University Press, 1989.

Cobb, L. Stephanie. *Dying to Be Men: Gender and Language in Early Christian Texts*. New York: Columbia University Press, 2008.

Cohen, Jeffrey Jerome and Bonnie Wheeler, eds. *Becoming Male in the Middle Ages*. New York: Garland, 2000.

Cole, Edwin Lewis, ed. *Man Power: The New Revival in America: The Call to African American Men for Spiritual Renewal*. Nashville, TN: Thomas Nelson, 1997.

Coltrane, Scott. *Family Man: Fatherhood, Housework, and Gender Equity*. New York: Oxford University Press, 1996.

Conant, Robert Warren. *The Virility of Christ: A New View*. Chicago, 1915.

Conn, Joann Wolski and Walter E. Conn, eds. *Horizons on Catholic Feminist Theology*. Washington, DC: Georgetown University Press, 1992

Conway, Colleen. *Behold the Man: Jesus and Greco-Roman Masculinity*. New York: Oxford University Press, 2008.

Courtwright, David T. *Violent Land: Single Men and Social Disorder from the Frontier to the Inner City*. Cambridge, MA: Harvard University Press, 1996.

Craig, Leon Harold. *The War Lover: A Study of Plato's Republic*. Toronto: University of Toronto Press, 1994.

Creesey, Frank Graves. *The Church and Young Men*. Chicago: Fleming H. Revell, 1904.

Cueva Merino, Julio de la. *Clericales y anticlericales: El conflicto entre confesionalidad y secularización en Cantabria (1875–1923)*. Santander: Universidad de Cantabria, 1994.

Cueva Merino, Julio de la and Ángel Luis López Villaverde, eds. *Clericalismo y asociacionismo católico en España: de la restauración a la transición: un siglo entre el palio y el consiliario*. Universidad Castilla-La Mancha, 2005.

Cullum, P. H. and Katherine J. Lewis. *Holiness and Masculinity in the Middle Ages*. Toronto: University of Toronto Press, 2004.

Dabbs, James M. *Heroes, Rogues and Lovers: Testosterone and Behavior*. With Mary Godwin Dabbs. New York: McGraw Hill, 2000.

Delap, Lucy and Sue Morgan. *Men, Masculinities, and Religious Change in Twentieth-Century Britain*. New York: Palgrave Macmillan, 2013.

Delgado Ruiz, Manuel, *La ira sagrada: Anticlericalismo, iconoclastia y anti-rritualismo en la España contemporánea*. Barcelona: Editorial Humanidades, 1992.

Delgado Ruiz, Manuel. *Las palabras de otro hombre: anticlericalismo y misoginia*. Barcelona: Muchnik Editores, 1993.

Delumeau, Jean, ed. *La religion de ma mère: La rôle des femmes dans la transmission de la foi*. Paris: Cerf, 1992,

Dinan, Susan E. and Debra Meyer, eds. *Women and Religion in the Old and New Worlds*. New York: Routledge, 2001.

Dittes, James E. *Driven by Hope: Men and Meaning*. Louisville, KY: Westminster John Knox Press, 1996.

Dixmier, Michel, Jacqueline Lalouette, and Didier Pasamonik. *La République et L'Église: Image d'une Querelle*. Paris: Éditions de la Martinière, 2005.

Doerne, Martin. *Der Mann vor Gott: Zur Grundlegung kirchlicher Männerarbeit*. Dresden: C. Ludwig Ungelenk, [1941].

Donnelly, John Patrick and Michael W. Maher. *Confraternities and Catholic Reform in Italy, France, and Spain*. Kirksville, MO: Truman State University Press, 1999.

Douglas, Ann. *The Feminization of American Culture*. 1977. New York: Noonday Press, 1998.

Dowd, Nancy E. *The Man Question: Male Subordination and Privilege*. New York: New York University Press, 2010.

Ducat, Stephen J. *The Wimp Factor: Gender Gaps, Holy Wars, and the Politics of Anxious Masculinity*. Boston: Beacon Press, 2004.

Eberly, Don E., ed. *The Faith Factor in Fatherhood: Renewing the Sacred Vocation of Fathering*. Lanham, MD: Lexington Books, 1999.

Eldridge, John. *Wild at Heart: Discovering the Secret of a Man's Soul*. Nashville, TN: Thomas Nelson, 2001.

Eliade, Mircea. *Rites and Symbols of Initiation: The Mysteries of Birth and Rebirth.* Translated by Willard R. Trask. New York: Harper Torchbooks, 1965.

Epstein, Barbara Leslie. *The Politics of Domesticity: Women, Evangelism, and Temperance in Nineteenth Century America.* Middletown, CN: Wesleyan University Press, 1981.

Erdozain, Dominic. *The Problem of Pleasure: Sport, Recreation and the Crisis of Victorian Religion.* Woodbridge, England: Boydell Press, 2010.

Evdokimov, Paul. *Woman and the Salvation of the World: A Christian Anthropology on the Charisms of Women.* Translated by Anthony P. Gythiel. Crestwood, NY: St. Vladimir's Seminary Press, 1994.

Farrell, Warren. *The Myth of Male Power: Why Men Are the Disposable Sex.* New York: Simon & Schuster, 1993.

Faull, Katherine M. *Masculinity, Senses, Spirit.* Lewisburg, PA: Bucknell University Press, 2011.

Fishburn, Janet Forsythe. *The Fatherhood of God and the Victorian Family: The Social Gospel in America.* Philadelphia: Fortress Press, 1981.

Fishman, Sylvia Barack and Daniel Parmer. *Matrilineal Ascent / Matrilineal Descent: The Gender Imbalance in American Jewish Life.* Waltham, MA: Brandeis University, 2008.

Flores, Edward Orozco. *God's Gangs: Barrio Ministry, Masculinity, and Gang Recovery.* New York: New York University Press, 2014.

Flowers, Ronald B. *Male Crime and Deviance: Exploring Its Causes, Dynamics, and Nature.* Springfield, IL: Charles C. Thomas, 2003.

Ford, Caroline. *Divided Houses: Religion and Gender in Modern France.* Ithaca, NY: Cornell University Press, 2005.

Fosdick, Harry Emerson. *The Manhood of the Master.* New York: Association Press, 1913.

Foxhall, Lin and John Salmon, eds. *Thinking Men: Masculinity and its Self-Representation in the Classical Tradition.* New York: Routledge, 1998.

Foxhall, Lin and John Salmon, eds. *When Men Were Men: Masculinity, Power and Identity in Classical Antiquity.* London: Routledge, 1998.

Frevert, Ute, ed. *Bürgerinnen und Bürger: Geschlechterverhältnisse im 19. Jahrhundert.* Göttingen: Vandenhoeck & Ruprecht, 1988.

Friend, Craig Thompson, ed. *Southern Masculinity: Perspectives on Manhood in the South since Reconstruction*. Athens: University of Georgia Press, 2009.

Gambill, Edward L. *Uneasy Males: The American Men's Movement 1970–2000*. New York: iUniverse, 2005.

Gibson, Ralph. *A Social History of French Catholicism 1789–1914*. London: Routledge, 1989.

Gilmore, David D. *Manhood in the Making: Cultural Concepts of Masculinity*. New Haven: Yale University Press, 1990.

Gilmore, David D. *The People of the Plain: Class and Community in Lower Andalusia*. New York: Columbia University Press, 1980.

Goldberg, Herb. *The Hazards of Being Male: Surviving the Myth of Masculine Privilege*. 1976. New York: Signet, 1987.

Goldwert, Marvin. "Machismo and Christ: The New Formula." *Contemporary Review* 145 (1984): 184.

Gondreau, Paul. *The Passions of Christ's Soul in the Theology of St. Thomas Aquinas*. Scranton: University of Scranton Press, 2009.

Good, Deidre J. *Jesus the Meek King*. Harrisburg, Pennsylvania: Trinity Press International, 1999.

Götz von Olenhusen, Irmtraud. *Jugendreich Gottesreich Deutschesreich: Junge Generation, Religion und Politik 1928–1933*. Cologne: Verlag Wissenschaft und Politik, 1987.

Götz von Olenhusen, Irmtraud, ed. *Wunderbare Erscheinungen: Frauen und katholische Frömmigkeit in 19. und 20. Jahrhundert*. Paderborn: Ferdinand Schöningh, 1995.

Gregory, Chad Alan. "Revivalism, Fundamentalism, and Masculinity in the United States, 1880–1930." Ph.D. University of Kentucky, 1999.

Grévy, Jérôme. *Le clericalisme? Voilà l'ennemi! Un siècle de guerre de religion en France*. Paris: Armand Colin, 2005.

Gross, Michael B. *The War against Catholicism: Liberalism and the Anti-Catholic Imagination in Nineteenth-Century German*. Anne Arbor: University of Michigan Press, 2004.

Grundmann, Herbert. *Religious Movements in the Middle Ages*. Translated by Stephen Rowan. Notre Dame. IN: University of Notre Dame Press, 1995.

Haliczer, Stephen. *Sexuality in the Confessional: A Sacrament Profaned*. New York: Oxford University Press, 1996.

Hall, Donald E., ed. *Muscular Christianity: Embodying the Victorian Age*. Cambridge: Cambridge University Press, 1994.

Harrington, Joel Francis. *Reordering Marriage and Family in Reformation Germany*. Cambridge: Cambridge University Press, 1995.

Hartel, Joseph Francis. *Femina ut Imago Dei in the Integral Feminism of St. Thomas Aquinas*. Rome: Editrice Pontificia Università Gregoriana, 1993.

Hartlieb, Elisabeth. *Geschlechtdifferenz im Denken Friedrich Schleiermachers*. Berlin: Walter de Gruyter, 2006.

Hartman, Mary S. and Lois Banner, eds. *Clio's Consciousness Raised*. New York: Harper & Row, 1974.

Hauke, Manfred. *Women in the Priesthood? A Systematic Analysis in the Light of the Order of Nature and Redemption*. Translated by David Kipp. San Francisco: Ignatius Press, 1986.

Healy, Róisín. *The Jesuit Specter in Imperial Germany*. Boston: Brill, 2003.

Hendrix, Scott H. and Susan C. Karant-Nunn, eds. *Masculinity in the Reformation Era*. Kirksville, Missouri: Truman State University Press, 2008.

Herzog, Dagmar. *Intimacy and Exclusion: Religious Politics in Pre-Revolutionary Baden*. New Brunswick, NJ: Transaction, 2007.

Higgs, Robert J. *God in the Stadium: Sports and Religion in America*. Lexington: University Press of Kentucky, 1995.

Hobbs, Angela. *Plato and the Hero: Courage, Manliness and the Impersonal Good*. Cambridge: Cambridge University Press, 2000.

Hobbs, June Hadden. *"I Sing for I Cannot Be Silent": The Feminization of American Hymnody, 1870–1920*. Pittsburgh: University of Pittsburgh Press, 1997.

Hockerts, Hans Günther. *Die Sittlichkeitsprozesse gegen katholische Ordensangehörige und Priester 1936/1937*. Mainz: Matthias-Grünewald-Verlag, 1971.

Hoffman, Shirl James. *Good Game: Christianity and the Culture of Sports*. Waco, TX: Baylor University Press, 2010.

Jaeger, Steffen. *Kirche braucht Männer – Brauchen Männer Kirche? Voraussetzungen und Perspektiven für kirchliche Männerarbeit*. Munich: GRON Verlag, 2007.

James, David C., ed. *What Are They Saying about Masculine Spirituality?* New York: Paulist Press, 1996.

Jewett, Paul K. *Man as Male and Female*. Grand Rapids: William B. Eerdmans, 1975.

Juster, Susan. *Disorderly Women: Sexual Politics and Evangelicalism in Revolutionary New England*. Ithaca: Cornell University Press, 1994.

Juster, Susan, and Lisa MacFarlan, eds. *A Mighty Baptism: Race, Gender, and the Creation of American Protestantism*. Ithaca, NY: Cornell University Press, 1996.

Kaeuper, Richard W. *Chivalry and Violence in Medieval Europe*. New York: Oxford University Press, 1999.

Kaeuper, Richard W. *Holy Warriors: The Religious Ideology of Chivalry*. Philadelphia: University of Pennsylvania Press, 2009.

Karras, Ruth Mazo. *Sexuality in Medieval Europe: Doing unto Others*. New York: Routledge, 2005.

Kemper, Theodore D. *Social Structure and Testosterone: Explorations of the Socio-Bio-Social Chain*. New Brunswick, NJ: Rutgers University Press, 1990.

Kimmel, Michael S. *The Gendered Society*. New York: Oxford University Press, 2007.

Knieling, Reinhard. *Männer und Kirche: Konflikte, Missverständnisse, Annäherungen*. Göttingen: Vandenhoeck & Ruprecht, 2010.

Krondorfer, Björn, ed. *Men and Masculinities in Christianity and Judaism: A Critical Reader*. London: SCM Press, 2009.

Krondorfer, Björn, ed. *Men's Bodies, Men's Gods: Male Identities in a (Post-) Christian Culture*. New York: New York University Press, 1996.

Kuefler, Mathew. *The Manly Eunuch: Masculinity, Gender Ambiguity, and Christian Ideology in Late Antiquity*. Chicago: University of Chicago Press, 2001.

Ladd, Tony and James A. Mathisen. *Muscular Christianity: Evangelical Protestants and the Development of American Sport.* Grand Rapids, MI: Baker Books, 1999.

Lamb, Michael E., ed. *The Role of the Father in Child Development.* 5th ed. New York: John Wiley & Sons, 2010.

Langlois, Claude. *Le catholicisme au féminine: Les congrégations françaises à supérieure générale au XIXᵉ siècle.* Paris: Cerf, 1984.

Le mouvement confraternel au Moyen Âge. Rome: École Française de Rome, 1987.

Leete, Frederick DeLand. *Christian Brotherhoods.* Cincinnati: Jennings & Graham, 1912.

Leeuwen, Mary Stewart. *My Brother's Keeper: What Social Sciences Do (and Don't) Tell Us about Masculinity.* Downers Grove, IL: InterVarsity Press, 2002.

Levi, Giovanni and Jean-Claude Schmitt, eds. *A History of Young People: Ancient and Medieval Rites of Passage*, Vol. 1. Translated by Camille Naish. Cambridge, MA: Belknap Press of the Harvard University Press, 1997.

Lindley, Susan Hill. *"You Have Stepped Out of Your Place": A History of Women and Religion in America.* Louisville, KY: Westminster John Knox Press, 1996.

Lippy, Charles H. *Do Real Men Pray? Images of the Christian Man and Male Spirituality in White Protestant America.* Knoxville, TN: University of Tennessee Press, 2005.

Lisón-Tolosana, Carmelo. *Belmonte de los Caballeros.* Princeton: Princeton University Press, 1983.

Lukatis, Ingrid, Regina Sommer, and Christof Wolf, eds. *Religion und Geschlechterverhältnis.* Opladen: Leske & Budrich, 2000.

Maccoby, Eleanor Emmons and Carol Nagy Jacklin. *The Psychology of Sex Differences.* Stanford, CA: Stanford University Press, 1974.

Malone, Edward C. *The Monk and the Martyr: The Monk as the Successor of the Martyr.* Washington, DC: Catholic University of America Press, 1950.

Marcoux, Marcene. *Cursillo: Anatomy of a Movement*. New York: Lambeth Press, 1982.

[Mariaux, Walther]. *The Persecution of the Catholic Church in the Third Reich*. [1942]. Gretna, LA: Pelican, 2007.

Matter, E. Ann. *The Voice of My Beloved: The Song of Songs in Western Medieval Christianity*. Philadelphia: University of Pennsylvania Press, 1990.

McDannell, Colleen. *Material Christianity: Religion and Popular Culture in America*. New Haven: Yale University Press, 1995.

McLeod, Hugh. *Religion and Society in England, 1850–1914*. New York: St. Martin's, 1966.

McLeod, Hugh. *Religion and the People of Western Europe 1789–1989*. New York: Oxford University Press, 1997.

McLeod, Hugh. *Secularization in Western Europe, 1848–1914*. New York, St. Martin's, 2000.

McMillan, James F. *France and Women 1789–1914: Gender, Society, and Politics*. London: Routledge, 2000.

Messner, Michael A. *Politics of Masculinities: Men in Movements*. Lanham, MD: AltaMira Press, 2000.

Michelet, Jules. *Du prêtre, de la femme, de la famille*. Paris: Ernest Flammarion, n.d.

Miles, Rosalind. *The Rites of Man: Love, Sex and Death in the Making of the Male*. London: Grafton Books, 1991.

Mitchell, Timothy J. *Passional Culture: Emotion, Religion, and Society in Southern Spain*. Philadelphia: University of Pennsylvania Press, 1990.

Moore, Stephen D. and Janice Capel Anderson. *New Testament Masculinities*. Atlanta: Society of Biblical Literature, 2003.

Moreno, Antonio. *Historia de la persecución religiosa en España*. Madrid: Biblioteca de Autores Cristianos, 1961.

Moreno Navarro, Isidoro. *Cofradías y hermandades Andaluzas: estructura, simbolismo e identidad*. Seville Editoriales Andaluzas Unidas, 1985.

Moreno Navarro, Isidoro. *Las hermandades Andaluzas: Una aproximación desde la antropología*. 2nd ed. Seville: Universidad de Sevilla, 1999.

Morgan, Edward S. *The Puritan Family: Religion and Domestic Relations in Seventeenth-Century New England*. New York: Harper & Row, 1966.

Morse, Samuel F. B. *Confessions of a French Catholic Priest*. New York: John S. Taylor, 1837.

Muchambled, Robert. *A History of Violence from the End of the Middle Ages to the Present*. Translated by Jean Birrell. Cambridge, England: Polity Press, 2008.

Mudie-Smith, Richard, ed. *The Religious Life of London*. London: Hodder & Staughton, 1904.

Murdock, Catherine Gilbert. *Domesticating Drink: Women, Men, and Alcohol in America, 1870–1940*. Baltimore: Johns Hopkins University Press, 1998.

Nabhan-Warren, Christy. *The Cursillo Movement in America: Catholics, Protestants, and Fourth Day Spirituality*. Chapel Hill: University of North Carolina Press, 2013.

Newman, Barbara. *From Virile Woman to WomanChrist: Studies in Medieval Religion and Literature*. Philadelphia: University of Pennsylvania Press, 1995.

Novak, Michael. *The Joy of Sports: End Zones, Bases, Baskets, Balls, and the Consecration of the American Spirit*. rev. ed. Lanham, MD: Madison Books, 1994.

Oakes, Edward T. and David Moss, eds. *The Cambridge Companion to Hans Urs von Balthasar*. Cambridge: Cambridge University Press, 2004.

Oates, James F. *The Religious Condition of Young Men*. Chicago: Young Men's Christian Association, n. d.

Obelkevich, Jim, Lyndal Roper, and Raphael Samuel, eds. *Disciplines of Faith: Studies in Religion, Politics, and Patriarchy*. London: Routledge & Kegan Paul, 1987.

O'Malley, John W. *The First Jesuits*. Cambridge, MA: Harvard University Press, 1993.

Ong, Walter. *Fighting for Life: Contest, Sexuality, and Consciousness*. Amherst: University of Massachusetts Press, 1989.

Ownby, Ted. *Subduing Satan: Religion, Recreation, and Manhood in the Rural South, 1865–1920*. Chapel Hill: University of North Carolina Press, 1990.

Parry, Jim, Simon Robinson, Nick J. Watson, and Mark Nesti. *Sports and Spirituality: An Introduction*. New York: Routledge, 2007.

Pasture, Patrick, and Jan Art. *Gender and Christianity in Modern Europe: Beyond the Feminization Thesis*. Louvain: Leuven University Press, 2012.

Payne, Stanley G. *Spanish Catholicism: An Historical Overview*. Madison: University of Wisconsin Press, 1984.

Payne, Stanley G. *The Spanish Civil War*. Cambridge: Cambridge University Press, 2012.

Pfitzner, Victor C. *Paul and the Agon Motif: Traditional Athletic Imagery in the Pauline Literature*. Leiden: E. J. Brill, 1967.

Phayer, Michael. *Protestant and Catholic Women in Nazi Germany*. Detroit: Wayne State University Press, 1990.

Pierce, Jason Noble. *The Masculine Power of Christ: or, Christ Measured as a Man*. Boston: Pilgrim Press, 1912.

Pinker, Stephen. *The Better Angels of Our Nature: Why Violence Has Declined*. New York: Viking, 2011.

Pitt-Rivers, Julian A. *The People of the Sierra*. Chicago: University of Chicago Press, 1971.

Podles, Leon H. *The Church Impotent: The Feminization of Christianity*: Dallas, TX: Spence Publishing, 1999.

Podles, Leon J. *Sacrilege: Sexual Abuse and the Catholic Church*. Baltimore: Crossland Press, 2008.

Popenoe, David. *Life without Father: Compelling New Evidence that Fatherhood and Marriage and Indispensable for the Good of Children and Society*. New York: Free Press, 1996.

Porter. James I. ed. *Constructions of the Classical Body*. Ann Arbor: University of Michigan Press, 1999.

Porterfield, Amanda. *Female Piety in Puritan New England: The Emergence of Religious Humanism*. New York: Oxford University Press, 1992.

Poska, Allyson M. "From Parties to Pieties: Redefining Confraternal Activity in Seventeenth-Century Ourense (Spain)." In Donnelly and Maher, *Confraternities and Catholic Reform*, 226–43.

Preece, Gordon, and Robert Hess. *Sport and Spirituality*. Adelaide: ATF Press, 2006.

Prelinger, Catherine M., ed. *Episcopal Women: Gender, Spirituality and Commitment in an American Mainline Denomination*. New York: Oxford University Press, 1992.

Price, Joseph L., ed. *From Season to Season: Sports as American Religion*. Macon, GA: Mercer University Press, 2002.

Prothero, Stephen. *American Jesus: How the Son of God Became an American Icon*. New York: Farrar, Straus & Giroux, 2003.

Pugh, S. S. *Christian Manliness: A Book of Examples and Principles for Young Men*. London: The Religious Tract Society, n. d.

Putney, Clifford. *Muscular Christianity: Manhood and Sports in Protestant America, 1880–1920*. Cambridge, MA: Harvard University Press, 2001.

Quéniart, Jean. *Les hommes, l'église et Dieu dans la France du XIIIᵉ siècle*. Paris: Hachette, 1878.

Raeburn, Paul. *Do Fathers Matter: What Science is Telling Us about the Parent We've Overlooked*. New York: Scientific American / Farrar, Straus & Giroux: 2014.

Rahner, Karl. "Der Mann in der Kirche." In *Sendung und Gnade: Beiträge zur pastoral Theologie*. 5th ed. Innsbruck-Vienna: Tyrolia-Verlag, 1988, 286–311.

Reed, John Shelton. *Glorious Battle: The Cultural Politics of Victorian Anglo-Catholicism*. Nashville, TN: Vanderbilt University Press, 1996.

Rémond, René. *L'anticléricalisme en France de 1815 à nos jours*. 2nd ed. Paris: Fayard, 1999.

Revenin, Regis, ed. *Hommes et masculinités de 1789 à nos jours*. Paris: Éditions Autrement, 2007.

Rhodes, Elizabeth. "Join the Jesuits, See the World: Early Modern Women in Spain and the Society of Jesus." In *The Jesuits II: Cultures, Sciences, and the Arts*, edited by John W. O'Malley, Gauvin Alexander Bailey, Steven J. Harris, and T. Frank Kennedy, 33–49. Toronto: University of Toronto Press, 2006.

Richardson, Ruth Drusilla. *The Role of Women in the Life and Thought of the Early Schleiermacher (1768–1806): An Historical Overview*. Lewiston, NY: Edwin Mellen Press, 1991.

Rodríguez, Pepe. *La vida sexual del clero*. 1995. Madrid: Suma de Letras, 2002.

Rohloff, Ivan. *The Origins and Development of Cursillo*. Dallas: National Ultreya Publications, 1976.

Roisman, Joseph. *The Rhetoric of Manhood: Masculinity in the Attic Orators*. Berkeley: University of California Press, 2005.

Roper, Lydal. *The Holy Household: Women and Morals in Reformation Augsburg*. Oxfrd: Clarendon Press, 1989.

Rosen, David "The Volcano and the Cathedral: Muscular Christianity and the Origins of Primal Manliness." In Hall, ed., *Muscular Christianity*, 17–44.

Ross, John Munder. *What Men Want: Mothers, Fathers, and Manhood*. Cambridge, MA: Harvard University Press, 1994.

Ruff, Julius R. *Violence in Early Modern Europe 1500–1800*. Cambridge: Cambridge University Press, 2001.

Sack, Birgit. *Zwischen religiöser Bindung und moderner Gesellschaft: Katholische Frauenbewegung und politische Kultur in der Weimarer Republik (1918/1933)*. Münster: Waxman Verlag, 1998.

Sanabria, Enrique A. *Republicanism and Anticlerical Nationalism in Spain*. New York: Palgrave Macmillan, 2009.

Sánchez Herrero, José. *La Semana Santa de Sevilla*. Madrid: Sílex, 2003.

Santos, Jose Leonardo. *Evangelicalism and Masculinity: Faith and Gender in El Salvador*. Lanham, MD: Lexington Books, 2012.

Scaraffia, Lucetta and Gabriella Zarri, eds. *Women and Faith: Catholic Religious Life in Italy from Late Antiquity to the Present*. Cambridge, MA: Harvard University Press, 1999.

Schindler, David L., ed. *Hans Urs von Balthasar, His Life and Work*. San Francisco: Ignatius Press, 1991.

Schleiermacher, Friedrich. *Christmas Eve Celebration: A Dialogue*. Edited and translated by Terrence N. Tice. Eugene, OR: Cascade Books, 2010.

Screiber, Theodore, ed. *Mann und Frau: Grundproblem theologischer Anthropologie*. Freiburg: Herder, 1989.

Schumacher, Michele M., ed. *Women in Christ: Toward a New Feminism*. Grand Rapids, MI: William B. Eerdmans, 2004.

Seibert, Dorette. *Glaube, Erfahrung und Gemeinschaft: Der junge Schleiermacher und Herrnhut.* Göttingen: Vanderhoeck & Ruprecht, 2003.

Setran, David P. *The College "Y": Student Religion in the Era of Secularization.* New York: Palgrave Macmillan, 2007.

Shaw, Russell. *To Hunt, To Shoot, To Entertain: Clericalism and the Catholic Laity.* San Francisco: Ignatius Press, 1993.

Smith, Helmut Walser, ed. *Protestants, Catholics and Jews in Germany, 1800–1914.* New York: Berg, 2001.

Smith, Katherine Allen. *War and the Making of Medieval Monastic Culture.* Woodbridge, England: Boydell Press, 2011.

Sosice, Janet Martin, ed. *After Eve: Women, Theology and the Christian Tradition.* London: Collins, 1990.

Spencer, Samia I., ed. *French Women and the Age of the Enlightenment.* Bloomington: Indiana University Press, 1984.

Spierenburg, Pieter. *A History of Murder: Personal Violence in Europe from the Middle Ages to the Present.* Cambridge, England: Polity Press, 2008.

Spierenburg, Pieter, ed. *Men and Violence: Gender, Honor, and Rituals in Modern Europe and America.* Columbus: Ohio State University Press, 1998.

Stark, Rodney and William Sims Bainbridge. *Religion, Deviance, and Social Control.* New York: Routledge, 1996.

Stearns, Peter N. *Be a Man! Males in Modern Society.* 2nd ed. New York: Holmes & Meier, 1990.

Stein, Edith. *Essays on Woman.* Translated by Freda Mary Oben. Washington, DC: ICS Publications, 1996.

Steinberg, Leo. *The Sexuality of Christ in Renaissance Art and Modern Oblivion.* Chicago: University of Chicago Press, 1996.

Stoller, R. J. *Presentations of Gender.* New Haven: Yale University Press, 1985.

Swanson, Robert Norman, ed. *Gender and Christian Religion: Papers Read at the 1996 Summer Meeting and the 1997 Winter Meeting of the Ecclesiastical History Society.* Woodbridge, England: Boydell Press, 1998.

Synnott, Anthony. *Re-Thinking Men: Heroes, Villains and Victims.* Farnham, England: Ashgate, 2009.

Tackett, Timothy. *Priest and Parish in Eighteenth-Century France*. Princeton: Princeton University Press, 1977.

Tallett, Frank and Nicholas Aitkin, *Religion, Politics, and Society in France since 1789*. London: Hambledon Press, 1991.

Téry, Gustave. *Les cordicoles*. Paris: Édouard Cornély, 1902.

Thiery, Daniel E. *Polluting the Sacred: Violence, Faith and the "Civilizing" of Parishioners in Late Medieval England*. Leiden: Brill, 2009.

Thomas, David. *Not Guilty: The Case in Defense of Men*. New York: William Murrow, 1993.

Thomas, Maria. *The Faith and the Fury: Popular Anticlerical Violence and Iconoclasm in Spain, 1931–1936*. Portland, OR: Sussex Academic Press, 2013.

Torrubiano Ripoll, Jaime. *Beatería y Religión: Meditaciones de un Canonista*. Madrid: Javier Morata, 1930.

Trzebiatowska, Marta and Steve Bruce. *Why are Women More Religious than Men?* New York: Oxford University Press, 2012.

Ullman, Joan Connelly. *The Tragic Week: A Study of Anticlericalism in Spain 1875–1912*. Cambridge, MA: Harvard University Press, 1968.

van Gennep, Arnold. *The Rites of Passage*. Translated by Monika K. Vizedom and Gabrielle L. Caffee. London: Routledge and Kegan Paul, 1960.

van Herik, Judith. *Freud on Femininity and Faith*. Berkeley: University of California Press, 1982.

van Osselaer, Tine. *The Pious Sex: Catholic Constructions of Masculinity and Femininity in Belgium, c. 1800–1940*. Louvain: Leuven University Press, 2013.

Vance, Norman. *The Sinews of the Spirit: The Ideal of Christian Manliness in Victorian Literature and Religious Thought*. Cambridge: Cambridge University Press, 1985.

Vandermeer, Philip R. and Robert P. Swierenca, eds. *Belief and Behavior: Essays in the New Religious History*. New Brunswick, NJ: Rutgers University Press, 1991.

Vauchez, André. *The Laity in the Middle Ages: Religious Beliefs and Devotional Practices*. Edited by Daniel E. Bornstein. Translated by Margery J. Schneider. Notre Dame, IN: University of Notre Dame Press, 1993.

Vázquez García, Francisco and Andrés Moreno Mengíbar. *Sexo y razón: Una genealogía de la moral sexual en España (siglos XVI–XX)*. Madrid: Akal, 1997.

Vincent, Catherine. *Les confréries médiévales dans le royaume de France XIIIe – XVe siècle*. Paris: Albin Michel, 1994.

von Balthasar, Hans Urs. *New Elucidations*. Translated by Mary Theresilde Skerry. San Francisco: Ignatius Press, 1986.

von Balthasar, Hans Urs. *The Glory of the Lord*. Vol. 1, *Seeing the Form*. Edited by Joseph Fessio and John Riches. Translated by Erasmo Leiva-Merikakis. San Francisco, Ignatius Press, 1982.

von Balthasar, Hans Urs. *Theo-drama: Theological Dramatic Theory*, Vol. 3, *The Dramatis Personae: Persons in Christ*. Translated by Graham Harrison. San Francisco: Ignatius Press, 1992.

von Hippel, Theodore Gottlieb. *Über die bürgerliche Verbesserung der Weiber*. Berlin: 1792.

von le Fort, Gertrud. *The Eternal Woman: The Timeless Meaning of the Feminine*. Translated and with a preface by Placid Jordan. Milwaukee, WI: Bruce Publishing, 1961.

Wagner, Ann. *Adversaries of the Dance: From the Puritans to the Present*. Urbana: University of Illinois Press, 1997.

Weber, Eugen. *Peasants into Frenchmen: The Modernization of Rural France, 1870–1914*. Stanford, CA: Stanford University Press, 1976.

Westerkamp, Marilyn J. *Women in Early American Religion 1600–1850: The Puritan and Evangelical Traditions*. New York: Routledge, 1999.

Wetzel, Franz Xaver. *Leitsterne für die männliche Jugend und strebsame Männer*. Ravensburg: Dorn'sche Verlagsbuchhandlung, 1896.

Wilcox, W. Bradford. *Soft Patriarchs, New Men: How Christianity Shapes Fathers and Husbands*. Chicago: University of Chicago Press, 2004.

Williams, Drid. *Anthropology and the Dance: Ten Lectures*. 2nd ed. Champaign: University of Illinois Press, 2004.

Wilson, Brittany E. *Unmanly Men: Reconfigurations of Masculinity in Luke-Acts*. New York: Oxford University Press, 2015.

Wohlgemuth, Anton. *Fragen der Männerseelsorgen*, Band 1 and 2. Saarbrücken: Saarbrücken Druckerei & Verlag, 1939, 1940.

Wöhrmüller, Bonifaz. *Mannhaftes Christentum: Nachdenkliche Kapitel für Männer und Frauen.* Munich: Verlag Josef Kösel & Friedrich Pustet, 1934.

Wolf, Eric, ed. *Religion, Power and Protest in Local Communities: The Northern Shore of the Mediterranean.* New York: Mouton, 1984.

Wolseth, Jon. *Jesus and the Gang: Youth Violence and Christianity in Urban Honduras.* Tucson: University of Arizona Press, 2011.

Zeldin, Theodore, ed. *Conflicts in French Society: Anticlericalism, Education and Morals in the 19th Century.* London: George Allen & Unwin, 1970.

Ziemann, Benjamin. *Sozialgeschichte der Religion.* Frankfurt-am-Main: Campus Verlag, 2009.

Zimmerman, Franz. *Männliche Frömmigkeit.* Innsbruck: Tyrolia-Verlag, 1936.

Index

Achilles, 11, 24

Agonism, 17, 28, 172, 174, 176, 178–80, 189–90, 203

Alcohol, 12, 19, 73, 87, 88, 157, 232,

Alpha Omega House, v, xi

Alienation. in male psyche, 13, from the clergy, 127; of men from the Church, ix, 4, 90, 213, 231, 241, 248; of women from the Church, 244, 245, 248

America: business in, 39; Catholicism in, 209, 242; gender roles in, 19, 66, 68, 106, 190, 231, 236, 238; Protestant revivalism in, 112, 132, 151, 202, 206–08, 229; political Christianity in, 226; temperance movement in, 87; violence in, 19, 78–80. *See also United States*

Andalusia, 10, 83, 171, 198, 201

Anger: in general, 22, 23, 26–27, 248; of God, 25, 29, 32, 40

Anglican Church, The, 89, 101, 106, 116, 223

Anticlericalism: American, 5, 111, 123, 128; Catholic, 138–40, 146, 182; in the New World, 110, 139, 143; and patriarchy, 132–38; political, 141; and sins of the clergy, 115; in Spain, 109, 162, 164, 192

Aquinas, Thomas, 27, 29, 50–51, 81

Aristotle, 24, 26, 27, 43, 50–51

Arnold, Franz Xaver, 45, 63

Art, sacred, 33, 35–36, 38, 206

Asceticism, 30, 207, 220

Athanasius, St., 53, 178

Athletics. *See also sports.*

Augsburg, 107, 154; Council of, 81

Augustine, St., 55, 81, 93, 120, 183

Baptist Church, 86, 88, 92, 97, 105, 227, 232, 237

Barcelona, 75, 168, 169, 170, 187

Barth, Karl, 4, 67–68

Barton, Bruce, 36, 39, 41

Bavaria, 154–55

Beecher, Henry Ward, 132, 138

Benedict, St., 178–79, 181

Bernard of Clairvaux, 3, 55–58, 61, 181, 185–86

Bert, Deputy Paul, 62, 118, 119, 139

Bible, 90, 161, 202, 224, 245

Body, the: gender biology of, 7–9; and the Eucharist, 31; of Christ, 35–36, 41; female, 51; and nuptial union, 53; and honor, 76; de-emphasis of, 89–90; and wages of sin, 97–98; mutilation of, 108, 170, 181; and redemption, 215, 223–24, 228; and Social Gospel, 232

Boston, 78, 209

Brakke, David, 178, 179

Bridal mysticism, xi, 33, 54, 58, 124, 185, 187, 192, 202, 207

Brothels, 80–82, 118

California, 78, 79, 96, 218

Calvin, John, 58, 92, 204–05
Canada, 100, 197
Catholicism: art of, 35–38; concept of the feminine in, 44–45; and dancing, 83–89; drinking and, 85, 87–88; family in, 82–83, 136–37; in France, 98; in Germany, 39, 145; in general, ix, x, 1, 4, 5; Irish men and, 88, 178; in Latin America, 143–44; masculinity in, 50, 70; sacred eroticism in, 62; and sports, 89
Celibacy: and Catholic clergy, 5; of Jesus, 30; as unnatural concept, 83, 117–18; and scandals, 122–23, 125, 127, 131; as a subversive concept, 133, 138–39, 150, 155; and anticlericalism, 159, 167, 180, 220
Cervantes, 162, 186
Charismatic Christianity, xi, 6, 217, 232, 235
Chastity: a woman's honor and, 76; men and, 81, 85; of priests, 117–20, 125–26; and pious women, 108, 148, 164; and commitment to Christ, 177, 180–81, 185; and Protestantism, 222
Chaucer, 104, 182
Children, 210, 217, 233–36, 239, 241–43
Chiniquy, Charles, 121, 136
Chivalry, 5, 181–84
Christen, Yves, 8, 11
Christendom, 182, 185–86
Christianity. See Catholic Church, Protestantism, liberal Christianity, fundamentalism.
Church attendance, 79, 94, 111, 173, 244
Church Impotent, The, xi,
Clergy: demanding male docility, 45; Catholic, 115–26; control over

families, 134–35, 137; critics of, 124–25; : losing the good portion and, xi, 4–5; sins of, 115–120; scandals of, 130–31, 155, 158; and social control, 71–114; as unmanly, 127–31, 138–39; and virtue, 38;
Clericalism, 40, 72–77, 98–111
Congregationalism, 36, 106, 223–24
Confession, and dancing; 96; and French clergy, 105–07; manuals for 118–22; as a Catholic issue, 127; and interference in the household, 85, 133–38; and women, 5, 141–42; as way to influence politics, 149–50; German attitudes toward, 152, 154, 160; Spanish anticlericalism and, 162, 165–67; and knights, 185; and Cursillo, 217
Conway, Colleen, 22, 30–31
Conflict: and masculinity, 16, 69; in life of Jesus, 31; as theme in the Christian life, 174; in Catholicism, 179, 180, 183, 195; as Protestant theme, 204, 211, 223
Confraternities: French, 95, 98–99, 194–97; Spanish, 101, 199–201; in general, 191–202; in Italy, 193, 195; Protestant opposition to, 195; replaced by Freemasonry, 196; in Latin America, 197, 201; in Canada, 197
Contraception, 83, 84, 119
Councils, Catholic: Seventh Ecumenical, 33; Fourth Lateran, 118, 120; First Vatican, 152; Second Vatican 191, 198; of Trent, 76, 120; of Avignon, 92; of Paris, 92; of Milan, 93; of Basel, 107;
Council of Augsburg, 81
Council of Baltimore, 95
Counter-Reformation, 81, 82, 103, 120, 195, 205

Courage: men and, 11, 19–20, 23, 26, 74, 76; secular ideas of, 126, 150; Christian, 29, 41, 176, 221
Crammer, Corinne, 46–48
Crucifixion, 31, 174, 192, 201
Crusades, The, 184–85, 192,
Cursillo, 5, 216–19
Cutten, George, 35, 106

Danger: and men, 10, 19, 23, 71, 74, 101, 240 ; of the vows, 48; of the clergy, 75, 94, 118; in life of Jesus, 30; of the Church, 151, 160, 165, 172; and work, 20, 228
De la Barre, execution of, 106–08
Domestic violence, 78, 204, 233
Driscoll, Mark, 37, 41, 238,
Dueling, 76, 126

Effeminacy: in Greco-Roman world, 11, 22; and Jesus, 4, 34, 35–37, 53, 62; of religion, 5, 61, 80, 154–55, 160, 210, 217, 219–22; of clergy, 117, 127, 129, 134, 138; of sin, 181; of liberal Christianity, 211
Egypt, 133
El Salvador, 197, 226
England: Anglican church in, 129, 246; anticlericalism in, 112; bridal mysticism in, 58, 61; clergy in, 116, 224; in general, 150, 202, 206, 247; sports in, 90, 222; violence in, 76; Victorianism, 77, 85
Enlightenment, The, 110, 132, 146
Episcopal Church, The, 202, 229, 246–47
Europe, 5, Christian manhood in, 69–70, 172; history of violence in, 72, 74–80; sexuality in, 93, 109, 110; anticlericalism in, 123, 141, 154; religious orders in, 192, 196; attitudes towards piety in, 198; contrast

with America, 207; war in, 213; politics in, 226, 244
Evangelicalism: religious experience in, 69; American, 86, 131, 207; clergy, 112; in modern Germany, 156, 160, 162; and masculinity, 6, 210, 217, 232, 235, 243

Family. *See fatherhood, husbands, wives, children.*
Fatherhood, 6, 16, 235
Fellowship of Christian Athletes, 225, 230
Feminine. *See also, women.*
Feminism, 53, 235
Festivals, 73–75, 92, 99–102, 195, 198
Feuerbach, Ludwig, 49
Fingerhuts, ix
Football (American), 91, 92, 127, 224, 230
Frontier,
France: spiritual role of women in, 155, 163, 196; virility and, 213, 229; male violence in, 76; vice in, 82, 83, 85, 89; repression in, 96, 98–99; clericalism in, 102; anticlericalism in, 122; women's rights in, 146; convents in, 147, 151; Sacred Heart in, 148; political downfall of, 162
Freemasonry, 124, 164, 165, 208
French Revolution, 5, 99, 146, 147, 196
Freud, Sigmund, 52
Fundamentalism, 5, 206, 210–11, 233

Germany, 63, 65, 102, 215; And Macho Jesus, 38; Nazi era in, 39; modern politics in, 145; political anticlericalism in, 149–62; Confession in, 119; Dancing and, 93, 94
Gertrude of Helfta, 56–57
Gilmore, David, 7, 30

Gladden, Washington, 224, 228
God the Father, 31, 48, 58
Good portion, the, xi, xii
Goss, Robert E., 123–24
Gray, A. Herbert, 62, 239
Great Awakening, 85, 207, 208
Greeks, 17, 23, 25–26, 174–76,
Greven, Philip, 68–69
Gospel: lay preaching of, 195; revival and, 209, 238; masculinity and the, 22, 69, , 183, 221, 238. *See also, Social Gospel.*

Hartel, Joseph, 50–51
Heroism: and manhood, 10, 17, 19, 21, 24; Christian, 161, 213–16, 221, 227; of Jesus, 30-32, 40–41, 214
Herrnhut, 61, 63
Higginson, Thomas, 127, 224
Higgs, Robert, 100, 182
Himmler, Heinrich, 155–56
Hitler, Adolf, 139, 156–57
Holy Spirit, The, 43–44, 100, 237
Homicide, 72, 75–78, 183,
Homosexuality, xi, 115, 117, 123, 156–58, 247,
Honor: and death, 21, 23, 184; and thumos, 26, 248; and Jesus, 29-32, 201; secular ideals of, 73, 76, 91, 114, 172; Christian ideals of, 77, 81, 176, 183, 213, 236; in worship, 101; as a theme in Christianity, 174; and Ignatius of Loyola, 186–87; and Cursillo, 218
Husbands, headship of, 60, 204, bond with wife, 14, 53, 132, 144; Christ as, 54, 58; sin and, 84; rivalry with priests, 121–22, 134–37, 150–51, 155; and family, 133, 164
Hybels, Bill, 237, 241
Hypocrisy, 114, 125, 138, 167
Hypermasculinity, 14, 15, 17, 211, 234, 238

Ignatius of Loyola, St., 186–89, 203
Iliad, The, 24
Infallibility, 152–53
Initiation: rites of passage, 13–14, 172, 174, 217; prospecting as, 80; and monks, 179–80, 183; conversion as, 208, 210
Inquisition, Spanish, 81, 120
Islam, 2, 6
Italy: church attendance in, 244; clergy in, 152, 195; confraternities in, 200; male unbelief in, 109, 111; pious women in, 108, 123, 137; and youth, 71

Jansenism, 34, 83, 97, 138
Jesuits: And devotion to the Sacred Heart, 34, 38; As educators, 189; As confessors, 165, 189; As male order, 138, 189, 190; As missionary order, 151, 189; in general, 5, 48, 188, 213; and Ignatius of Loyola, 186; Pedophilia and, 152, 154; Suspicion regarding, 139, 152, 154, 155, 173.
Jesus Christ: As Leader and Friend, 248; as member of holy family, 205–06; masculine images of, 4–5, 210, 214, 238; Social Gospel and, 227; as model, 156, 175, 192, 231–32; sacred eroticism and, 57–58, 61–63, 237; masculinity of, 22, 29–33, 67; Sacred Heart devotion to, 33–34, 121, 166; Protestant image of, 37–38; macho Jesus, 39-42
Jerome, St., 177, 180,
Jerusalem, 39
John the Baptist, St.,
John of the Cross, St., 57
Judaism, 2, 203
Jules Michelet, 58, 121, 133–35

Kingsley, Charles, 220–21
Knights of Columbus, 96, 202
Knights Templar, 185–86
Kulturkampf, 147, 153, 155

Latino culture,
Liberal Christians, 4, 211, 222–24, 235
Liberals: anti-Catholic sentiment of, 5, 151–56, 160, 166; and the family, 133–4; in Italy, 109; on women in public life, 145; and women's suffrage, 135, 137, 141–43;
Ligouri, Alphonsus, St., 62, 84
Leonhardt, 65, 206
Lippy, Charles, 230, 246
Losingthegoodportion.com, x
Luther, Martin, 82, 93, 195, 203, 206
Lutheranism, 87, 203, 204
Lyon, 93, 99, 106

Macho Jesus, 38, 41
Madrid, 164, 166, 168–69
Margaret Mary Alacoque, St., 33, 57–58
Marriage: anticlericalism and, 126, 132–34, 166, 170, 172; to Christ, 56–57, 59–60; and clergy, 117–18, 150; and fatherhood, 204–05; and Fundamentalism, 211; history of, 74, 80–83, 93; and men in the Church, 50; and Protestant revivalism, 220, 232
Martyrdom, 175, 177–78, 180
Mary: images of, 37; as member of the Holy Family, 205–06; as model for men, 50, 190, 103, 126; as perfect woman, 43, 45, 67; as prototypical disciple, 47; virginity of, 187; as unsuitable role model, 214
Masculinity. *See husbands; hypermasculinity; Jesus Christ, masculinity of; thumos; youth.*

McCartney, Bill, 230-31
McMillan, James, 146–47
McLeod, Hugh, 105, 109
Mediterranean, 4, 21, 22
Men and Religion Forward Movement, 6, 37, 39, 229–31
Methodism, 88, 112–13, 130–31
Mexico, 100, 143–44
Michelet, Jules, 58, 121, 133–35, 154–55
Middle Ages: 72–73, 75–76, 78, 81, 88, 117, 142, 162, 205
Monasticism, 5, 40, 178, 180–82, 185, 213
Moravians, 61, 63
Morgan, David, 34, 37
Muscular Christianity, 91, 219–25
Music, 17, 62, 74, 96, 99, 100, 107, 237
Moses, 22, 27

Napoleon, 94, 148
Napoleonic Wars, 94, 104, 147
National Socialism, see Nazism.
Nazism: attack on confession, 160; Christian resistance to, 215–16; in general, 5, 138, 159, 162; opposition to clerical pedophilia, 157–58; origins in Munich, 156.
New England, 60, 128,
New Testament, The, 4, 25, 26, 29
Newman, John Henry Cardinal, St., 220, 222
Nicomachean Ethics, 26–27
North America, 68, 211

Obedience: and femininity, 38, 44, 46–47; and religion, 40, 69–70, 103, 105, 157, 180, 185; of children, 108; and social control, 153–54
Odysseus, 24
Ong, Walter, 70, 190
Origen, 54–55, 177

Papacy, 103, 147. *See also popes.*

Patriarchy. *See fatherhood, fundamentalism, husbands, liberals.*

Paul, St., 31, 32, 174, 176

Pedophilia, 124, 154

Pentecostalism, 212, 232, 234, 236

Philosophers, 26, 102, 175–76

Pietism, 4, 61, 63

Plato, 25-26, 65, 175, 221,

Podles, Leon, iii, iv

Podles, Madie, iii

Popes: Benedict XV, 97, 142; Benedict XVI, 173; Clement VII, 195; Innocent III, 103; John Paul II, 1, 46, 48, 50; Pius V, 89; Pius X, 104; Pius XII, 35; Urban II, 184

Poverty, 86–87, 180, 185, 192, 235

Priesthood, 115–26. *See also anticlericalism, clericalism, confession.*

Prison system, 18, 80

Progressive Movement, 227–28

Prohibition: in Britain, 86; in America, 87–88, 228

Promise Keepers, 6, 217, 230–33

Prostitution, 74, 81–82, 85

Protestantism, 4, 40, 60, 105–06, 127, 129, 206, 208, 217, 229, 233, 235

Preaching, 128, 139, 208–09, 248

Presbyterianism, 112, 121, 244

Puritanism, 59, 87, 207

Quakers, 105–06

Rahner, Karl, 1, 240

Rape, 5, 74, 82, 112, 158

Rauschenbusch, Walter, 226, 229

Rebellion, 4, 112,138

Rebirth: as masculine theme, 5, 13, 14; male cycle for piety, 65, 240; as theme in the Christian life, 174, 180, 183, 208, 212; Cursillo as, 217

Reformation, The, 5

Reformers, the, 40, 76, 81–82, 195,

Religion, *see anticlericalism, clericalism, Social Gospel*

Revivalism, 5, 131, 151, 206–10, 229

Rome, ancient, 22–24, 176

Ruff, Julius, 73, 78

Ruiz, Manuel Delgado, 109, 172

Sabbath, 8, 90–91, 112

Samuel F. B. Morse, 122–23

Santiago de Compostela, 173, 216

Sawyer, Stephen, 41

Satan, 29, 30, 69, 96, 177–78, 183, 188, 203, 213, 231,

Schell, Herman, 155

Schleiermacher, Friedrich, 4, 63–67

Sergardi, Cardinal Ludovico, 118–19

Sin: conquered by Jesus, 29; of the clergy, 115, 120, 130, 152, 159–60, 166; judgment and, 37; and manhood, 91, 130, 175, 177, 203; medieval expiation of, 180, 184–85; mercy and, 239; passivity as, 27; sexual, 81, 83; and social control, 144; spirituality and, 207–08, 217, 231; sports and, 225; temperance and, 88

Social Gospel, 5, 41, 226–29

Socialists, 108, 145, 148, 173, 199, 226

Socrates, 28, 31

Song of Songs, 53, 55, 60, 192; Bernard of Clairvaux on 185; Origen on, 54–55.

South, The, 86, 91–92, 113–14, 131, 224, 227

South Carolina, 114, 207

Spain: influence of the Church in, 81–82, 101; male attitudes to the Church in, 110, 142–43; clergy in, 120, 125; anticlericalism in, 162–63, 168–72; secularism in, 173; confraternities in, 193, 198–201; Cursillo in, 216

Spanish Civil War, 5, 186, 216
Spierenburg, Pieter, 76,
Sports: in late antiquity, 88; Medieval
and Renaissance, 89; in modern
era, 91, 112; analogy to martyrdom, 175; Protestantism and, 212;
in Nazi Germany, 215; targeting
men and, 222–26, 231
Stoicism, 20, 22
Stott, Richard, 79, 86
Sunday: sports and, 89–91, 112;
dancing and, 93–94; attitudes on
church attendance and, 101, 196,
200, 205, 227; Bonnefond and,
106; Sunday school and, 39, 128,
210, 242

Tanner, J.M., 7
Temperance movement, 86–88, 197,
202, 222
Teresa of Avila, 57,
Tertullian, 53, 175,
Téry, Gustave, 108, 148
Theology, 30, 32, 39, 49, 63–65, 98,
118, 161, 211, 228
Therese of Lisieux, Saint, 1, 124
Thumos, and antiquity, 24–26; and
Christian life, 5; and honor, 28;
and Jesus, 32; as male energy, 101,
221, 239–40; and unchurched men,
168, 248
Tomás Sánchez, 118–19
Toronto, 88, 198
Trinity, 48, 179
Twain, Mark, 79, 123

Ultramontanism: and liberals 5, 152;
and women, 147, 150; and men,
153; in Germany, 155; and Spain,
166
Unitarianism, 128, 150, 208, 224, 225
United States, The: workplace accidents
in, 20; images of Jesus in, 35; vice
in, 80, 85–87; sports in, 91, anticlericalism in, 122, 159; confraternities
in, 201; sports in, 223; social Gospel
in, 226; domestic violence in, 233;
black churches in, 236; male church
attendance in, 113, 243, 245. *See also*
America

Vengeance, 27, 29, 30, 73
Vianney, St. John, 94, 95, 107,
Violence, 72–82. *See also: anticlerica-*
lism, French Revolution, Spanish
Civil War, thumos, youth
Virginia, University of, xi
Voltaire, 108, 124, 139, 146
von Balthasar, Hans Urs, 4, 45–49
von Zinzendorf, Count Nicolas Lud-
wig, 61, 63–64

Waldbreitbach trial, 156–57
Wilcox, Brad, 233-34
Willow Creek Church, 237, 241
Wives, 51, as moral leader in the family, 80, 209; influence of husbands on, 219, 233, 236, 239;
influence of priests on, 84, 112,
120–21, 123, 134–37, 150; piety of,
109, 211; seduction of, 146, 144; secular criteria for, 149
Women, xi: and church membership,
101, 111, 207–09, 228, 241–47; corruption by priests, 118–15, 141–45,
165–73; emotion in, 51–53; gender
role of, 7–15; manliness required
in, 178–80; perceived as religious
sex, 1–4; and religious associations, 187–92, 197, 219, 226; religion
and home life of, 85–87, 203, 232–
35; receptivity to grace in, 44–50;
sacred eroticism and, 33–38, 53–
63; secular attack on, 150–55.

Women's suffrage, 44, 132, 142–45
World War I, 62, 78, 97, 157, 186, 213–14
World War II, 216

YMCA, 223-25
Youth: Christ as a, 56; Medieval, 71–78; American, 78–79; sex and, 80–85; temperance and, 85; church societies for, 98–102